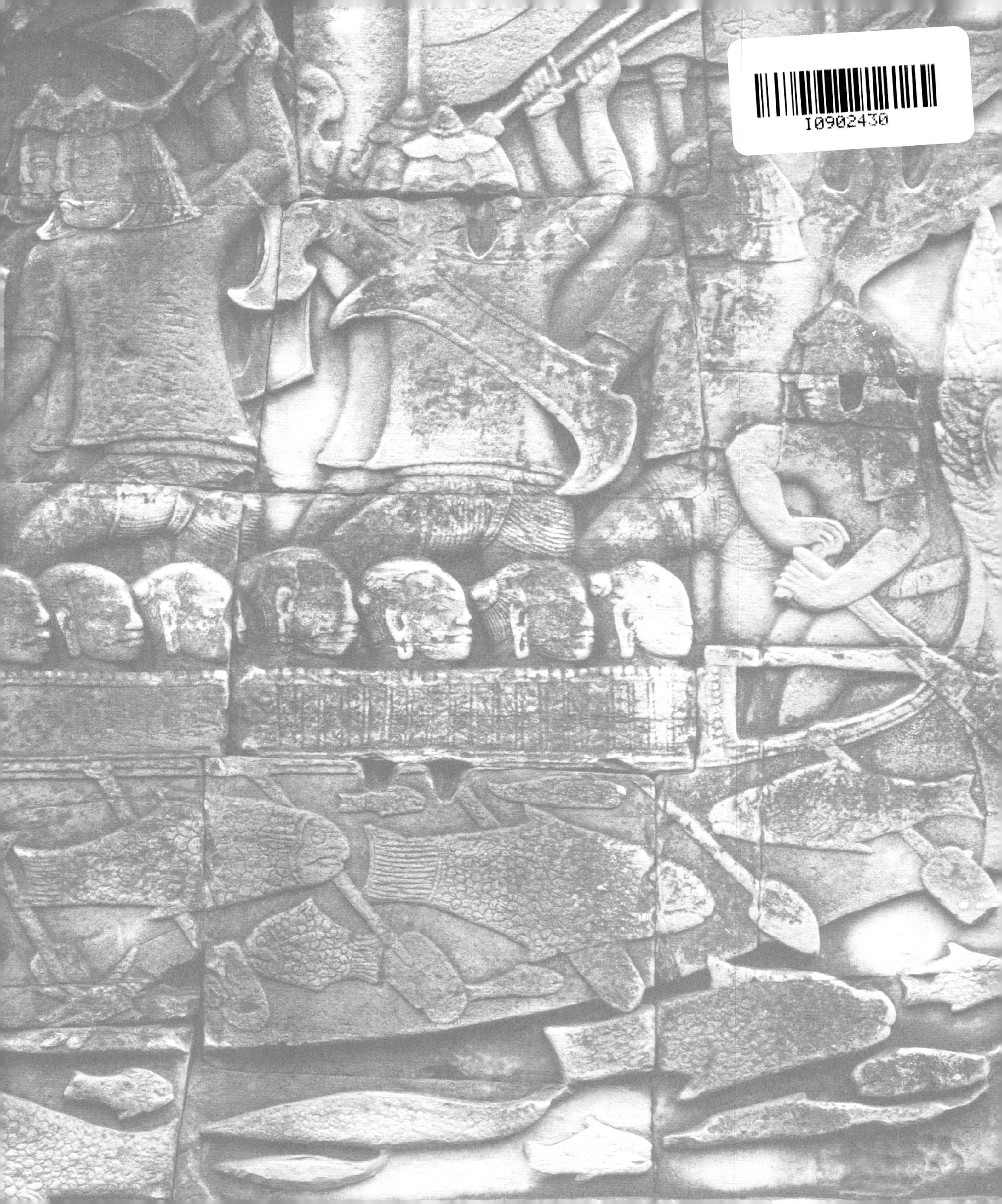

Presenting

CAMBODIA

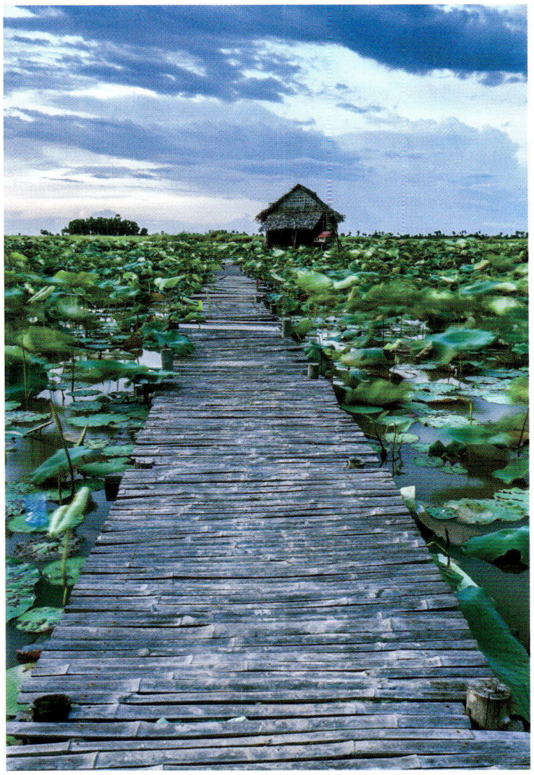

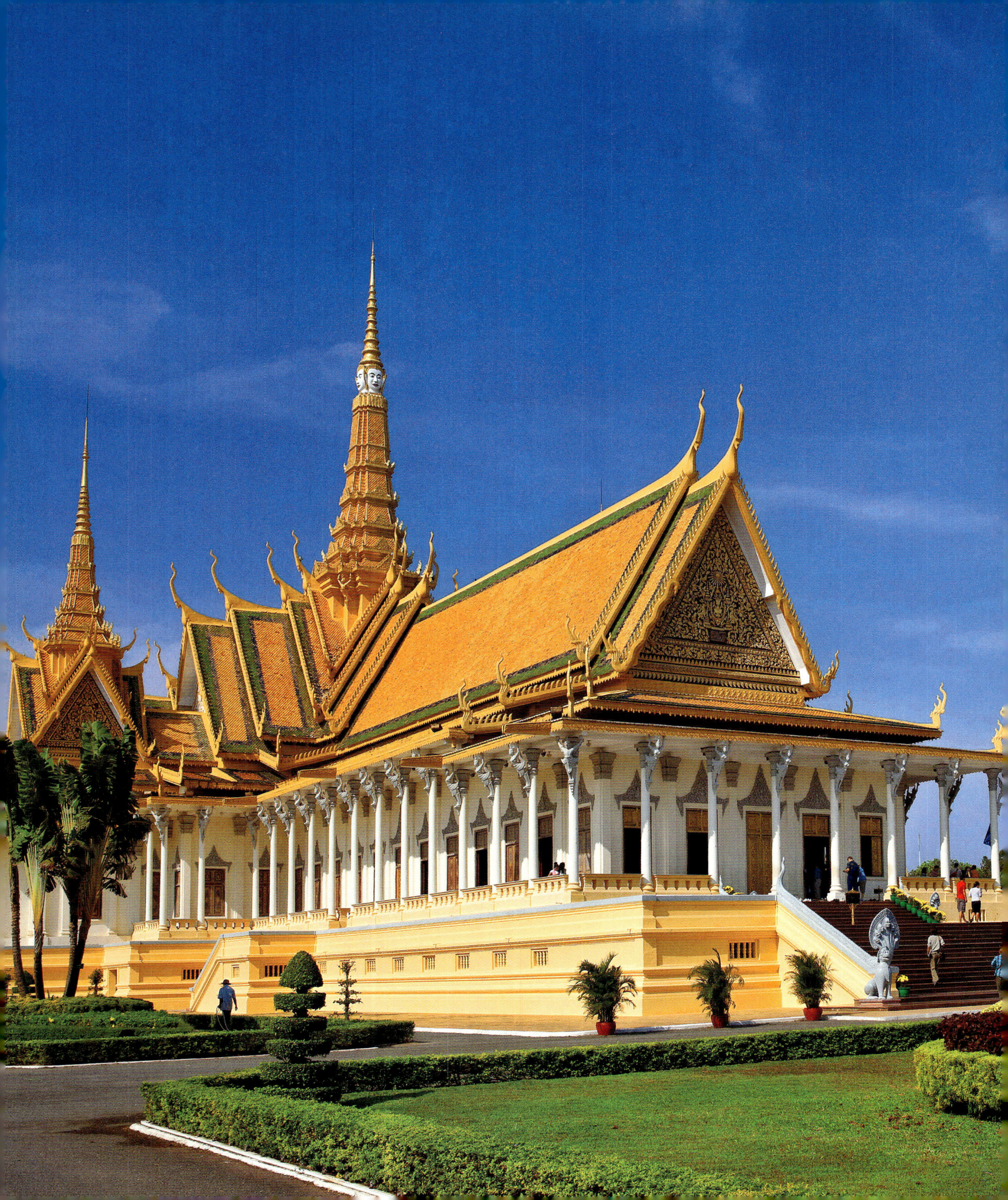

Presenting CAMBODIA

The Kingdom of Wonder

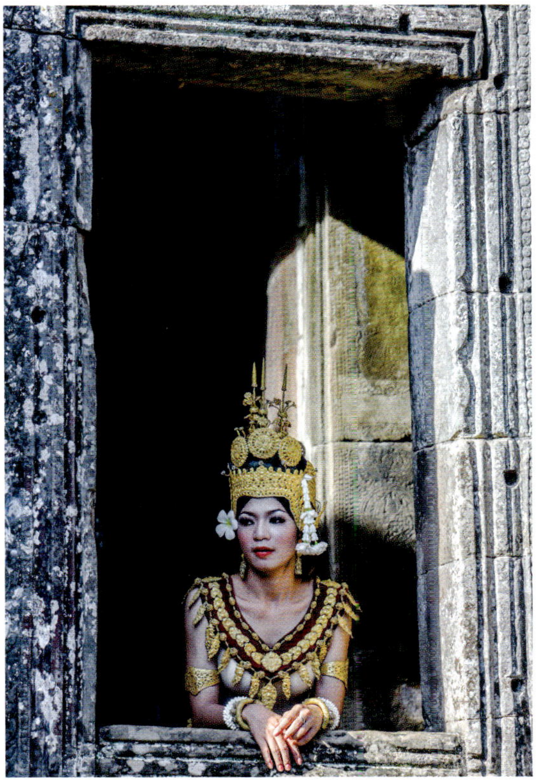

MICK SHIPPEN

JOHN BEAUFOY PUBLISHING

ASIA BOOKS

Published and distributed in Thailand by Asia Books Co., Ltd.
Berli Jucker House, 14th Floor, 99 Soi Rubia, Sukhumvit 42 Road,
Phrakanong, Klongtoey, Bangkok 10110, Thailand
Tel: (66) 2-715-9000; Fax: (66) 2-715-9197
Email: information@asiabooks.com
www.asiabooks.com

First published in the United Kingdom in 2013 by John Beaufoy Publishing,
11 Blenheim Court, 316 Woodstock Road, Oxford OX2 7NS, England
www.johnbeaufoy.com

ISBN 978-1-906780-99-9

Design: Glyn Bridgewater
Cartography: William Smuts
Project management: Rosemary Wilkinson

Printed and bound in Singapore by Tien Wah Press (Pte) Ltd

Front cover: The Independence Monument in Phnom Penh lit up at night.

Back cover: One of Angkor Thom's five imposing arched entranceways.

Page 1: A wooden walkway leading to a small bamboo house in the middle of a lotus farm outside Siem Reap.

Page 2: The Throne Hall at the Royal Palace, Phnom Penh.

Page 3: An Apsara dancer takes a break from performing for tourists at the Bayon.

Page 5: The large bronze Buddha image within the central hall of Wat Phnom, Phnom Penh.

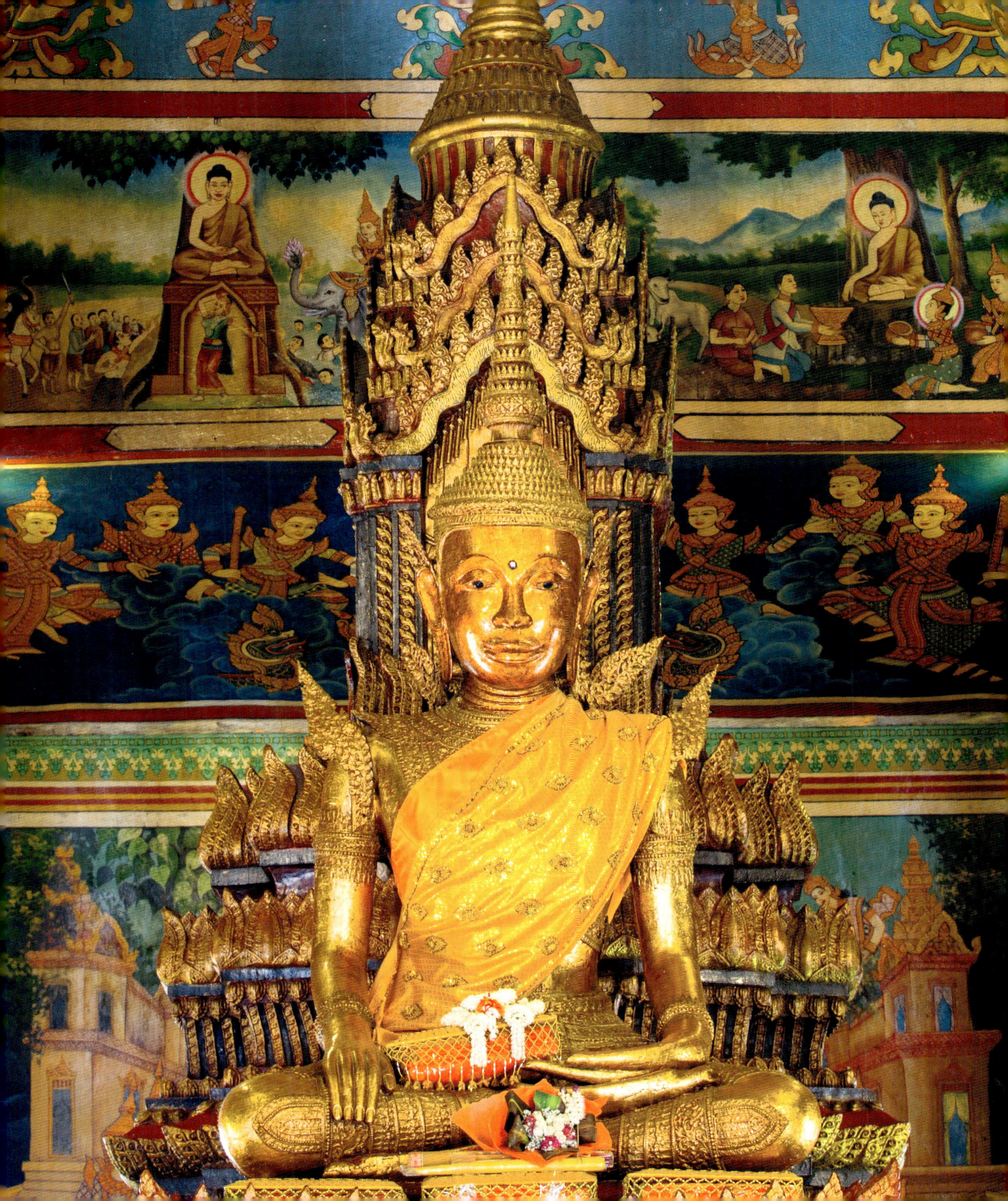

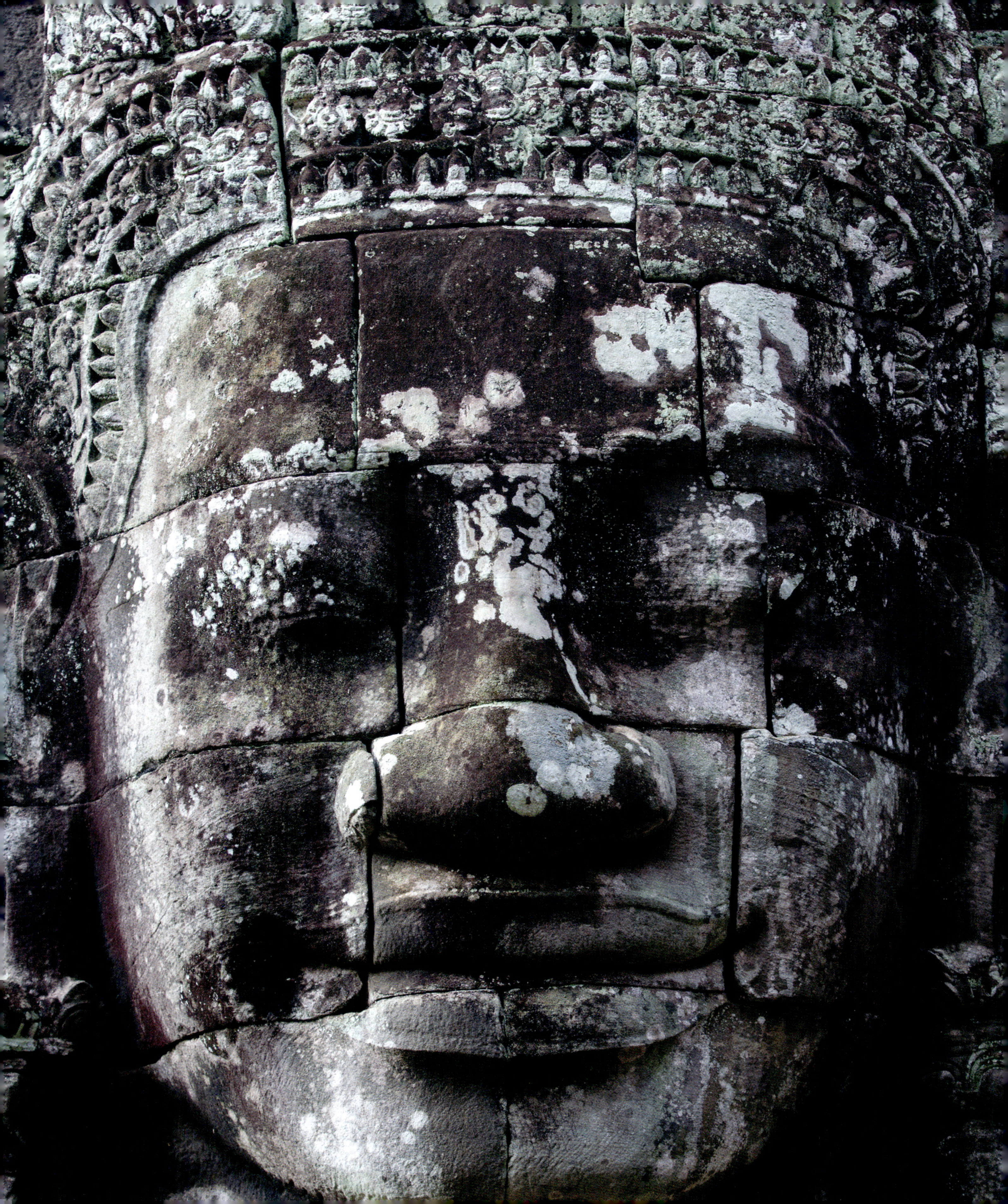

CONTENTS

Opposite: The huge carved faces of Bayon in the Angkor Archaeological Park are the most enigmatic and recognizable images of Asia.

INTRODUCTION

Cambodia's numerous attractions, fascinating culture and its charming people make it a truly rewarding destination for adventurous travellers.

Just two decades ago it was impossible to even consider Cambodia as a tourist destination. At the beginning of the 1990s, the troubled Southeast Asian nation was emerging from a brutal civil war that was to go down in history as one of mankind's darkest moments. Yet, in a short period of time, the country has rebuilt its infrastructure and society and now welcomes travellers from around the globe.

Cambodia's achievements should not be underestimated. In 1993 when King Norodom Sihanouk was returned to the throne and the wicked ideology of the Khmer Rouge had been confined to the pages of history, there were just 120,000 recorded foreign visits to the country, the majority of which were by aid workers, NGOs and UN staff. Today, over three million tourists a year discover why Cambodia has been dubbed the 'Kingdom of Wonder'. It's a remarkable success story and testament to the resilient and naturally hospitable character of the Khmer people, and of course, the country's incredible beauty and engaging traditions.

Tourism, however, is not new to Cambodia. In the 1920s and 30s, Phnom Penh and the ancient ruins of Angkor attracted cultured travellers from Europe – the likes of W. Somerset Maugham and Noel Coward – and even stars of Hollywood's silver screen, including Charlie Chaplin and his entourage. As they discovered, few sights are more inspiring than Angkor. A magnificent expression both of centuries of regional dominance by the Khmer Empire and of sublime creativity, it is as one of the world's largest and greatest historical sites. The centrepiece is the stunning Angkor Wat, yet this is just one of dozens of temples in the immediate area and hundreds scattered across the country, each built by a civilization that held sway over much of Southeast Asia from the ninth to the 15th centuries.

Rich and fascinating as the country's history is, it does not define the nation. Today's Cambodia is youthful and vibrant and is eagerly embracing a brighter future. In Phnom Penh the energy of this revitalized nation is palpable. The streets are clogged with motorcycles and SUVs, gleaming new buildings reach skywards and an emerging middleclass flaunts newfound wealth. For the traveller, the city offers chic bars and restaurants, trendy boutiques, and a burgeoning arts and entertainment scene. Of course in Phnom Penh, there are also the Royal Palace, the National Museum, the sobering Tuol Sleng Genocide Museum, the Killing Fields and more, all of which are must-see sites, but just beyond the city, Cambodia's countryside beckons. Visitors can relax with locals at the popular riverside picnic site of Kien Svay, enjoy day-trips to the former capital of Oudong, or explore floating villages that hug the shoreline of Tonlé Sap.

In the country's heartland, Siem Reap is the base for exploring Angkor but the booming town's nightlife and dining scene also provide a welcome break from too much temple time. Likewise, Battambang enchants travellers with rows of French-era shophouses, cosy coffee shops and pleasantly bucolic countryside. To the east, cultural travellers can follow the Mekong River upstream to Kompong Cham and Kratie, two endearing riverfront towns where time can be allowed to slip away over an ice-cold Angkor beer and local delicacies. Further east, adventure awaits in Mondulkiri and Ratanakiri with treks to hill villages, volcanic lakes, elephant camps and waterfalls.

In recent years, Cambodia has also begun to attract beach lovers. Most head for Sihanoukville but the coast is lined with deserted beaches and its waters dotted with islands where visitors can still take advantage of the tranquillity before the inevitable development arrives. Head east along the coast to Kampot and Kep, both former haunts of the French colonialists, and national parks, pepper farms and a fabulous crab market top the traveller's itinerary.

Cambodia's numerous attractions, fascinating culture and its charming people make it a truly rewarding destination for adventurous travellers. Whether exploring ancient jungle-shrouded temples, lazing on a beach, admiring Buddhist or colonial architecture, enjoying the grace and beauty of traditional dance, or savouring the delights of local cuisine, Cambodia rewards all who visit with memories that endure.

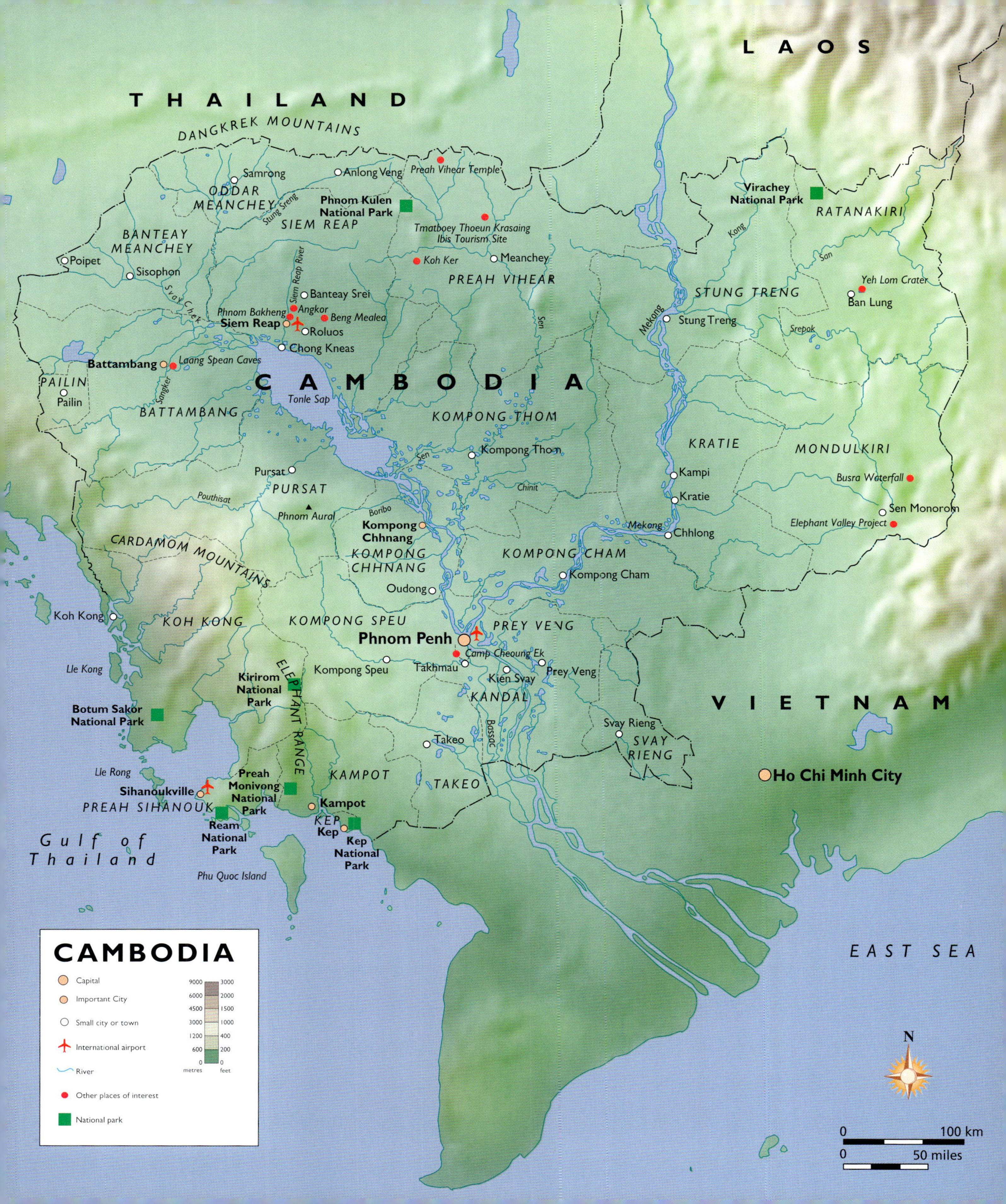

LAOS
THAILAND
DANGKREK MOUNTAINS
Samrong
Anlong Veng
Preah Vihear Temple
ODDAR MEANCHEY
Phnom Kulen National Park
Stung Sreng
SIEM REAP
Tmatboey Thoeun Krasaing Ibis Tourism Site
BANTEAY MEANCHEY
Koh Ker
Meanchey
Poipet
Sisophon
PREAH VIHEAR
Svay Chek
Siem Reap River
Banteay Srei
Phnom Bakheng
Angkor
Beng Mealea
Siem Reap
Roluos
Chong Kneas
Battambang
Laang Spean Caves
PAILIN
Pailin
Sangker
BATTAMBANG
CAMBODIA
Tonle Sap
KOMPONG THOM
Kompong Thom
Sen
Chinit
Pursat
PURSAT
Pouthisat
Phnom Aural
Boribo
Kompong Chhnang
KOMPONG CHHNANG
CARDAMOM MOUNTAINS
Oudong
Koh Kong
KOH KONG
KOMPONG SPEU
Phnom Penh
Camp Cheoung Ek
Takhmau
Kompong Speu
Ile Kong
Kirirom National Park
ELEPHANT RANGE
Botum Sakor National Park
KANDAL
Kien Svay
Prey Veng
PREY VENG
Bassac
Takeo
TAKEO
KAMPOT
Ile Rong
Sihanoukville
Preah Monivong National Park
PREAH SIHANOUK
Ream National Park
Kampot
KEP
Kep
Kep National Park
Gulf of Thailand
Phu Quoc Island
Virachey National Park
RATANAKIRI
Kong
San
Yeh Lom Crater
Ban Lung
STUNG TRENG
Mekong
Stung Treng
Srepok
Sen
KRATIE
MONDULKIRI
Kampi
Kratie
Busra Waterfall
Sen Monorom
Elephant Valley Project
Mekong
Chhlong
KOMPONG CHAM
Kompong Cham
VIETNAM
Svay Rieng
SVAY RIENG
Ho Chi Minh City
EAST SEA
CAMBODIA
Capital
Important City
Small city or town
International airport
River
Other places of interest
National park
9000 3000
6000 2000
4500 1500
3000 1000
1200 400
600 200
0 0
metres feet
N
0 100 km
0 50 miles

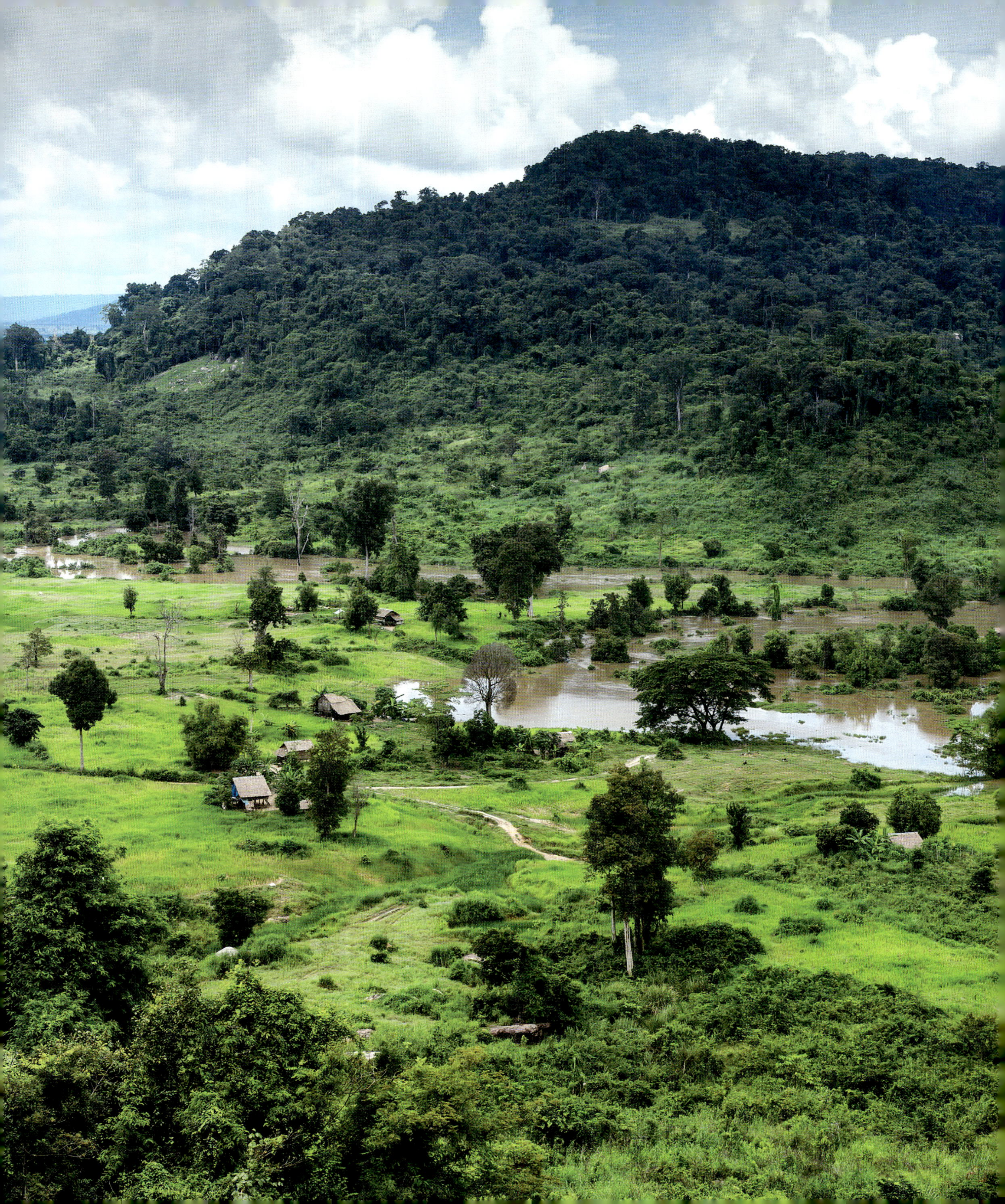

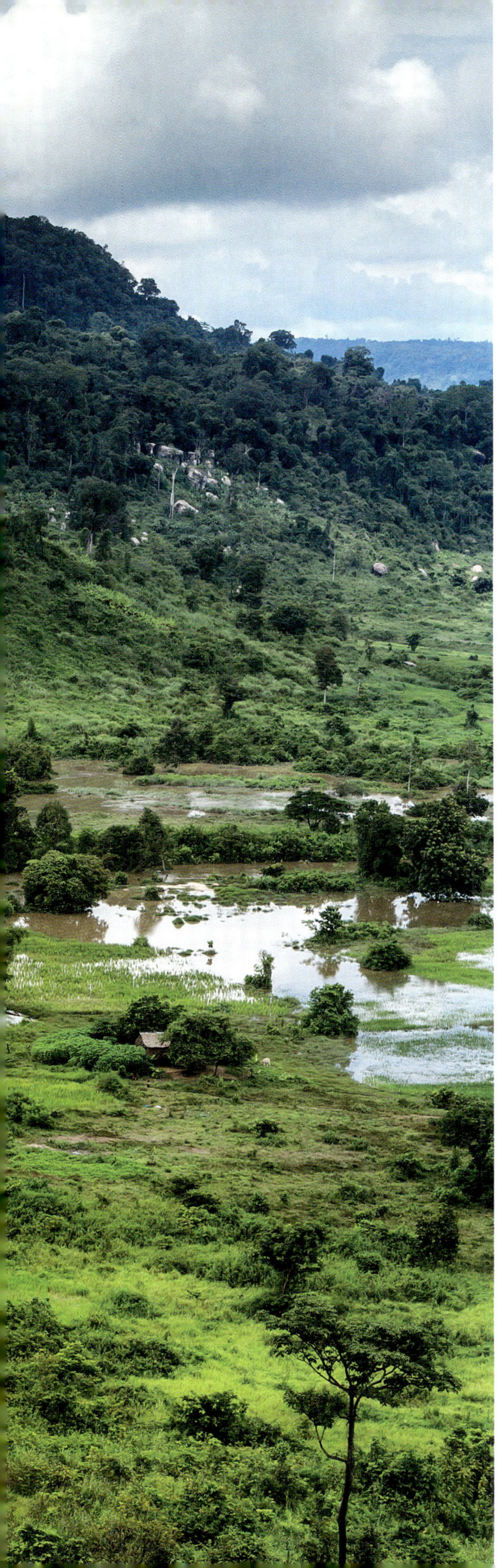

CHAPTER I

An OVERVIEW of CAMBODIA

Kingdom of Wonder

Cambodia is embraced by three neighbouring countries: Thailand to the west and north, Laos to the north, and Vietnam to the east and south. It also has a 450-km (280-mile) coastline to the south-west bordering four provinces and a sea scattered with islands. The country encompasses 180,040 km^2 (69,515 sq. miles) or roughly half the size of neighbouring Vietnam, and comprises 23 provinces.

Left: The view from Phnom Kulen. The sacred mountain lies within a national park one hour's drive from Angkor. It was here in 2013 that a team of archaeologists from the University of Sydney discovered the remains of an ancient city called Mahendraparvata. Believed to predate Angkor by 350 years, it is one of the most significant finds in Cambodia for many years.

GEOGRAPHY AND CLIMATE

Blessed with a tropical, three-season climate of cool, dry and wet, the temperature and humidity are high and constant throughout the year with only small variations from an average temperature of 25°C (77°F). The best time to travel in Cambodia is during the cool season which runs from November to February, but this is also the busiest period for tourism particularly at Angkor which draws upwards of three million visitors a year. Even during the cool season temperatures can still reach 30°C (86°F) during the afternoons but it is usually pleasantly cool in the early morning and evening. The hot season follows from March to May when temperatures can reach an uncomfortable 40°C (104°F). The annual rains begin in June, gradually building to a peak in October. At its height, downpours can be a daily occurrence but are usually brief and dramatic, clearing the air before the humidity rises again.

The fertile central plain is the rice bowl of Cambodia, particularly in Battambang, the country's fifth largest province. More than 2,500 km² (965 sq. miles) of Battambang are under rice cultivation, producing an annual harvest in excess of 500,000 tonnes (550,000 tons) of Cambodia's staple grain. Agriculture in the area also includes sugarcane, corn, soy beans, cassava and a variety of fruits.

From its source on the Tibetan Plateau, the mighty Mekong River flows 4,200 km (2,610 miles) before entering Cambodia at the Khone Falls on the border with Laos, then continues its course through the country into Vietnam where it fertilizes the Mekong Delta. The river and its floodplains are enormously important in all three countries.

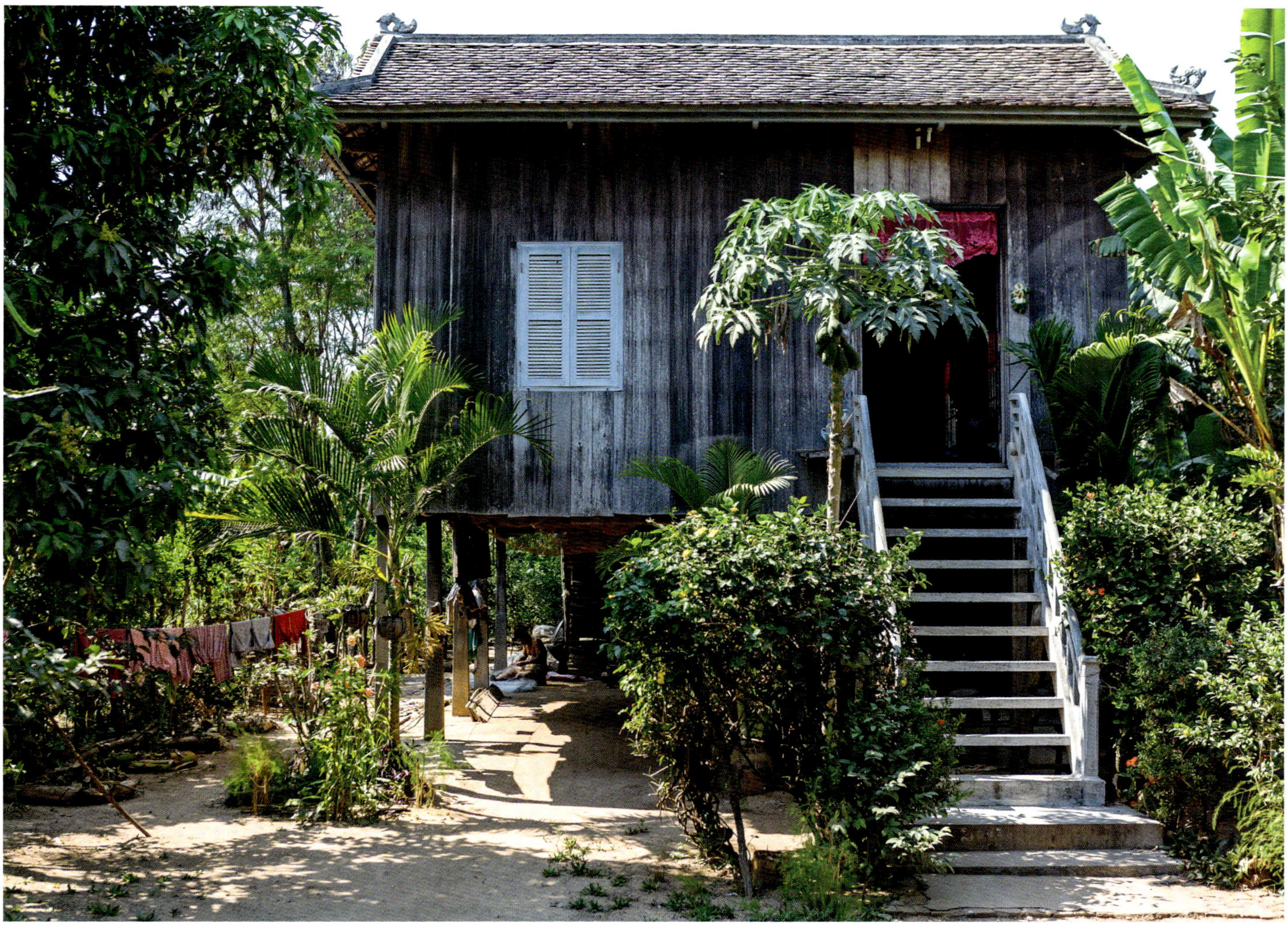

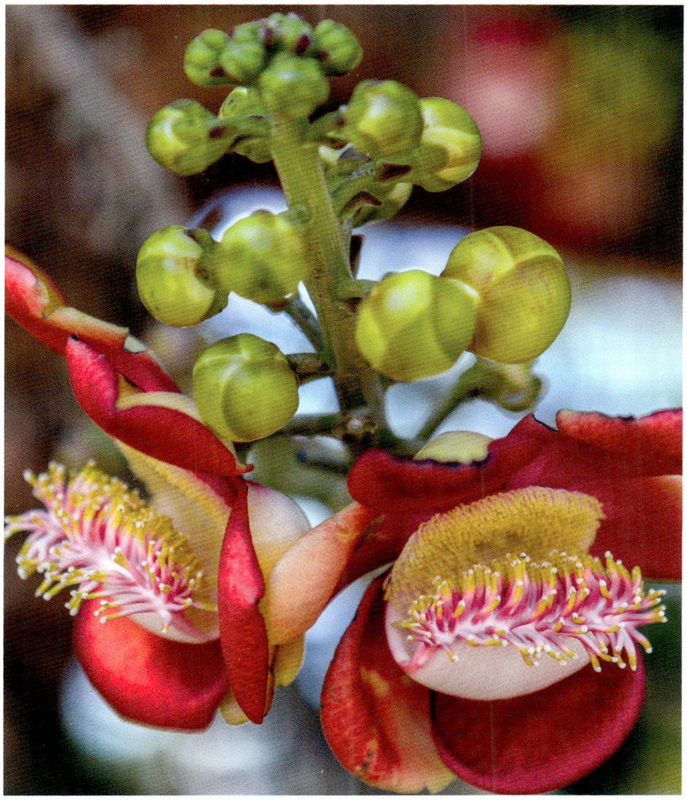

Left: The flowers of the Sal tree (*Shorea robusta*). Commonly found growing in the grounds of Cambodian temples, in Hindu mythology the Sal tree is said to be a favourite of Vishnu.

Below: Three ladies walking past rice fields in Battambang wearing a *krama* (see page 50) to protect themselves from the sun.

Opposite: Homes in rural areas are typically wooden and raised on stilts which keeps them cool and offers protection in times of flood.

In Cambodia, the 486-km (290-mile) stretch of river provides water and food security, with an estimated 85 per cent of the population's protein coming from fish caught in its waters. North of Kratie (pronounced Kra-chay) the river flows through a series of rapids in an area known as one of the best places to see the Irrawaddy Dolphin (see page 154). Below Kompong Cham, the river winds its way through a fertile lowland landscape with expansive floodplains, wetlands and paddy fields. When the river reaches Phnom Penh, it meets the Bassac and Tonlé Sap rivers, creating a 100 km (62-mile) channel that flows into the Tonlé Sap itself. At the confluence of the three rivers are large islands and sand banks, and south of the city, a fertile delta in the provinces of Kandal and Prey Veng which extends to over

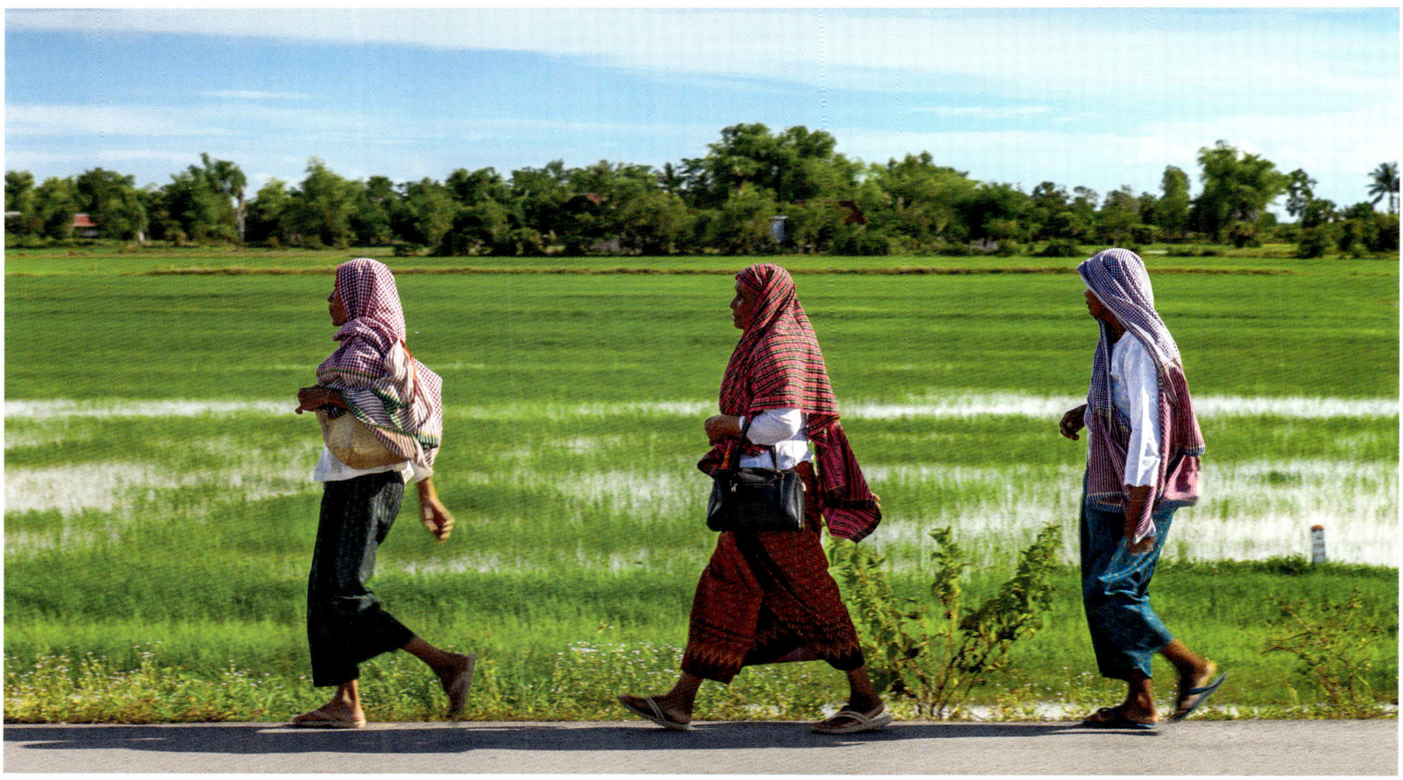

16,000 km² (6,200 sq. miles). The Mekong River is greatly affected by seasonal change and water levels drop to their lowest in the dry season months of April and May, allowing farmers to cultivate the fertile riverbanks and islands with quick-growing cash crops. With the start of the monsoon rains in June, the river begins its gradual rise before peaking in October.

In late 2012, the Cambodian government announced a plan to dam one of the Mekong River's major tributaries, the 3-S river basin that encompasses the Sekong, Sesan and Sre Pok Rivers near the borders of Cambodia, Laos and Vietnam. The announcement sees Cambodia join China and Laos in a controversial drive to harness hydroelectric power from the region's most important river. Millions of people in the Mekong River basin rely on it directly for food and the irrigation of crops. Damming the river will undoubtedly have a major negative impact on fisheries and agriculture. Some 66 per cent of fish species in the Mekong River are migratory and the dam, the first of several that have been proposed, will hurt the livelihood of those living downstream. The Mekong River also feeds the Tonlé Sap and is home to threatened species including the Irrawaddy Dolphin, the Mekong Giant Catfish and the Giant Freshwater Stingray, all of which can reach 300 kg (660 lb).

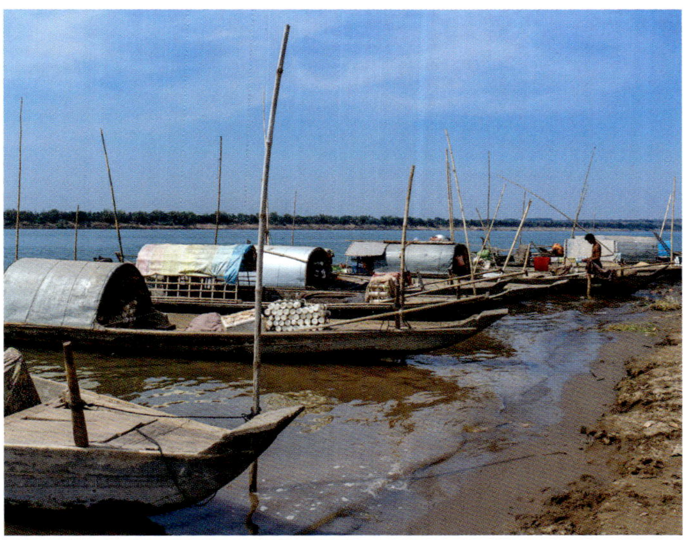

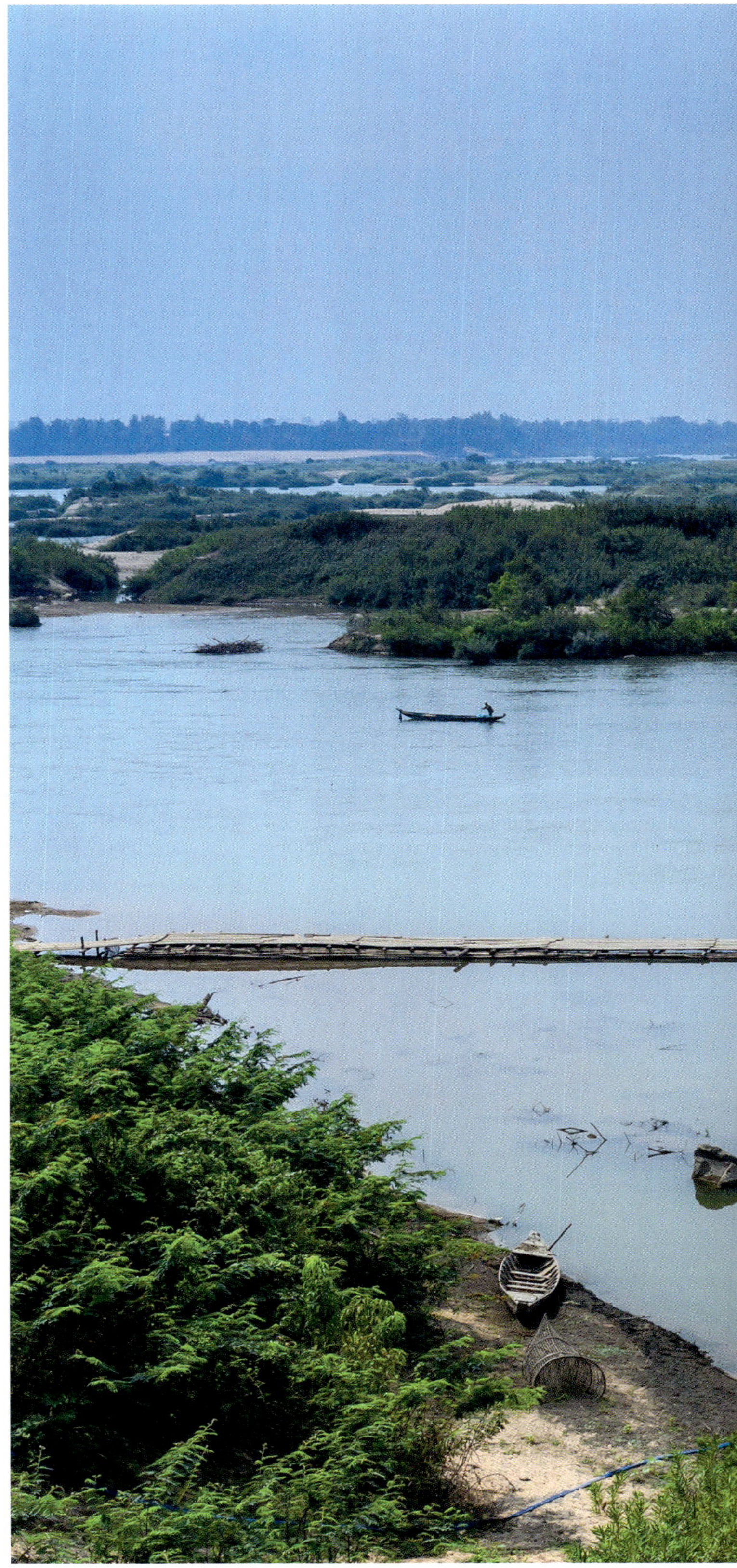

Above: Fishing boats moored on the shore of the Mekong River.
Right: Kampi village is the best spot to see Irrawaddy Dolphins. Nearby, during the dry and cool seasons when the water is low, temporary restaurants set up, attracting hundreds of locals.

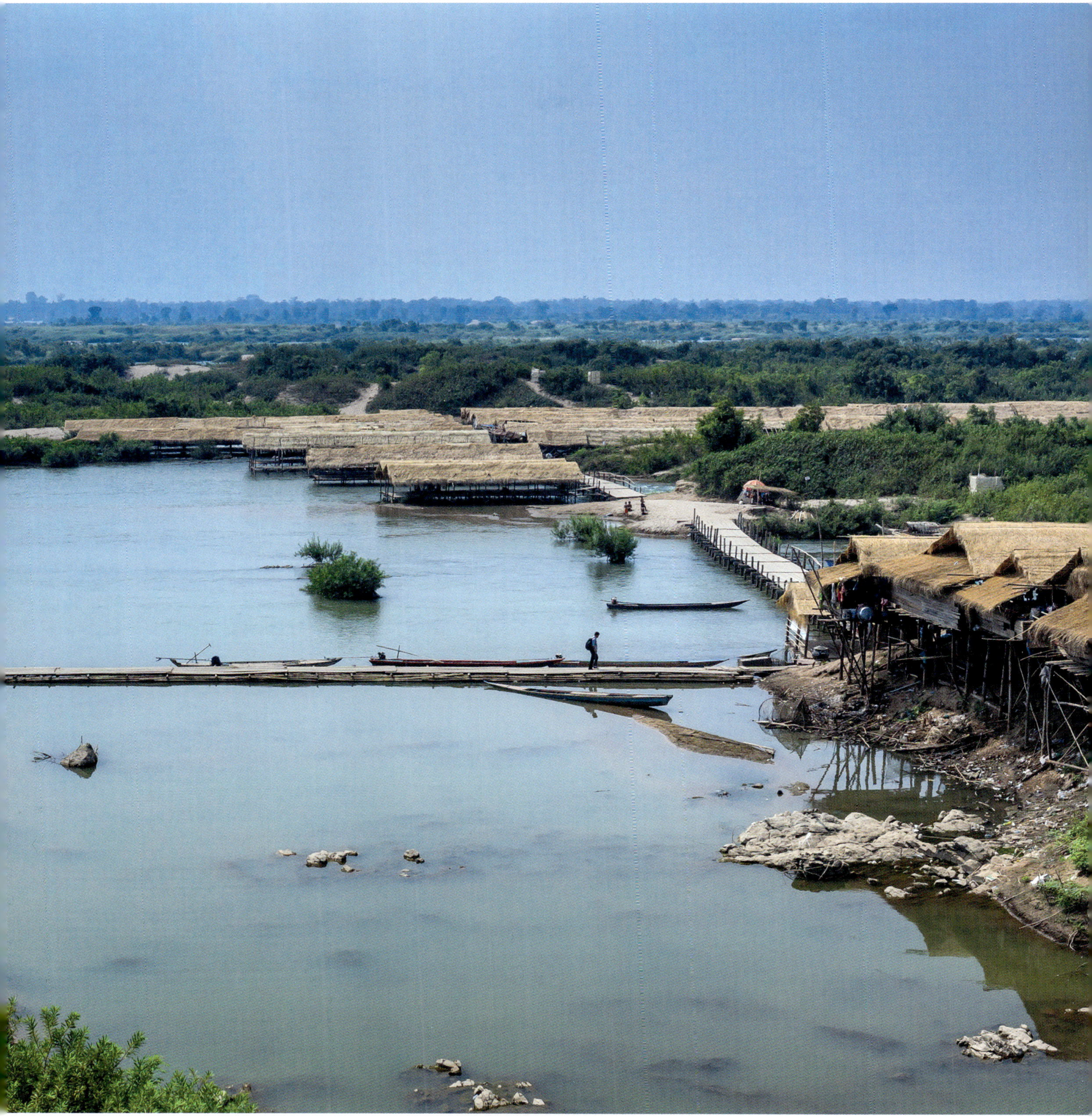

RICE CULTIVATION

A largely agrarian society, Cambodia is known to have been cultivating rice for more than 2,000 years. Eighty per cent of land given over to agriculture is used for growing rice with 2.8 million hectares (6.9 million acres) producing an annual yield of 7.6 million tonnes (8.4 million tons). With 80 per cent of farmers planting the crop, it is the mainstay of the rural economy. According to the International Rice Research Institute, during the Khmer Rouge years Cambodia lost many of its heritage rice varieties because farmers, unable to plant rice, ate the seed. However, between 1981 and 1990, the International Rice Genebank multiplied conserved stock of Cambodia's 766 traditional rice varieties and returned the seed. Such has been the success of the programme and rice cultivation that Cambodia is now able to export a large tonnage of excess production.

Many of Cambodia's paddy fields are still ploughed with oxen or buffalo when the soil is wet in June or July, and seed is broadcast by hand. Seedlings are transplanted from the nursery to the main paddy field from July through to September and are ready for harvest by December. Harvesting and threshing are also commonly done by hand. It's backbreaking work but the farmers are seldom without a smile. In some rice-growing areas that have access to a plentiful source of water, typically those close to the Tonlé Sap, fields are irrigated throughout the dry season, enabling the farmers to benefit from two or even three crops a year.

Domestic Asian Water Buffalo (*Bubalus bubalis*) are an essential part of rural life. Cambodia is also home to the endangered Wild Water Buffalo (*Bubalus arnee*). One of the few remaining populations is in Mondulkiri Province.

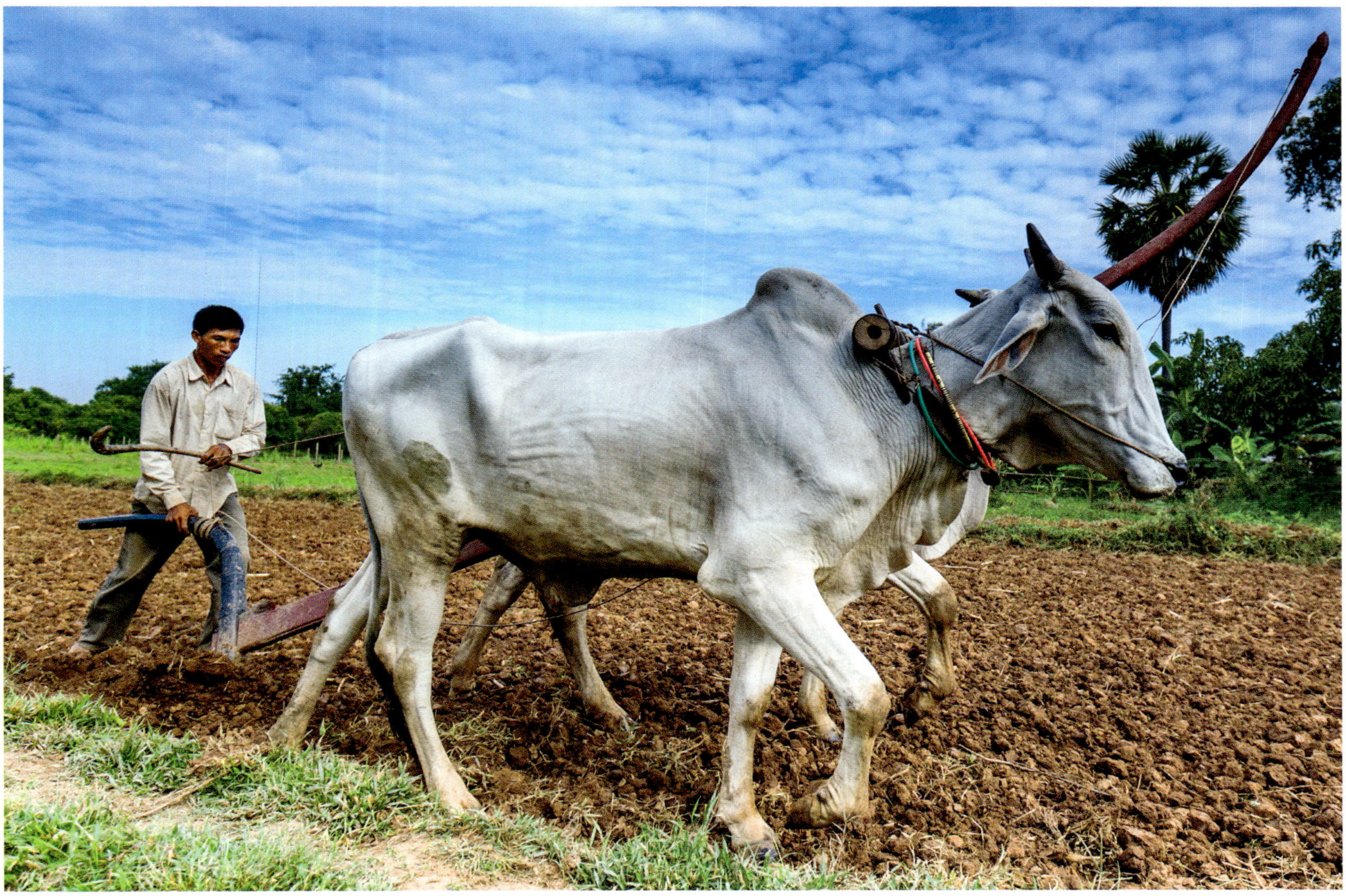

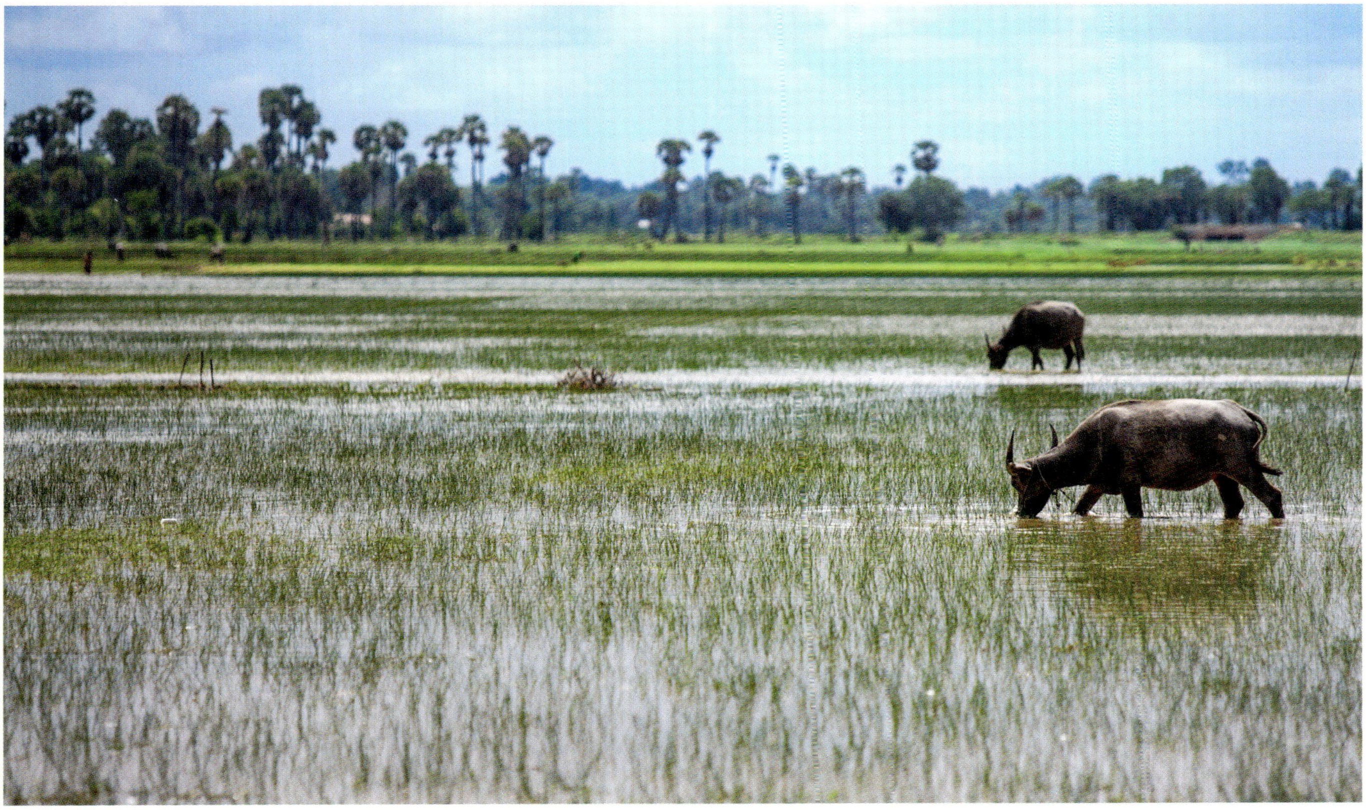

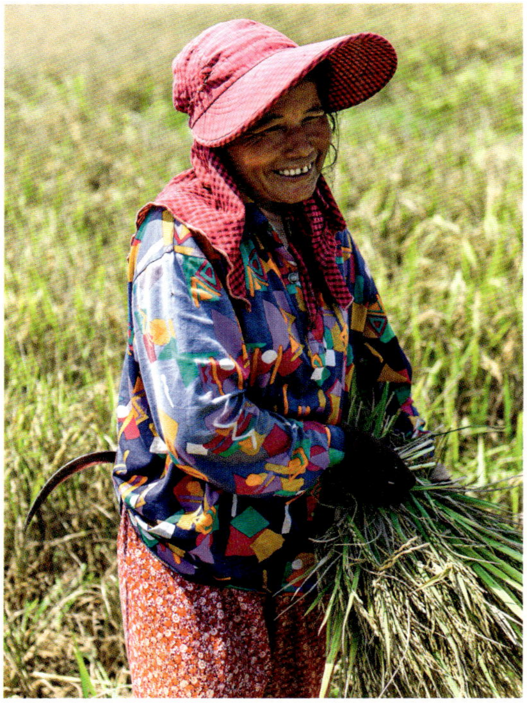

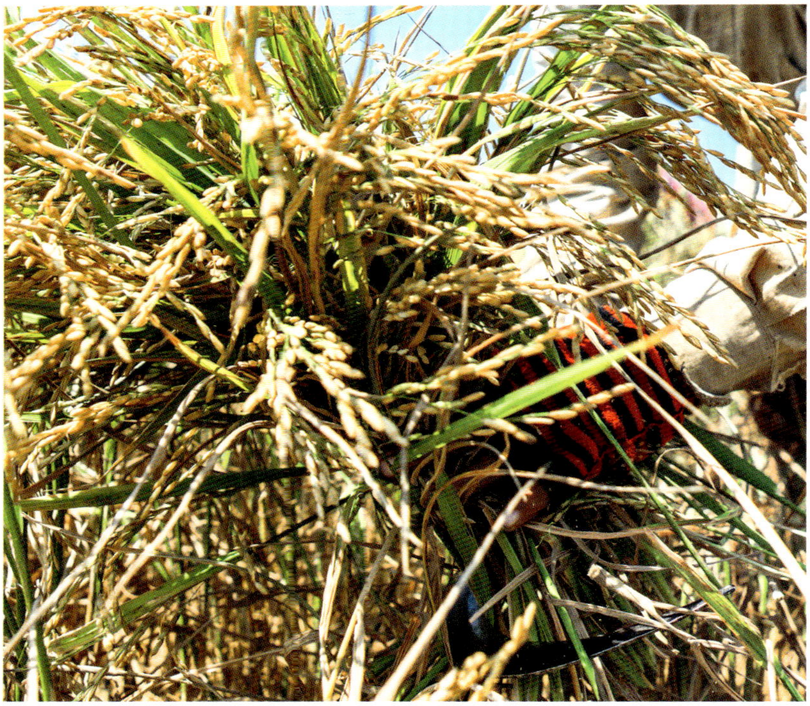

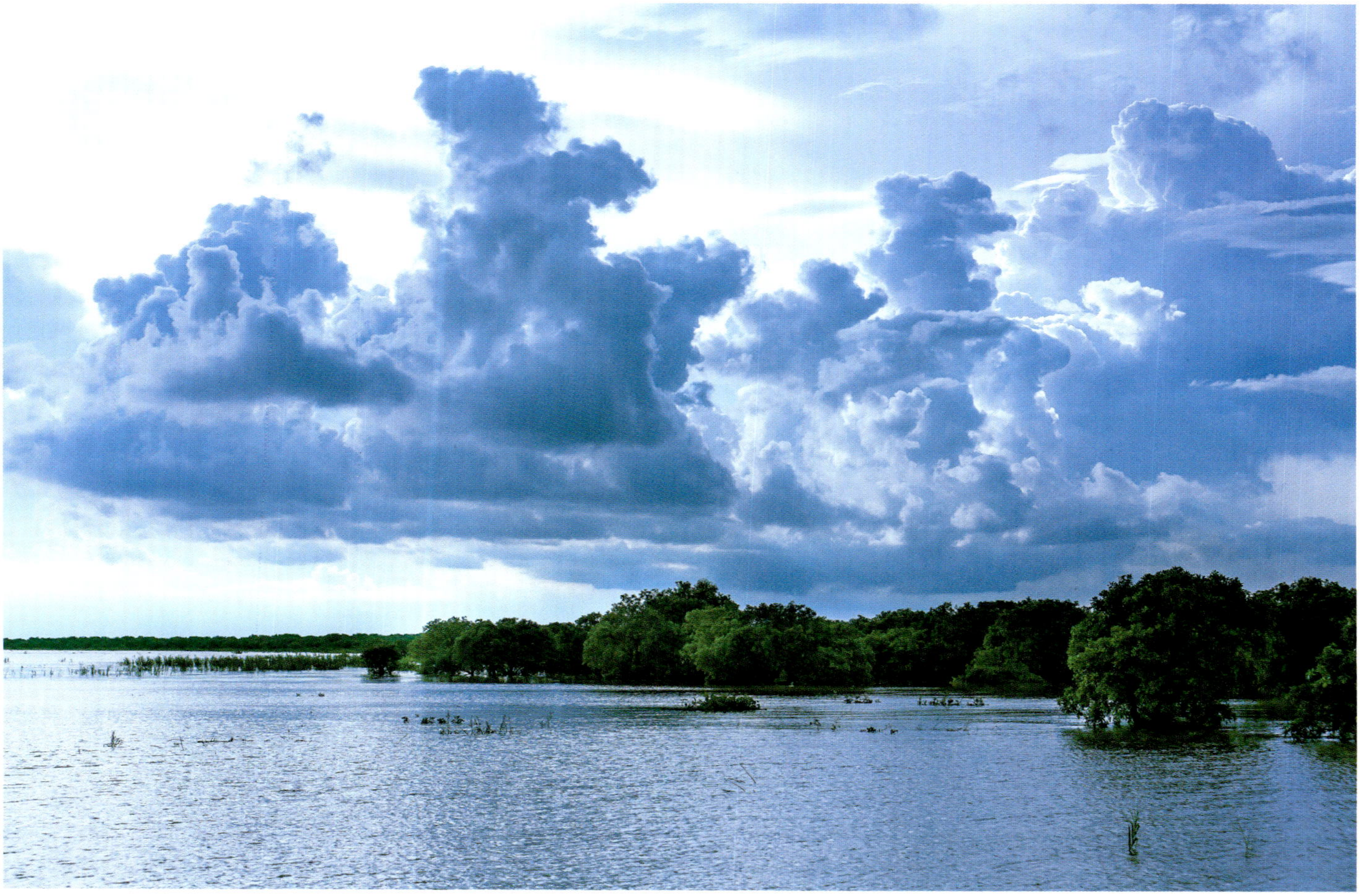

Above: Storm clouds gather over the Tonlé Sap. When the rains come the waters rise, inundating forests and covering a huge expanse of land.

Below: A woman making fishing nets.

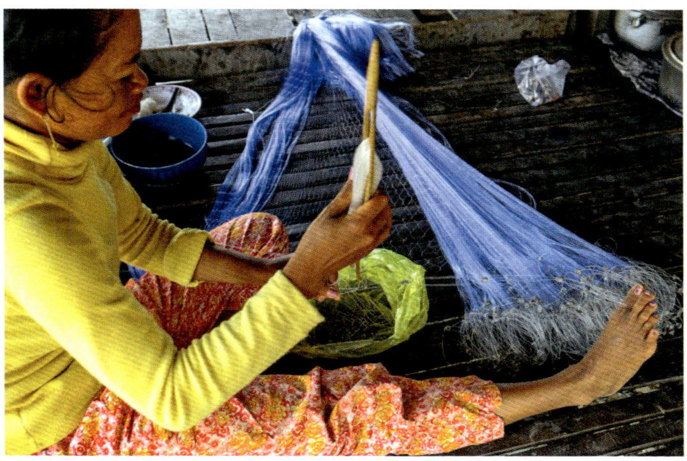

Inextricably linked to the ebb and flow of the Mekong River is the Tonlé Sap, Cambodia's great lake and the largest in Southeast Asia. Situated in the country's north-west, the lake environs include an expanse of open water surrounded by forest and grasslands bordering six provinces: Siem Reap, Kompong Thom, Battambang, Banteay Meanchey, Pursat and Kompong Chhnang, all of which are inundated with floodwaters every rainy season.

What makes the lake unusual is that twice a year, the flow of water changes direction. In the cool and dry season months from November to May, the waters of the Tonlé Sap drain into the Tonlé Sap and Mekong rivers but as the monsoon rains arrive in June they reverse course, flowing back into the lake. This extraordinary natural event sees the lake increase its dry-season size from 2,500 km² (965 sq. miles) up to 15,000 km² (5,795 sq. miles). The lake and the surrounding area provide habitats for incredibly diverse birdlife including pelicans, ibis,

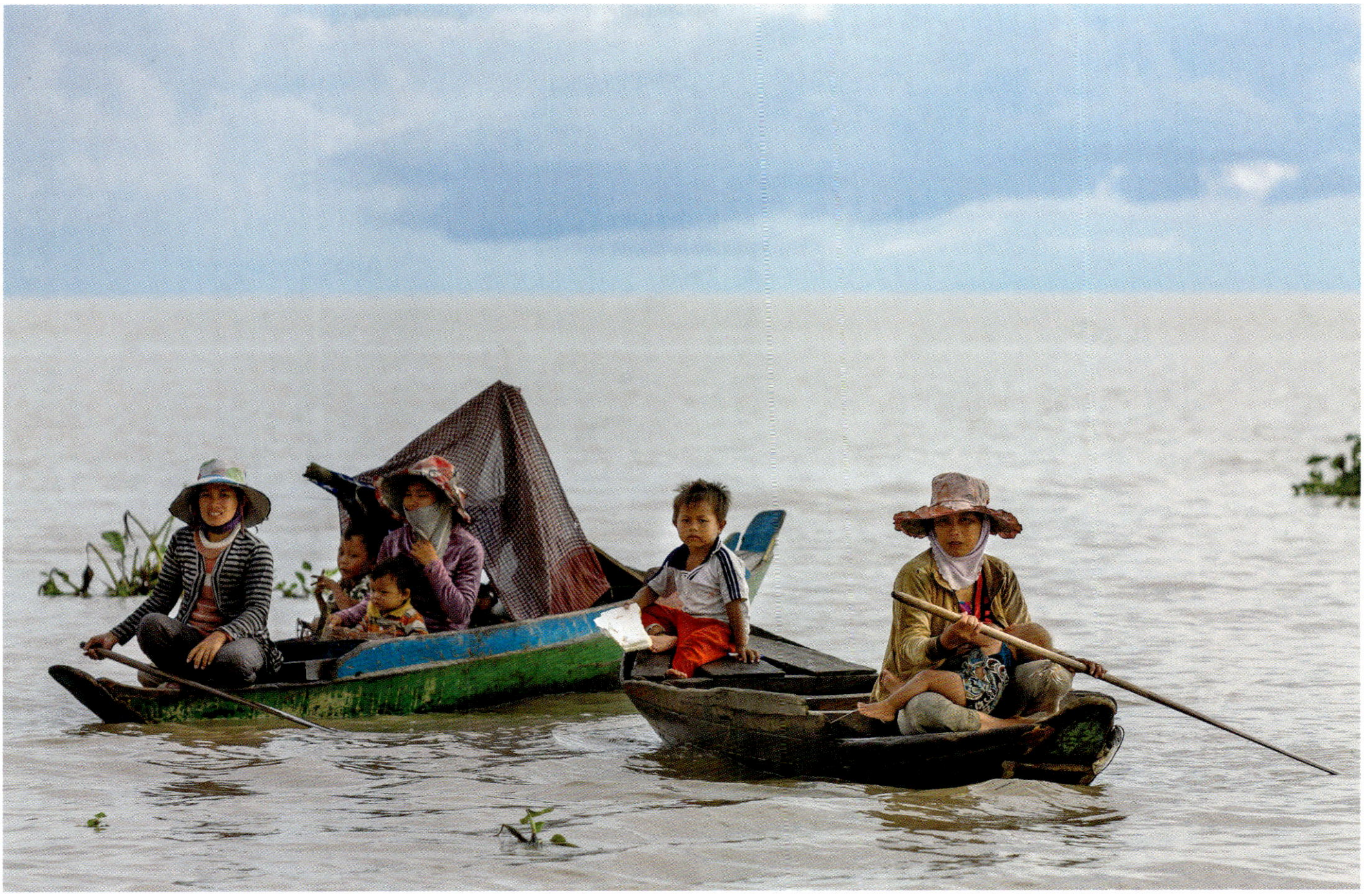

storks and fish eagles. Of the 100 bird species that live on the lake, 16 are endangered. As one of the world's richest inland fisheries, the lake also supports an estimated 1.5 million people who live on and around its shoreline.

However, despite the creation of protected areas, such as the Tonlé Sap Biosphere Reserve, which encompasses the Prek Toal Bird Sanctuary, the great lake's delicate ecosystem is threatened by overfishing, the illegal collection of bird eggs, deforestation, pollution and now the upstream damming of the Mekong.

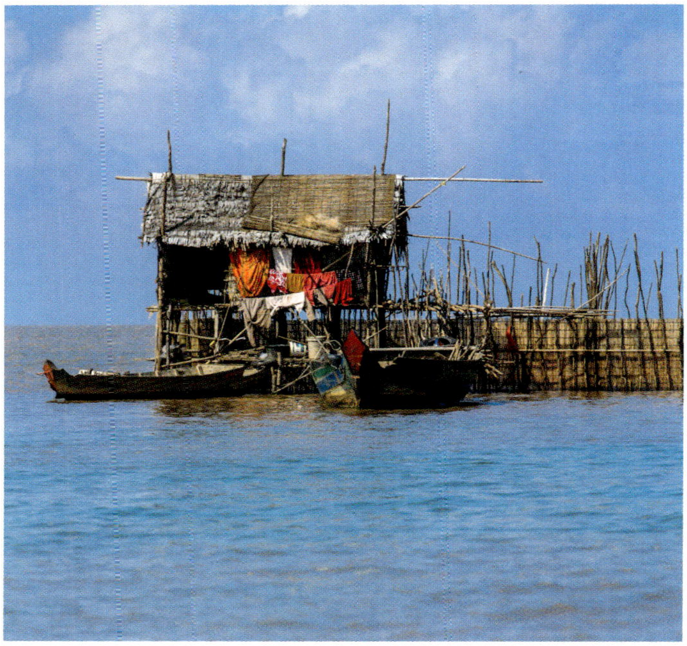

Above: The Tonlé Sap's bountiful fish supports a number of large communities. Many are originally from Vietnam and live in floating homes that are moved with the annual rise and fall of the waters. **Right:** When the flood waters of the Tonlé Sap are at their peak, temporary homes are often set up out in the lake along with bamboo corrals and netting in which to drive the fish.

FLOODED FOREST

When the flow of the Mekong and Tonlé Sap rivers reverse, the protected forest surrounding the lake, which covers 6.5 million hectares (16 million acres) and supports more than 200 plant species, becomes flooded from August until November, creating an important breeding ground for migratory fish.

At Kompong Phluk, near Siem Reap, when the waters are high, visitors can travel by boat through a series of stilted villages and into the nearby flooded forest. Drifting silently through the trees as the light dances on the water is a magical experience. The main waterway cuts through the forest and leads to the Tonlé Sap. This picturesque area has become an essential destination on the traveller's itinerary.

Walkways have also been built through the trees where birds and crab-eating macaques can be seen.

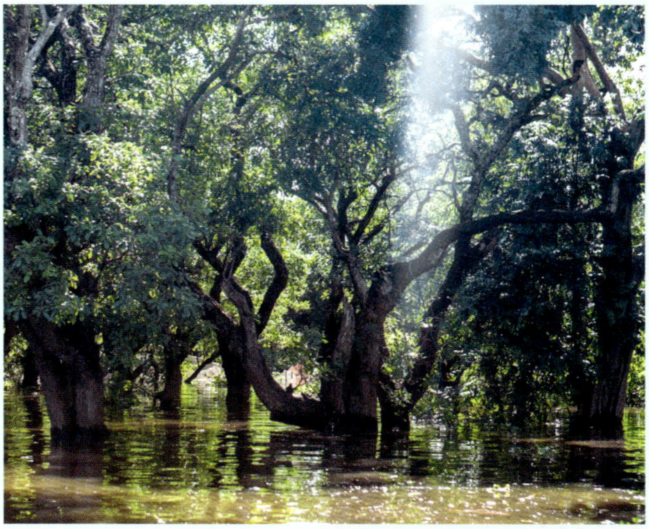

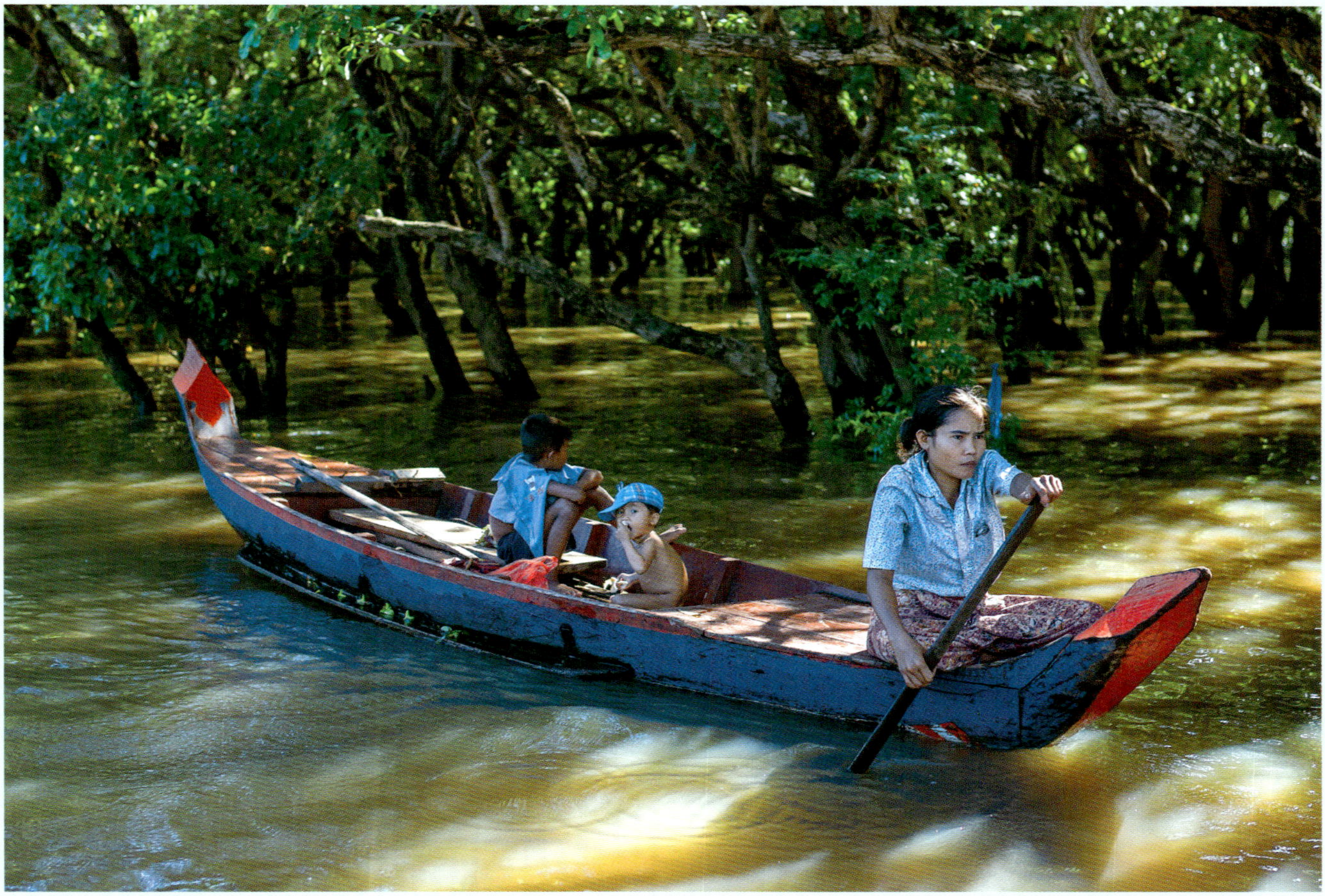

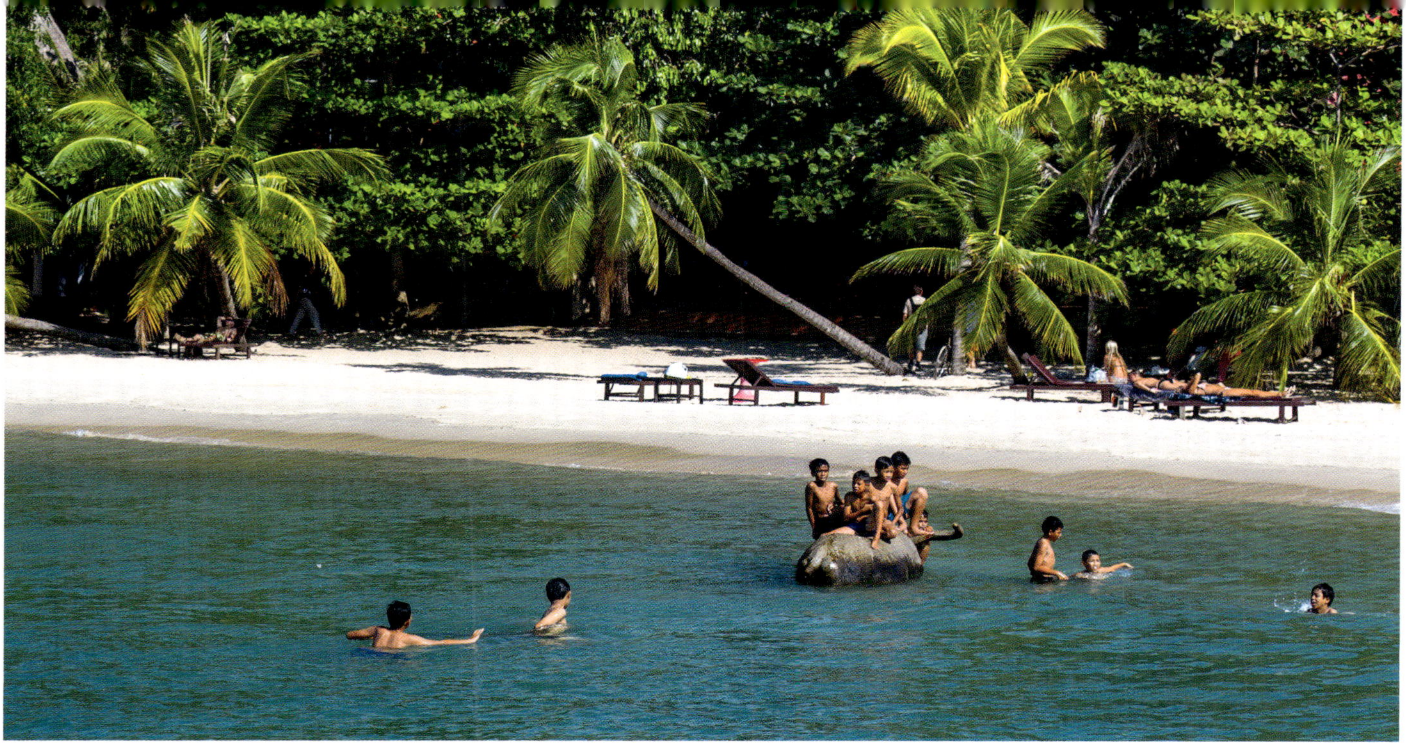

Cambodia's south-west is home to the Krâvanh or Cardamom Mountains. The range includes the country's highest peak, the 1,770-m (5,800-ft) Phnom Aural. The area extends to 4.42 million hectares (10.9 million acres) of rainforest and is one of Southeast Asia's most important wildlife conservation areas. As such it is still largely unexplored but surveys in small areas have identified 30 large mammal species, including elephants, Clouded Leopards, Tigers, gibbons and Sun Bears, 30 small mammal species, more than 450 birds including bee-eaters, hornbills, owls and woodpeckers, 64 reptiles, 30 amphibians, and numerous plants and insects. Visitors to Koh Kong in the foothills of the Cardamom Mountains can embark on guided treks and river journeys through the jungle, with the possibility of staying overnight in remote villages or temporary camps. Running south of the Cardamoms is the Dâmrei or Elephant mountain range that extends through the Kirirom and Bokor National Parks, at times rising to elevations of 1,000 m (3,280 ft).

Cambodia's coastline and its islands are still largely under-developed. Visitors can relax on beaches at Sihanoukville, Kep and Kampot or hop over by boat to nearby Rabbit Island and a handful of others, all trimmed with talcum powder beaches and turquoise waters. With the exception of Sihanoukville that now attracts more than its fair share of tourists, most of the beaches and islands along Cambodia's 450-km (280-mile) coastline offer the peace and tranquillity that first attracted travellers to Thailand more than two decades ago; at least for now.

DISAPPEARING FORESTS

With trees growing on a total of 10.094 million hectares (24.94 million acres) or nearly 57 per cent of its land area, Cambodia is a high forest-cover country. However, it also has one of the worst deforestation rates in the world and has lost 2.85 million hectares (7 million acres) of trees in the last two decades. Since 1970, it has felled 70 per cent of its primary rainforest through logging, both legal and illegal. Today, just three per cent or 322,000 hectares (796,000 acres) of primary forest remain. The growing exploitation of hardwoods and other natural resources has done irreparable damage to one of Southeast Asia's richest ecosystems, including the forest of the Cardamom Mountains. Numerous concessions have been granted to foreign logging and mining companies, even in protected areas, who are felling trees, impacting negatively on wildlife and fragmenting local communities.

Above: Cambodia's beautiful, palm-lined beaches are starting to attract an increasing number of international travellers.

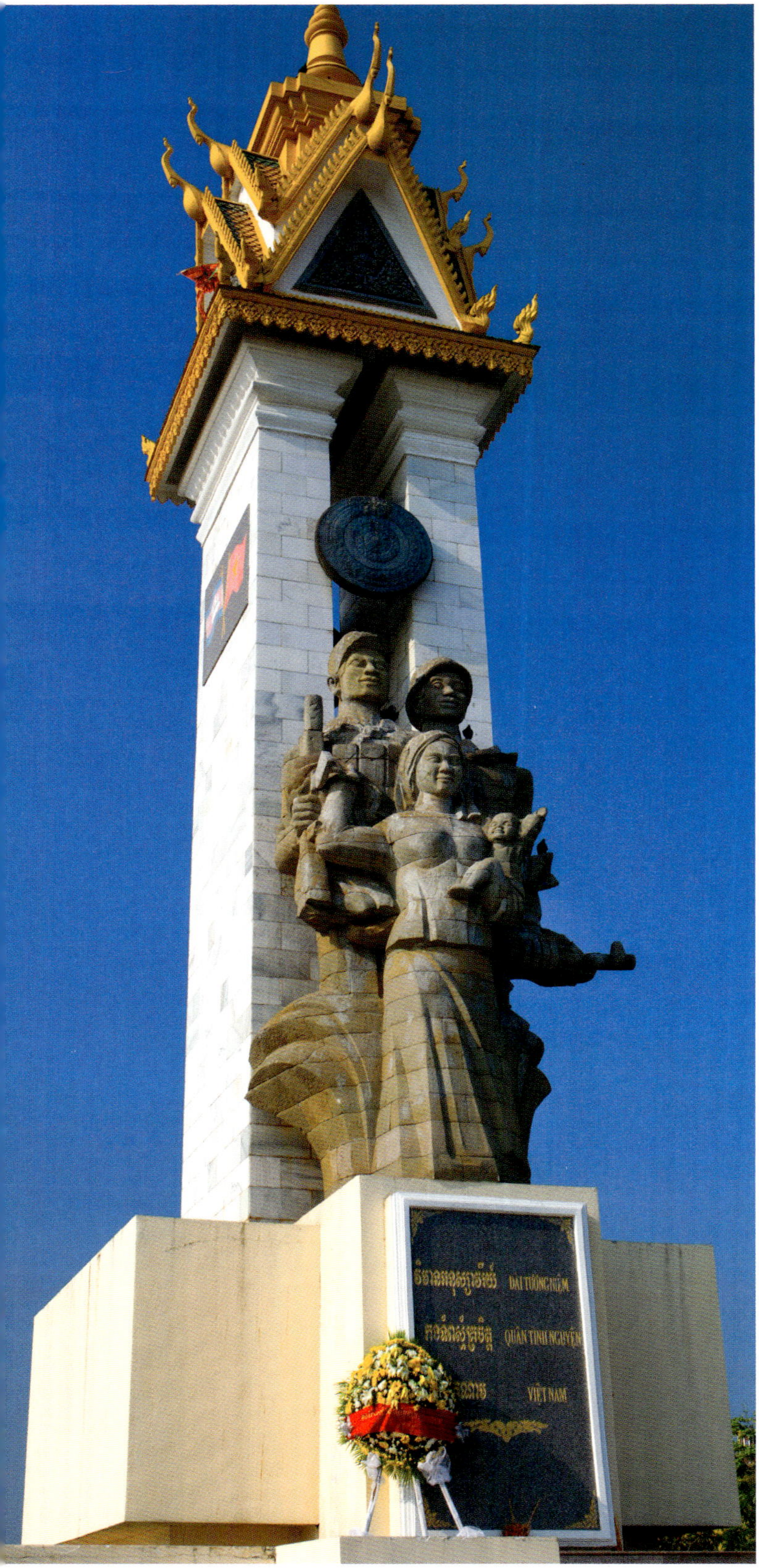

HISTORY OF CAMBODIA

Cambodia's history is both fascinating and deeply disturbing. At its peak, the might of the Khmer Empire extended over much of Southeast Asia and its culture, rich in art, music, dance and religion, created a heritage that can be still experienced today. For many years, however, the glories of the past were overshadowed by the genocide committed by the Khmer Rouge, an era of unfathomable inhumanity that still haunts its survivors.

Archaeologists believe that shards of pottery unearthed at the Laang Spean caves near Battambang in north-west Cambodia date from the sixth millennium BC and are the earliest evidence of human habitation in the country. There have also been significant Neolithic and Bronze Age finds around Siem Reap which have been dated to between 3,000 and 500 BC. These discoveries include primitive stone tools, such as adzes, as well as earthenware pottery.

It is also known that as long ago as the first century AD the Khmer established coastal settlements in what is now southern Vietnam where they traded with Chinese and Indian merchants. Later, from the sixth century onwards, fertile areas along the Tonlé Sap and Mekong supported communities that thrived by cultivating rice and fishing. During this early period, Funan was the most important of a loose amalgamation of separate states that would eventually be unified to form the Khmer Empire., with Angkor as its seat of power.

At its zenith, the mighty Khmer Empire encompassed what is present-day Cambodia, north-east Thailand, southern Laos and southern Vietnam, all of which have ancient temple remains that bear testament to the kingdom's extensive reach and power.

Jayavarman II is hailed as the first king of the Angkor period (802 to 1431). Although little is known about him, he is widely credited with the introduction of a sophisticated irrigation system that allowed the society to flourish. Reigning from 802–850 AD, he moved the site of the capital several times before finally settling at the sacred Mount Mahendraparvata, today known as Phnom Kulen, 40 km (25 miles) north-east of Angkor Thom. Inscriptions discovered at the site reveal that he created the Devaraja god-king cult and immodestly declared himself the universal ruler in 802 AD, an event that marked the beginning of the Angkor era. Later, he once again relocated the capital to Hariharalaya, today known as Roluos, where he ruled until his

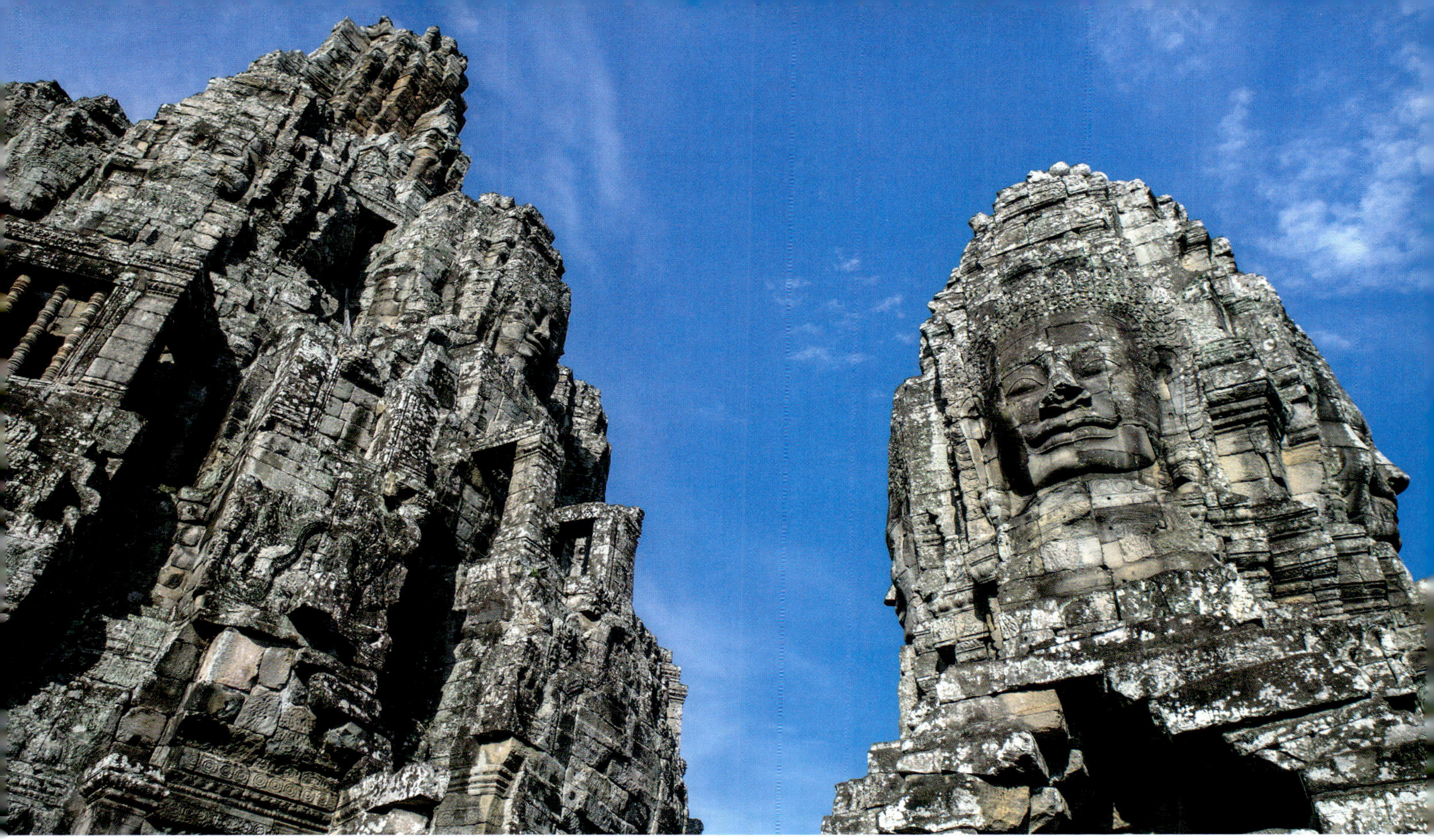

death in 850 AD. Roluos remained the capital until 905 AD when it was moved to Bakheng.

During its formative years, Angkor had established important strategic alliances but during the 10th and 11th centuries there was a series of conflicts and power struggles. What enabled the kingdom to prosper, however, was its extensive irrigation system. Water was held in *barays* – vast reservoirs that could measure up to 8,000 by 2,000 m (8,750 by 2,185 yds). It has been suggested that water from the *barays* was used to irrigate rice fields via a network of canals while other scholars claim that it was only used by the local population for drinking and bathing. What is certain, however, is that the excavation of a *baray* was an important factor in establishing a king as the ruler and protector of his people. *Barays* also held religious significance and usually included a temple on a manmade island in the centre. One of the largest that is still filled with water today is the West Baray, located just west of Angkor Thom.

Under the reign of Suryavarman II (1113 to around 1145-1150), the monarch who commanded the construction of Angkor Wat, the country became embroiled in tit-for-tat wars with Champa or what is today central Vietnam. Although Champa mounted a revenge attack in 1177, sacking Angkor and executing King Dharanindravarman II, a year later they were defeated by Khmer forces and Jayavarman VII took to the throne.

It was during Jayavarman VII's reign from 1181 to 1218 that many of Angkor's greatest architectural wonders were realized, most notably Angkor Thom and its magnificent Bayon, the temple renowned for its enormous enigmatic stones faces and exquisite craftsmanship. This was also the period during which other jewels of Angkor were built, in particular, the other-worldly Preah Khan and Ta Prohm.

Above: Bayon is one of Angkor's finest temples, a monument to the brilliance and artistry of Khmer stone carvers.

Opposite: The Cambodian-Vietnamese Friendship monument in Phnom Penh was built to commemorate the Vietnamese invasion that overthrew the Khmer Rouge.

Overleaf: The exquisitely carved Banteay Srei, often referred to as the pink temple, was constructed during the 10th century and dedicated to the Hindu god, Shiva.

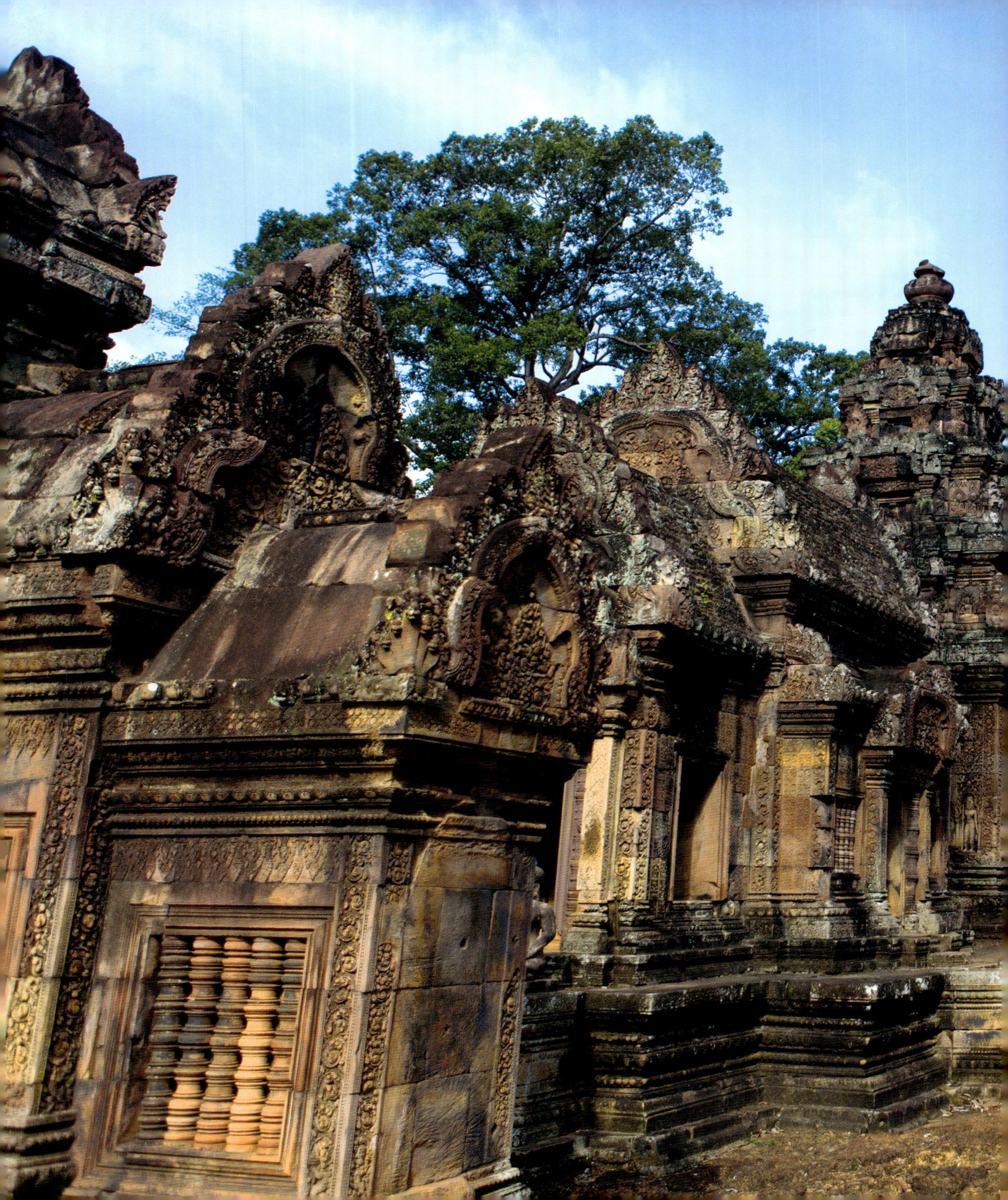

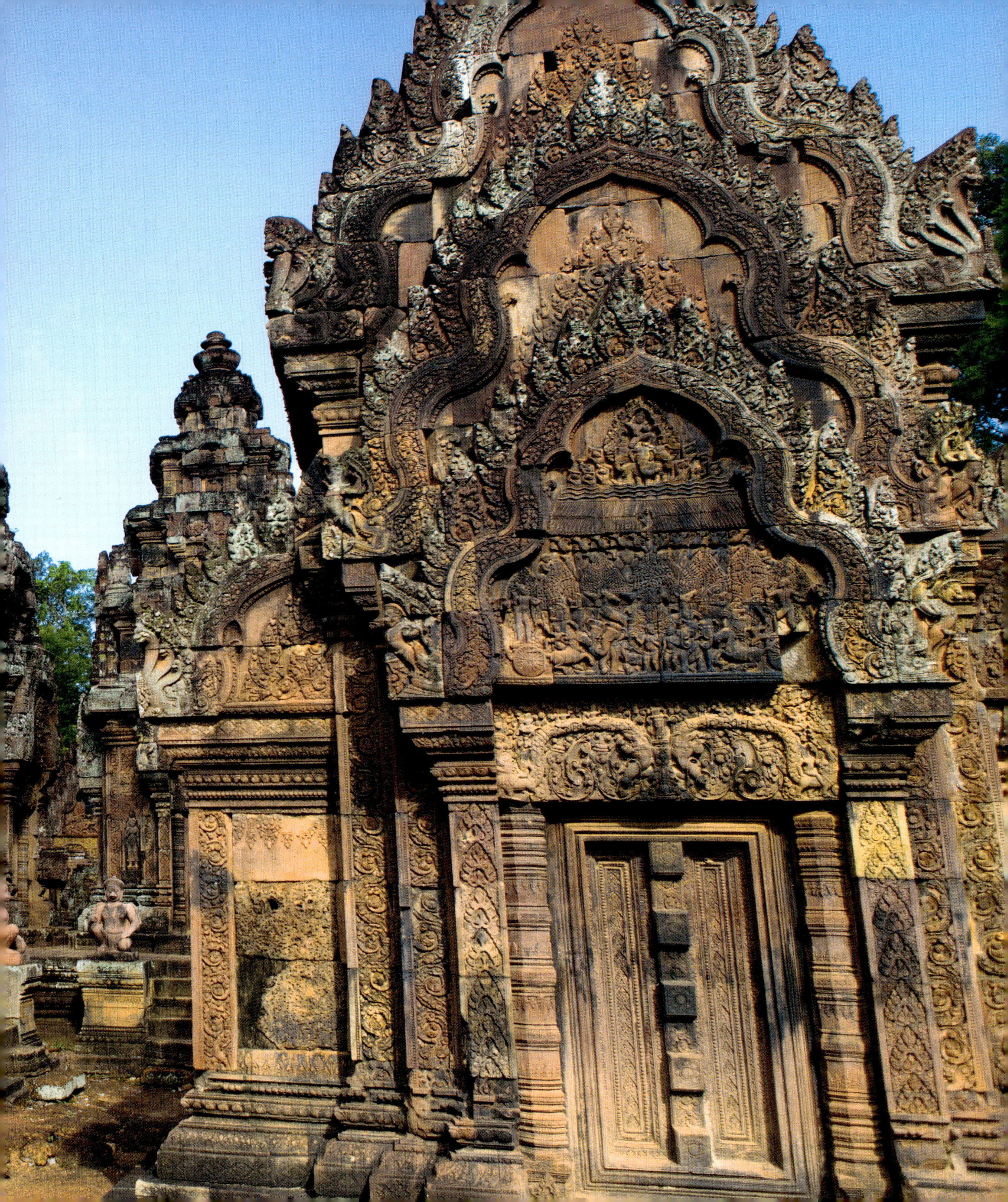

KHMER TEMPLES IN THAILAND

The largest and most spectacular of the Khmer-built temples in Thailand is Prasat Hin Phimai. It is believed that the construction and design that reflect that of Angkor Wat were instigated by Suryavarman I during the 10th century. Laid out in a rectangle measuring 565 by 1,030 m (1,855 by 3,380 ft), the ancient monument is surrounded by a moat and features an inner courtyard with three elegant, lotus-shaped towers that are representations of the Mount Meru of Hindu mythology and indicative of Khmer style. The main tower, unlike many Khmer structures, faces south towards Angkor, instead of the more typical east. The outer walls and lintels are decorated with beautiful carvings depicting episodes from the *Reamker*, the Khmer interpretation of the Hindu epic tale, the *Ramayana*. Construction of temples such as this, consists of huge sandstone blocks built over a brick and laterite structure, much of which has become exposed over time as the buildings have weathered or collapsed.

Prasat Hin Phimai is one of many Khmer-style temples scattered across north-east Thailand that show the reach of the former empire.

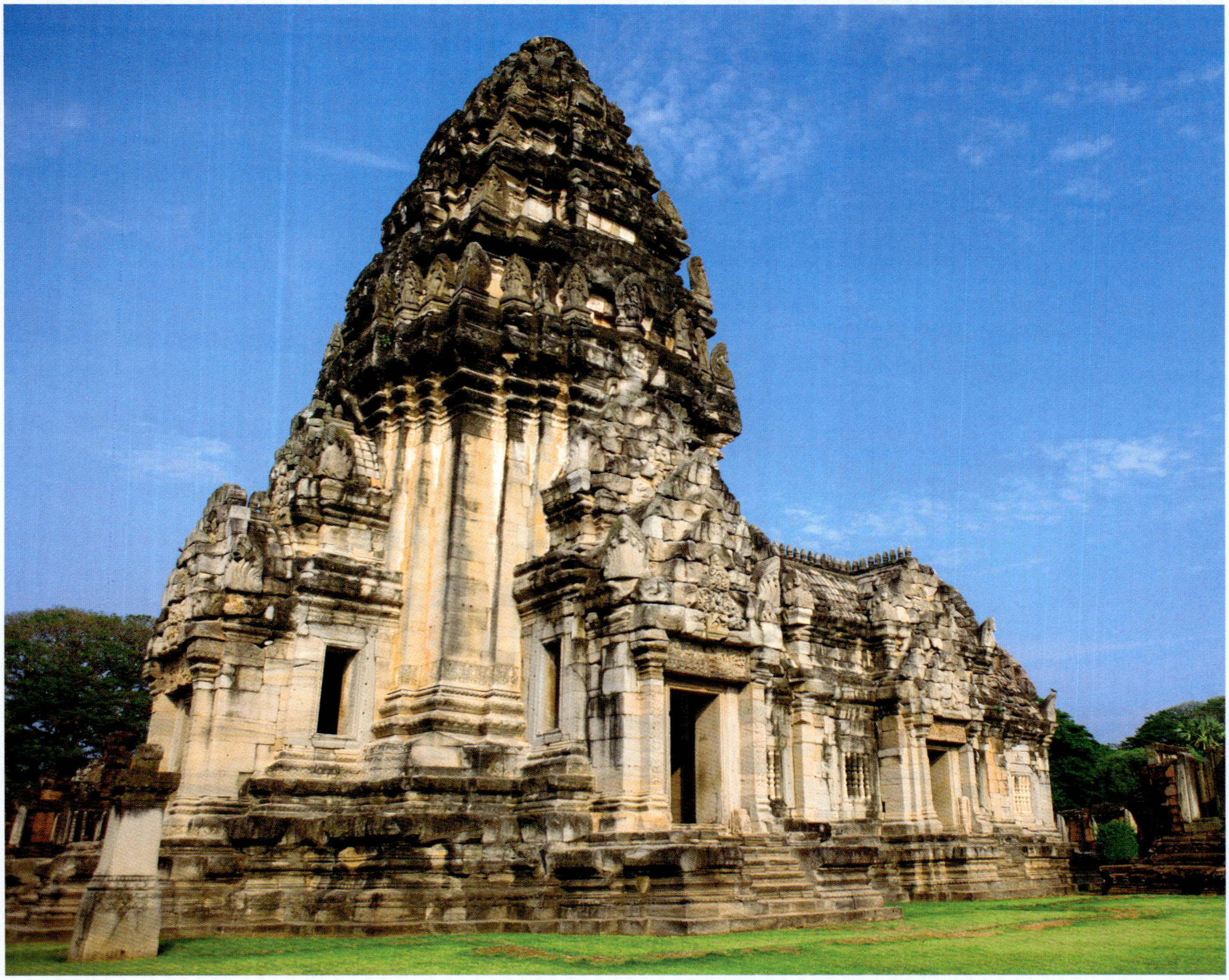

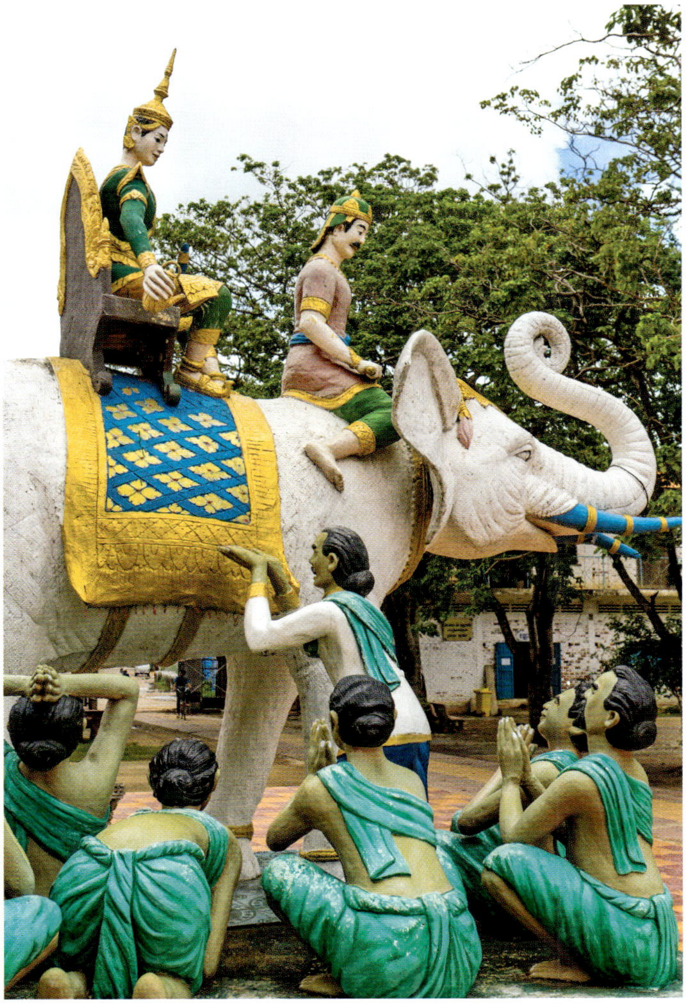

After five centuries of regional dominance, the power of the Khmer Empire began to diminish. Several factors have been attributed to its demise including long periods of drought, rivalries and religious differences, civil wars, and the loss of control at the outreaches of the empire. The Thais, with kingdoms in Sukhothai and later Ayutthaya, also became increasingly powerful and in 1431 attacked Angkor, holding sway over the provinces of Siem Reap and Battambang until 1794. Khmer ruler, Preah Ponhea Yat (1393–1463), left Angkor in favour of a new capital at Phnom Penh from 1432 to 1505, followed by a succession of sites including Tuol Basan (now known as Srey Santhor) in Kompong Cham province, Pursat, Longvek and later Oudong from 1618 to 1866. During much of this time Cambodia was ruled as vassal states by its neighbours, Thailand and Vietnam.

With the arrival of the French in the region in 1863, King Norodom I saw an opportunity to save the country from Thai and Vietnamese rule. In 1863 he signed a treaty as a French protectorate and one year later, despite a Khmer rebellion, Cambodia was annexed and became a French colony. In 1866 King Norodom I returned the capital to Phnom Penh establishing the government and building of the Royal Palace. For the next 87 years of French rule, Cambodia's monarchy was little more than symbolic, yet King Norodom's tactical move had ensured the survival of the royal court and the country. It was during this period that the French also helped win back control of Battambang and Siem Reap (which literally means "Thais flattened" in the Khmer language) from Thailand.

Although French rule was viewed by royalty as a necessary measure to save the country from Thai and Vietnamese dominance, resistance to the occupation was growing within the general population. After the Second World War the Khmer Issarak or "Free Khmer" movement was formed and the fight for independence began. In 1953, King Norodom Sihanouk gave his support to the country's desire for freedom. He dissolved parliament, declared martial law and began an international campaign to garner support for independence. On 9 November 1953, Cambodia declared independence from France.

During America's war on Vietnam (1 November 1955 to 30 April 1975), Sihanouk, who had a deep distrust of America, declared Cambodia to be neutral although he also allowed the North Vietnamese army to use Cambodian territory for bases and supply lines. Nixon, with the backing of his national security advisor, Henry Kissinger, began carpet-bombing eastern Cambodia with B52s on 9 March 1969. Over the next 14 months a total of 3,630 bombing missions were carried out over Cambodia by the US Air Force. At Kissinger's suggestion, all operations were conducted in secret. Despite the months of bombing designed to disrupt the supply lines of the North Vietnamese Army, it had little effect. The Vietnamese moved further into Cambodia and America's secret bombing raids continued. Thousands of Cambodians were killed and countless more became refugees.

Above: A statue outside Wat Damrey Sar in Battambang, also known as the White Elephant Temple, depicts peasants making offerings to a former king mounted on an auspicious white elephant.

In 1970, Sihanouk was ousted by Cambodia's elected lower house of parliament, the National Assembly, and went into exile in Beijing. Three years later, the US began another secret bombing campaign that lasted eight months and dropped hundreds of thousands of tons of bombs across Cambodia and forcing many rural Cambodians to seek refuge in Phnom Penh, swelling the population to over two million. During this time, the Khmer Rouge, a group of socialist, Paris-educated, left wing politicians with a hatred of Sihanouk and lead by Solath Sar, or Pol Pot as he became known, enjoyed increasing support among the rural population.

Following battles in the countryside, Pol Pot and his henchmen gradually tightened their grip on Phnom Penh, eventually taking the city on 17 April, 1975. It was to be the beginning of Cambodia's darkest days.

The Khmer Rouge ordered Cambodians to evacuate almost the entire population of Phnom Penh and forced them to work in collective farms. Pol Pot's bizarre and brutal political doctrine declared that the Cambodian calendar would be reset at the Year Zero, currency abolished and the country known as Democratic Kampuchea. During the three terrible years of Khmer Rouge rule, it is thought that up to two million people were massacred and countless more died of hunger and disease.

In December 1978, the Vietnamese army invaded Cambodia with the intention of freeing the country from the scourge of the Khmer Rouge. Although they quickly defeated Pol Pot's forces, the Vietnamese remained in Cambodia for over a decade. However, when they did eventually withdraw due to international pressure in September 1989, civil war soon broke out and several groups, including the Khmer Rouge, tried to take power. Following a peace settlement brokered by the United Nations, elections were held in 1993 and Norodom Sihanouk was returned to the throne. The Khmer Rouge leader, Pol Pot, escaped justice and died in rural Cambodia in 1998 aged 73.

In 2001, King Sihanouk signed legislation for a special tribunal to prosecute members of the Khmer Rouge. A series of politically motivated squabbles over financing of the UN-backed trial constantly prevented the judicial process from moving forward. Those who have faced the courts received light sentences, and the victims of the atrocities and their families have been denied justice.

Since 1985, Cambodian politics has been dominated by Prime Minister Samdech Hun Sen, an extremely controversial figure and a former Battalion Commander with the Khmer Rouge. Today, Cambodia is a society with great divisions between the relatively small ruling middle class and the majority rural poor. However, the country is experiencing considerable growth and development which offers increased opportunity for the young. More importantly, despite the many challenges, the country is enjoying a welcome period of peace and stability. Investment is pouring in from China, Korea, Japan and Singapore, and the country is one of Asia's most popular tourist destinations, all of which would have been unthinkable just two decades ago.

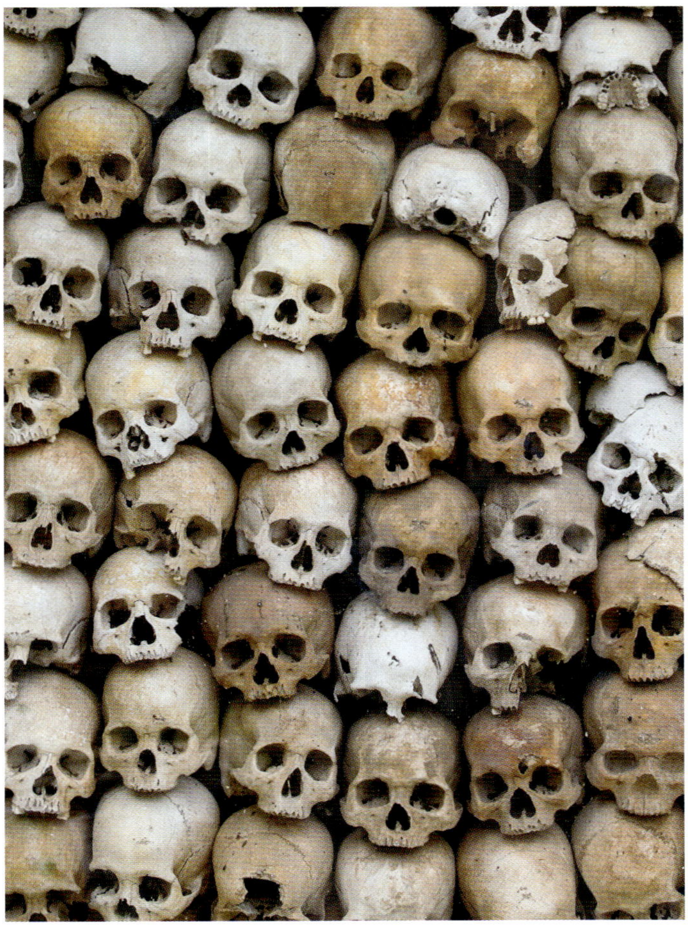

Opposite top: The national flag fluttering in the wind on Phnom Penh's riverfront.

Left: At the Killing Fields memorial outside Phnom Penh the skulls of those murdered by the Khmer Rouge are displayed as a gruesome reminder of their appalling atrocities.

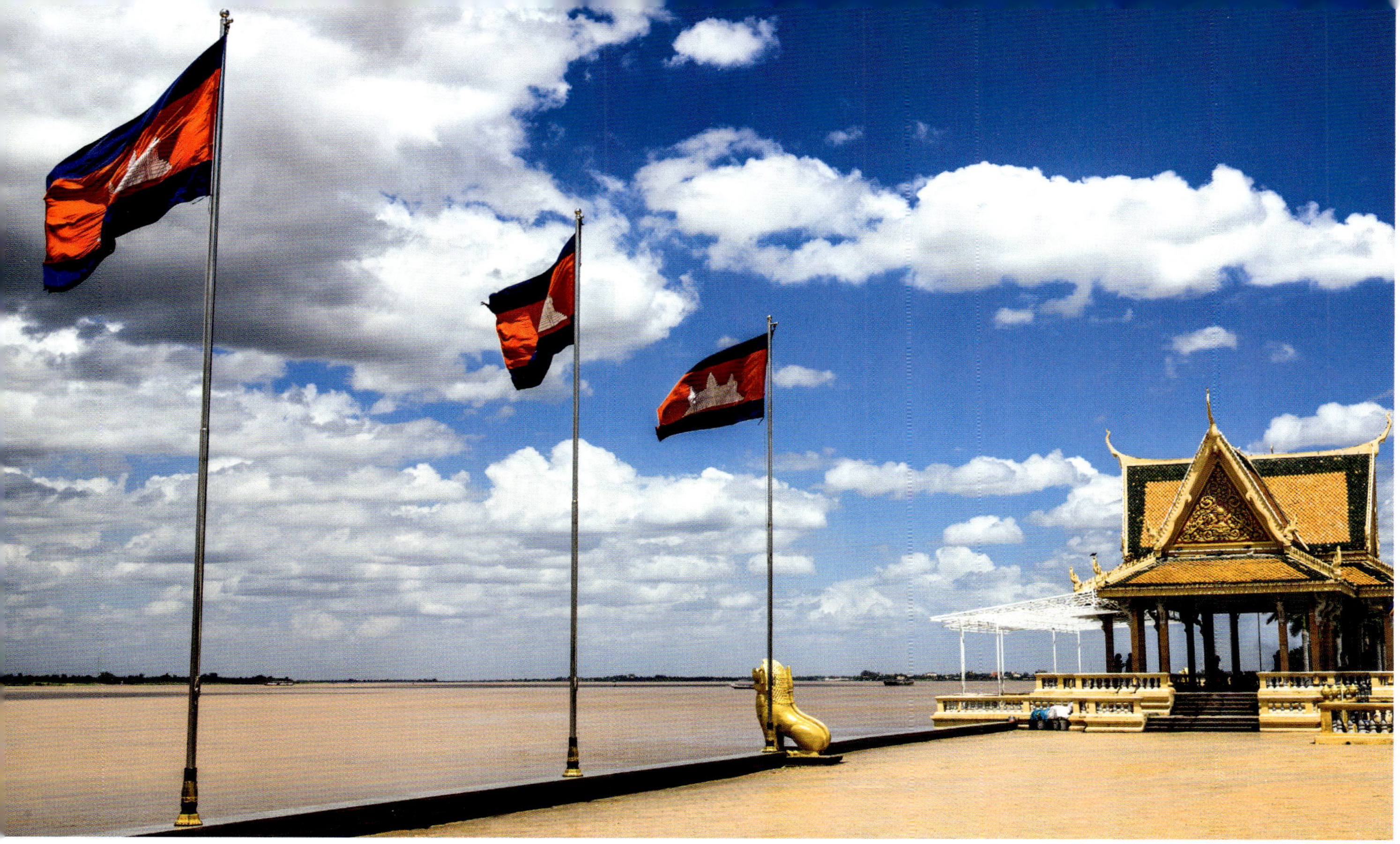

CAMBODIAN LANDMINE MUSEUM

America's enduring legacy in Cambodia is unexploded ordnance (UXO) that continues to claim victims. Over 40,000 Cambodians have been maimed by landmines. Cambodia's deadly hidden explosives are also the result of 35 years of civil war and were used by all sides of the conflicts including Cambodians, Americans and Vietnamese. To highlight the problem, the Cambodian Landmine Museum Relief Facility was established near Siem Reap in 1997 by an ex-child soldier, Aki Ra. It is estimated that 5,000,000 landmines manufactured in China, Russia, Vietnam and the United States, and an equal number of other UXOs, such as rockets, missiles, mortars and grenades, remain scattered across the Cambodian countryside. Thanks to raised awareness and on-going, systematic, mine-clearance projects, the casualties from the hidden explosives, who are usually poor farmers or children, have fallen from an annual high of 4,320 in 1996 to 286 in 2010. At the Cambodian Landmine Museum Relief Facility visitors can gain valuable insight into the extent of this insidious problem.

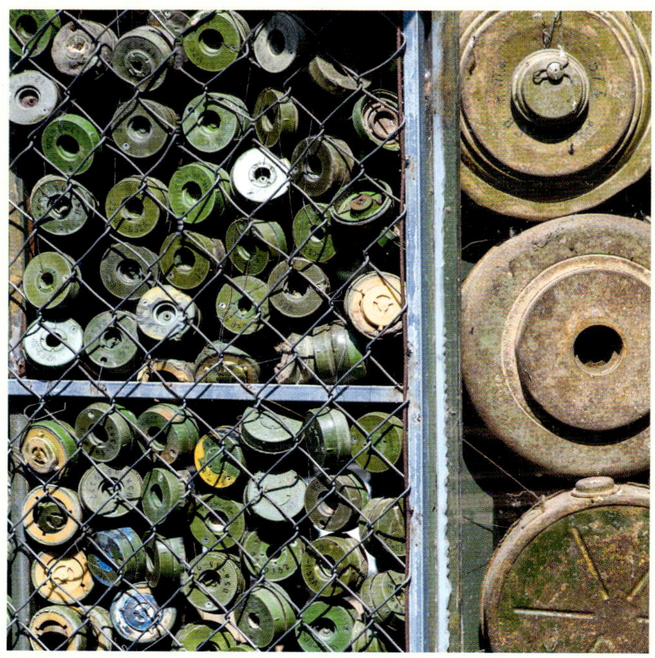

THE END OF A ROYAL ERA

King Norodom Sihanouk died of a heart attack aged 89 on 15 October 2012, while living in Beijing. A colourful and often controversial character, he first ascended the throne in 1941 aged 19 before abdicating in 1955. Sihanouk was a political survivor who aligned himself with the Khmer Rouge, although they later placed him under house arrest. In 1991, following peace negotiations with a coalition government and Hun Sen's People's Republic of Kampuchea, a treaty was signed in Paris and Sihanouk returned to the country. He was restored to the throne in 1993. In 2004, he abdicated for the second time in favour of his eldest son, Norodom Sihamoni. Despite long periods living in exile in both North Korea and China, Sihanouk remained an important figure for many Cambodians because he had helped regain independence from the French and worked to stabilize the country during the 1990s. When his funeral was held in Phnom Penh 100 days after his death, thousands of rural Cambodians lined the city streets to watch his embalmed body escorted to the funeral pyre in front of the National Museum.

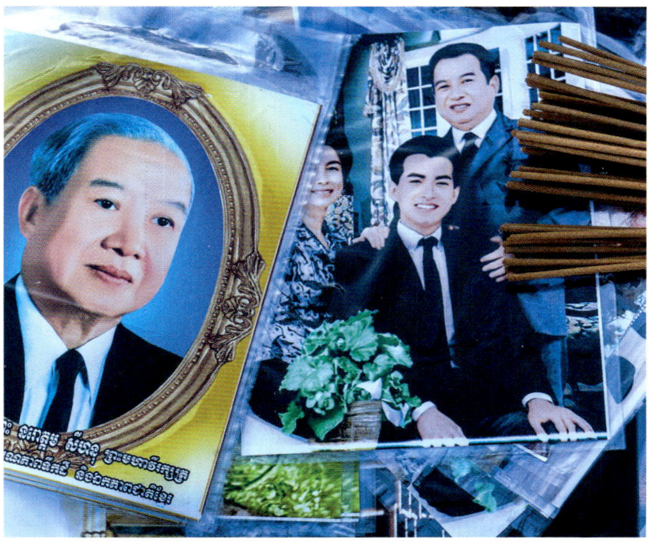

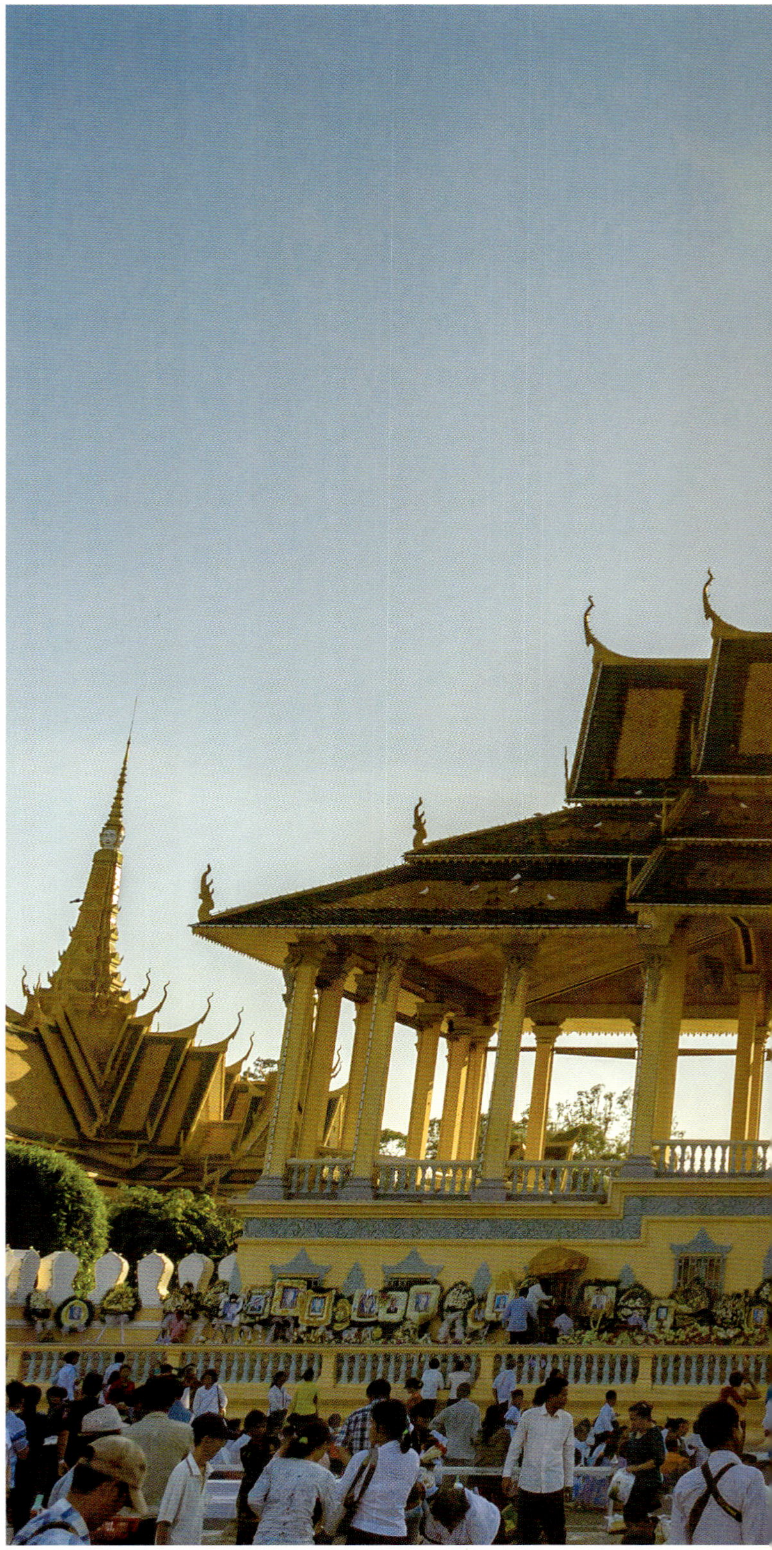

Above: Posters of Cambodia's popular King Sihanouk and his family for sale at his funeral.

Right: Following the death of King Sihanouk, thousands of Cambodians poured into Phnom Penh to offer their respects while his body lay in state at the Royal Palace.

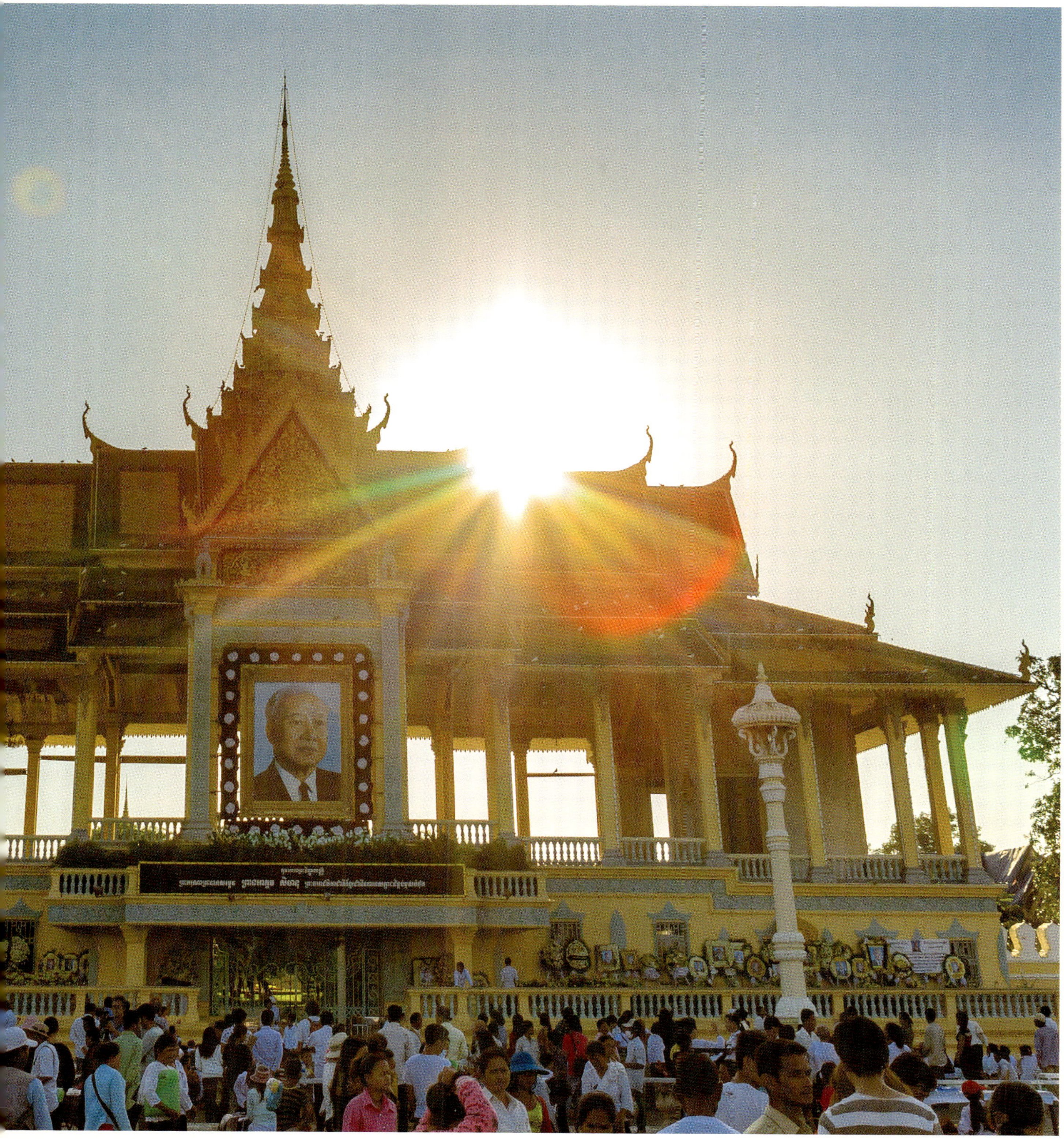

THE PEOPLE

Cambodia has a population of almost 15 million and is growing at a rate of two per cent a year, meaning that it will top 20 million by 2028. In recent years, Phnom Penh has experienced an influx of people from rural areas seeking work and the city is now home to more than 1.5 million.

The majority of the population is ethnic Khmer and almost all are Buddhist. Cambodia also has a long history of immigration and the population includes large numbers of Chinese, Vietnamese and Cham Muslims. There are also various ethnic groups in the mountainous north-west. These include the Kui in Preah Vihear, the Pnong in Mondulkiri, Ratanakiri, Kratie and Stung Treng, and the Krung also in Ratanakiri and Stung Treng.

Cambodia's ethnic Khmer make up around 86 per cent of the population. It is believed that they migrated down from Tibet and southern China 3,000 years ago. Related to the Mon who settled in Myanmar, they speak Khmer, which is part of the larger Mon-Khmer linguistic family. Today there are several regional dialects, but the Khmer standard is the dialect spoken in Phnom Penh. In common with other Southeast Asian cultures, the Khmer were heavily influenced by the religion and culture of India and Sri Lanka brought to the region by early traders. Over the years, the Khmer have assimilated with migratory people including the Malays and Javanese who arrived during the eighth century and the Thais during the 15th century, as well as waves of Vietnamese and Chinese during the 17th and 18th centuries respectively.

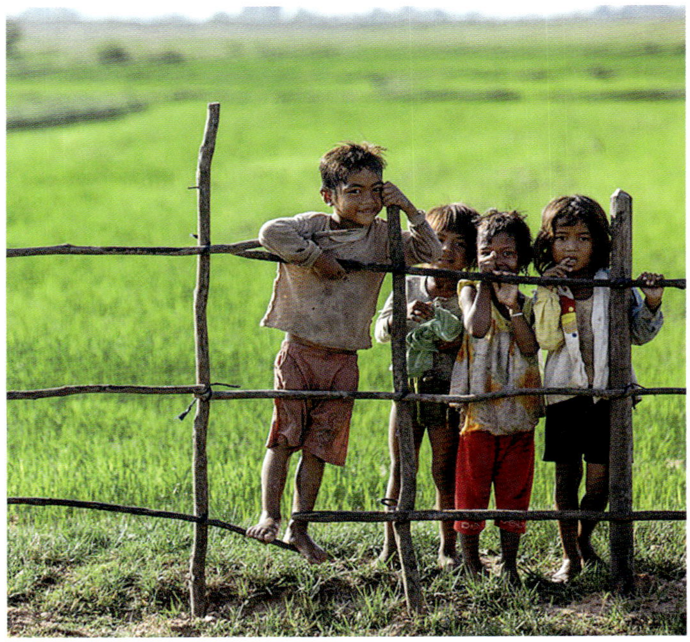

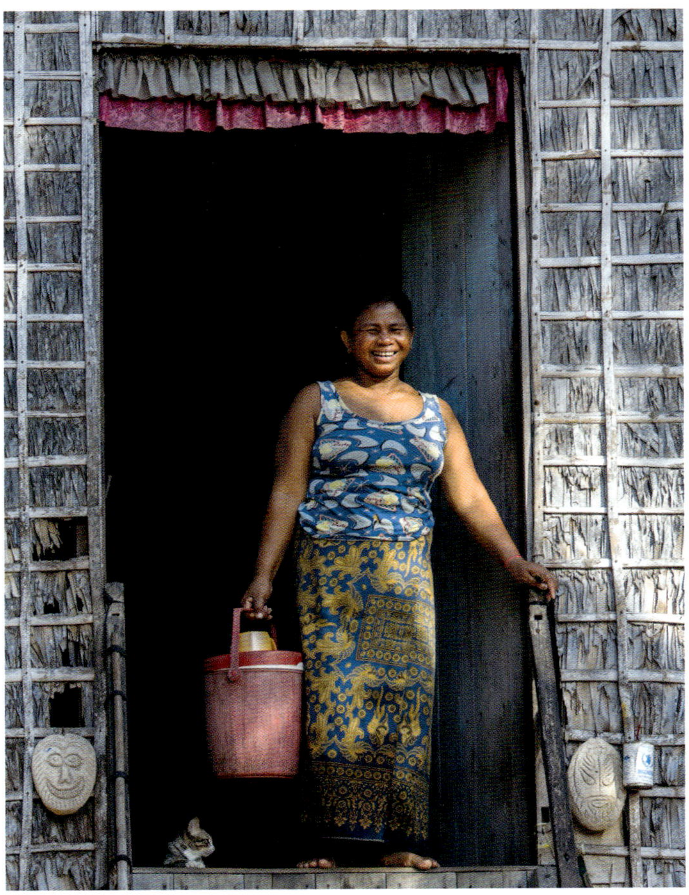

This page and opposite top: Rural Cambodia is populated by resilient people, many of whom live a hard subsistence existence, but they remain warm and welcoming. In recent years, however, increasing numbers have been drawn to Phnom Penh where they can make a better living selling food in the streets or working in factories.

Opposite below left: The majority of Cambodians are devout Buddhists and regularly visit temples to pray and make offerings of incense and flowers.

Opposite below right: The country's large population of Vietnamese live mainly in stilted homes and houseboats on the Tonlé Sap and along the banks of Mekong River.

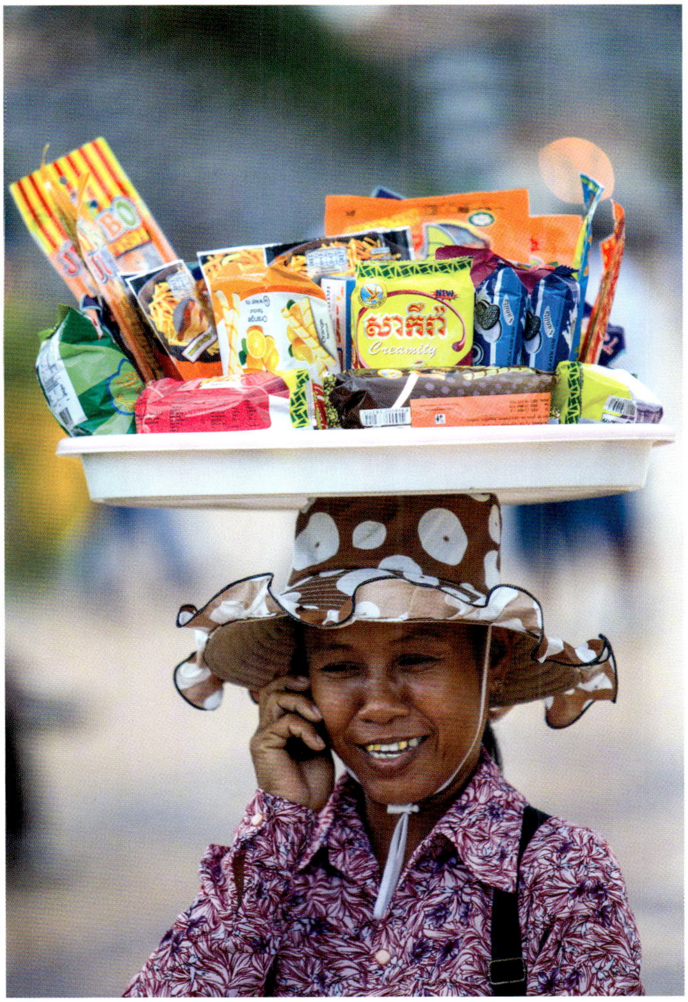

At five per cent of the population, the Vietnamese are Cambodia's largest ethnic minority. Although the official figure is 740,000, it is thought that there may be up to two million Vietnamese living in Cambodia. They moved into Cambodia from the Mekong Delta in the 17th century, and were also brought in by the French around 1860 to work in plantations or within local administration. During the Khmer Rouge years, many were persecuted or killed, causing thousands to flee back to Vietnam. Even today, relations between the Khmer and the Vietnamese are strained and they have not been allowed to integrate like the Chinese. There are substantial Vietnamese communities in Phnom Penh and other large towns but the majority live along the Mekong and Bassac rivers and around fringes of the Tonlé Sap in stilted houses or floating villages where they earn a living farming fish. Many others are involved in the construction industry, particularly with timber.

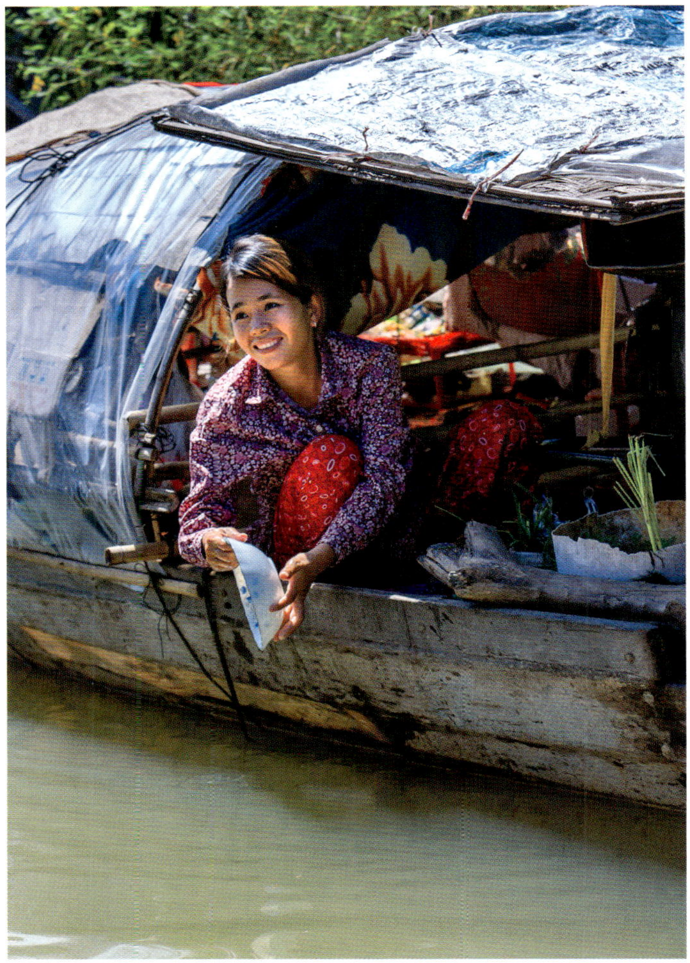

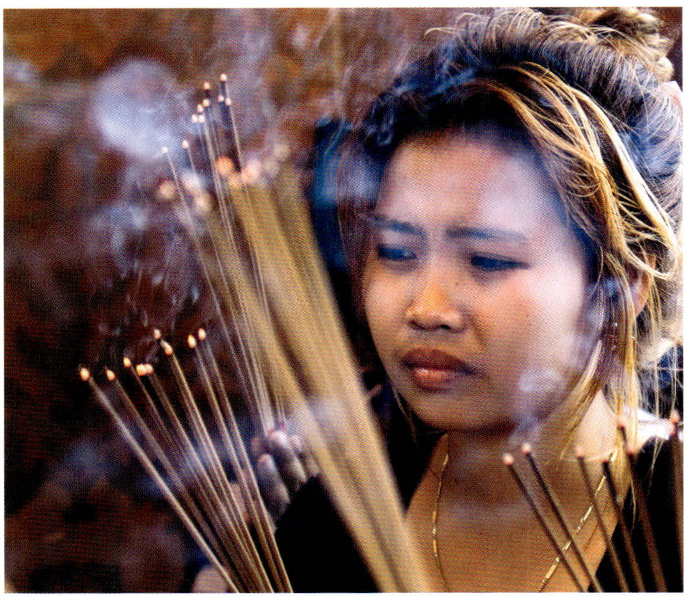

THE SAMPEAH

Cambodian people are disarmingly friendly and welcoming. When meeting locals, visitors will often receive a *sampeah*, a traditional greeting of palms pressed together in front of the chest in a prayer-like gesture, and accompanied by a slight bowing of the head. It is considered a way of showing respect to a guest. When greeting friends of a similar age, the hands are held at chest level. For elders or an employer, the tips of the fingers are at lip level, while for greeting parents or teachers they are at nose level and at eyebrow level for royalty or monks.

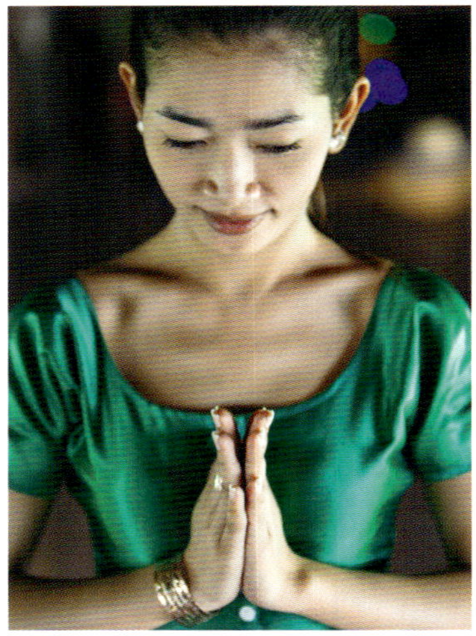

The *sampeah* can also be offered as an apology or a plea for sympathy. When kneeling in prayer, the hands are held higher in front of the nose or forehead before lowering the head and hands to the ground three times. Similar to the Thai *wai* or the Indian *anjali mudra* from which it is most likely to have been derived, the Cambodia *sampeah* is an enchanting greeting. It is often accompanied by the words, *johm riab sua*, or 'hello'. The gesture has long been used in Khmer society and can be seen in temple carvings dating back to the ninth century.

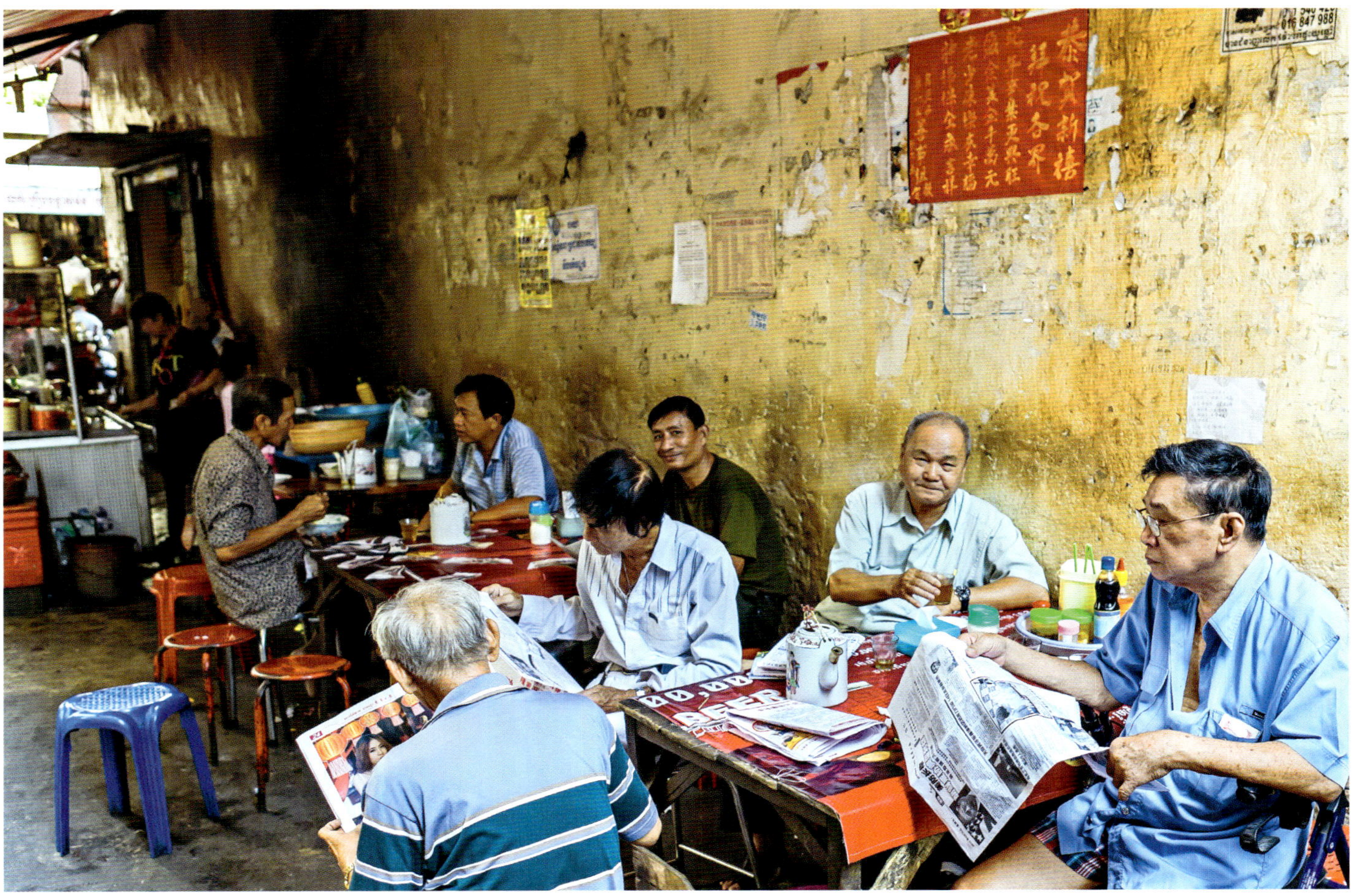

Although there are fewer Chinese in Cambodia than Vietnamese (estimates vary from half to one million) they have almost completely assimilated into society to the extent that they dominate banking and commerce. They are also active in government at a local and national level. There are five ethnic Chinese groups in Cambodia: the Teochew and Cantonese, who have large communities in Phnom Penh and Kompong Cham, the Hainanese, who are said to have originally started the pepper farms in Kampot, and the Hakka and Hokkien, who are involved in banking. In recent years, the Chinese community has begun to increase rapidly due to close political ties between the two countries and huge investment in a range of industries, including mining and forestry.

Opposite below: Khmer-Chinese men enjoying tea and the morning paper at a food stall in one of Phnom Penh's older districts.

THE CHAM

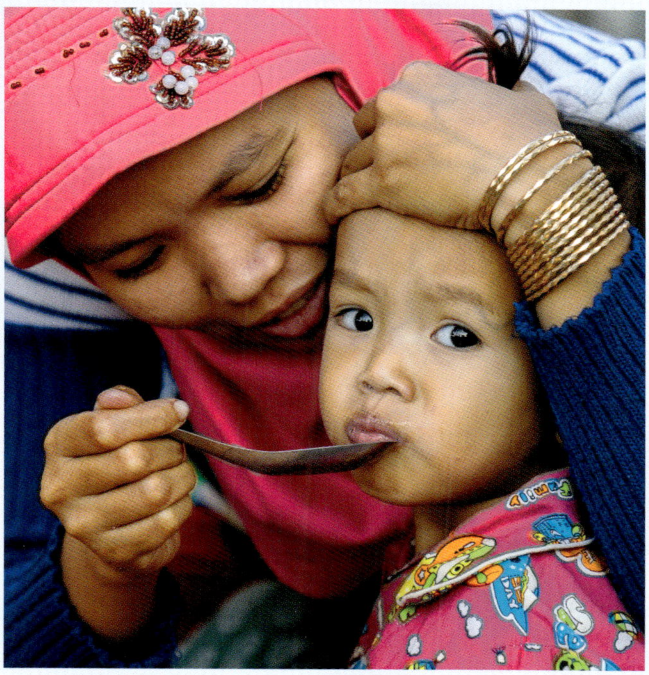

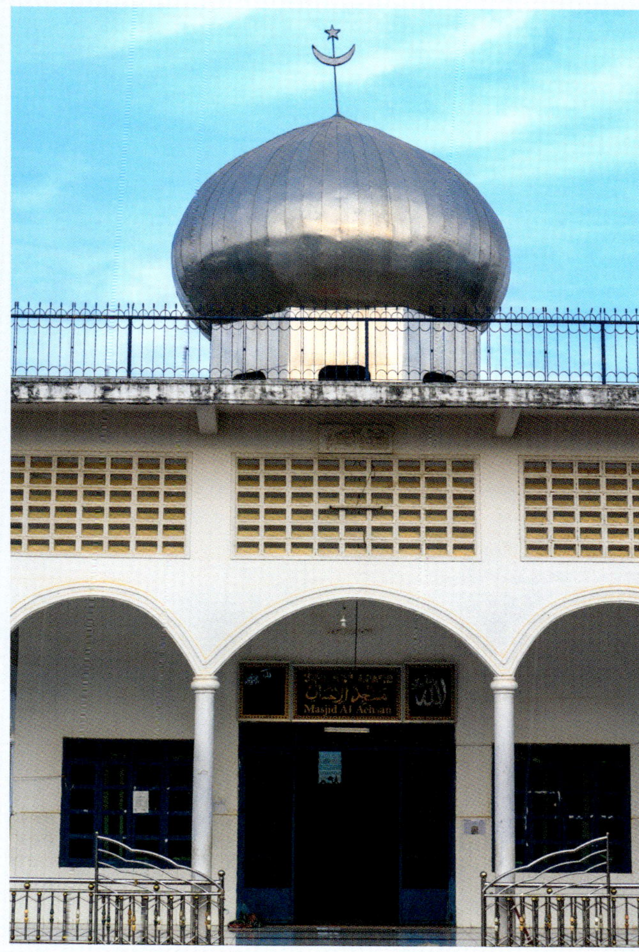

Many visitors to Cambodia are surprised to learn that the country has a significant population of Cham or Khmer Muslims who adopted Islam from Malay traders during the 17th century. Descendants of the former kingdom of Champa, which was located along the central coast of present-day Vietnam, they were heavily persecuted by the Khmer Rouge, their leaders executed and mosques destroyed. Today the majority of Cham Muslims, who number around 400,000, live in 400 or more villages located beside the Mekong River and Tonlé Sap in Kompong Cham and Kompong Chhnang provinces. The Cham make a living from fishing but are also farmers and tend crops such as rice, corn, tobacco, peanuts, beans and vegetables. The Cham are easily recognized by their distinctive sarong which is worn by men and women. The women also wear a characteristic Muslim headscarf.

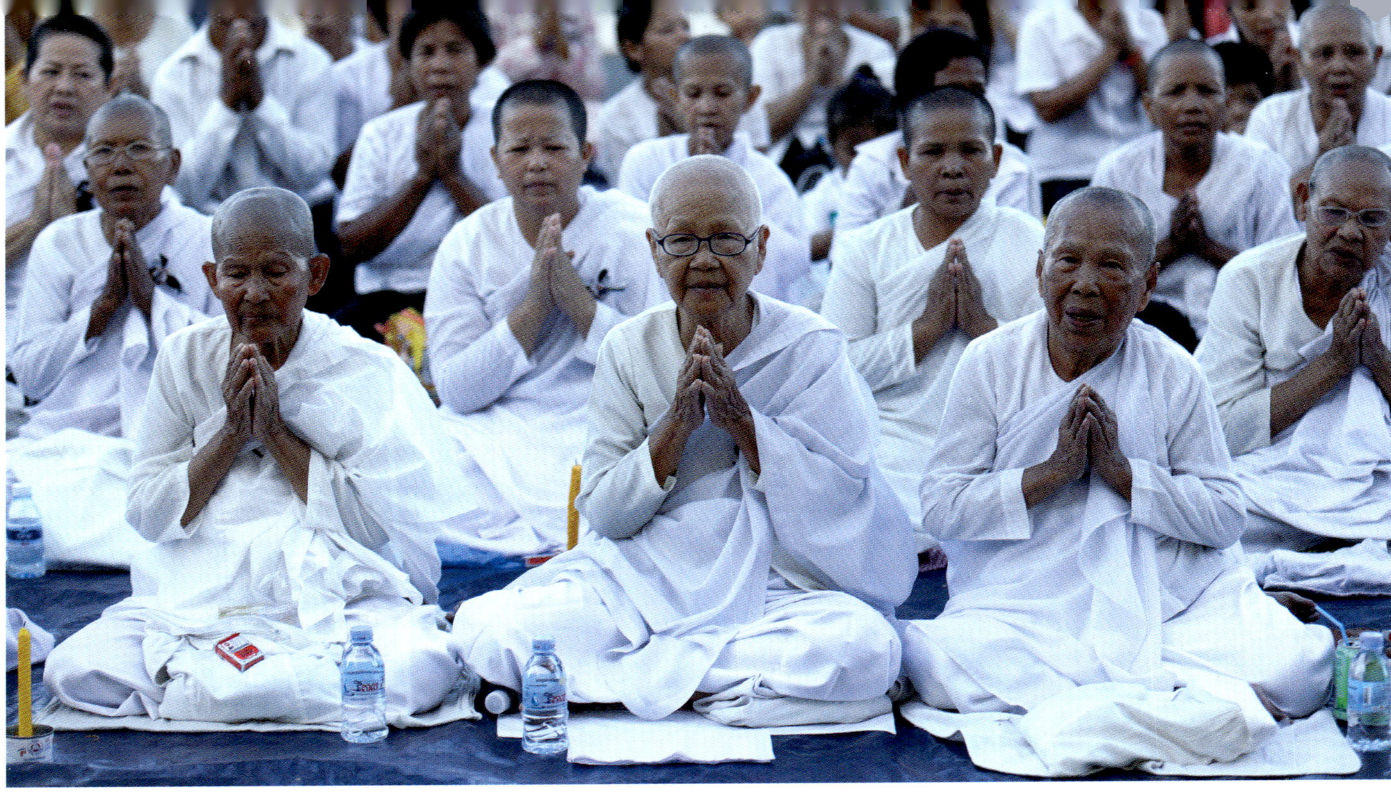

RELIGION

Buddhism is the official religion of Cambodia. Both Mahayana and Theravada Buddhism were brought to Cambodia but during different periods. It is thought that Mahayana Buddhism, or the 'great vehicle', may have arrived via Indonesia, then the former Kingdom of Srivijaya, as early as the fifth century. This school of Buddhism was at its most popular during the reign of Jayavarman VII in the late 12th and early 13th centuries. Central to the belief system is the Bodhisattva, or Enlightened Being, who has gained sufficient merit to enter Nirvana but chooses instead to return to earth to help mankind. Bodhisattvas feature as Angkor-period sculptures and reliefs. Theravada Buddhism appeared much later, having arrived from Sri Lanka via Myanmar and Thailand from the 11th century onwards, eventually displacing Mahayana Buddhism and spreading throughout all levels of society. It was during the 13th century when Angkor's decline began that Theravada Buddhism became the official religion of Cambodia. Today, around 90 per cent of the population follows Theravada Buddhism, although elements of animism and ancestor worship have also been integrated into many Buddhist rituals and festivals. Hinduism was also present in Cambodia from about the first century and existed alongside Buddhism. During the Angkor period, several popular cults inspired by Hindu deities began and ended, including Jayavarman II's Devaraja god-king cult in the eighth century, Shivaism in the ninth and 10th centuries, and Vishnuism in the 11th century.

Buddhism lies at the heart of Cambodian society. In life, it builds and maintains strong bonds within communities through regular religious festivals, and provides rudimentary education for orphans and the poor at temple schools. In death, it guides the passage into the next life and offers comfort for the bereaved. During the Khmer Rouge years, Buddhism was declared a reactionary force and was targeted as part of their attempts to dismantle society. Many monks were killed or endured forced labour in the fields, and hundreds of temples and Buddha images destroyed. When the country was released from the terrible spectre of Pol Pot and his cadres, there were very few monks left but the restoration of Buddhism was considered essential in helping the country rebuild itself. In 1979, Theravada monks from Vietnam re-ordained the surviving monks and the new Cambodian government welcomed further ordinations. It also encouraged the restoration of temples and the production of Buddha images. By the early 1980s religious festivals had been revived and hundreds had entered the monkhood.

Today, there are more than 50,000 monks in Cambodia and Buddhism is enshrined in the national constitution as the state religion. The Cambodian Buddhist assembly or Sangha is divided into two distinct sects: the majority Mahanikaya sect that includes 90 per cent of the monks and the remaining, smaller Thammayut sect that was introduced by Buddhists from Thailand in the mid-19th century. Thammayut means 'those holding to the law' and was originally founded by Thailand's King Mongkut (1851–68). The movement advocated stricter compliance with religious practice and also sought to modernize Buddhism by encouraging rationalism over superstition. In Cambodia, as in Thailand, it became popular with royalists and the country's ruling class.

The Cham communities in the south-east practise Islam. Although many mosques were destroyed during the Khmer Rouge rule, today there are estimated to be around 250 in the country, many of which are in Kompong Cham Province. There are small groups of Christians in Cambodia among some of the Chinese and Vietnamese communities, though they too are predominately Buddhist, and animism is practised by the country's hill peoples.

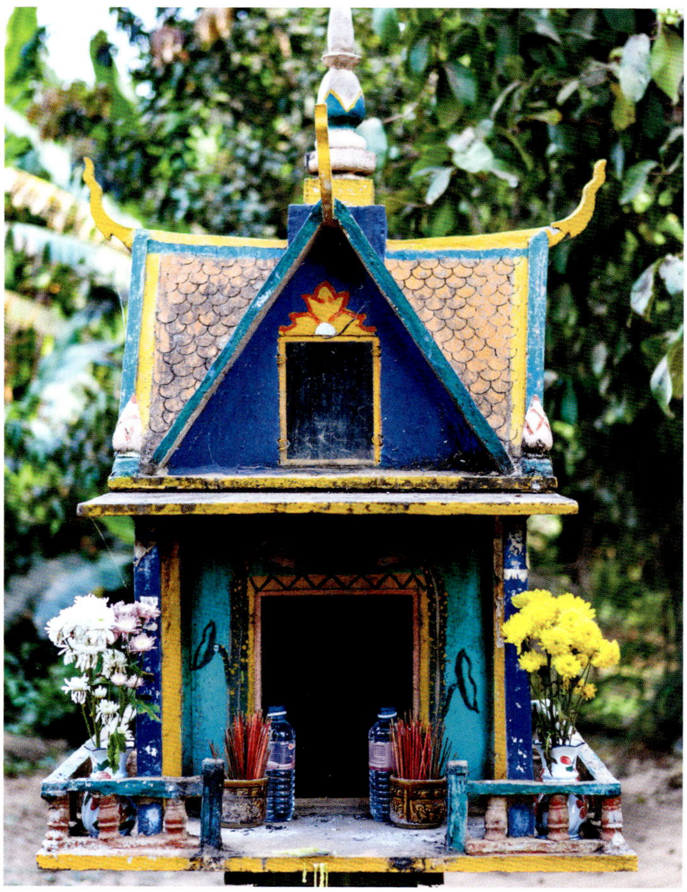

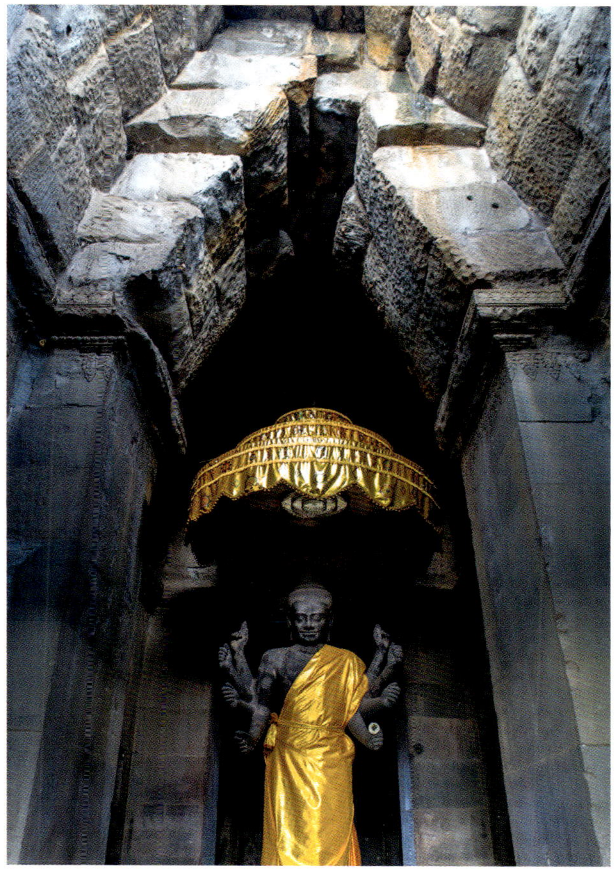

VISHNU AT ANGKOR WAT

In a western *gopura*, or arched entranceway, of Angkor Wat's outer corridor stands a magnificent eight-armed statue of Vishnu. Known locally as Ta Reach, the five-metre (16-ft) tall image is revered by Hindus and Buddhists alike. It also illustrates the transition of religious beliefs in Cambodia. Angkor Wat was originally built as a Hindu temple but the head of Vishnu has been replaced with that of Buddha. Shaded by a multi-tiered parasol and draped with an orange robe, the image is worshipped by Buddhists who offer flowers, and light candles and incense.

Left: Small spirit houses where Buddhists make daily offerings are situated outside almost every home.

Opposite: A gathering of nuns holding a prayer vigil for King Sihanouk in front of the Royal Palace.

THE BUDDHIST LIFE

Theravada Buddhism, which translates as 'the doctrine of the elders', is based on three concepts: *dharma*, the doctrine of the Buddha; *karma*, the belief that future incarnations are related to your deeds and misdeeds in this life; and *sangha*, the religious community where man can improve his *karma*. Making merit is therefore central to the life of a Buddhist. The daily ritual of offering food to monks, worship and giving donations are all considered merit-making actions.

Theravada Buddhism does not believe in supernatural solutions to worldly problems, instead it teaches that an individual can achieve enlightenment through meditation. Every young Buddhist man is expected to enter the monkhood for a short period of his life, an act which earns merit for the family. The Buddhist order's 227 rules for the monastic life include refraining from causing harm to living beings, refraining from taking that which is not freely given, refraining from sexual misconduct, refraining from lying and gossip, and refraining from intoxicating drink and drugs. Monks and nuns are also not permitted to eat from midday until daybreak, and must not handle money.

Below: After monks return to the temple from collecting alms they sit together in silence and eat the last meal of the day, usually at about 11.30 a.m.

Opposite top left: A Buddhist monk reading the scriptures at Angkor Wat. The faithful bring him offerings in the morning. In return they receive a blessing and are sprinkled with holy water.

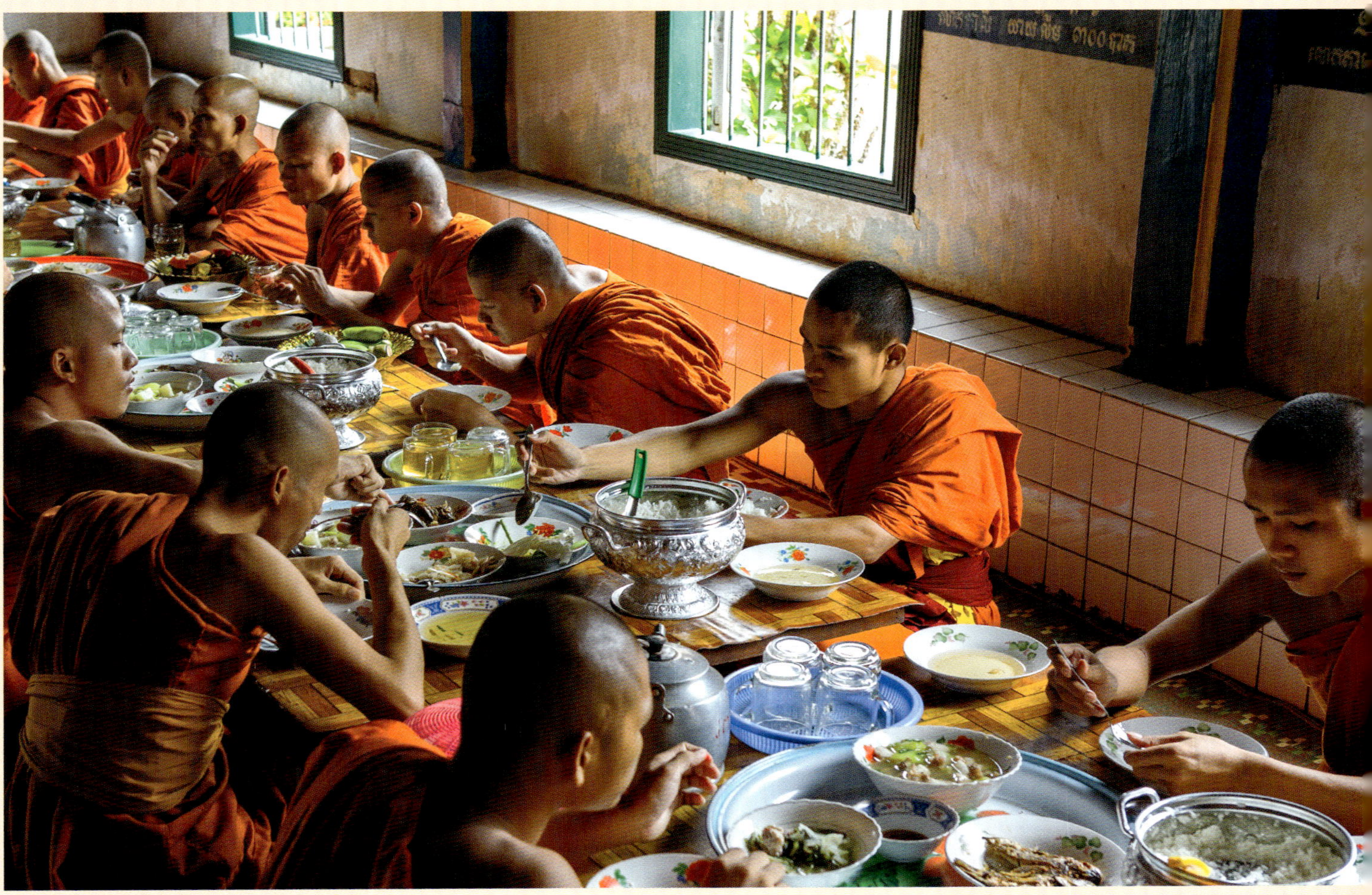

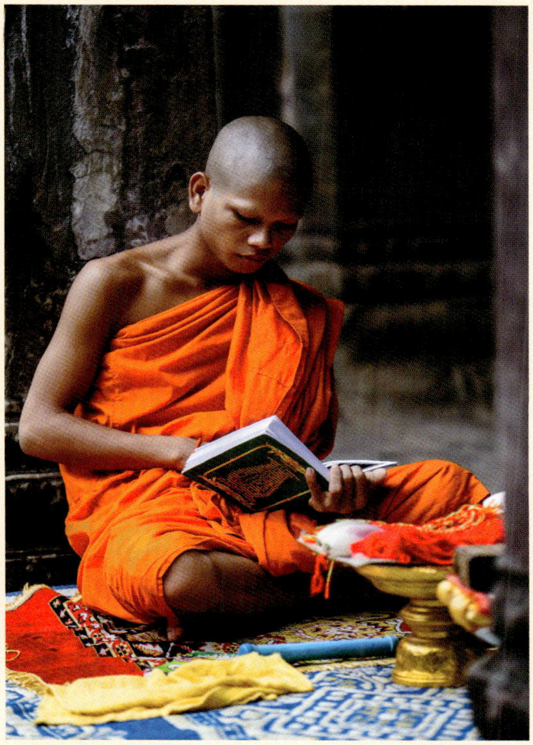

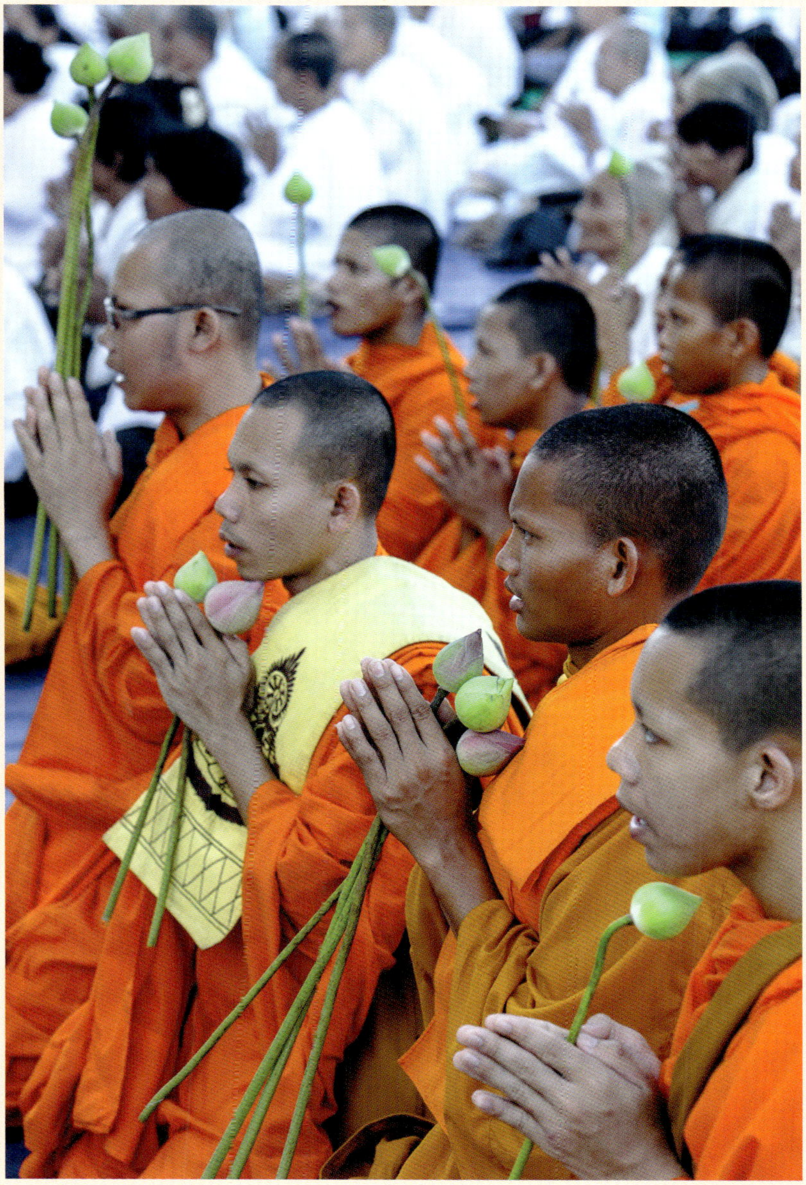

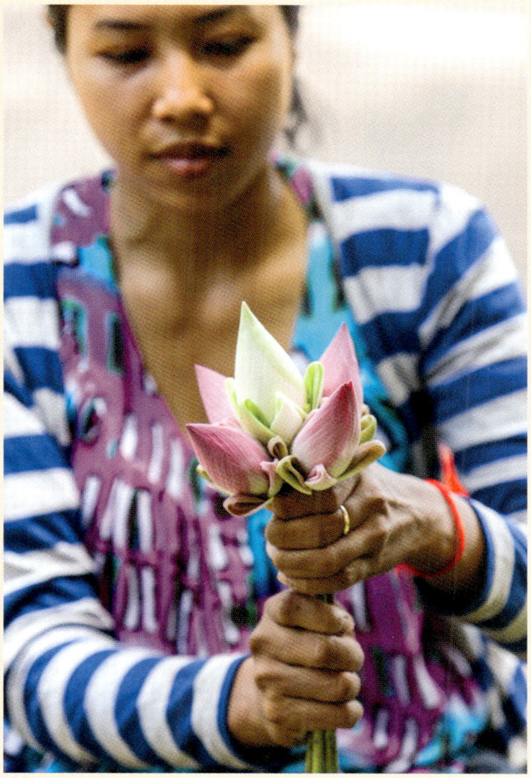

Above: Monks at prayer and holding lotus flowers that will be offered to an image of Buddha. In Buddhism, the lotus is symbolic of the path to enlightenment. The plant is rooted in mud yet grows through murky waters, emerging and blossoming in bright sunlight. White lotus flowers are said to symbolize purity of mind and body, while pink blooms are associated with Buddha himself.

Left: A flower seller at a temple folding the petals back on lotus blossoms to create a beautiful offering for worshippers. The flowers will be offered to Buddha along with incense and a candle.

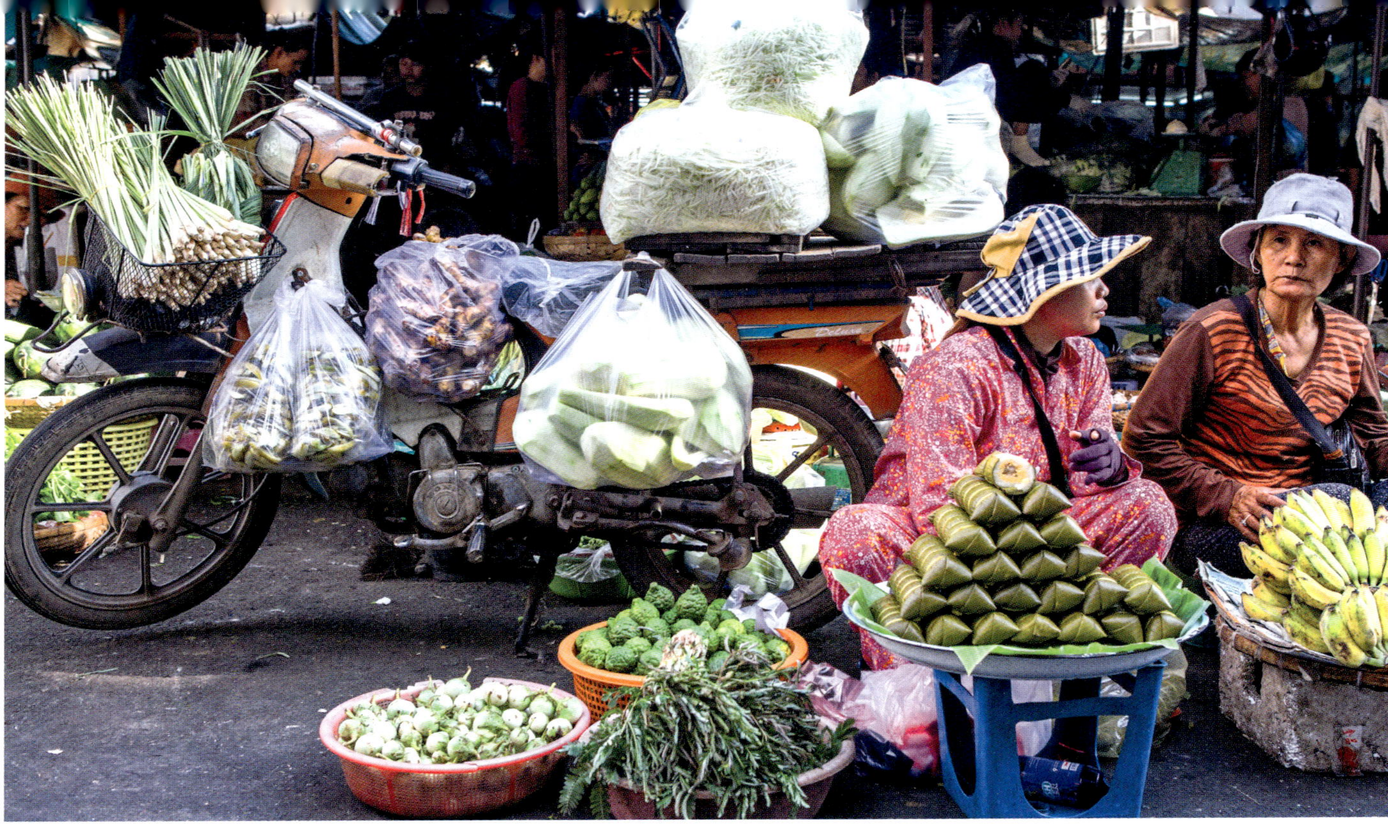

CAMBODIAN CUISINE

Cambodian food is probably one of the Asia's least known cuisines, having undoubtedly been overshadowed by that of Thailand and Vietnam. Nevertheless, it is delicious, varied and currently enjoying an exciting renaissance driven by a resurgence of interest in local culture, a blossoming restaurant scene and increased wealth. Like all Khmer arts, many of the country's skilled cooks, culinary traditions and recipes were lost during the days of the Khmer Rouge. Today, thanks to a few dedicated chefs who have freely passed on their knowledge, the cuisine has been revitalized and travellers to Cambodia can explore an array of unfamiliar ingredients and enticing flavours, from simple street-side bites to innovative, upmarket, à la carte dining. However, it is often best to avoid many of the restaurants that cater to tourists as the food generally lacks the depth of flavour and complexity that can be found at popular local eateries.

Steamed rice is the mainstay of the Khmer diet. Indeed the literal translation of the Khmer word to eat or *nam bai* means "eat rice". To further emphasize its importance, rice also features in religious ceremonies and is celebrated in song and dance. Rice flour is used for making noodles and a variety of desserts. Sticky rice, which is eaten as an accompaniment to the main meal, is also commonly used in desserts. Typically diners eating together will order rice accompanied by a selection of dishes that may include a fish, grilled, steamed or fried, a soup or curry, vegetables and a meat dish. Desserts are ordered after the savoury dishes. There are street vendors who specialize in desserts and it's a popular thing to buy and take home to eat.

The best Cambodian cooks are intuitive, drawing influences from Laos, Thailand and Vietnam to create their own distinctive dishes. Flavoursome yet without the searing chilli heat of Thai food, the base of most dishes is a *kroeung*, or herb paste. There are many recipes for aromatic *kroeung* but the basis of each is usually lemongrass, kaffir lime, galangal, lesser galangal, turmeric, garlic and shallots, all pounded with a mortar and pestle. Depending on the requirements of the dish, these ingredients are further enhanced with dried chillies, peanuts, shrimp paste and herbs. Red, yellow and green *kroeung* can be used in soups, curries and stir-fries. Favourite local dishes include *somlar machu banle*, a sour fish soup, *somlar chapek*, pork soup with ginger, *samla kh'tih m'noas*, spare rib and pineapple curry, *nhoam kra-ao chhouk*, lotus root salad, and *kang kep baob*, curried frog stuffed with pork.

In common with all Southeast Asian nations, Cambodia's culinary scene has been strongly influenced by the Chinese. Street stalls and basic shophouse restaurants sell a variety of noodle and rice dishes with roast pork and roast duck. The French also left their mark on the local cuisine and crusty baguettes are widely available. Street vendors, often Vietnamese, sell baguettes smeared with pork pâté, then dress it up with raw papaya, tomatoes, cucumbers and chilli sauce for the perfect hearty breakfast or lunch. Vietnamese shophouse restaurants also offer steaming bowls of *pho,* noodle soup, and stir-fried noodles with beef.

Opposite: Vendors in Psar Kandal, one of Phnom Penh's many vibrant markets. Most open in the early morning and again in the late afternoon.
Right: The large Vietnamese population in Cambodia has influenced the food. Popular dishes include noodle soup, shown here ready to be delivered to a market vendor for breakfast.
Below: Light and healthy, Vietnamese-style fresh spring rolls are also enjoyed, like the ones sold at this stall outside Central Market in Phnom Penh.

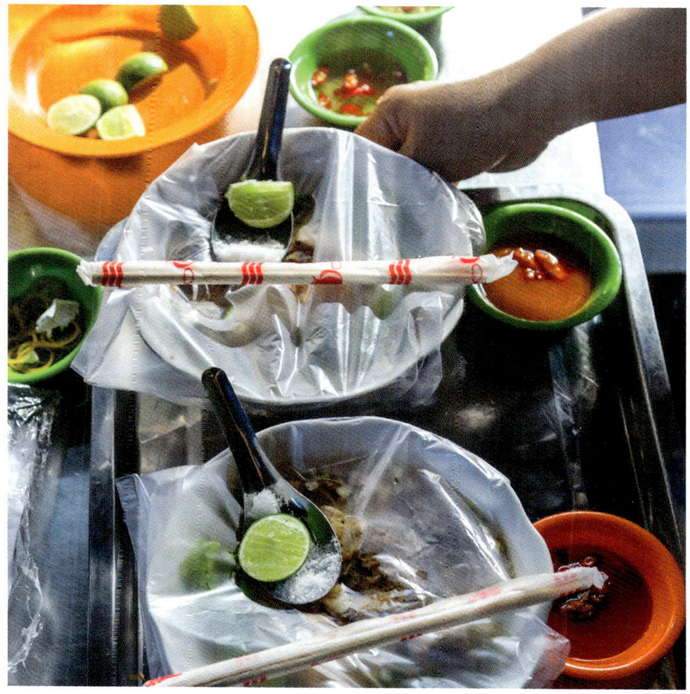

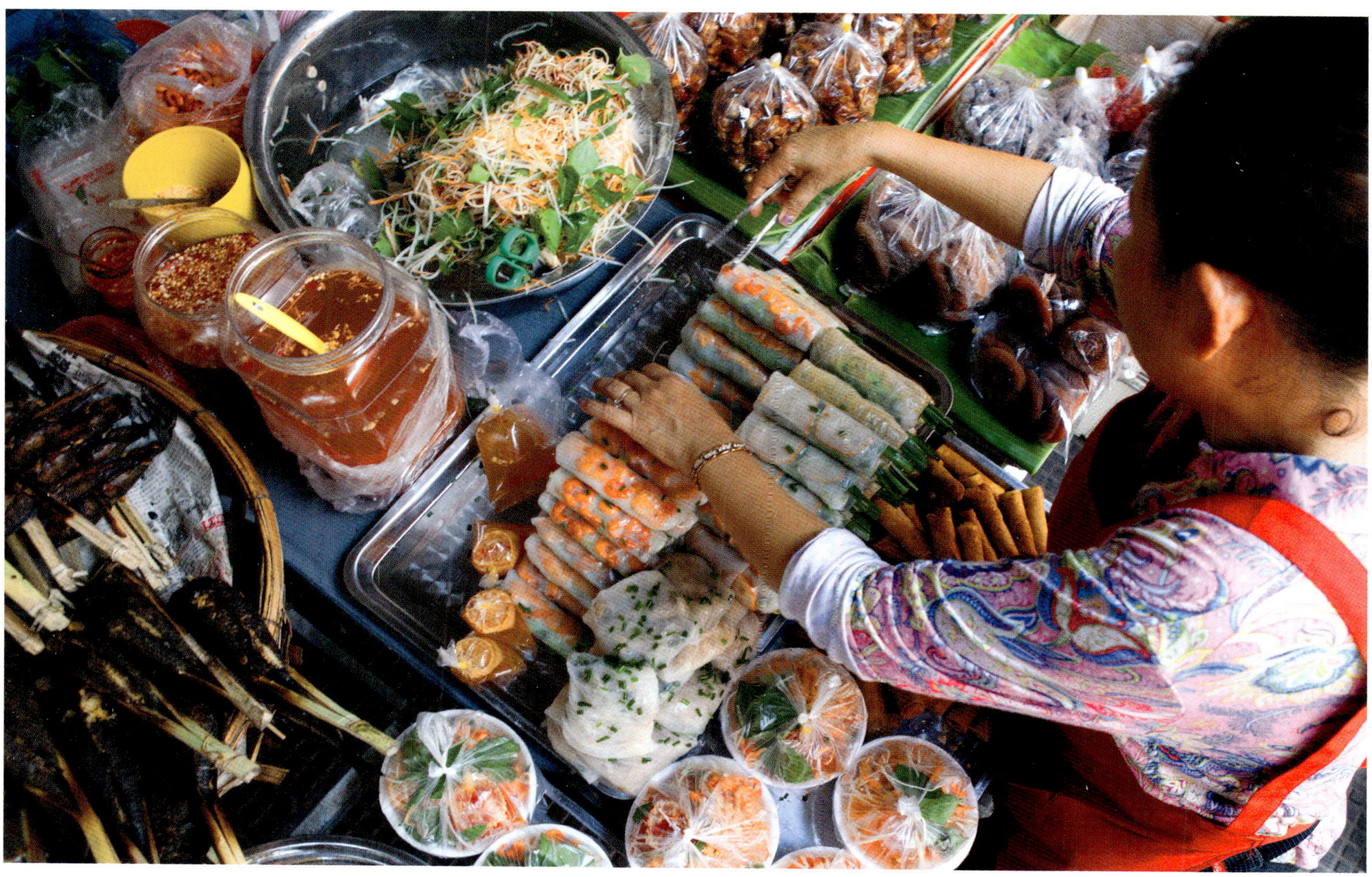

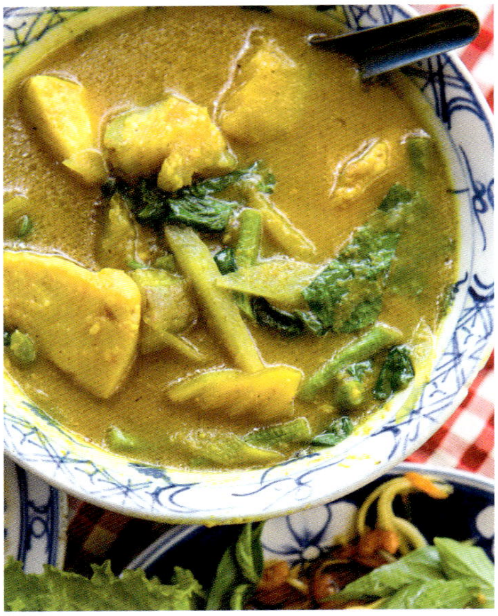

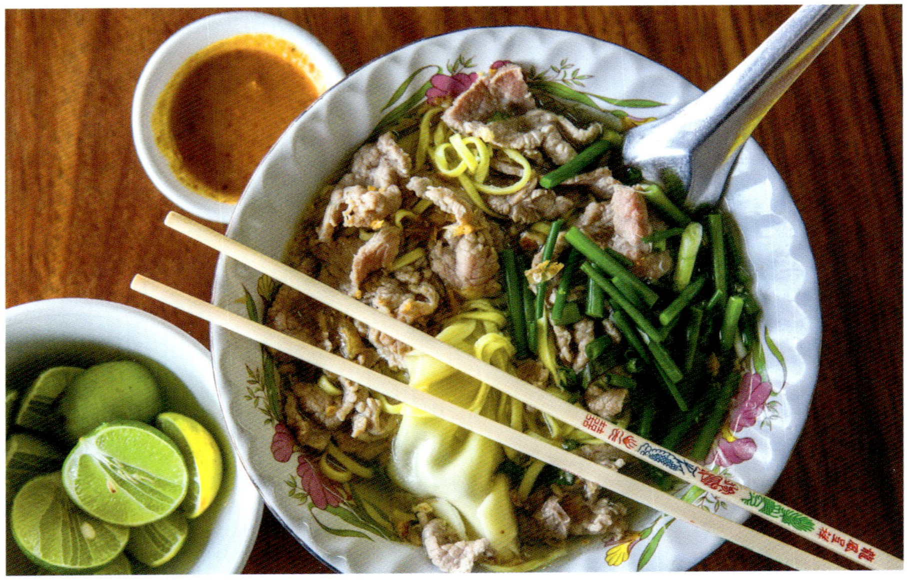

Above: Flavourful Khmer curries are made using a complex mix of herbs and spices, usually in the form of a paste known as *kroeung*.
Above right: Chinese and Vietnamese noodle dishes are eaten day and night. Beef is a popular meat in Cambodia, much more so than in neighbouring Thailand where it is rarely eaten.
Right: Several contrasting dishes are served at the same time, like this spicy soup and fresh vibrant salad.
Below: A meal of banana flower soup plus beef and pineapple with cashew nuts, and a bottle of the national brew, Angkor Beer.

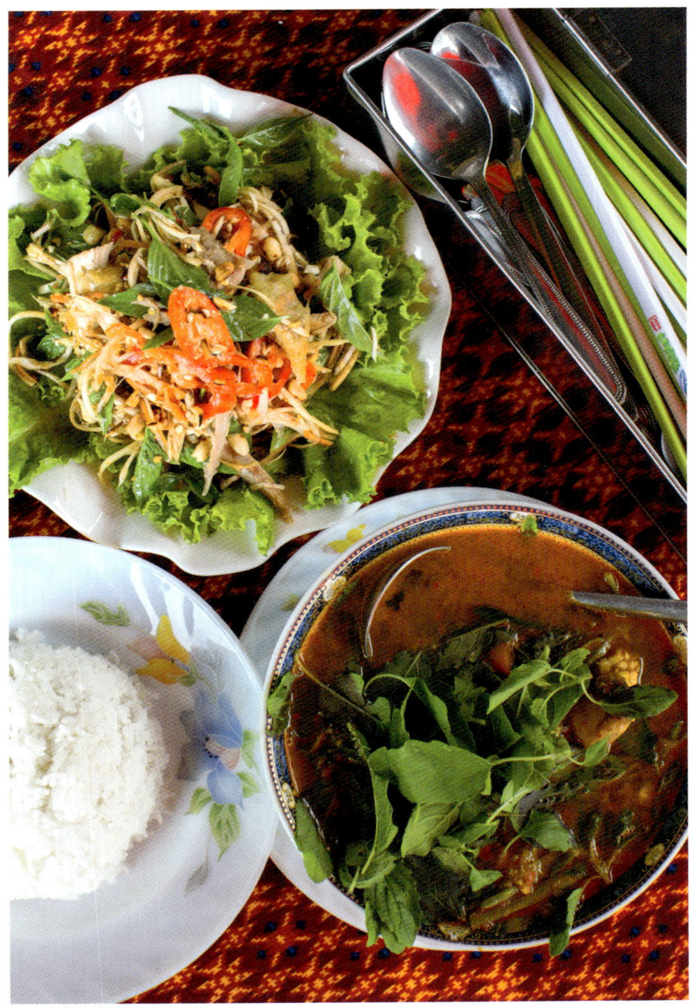

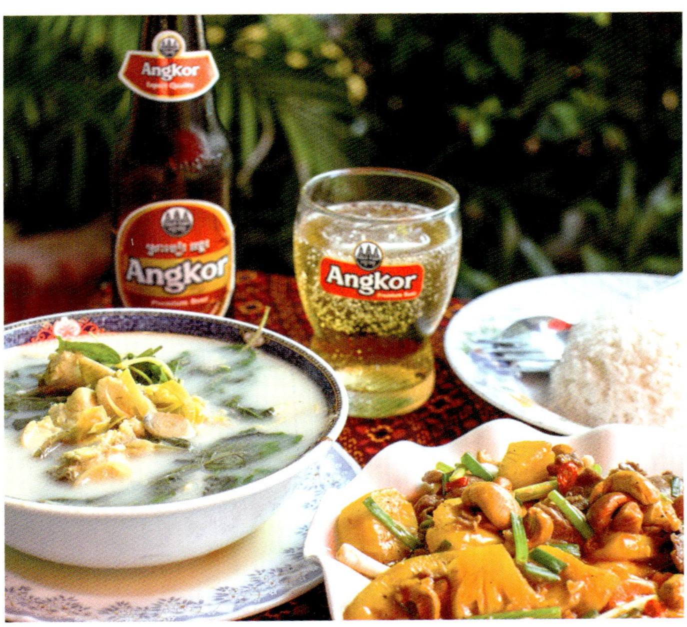

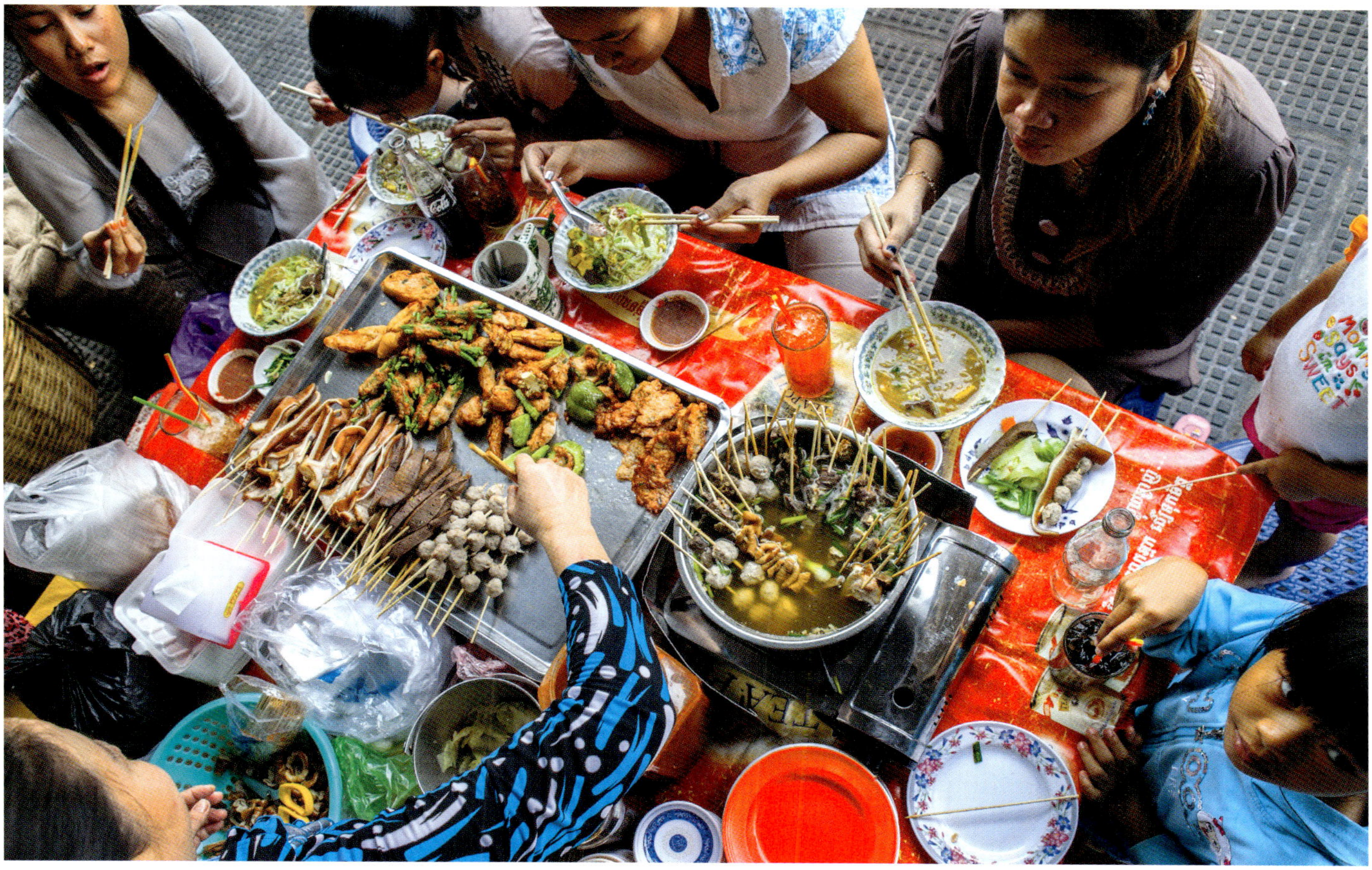

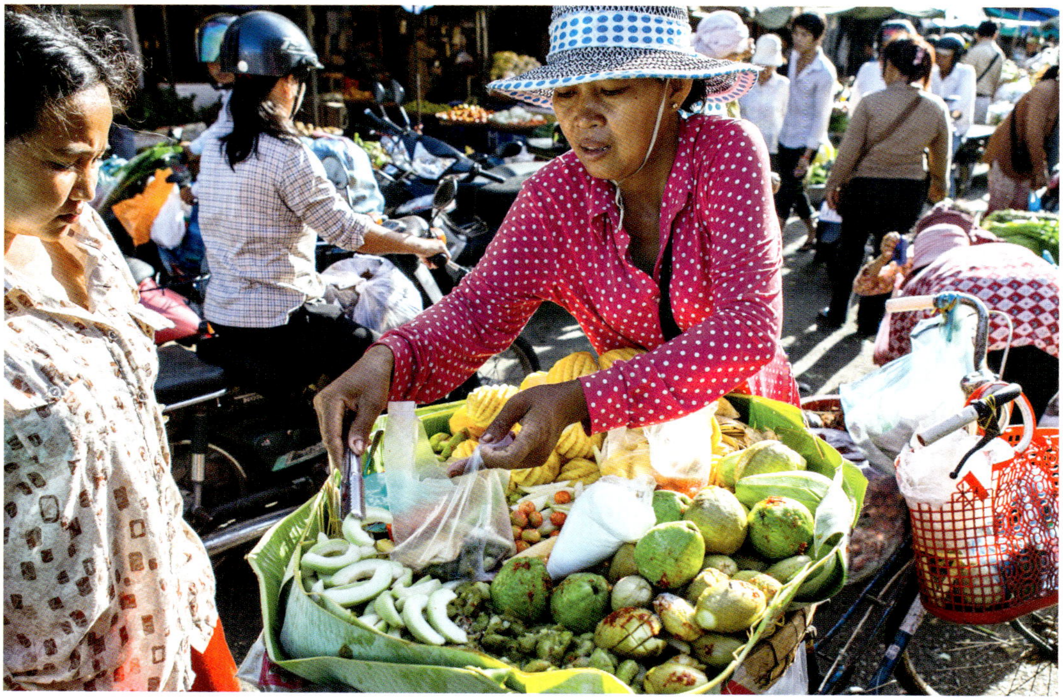

Above: In Cambodia food seems to be available anywhere and at any time. Here, diners share a table at a stall selling fried chicken, skewered meatballs and offal. **Left:** Fresh fruit vendors ply the streets with baskets strapped to the back of bicycles. An essential accompaniment to guava, mango and other fruits is a dip made from sugar, salt and chillis.

Right: *Amok* is one of Cambodia's most famous dishes. The lightly spiced and aromatic curry is traditionally made using freshwater fish but today it is not uncommon to see versions made with chicken or vegetables. In addition to the *kroeung* paste, the dish includes delightfully bitter amok leaves, also known as *nhor*. The vibrant orange colour comes from the use of annatto seeds.

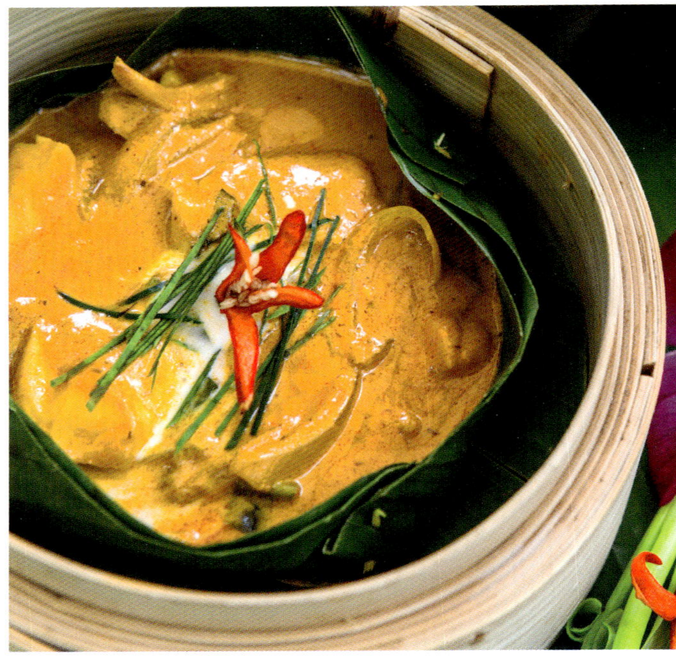

The classic Khmer dish is *amok*, a fragrant mix of succulent fish, coconut milk and a *kroeung* made from lemongrass, herbs and spices. The dish was traditionally steamed gently in a small banana leaf basket, resulting in an almost mousse-like texture. However, these days few chefs take the time to steam the mixture and more often than not cook it in a saucepan, then simply ladle it into the baskets and serve as a thick curry.

Visitors to Cambodia may be surprised at the local appetite for what many would consider unsavoury snacks. Wild food, which can include anything from fried crickets, gruesome-

FERMENTED FISH PASTE

Many hate the smell of *prahoc*, or fermented fish paste, and *tik trei*, fish sauce, but they are essential ingredients in Cambodian cuisine, adding depth of flavour and saltiness to dishes, and no self-respecting Cambodian chef would be without them. Several villages in Siem Reap and Battambang have a reputation for producing high quality *prahoc*, an annual activity that begins in the rainy season.

The process is said to have existed since before the Angkor period and starts by the cleaning of whole fish, rubbing them with salt and leaving them in the sun for a day. More salt is rubbed in over several days until the fish begin to ferment. They are then placed in huge wooden vats with more coarse salt, sealed and left for several months or up to one year until the paste is ready.

In the coastal town of Kampot, there are factories making *tik trei* from anchovies that are also fermented in wooden vats and distilled several times over a period of months before being siphoned into ceramic jars, then left in the sun for another two months to complete the fermentation process.

Smoked and fried fish and *kapi*, or shrimp paste, are also widely used Cambodian cooking.

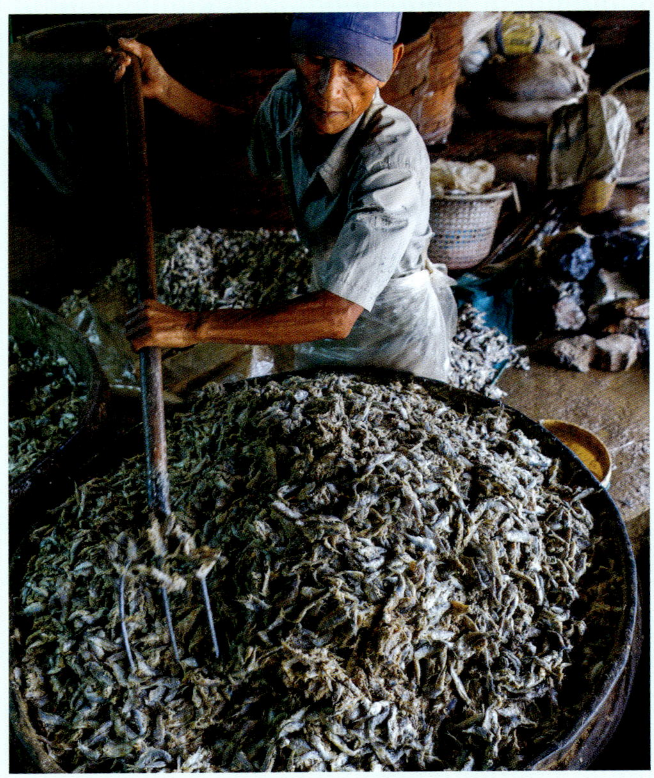

looking tarantulas, ant eggs, bee larvae, freshwater snails and grilled snakes, is extremely popular. It has been said that Cambodians developed a taste for such things when food was scarce under the Khmer Rouge but in truth delicacies from the wild larder are enjoyed throughout Southeast Asia because they are delicious and a high source of protein. A plate of crispy, deep-fried crickets sprinkled with a little white pepper, fried kaffir lime leaves and a dash of fish sauce makes a very tasty beer snack. In fact Nusara Thaitawat in her book *The Cuisine of Cambodia* suggests frying plump crickets in butter with coconut meat, ground peanuts and a glass of Champagne. For those who have difficulty with the thought of eating an insect, consider a cricket merely as a land shrimp!

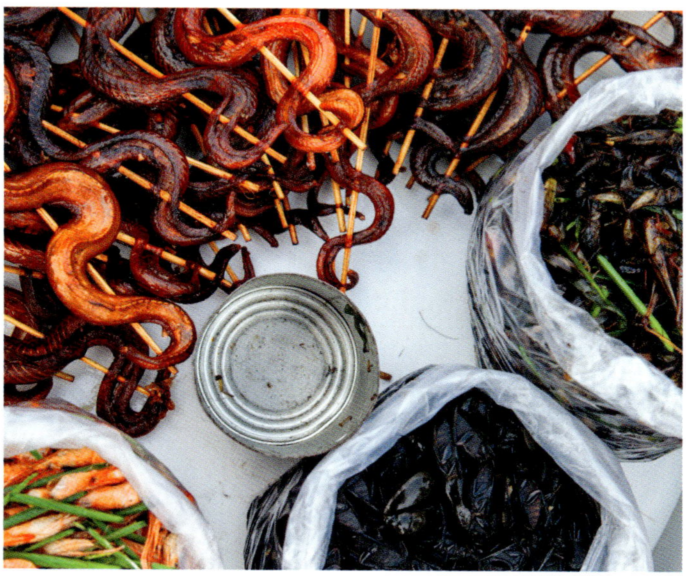

Walk around a street market in Cambodia and you may be stopped in your tracks by the powerful aroma of durian. There's no sitting on the fence with this fruit – it's a love-it-or-hate-it experience. Although banned from buses, trains and public buildings because of its pungent smell (it's transported by motorcycle), the durian is adored by most Asians yet despised by many Westerners. The king of fruits is mainly grown in the provinces of Kampot and Kompong Cham.

Buying a durian is a delightful, almost ritualistic process. First tell the vendor how you like to eat your durian – hard, soft or somewhere in between – then stand by and watch as he goes through the process of selecting it. Reaching out for this most

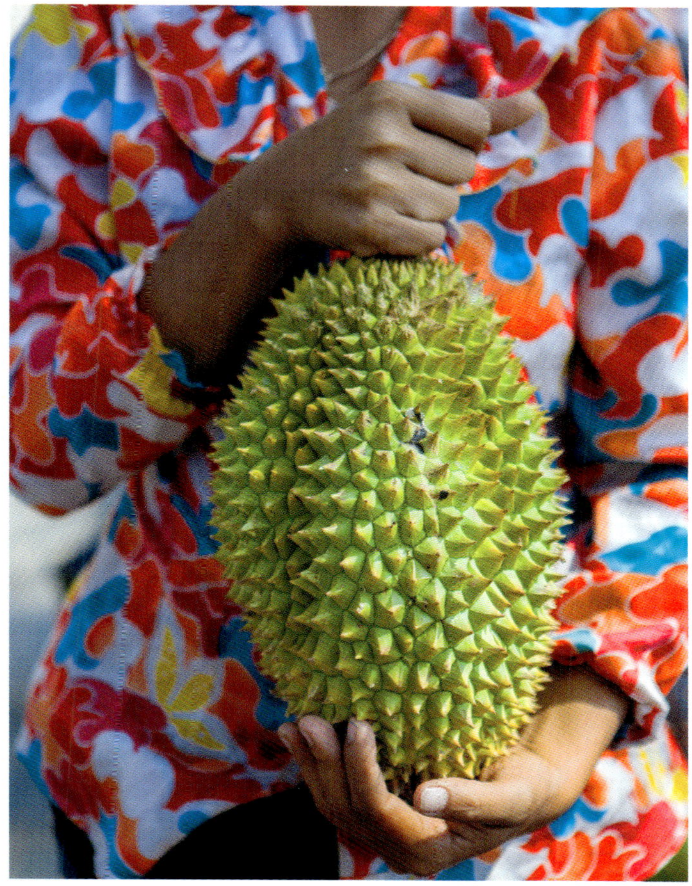

unlikely of fruits, his fingertips defy the armoured exterior as he lifts it up, taps it with the blade of a machete and listens for the hollow sound that tells him it is ripe. A small section of the shell is then cut and pulled back, just enough so you can insert a finger and test the softness of the fruit. Some vendors will pull the spiky fruit dangerously close to their face. With eyes closed and inhaling deeply they respond to its pungency with a knowing smile before finding a weak spot, and carefully inserting a slender blade to break the seal. With its defences breached, the durian yields to further pressure eventually cracking to reveal its treasure – two golden pillows of succulent flesh. The fruit is eaten raw. Some like it a little under-ripe when it is firm but when it is ripe, soft and creamy, it is sublime!

Above: The durian is the most unlikely looking fruit. Vendors are skilled at judging ripeness according to a buyer's preference.
Above left: The wild larder is an important part of the Cambodian culinary repertoire. Delights include fried crickets and grilled snake.

ARTS AND CRAFTS

It doesn't take a trained eye to appreciate the fact that Cambodian craftsmen and women possess a unique aesthetic. Bolstered by increased tourism and access to the global marketplace, artisans have developed and refined their skills and now recreate classic forms as well as contemporary interpretations of traditional Khmer arts to enhance the modern home. Chic boutiques in Siem Reap and Phnom Penh offer a range of highly accomplished lacquerware, silk weaving, silverware, pottery and stone carving, as well as fragrant herbal beauty and spa products made using indigenous herbs and spices.

The crafts were given new life in Cambodia by *Artisans Angkor*, an inspirational project designed to provide villagers in rural areas with new skills and an improved livelihood. Since the project began at the tail end of the 1990s as an EU-funded educational initiative by Chantiers-Ecoles de Formation Professionnelle, *Artisans Angkor* has opened 42 workshops in the Siem Reap area, employs more than 1,000 people and sources high-quality products from 900 artisans. In Siem Reap, visitors can buy items at a boutique in the town centre and watch crafts being made at a nearby workshop. There is also a silk farm on the outskirts of town and another boutique in Phnom Penh.

The art of the stonemason that gave life to the magnificent temples of Angkor and dozens of other ancient monuments is still alive and well in Cambodia. To the craftsmen of yesteryear, however, the tool kit of today's artisan would look unfamiliar. Although a selection of traditional tools are employed to shape stone and marble, much of the work is now done using angle grinders and drills. With a practiced eye and a dexterous hand, they create enormous Buddha images and intricate bas reliefs. Wood carvers also fashion smaller Buddhas, kitchenware and decorative items from hardwoods.

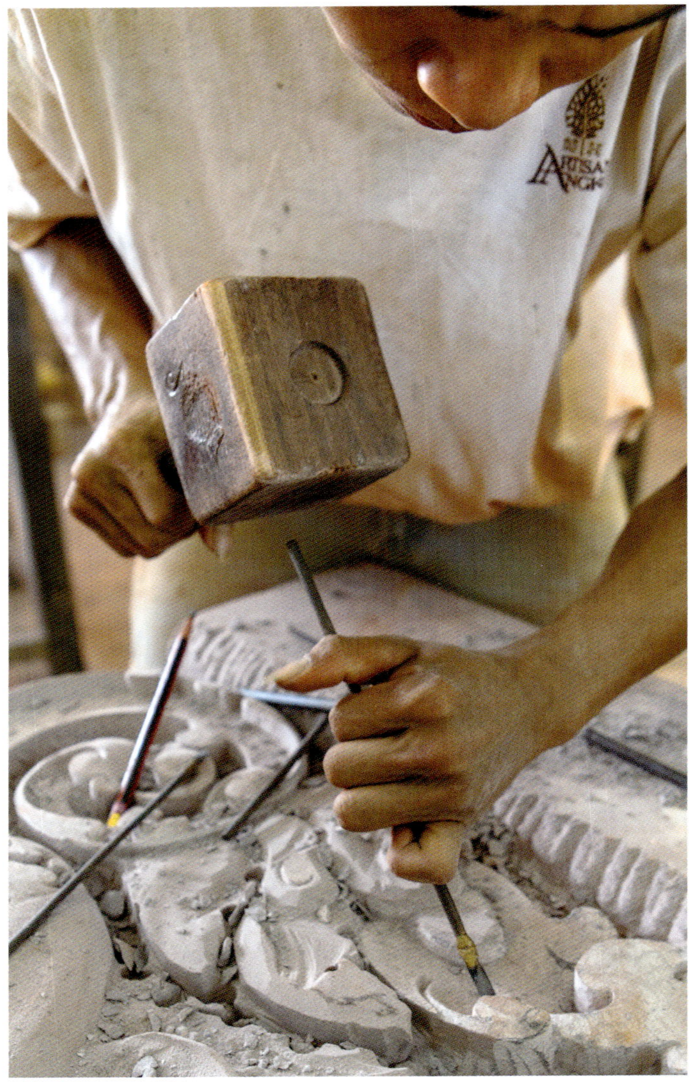

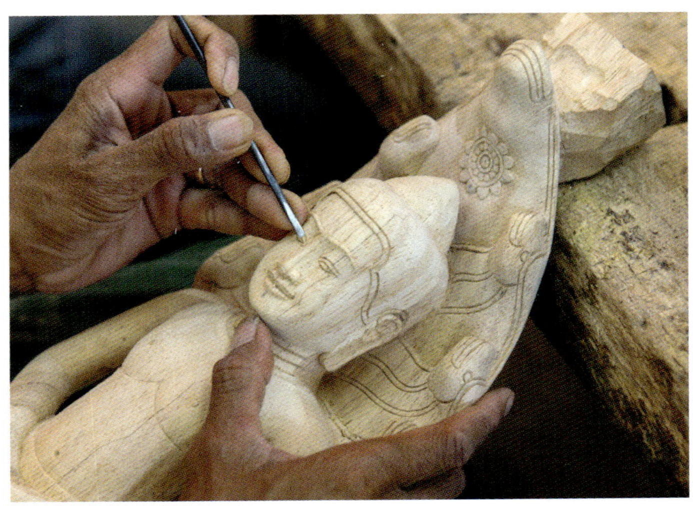

Above and opposite top: Reproducing the designs of the Angkor period, the work of the highly skilled stonemasons is in great demand for temples, resorts and public monuments. Around Siem Reap there are many roadside workshops where craftsmen can be seen in action.

Right: The revival of Cambodian crafts has benefited many rural people. From wood carving to handwoven silk and a wide range of contemporary home décor products, visitors are spoilt for choice.

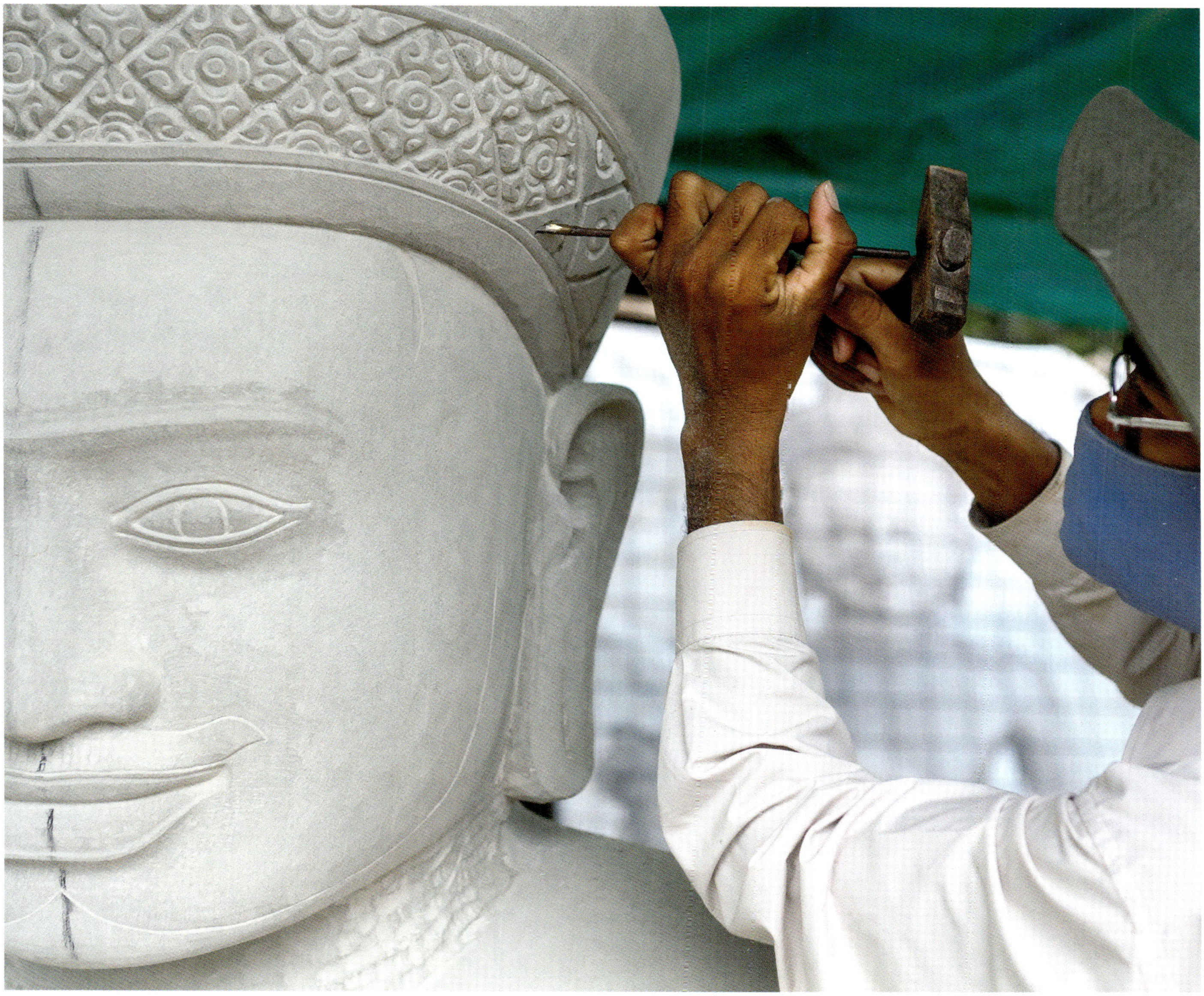

Cambodia is known primarily for its historic, glazed, high-fired ceramics. It is believed that production of such ware may have begun in the ninth century, although the finest pieces are said to have been made a little later during the 11th and 12th centuries, a time when production also reached its peak. Bowls and storage jars as well as oil lamps, animal-shaped pots and ritualistic items were produced and usually decorated with a dark brown or Celadon glaze. Ancient Khmer ceramics have been discovered in Indonesia showing that pots were clearly a valued trade commodity. Today the art of glazed stoneware has been revived by NGO groups but the majority of the work is copies of the old pots, sold as gifts. The glazed ware found in markets is mass produced and imported from Vietnam.

In rural Cambodia many communities live without mains electricity or a piped water supply. Traditional earthenware pottery is therefore still used for water storage. Cooking pots and charcoal-burning stoves, also made from earthenware clay, are essential in the rural kitchen. Earthenware pottery can be seen being made at the village of Ondoung Rossey near Kompong Chhnang, and at Bhumi Dom Dek, near Kompong Speu, just to the west of the capital Phnom Penh.

Cambodia has a long history of weaving with both silk and cotton threads. Mulberry trees are grown for leaves to feed the silkworms but to meet demand for their products weavers also have to import raw silk from China and Vietnam. However, locally produced golden silk, so-called because of its vibrant yellow colour, is highly prized and Khmer weavers produce lengths of intricately patterned *ikats* or *hol* under their houses around Siem Reap, on Koh Dach, also known as Silk Island and located a short distance from Phnom Penh, and at Phnom Srok District in Banteay Meanchey Province, an area renowned for its high quality silk.

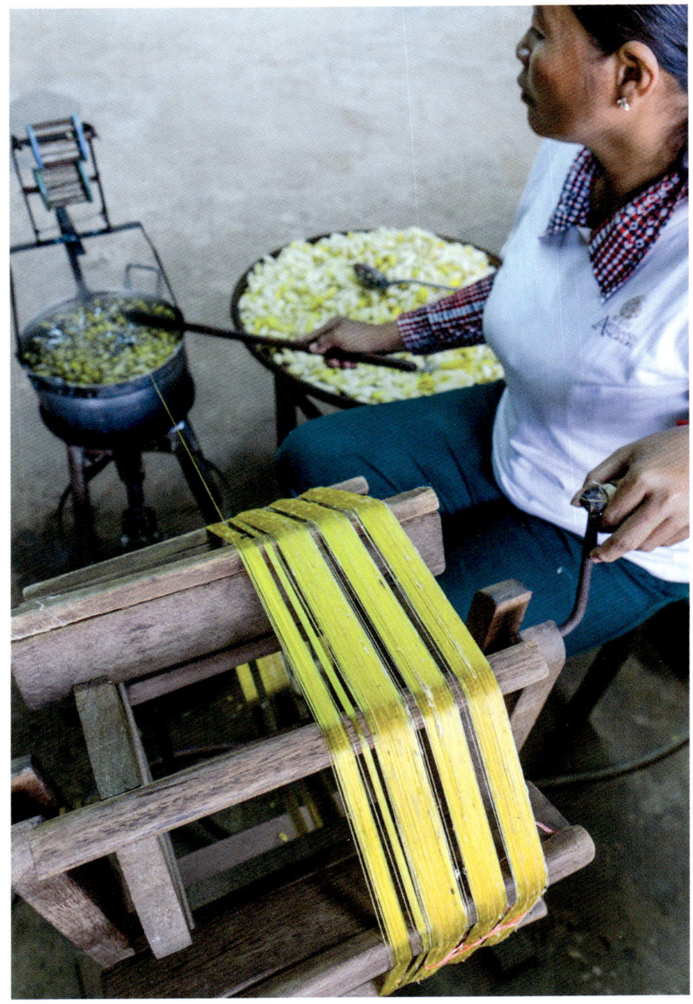

These pages: Cocoons of the silkworm are boiled in water and the golden threads carefully reeled onto a wooden frame. The silk can then be dyed and woven on a traditional loom. Larger factories now use more modern methods.

Below: As the name implies, on Koh Dach, or Silk Island, there are dozens of weavers producing high-quality silk.

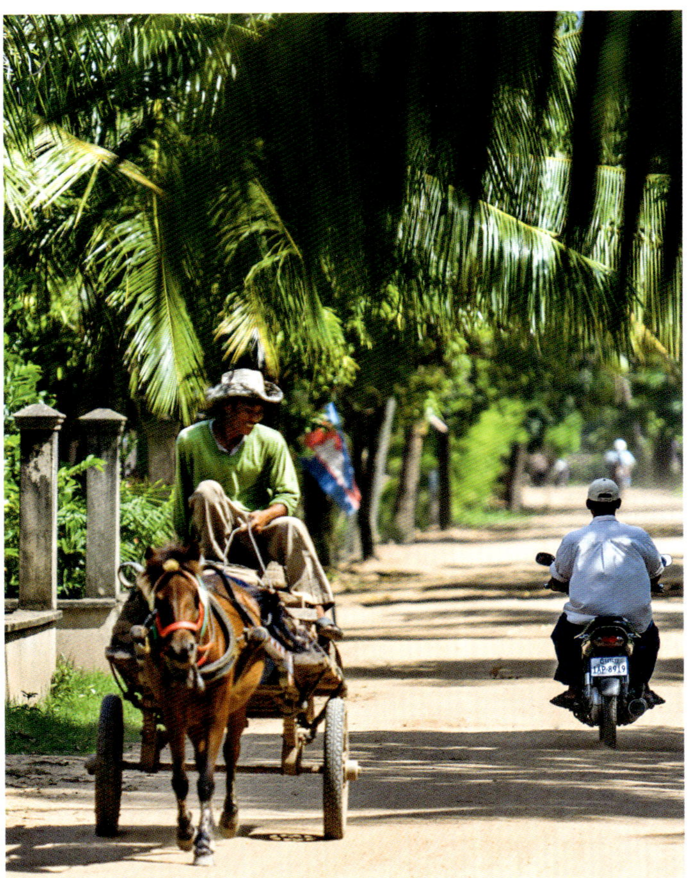

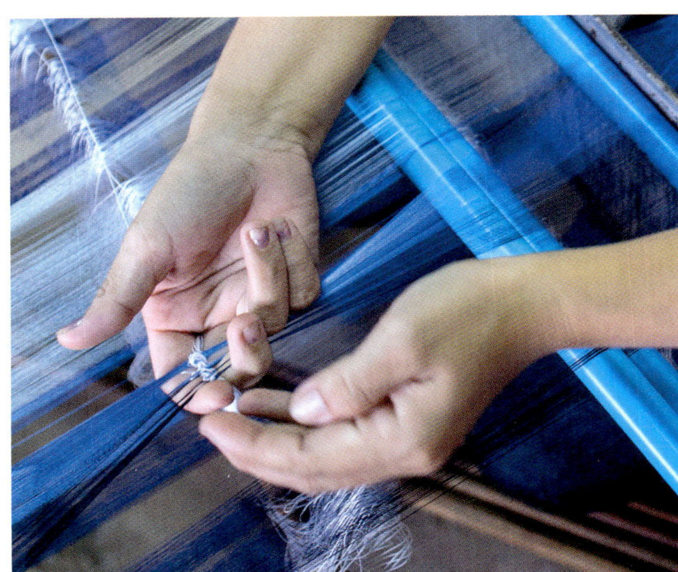

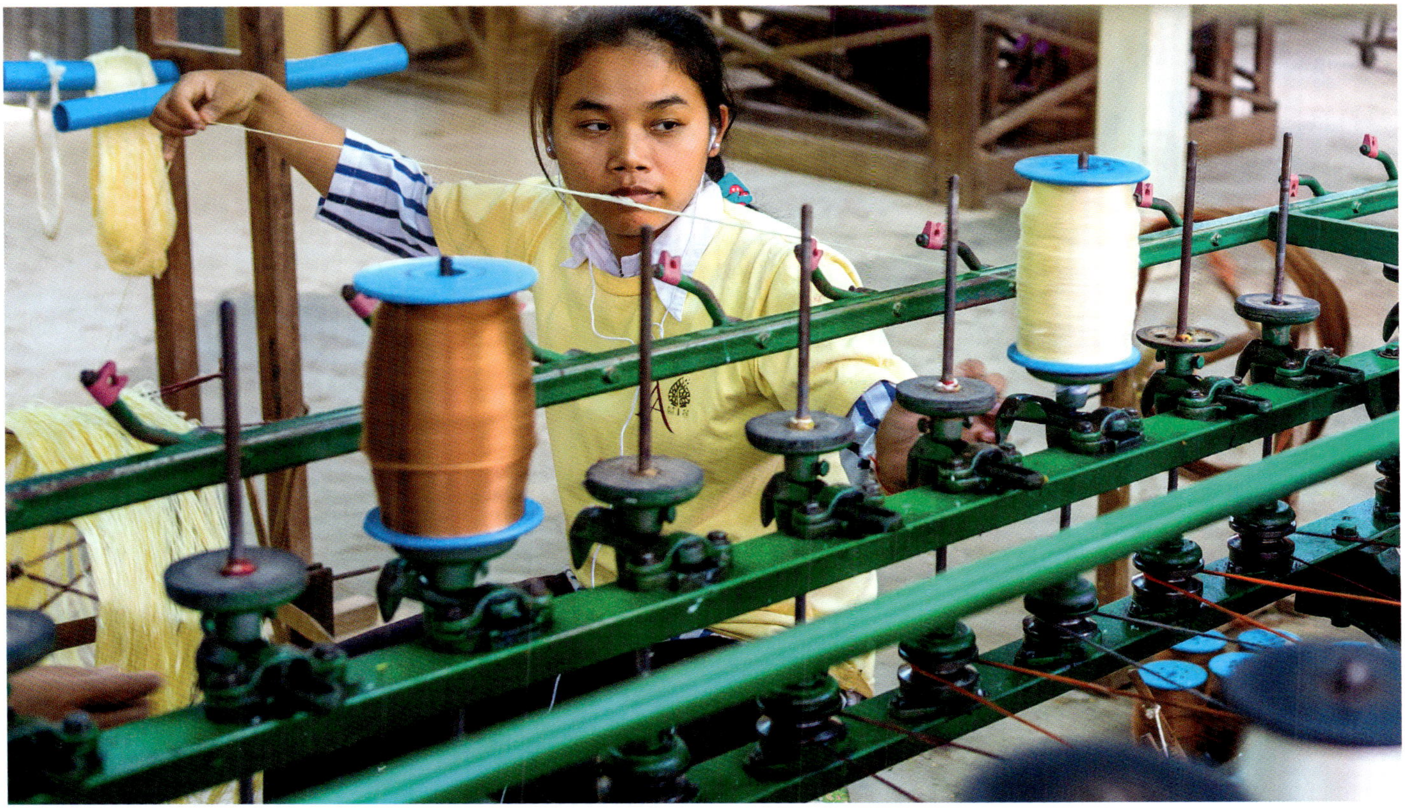

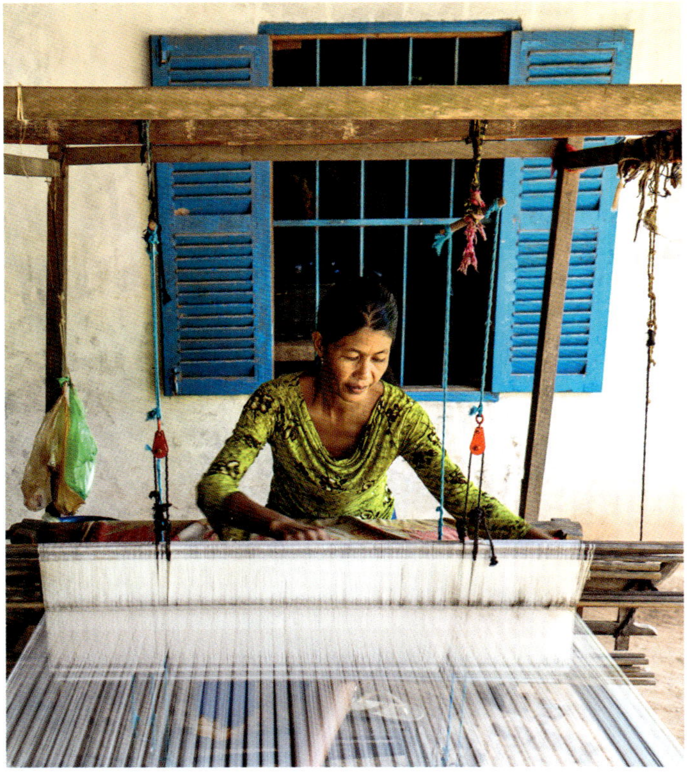

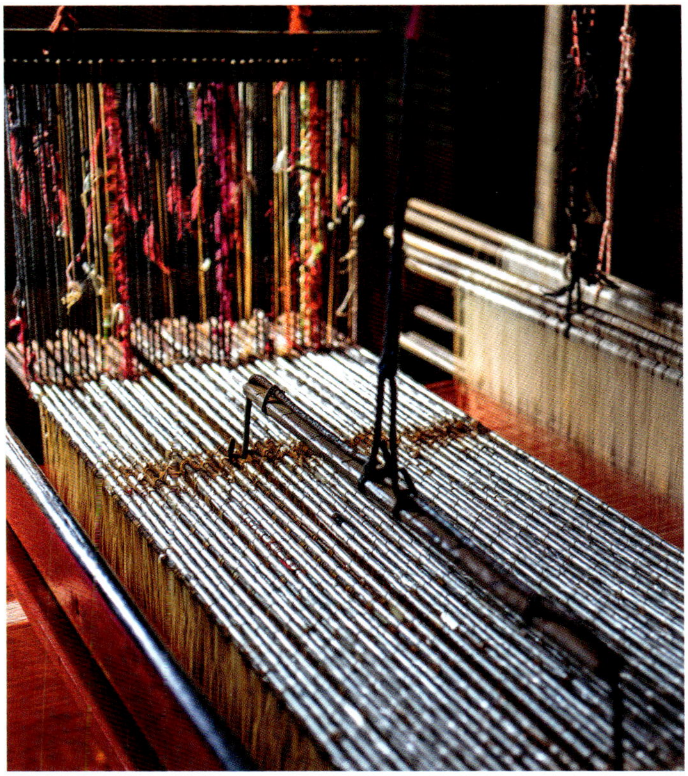

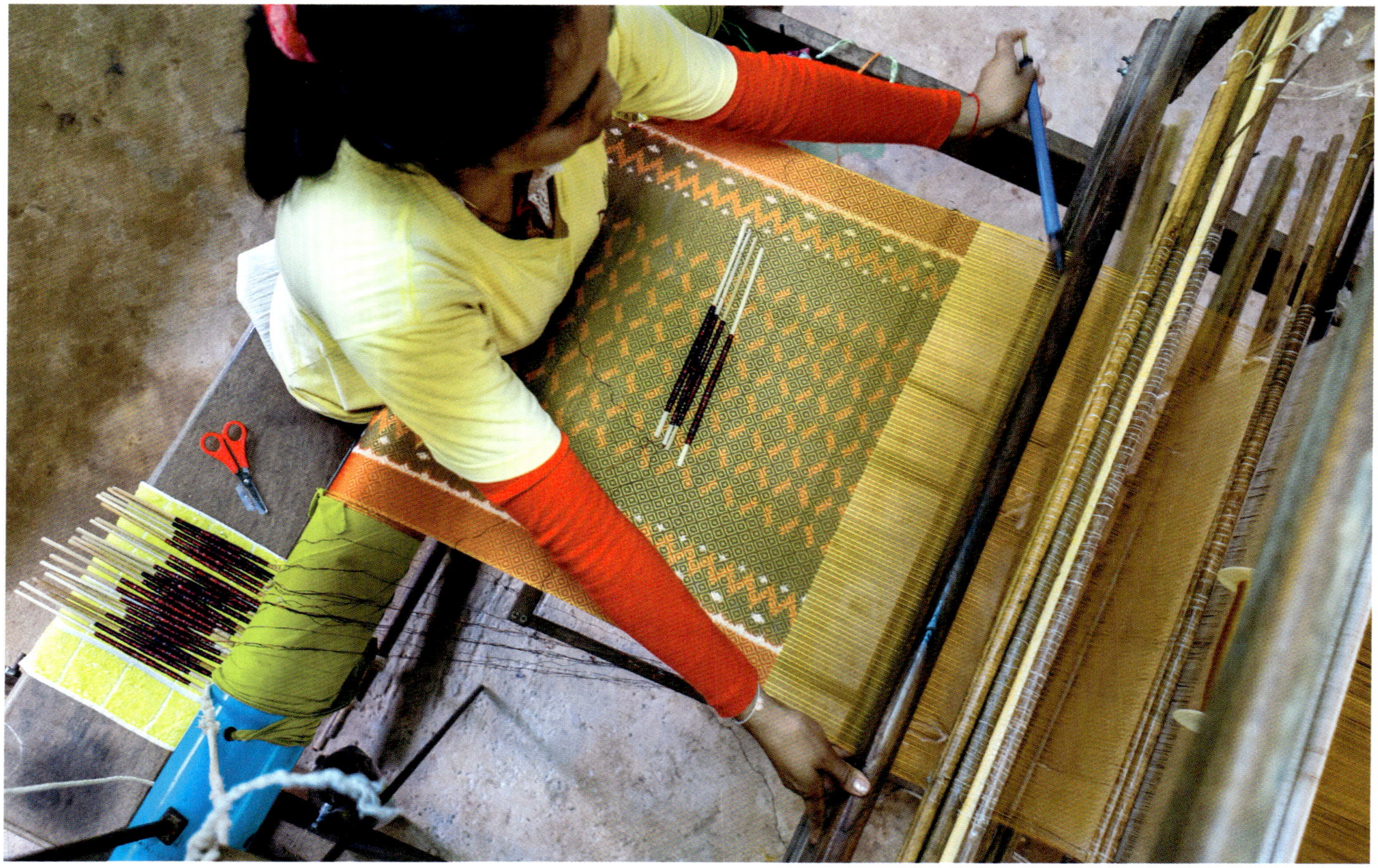

THE KRAMA

Cambodia's most famous woven fabric is the *krama*, or Khmer scarf. The *krama*, a length of woven cotton or silk with a simple chequered pattern, is essential attire for most rural Cambodians. The multi-purpose length of cloth is commonly used as a headscarf by market traders and farmers, protects the faces of travellers from sunburn and dust, is used to secure babies to the backs of their mothers and has a dozen or more uses besides. Available at every market in Cambodia, it also makes the perfect gift.

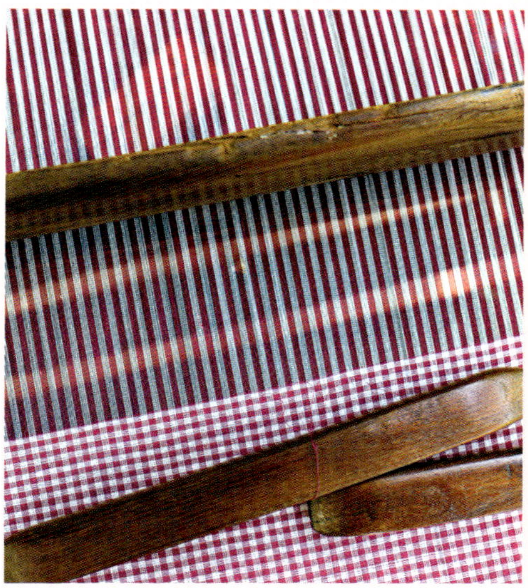

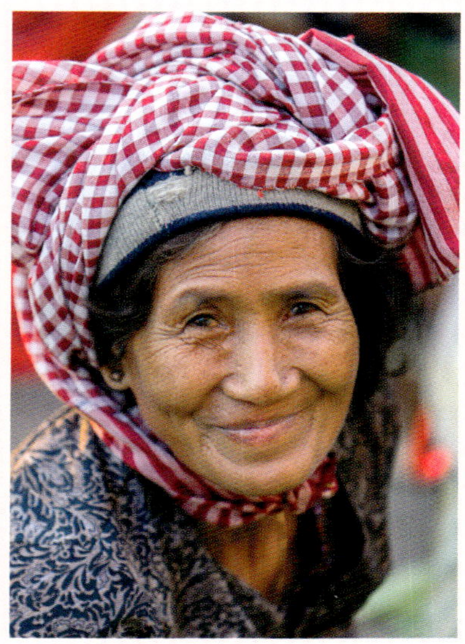

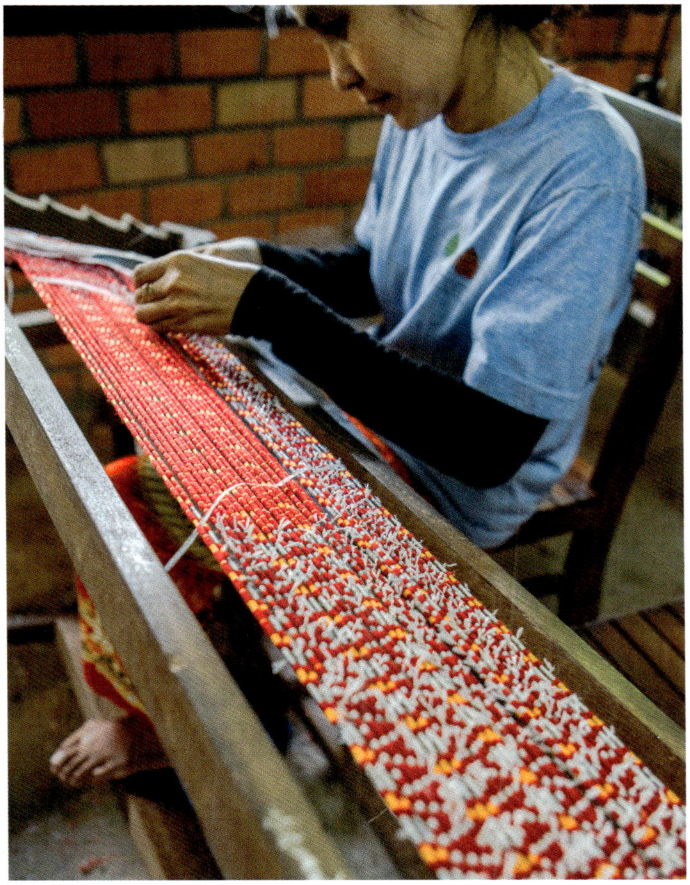

These pages: The national dress of Cambodian women is the *sampot*, or sarong, the origins of which date back centuries and can be seen in bas-reliefs at Angkorian temples. Hand-woven silk is prized and an expert weaver's work can command high prices, as it can take several weeks to create a length of fabric. The colours of a *sampot* are usually vibrant and the patterns complex. It can take two to three days just to prepare a loom for weaving. The warp is from 40–80 m (130–260 ft) in length and includes up to 4,500 threads. A skilled weaver working on an intricate pattern on a traditional, wooden, hand loom can only advance a few centimetres each day.

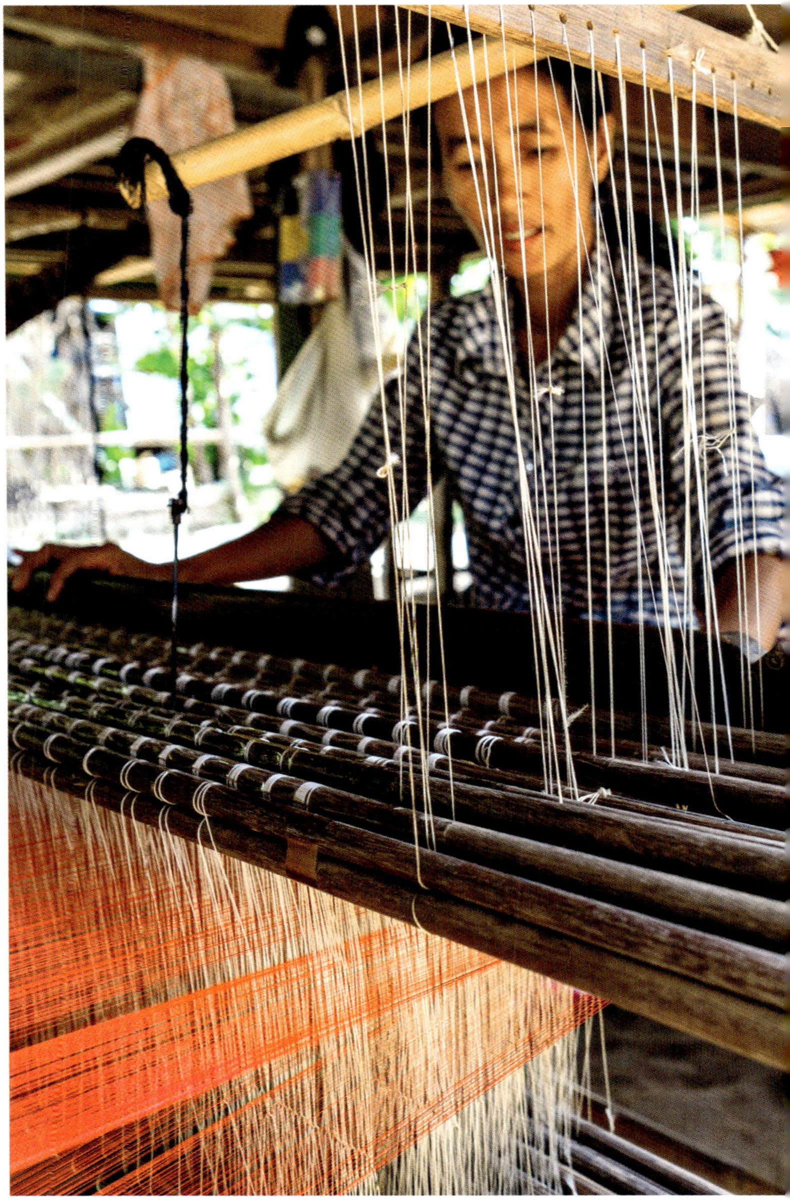

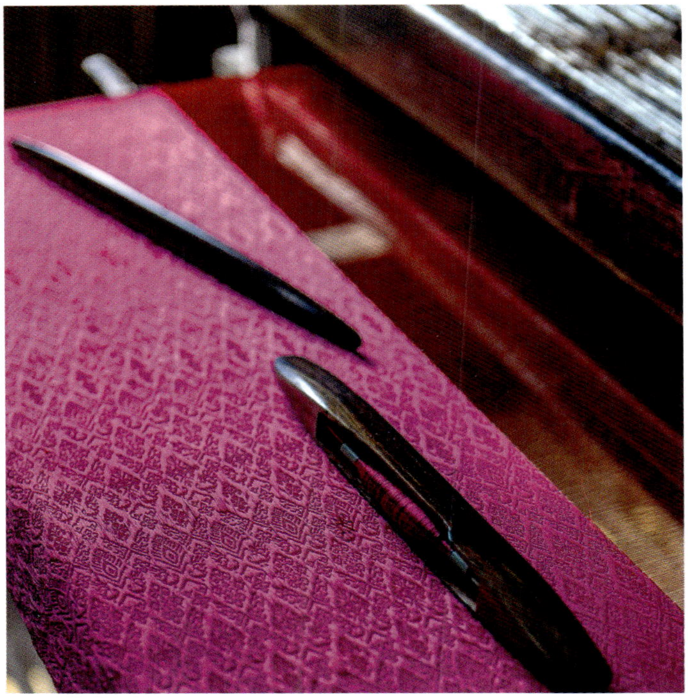

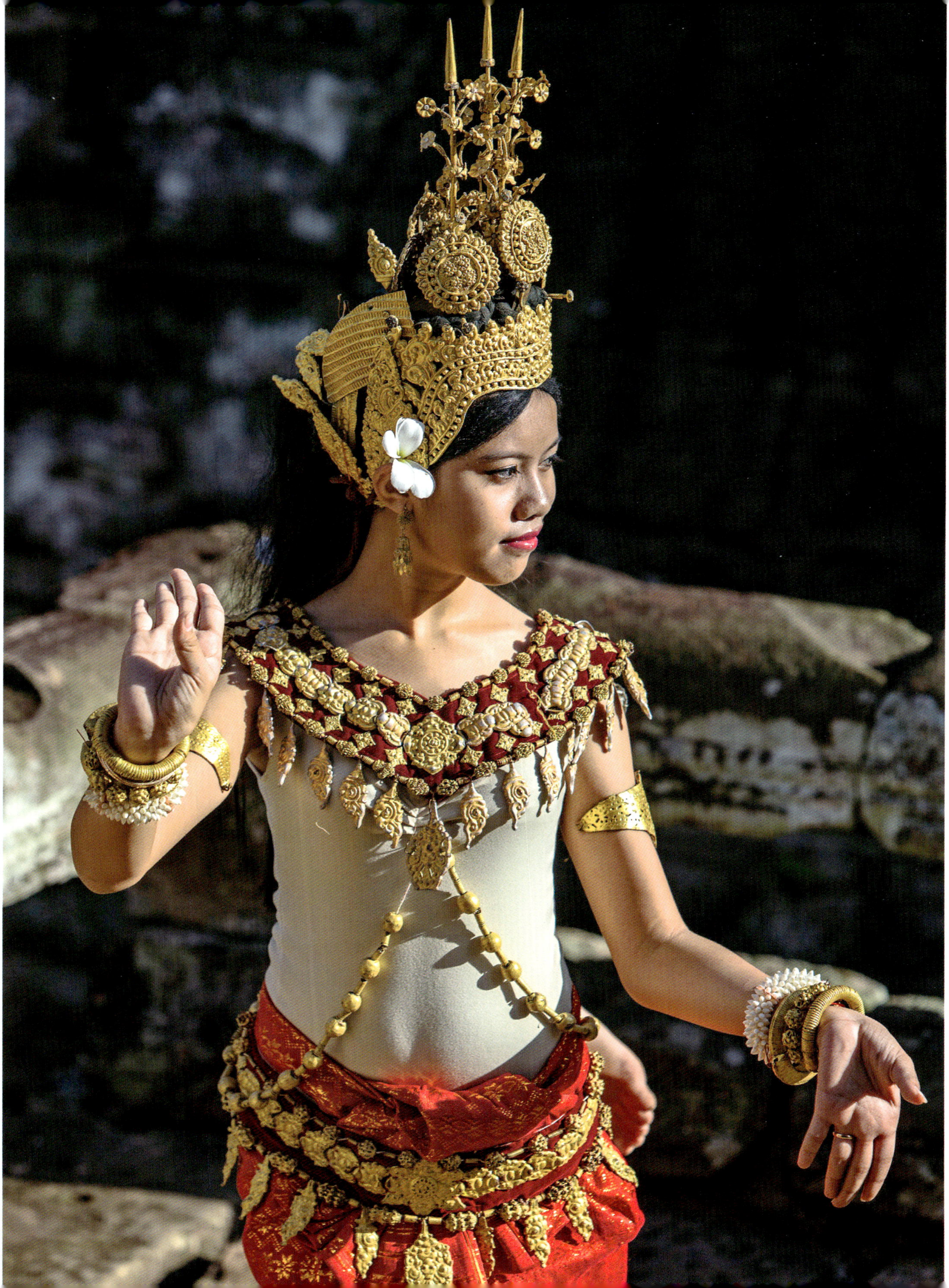

When the Chinese emissary, Zhou Daguan, travelled throughout Cambodia in 1296, he noted the importance of dance in the royal court and at temple celebrations, highlighting one festival in particular known as *ngai-lan*, a Khmer word for dance. He went on to document a ritual procession and described hearing "musical instruments rendering a clamorous noise that charms the spirit....and all around the dancing of men and women".

Cambodian classical dance drama is based on the Hindu epic poem, the *Ramayana*, known as the *Reamker* in Khmer. Written about 2,000 years ago and attributed to the India sage and poet, Valmiki, the 50,000-word poem is a moral story that describes the life of Rama and his wife Sita. The adventurous tale is full of gods, demons, magic spells and heroes doing battle with evil enemies. The female dancers that feature in the epic story are incarnations of Apsaras (see page 119). The images of these celestial beauties along with scenes from the *Reamker* dating from the 12th century and earlier can be seen carved on walls throughout the temples of Angkor.

In his book, *Theatre in Southeast Asia*, James R. Brandon asserts that, although the roots of Khmer dance are clearly Indian, it has also been influenced by the Javanese. When the Thais attacked Angkor in 1431, they are known to have enslaved dancers and taken them back to the Thai court of Ayutthaya. To this day, nationalistic Thais and Cambodians dispute the origins of many aspects of their cultures and traditions, including dance.

Having gone through a period of decline when the Angkor region was under Thai rule until 1794, and for a further century, the art of dance began to enjoy renewed interest, this time in Europe. In 1906, a troupe of dancers joined King Sisowath on his visit to France and performed at the French Colonial Exposition in Marseilles. The artist Auguste Rodin (1840–1917) was captivated by their grace. Described as his final passion, he famously made 150 pencil sketches and watercolours of the dancers in a week of intense creativity. He said of the beautiful nymphs, "They have even found a new movement, of which I was unaware: the jolts their body gives as it moves downward. And then their great strength lies in the fact that they keep their legs permanently bent, like a spring box, from which they can bounce or rise upwards as they wish, make themselves taller, at any given moment. It is a movement all of their own and unknown to us".

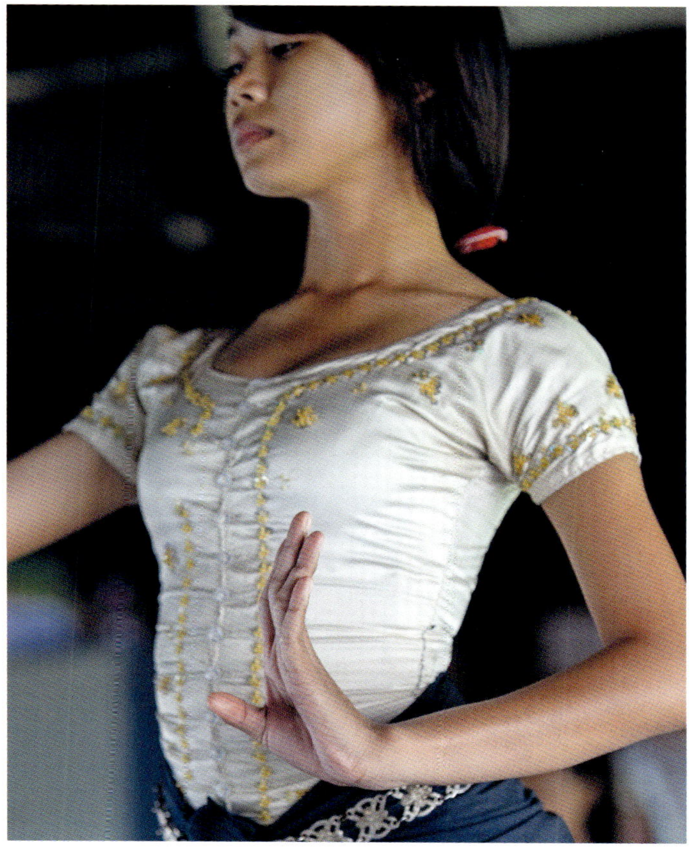

The greatest challenge to the dancer's art, however, was under the cloud of the Khmer Rouge. Seen as aristocratic, it was frowned upon and was almost extinguished when musicians, dancers and choreographers were executed by the Khmer Rouge. In later years when stability had returned to Cambodia, a few survivors who had managed to flee across the border into Thailand were tracked down and asked to help revive the tradition by teaching a new generation of performers.

Lengthy performances of scenes from the *Reamker* are seldom performed. More common are shows that offer an overview of classical and theatrical folk dance. Often the first dance of the evening is the dance of the Apsara which was created in the 1940s by Queen Sisowath Kossamak and performed by her granddaughter and protégé, Princess Bopha Devi.

Above: A student practises her hand gestures at one of the many schools now teaching the art of traditional Khmer dance.

Opposite: A beautiful young Khmer woman dressed as a mythical Apsara strikes a graceful pose for a tourist.

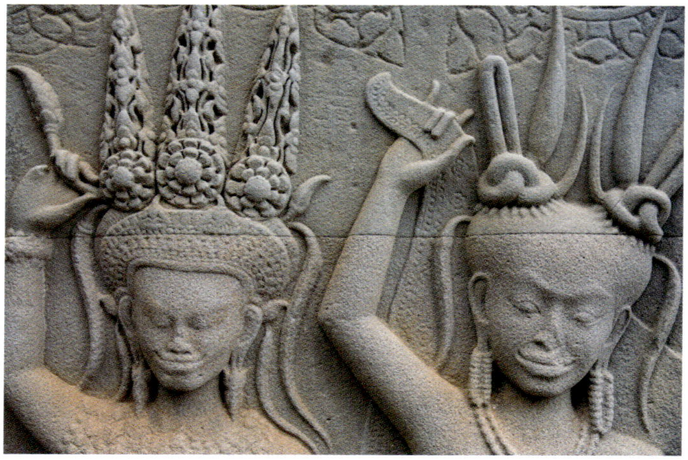

Apsara dancers dress in glittering costumes and the elaborate headwear that is recorded by the carvings at Angkorian temples. Postures and movement are also inspired by the stone-hewn images. Although the dance tradition was introduced from India, the classical dance movements in the Khmer form are slower, more considered and sublimely graceful. Elegant posture, arched backs and fingers, enigmatic expressions and economy of movement combine to create a truly mesmerizing performance. Classical dance is accompanied by a wind and percussive ensemble, known as *pinpeat*, who sit in the wings of the stage. Each act is also separated by a narrative that explains the intricacies of the drama.

More playful folk dances, such as the fishing dance, were developed during the 1960s. The storylines of this and other dances are easily interpreted and usually present an idealized view of rural life, with flirtatious men pursuing, and often being rebuffed by, shy young women. But folk dance, it has to be said, is far less engaging than the highly stylized classical dance.

The success of the Princess Bopha Devi's efforts together with other highly accomplished dancers to revive one of Cambodia's most refined arts is a triumph but it would not have been possible without the growth in tourism. In Phnom Penh visitors enjoy regular performances by troupes such as the Children of Bassac and at the National Museum. In Siem Reap, five-star hotels, such as La Résidence d'Angkor, host regular performances of Apsara dance drama accompanied by live music.

Above: The costumes that dancers wear today have been styled on ancient carvings of Apsaras at Angkor Wat and other temples.

A LIVING TRADITION

The revival of classical Khmer dance is a remarkable success story. Today, there are several classical dance schools in Phnom Penh and Siem Reap. Typically students start to learn the art at a very young age when their bodies are still flexible. Daily classes begin with a series of stretching exercises to keep the limbs supple and train the fingers to arch backwards and form the characteristic hand gestures before moving on to classic poses and movements. It takes many years of discipline and hard work to become an accomplished dancer. Emphasizing the importance of maintaining the tradition for future generations, Khmer classical dance was proclaimed a Masterpiece of Oral and Intangible Heritage of Humanity by UNESCO on 7 November 2003.

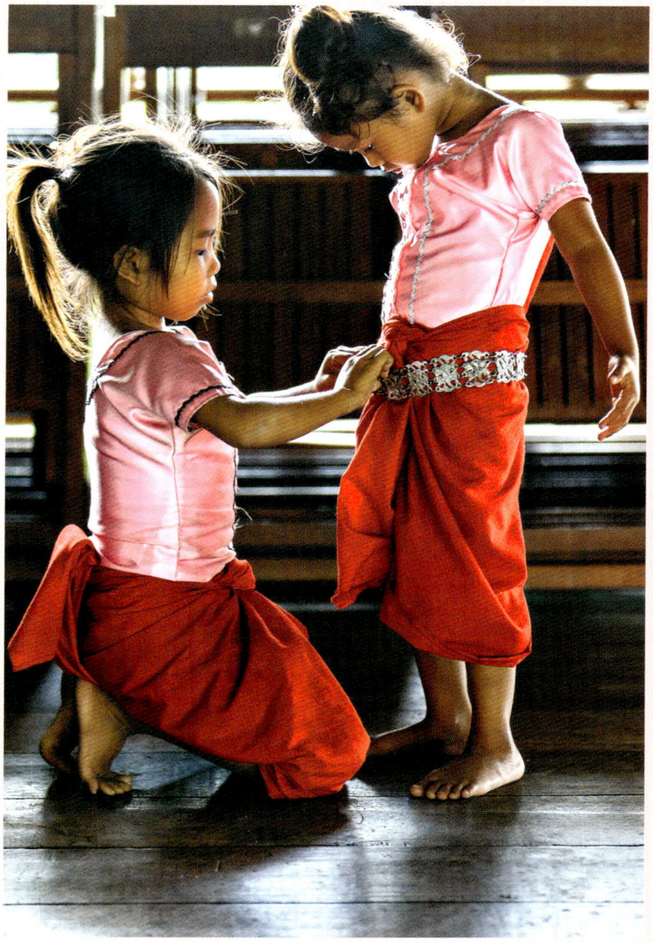

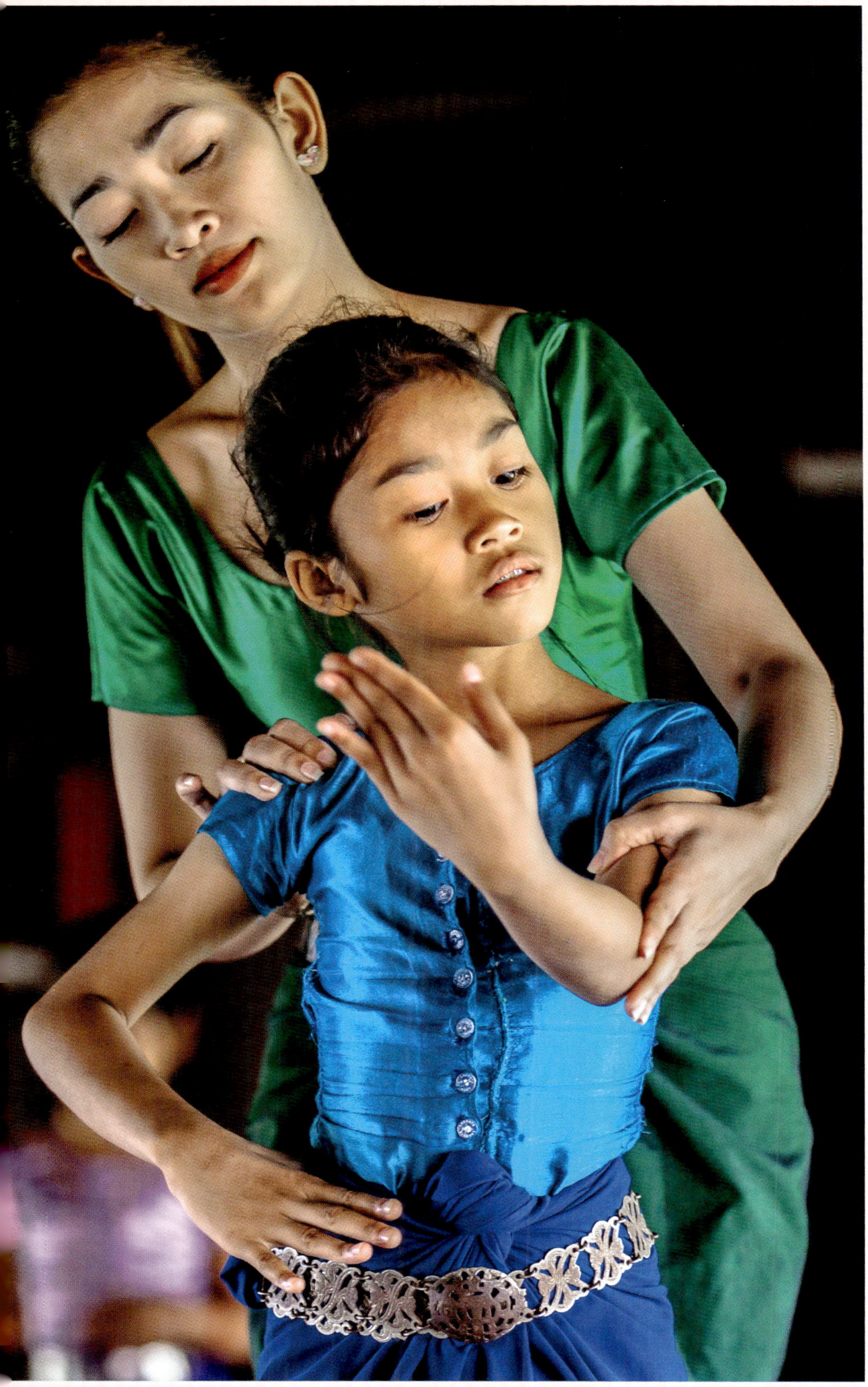

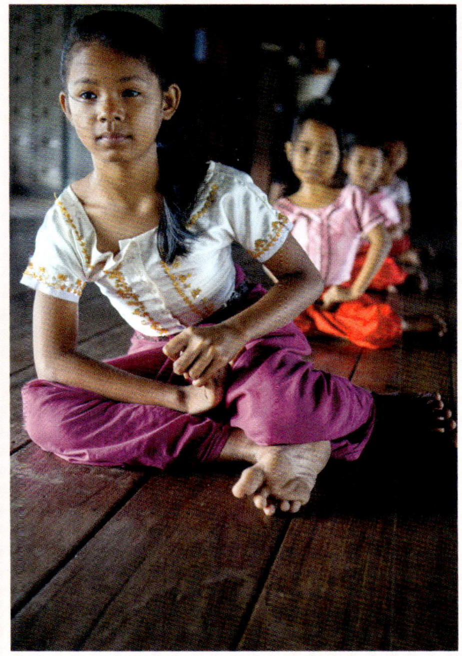

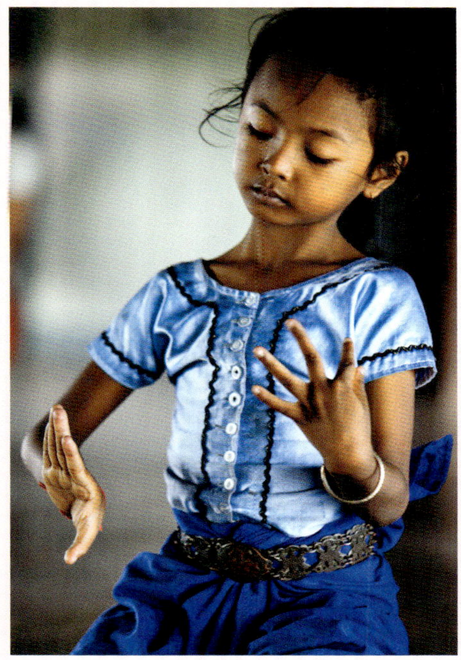

This page and opposite below: Girls begin to learn Khmer dance as young as four years of age. Their daily classes require dedication, discipline and many years of practice to perfect the art.

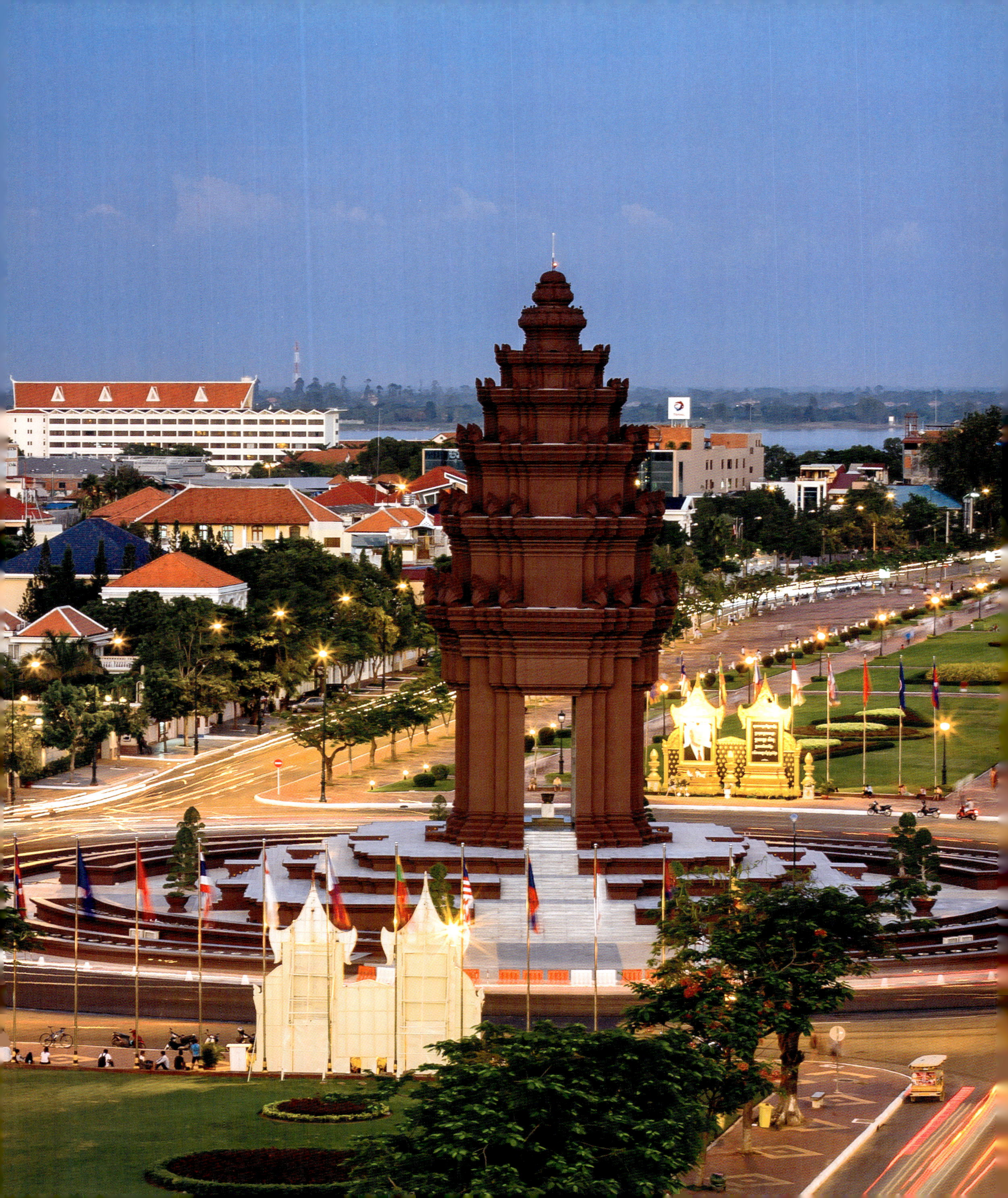

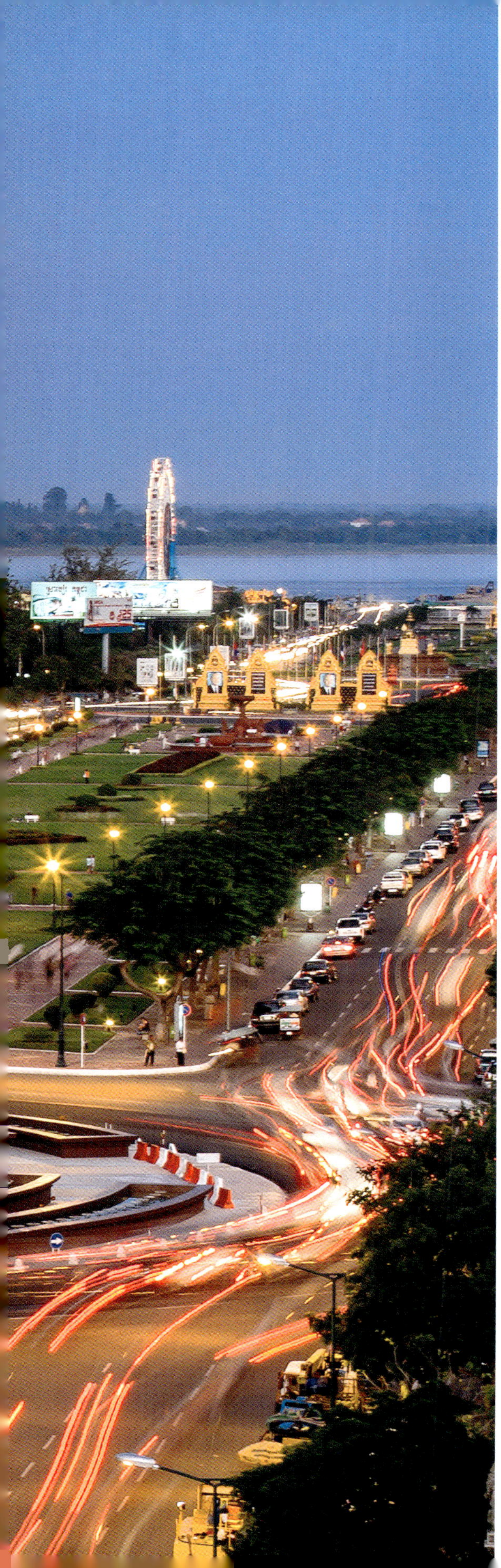

CHAPTER II

PHNOM PENH *and* SURROUNDS

The Charming City

Just two decades ago, following years of civil war, Phnom Penh was a city in tatters. The only foreign visitors it attracted were UN staff, NGOs and a handful of journalists and photographers. Following years of development and investment, the city is now experiencing a remarkable social and economic boom. Phnom Penh is a city on the move.

Left: Independence Monument ringed by traffic trails at dusk. The Phnom Penh landmark stands at the intersection of the broad Norodom and Sihanouk boulevards. The area around the monument is the focus of celebrations for Independence Day on 7 January and Constitution Day on 24 September. The boulevards are often decorated with flags as a welcome to foreign dignitaries.

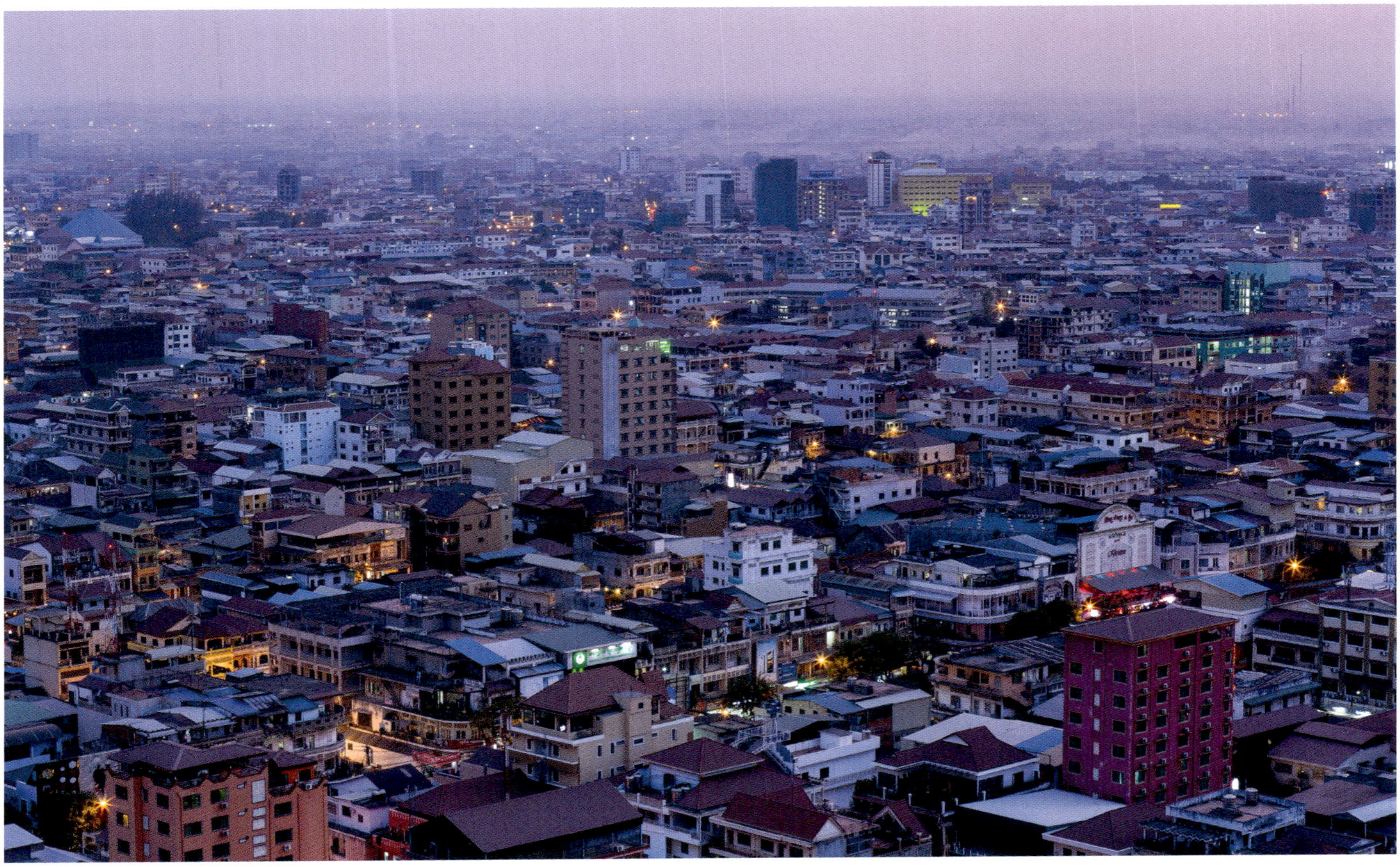

Phnom Penh was established as the capital by Preah Ponhea Yat in 1432 before being abandoned in 1505 as a result of political power struggles. In 1866, King Norodom I returned the seat of government to Phnom Penh and it once again became the capital city. Situated at the confluence of three rivers, the Mekong, the Tonlé Sap and the Bassac, it flourished during the French occupation, particularly from 1870 onwards when the city's easily navigated grid layout was put in place and some of its grandest buildings constructed. The Royal Palace and the National Museum, arguably the finest of Cambodia's many architectural gems, were built during this period.

In recent years, Phnom Penh's population has swelled to two million and the once-deserted roads are now clogged with traffic. It is, however, an easy city to get around and a pleasure to explore on foot. Riding on the back of massive investment from China, Korea, Singapore and Japan, the skyline of Phnom Penh seems to change on an almost weekly basis. High-rise buildings, all gleaming glass and steel, now overshadow humble shophouses and many more ambitious development projects are on the way. For the visitor, discovery waits in historic temples, vibrant fresh food markets and fascinating neighbourhoods navigated through a network of shaded alleyways. It is here that the real Phnom Penh can be uncovered.

But despite the welcome drive for modernity, Phnom Penh's history cannot and should not be ignored. Disturbing but necessary insight into the true horror of the atrocities committed by the Khmer Rouge can be gained at Tuol Sleng Genocide Museum, a former secondary school where the ghosts of the past still haunt the classrooms. Fifteen kilometres (nine miles) away at Camp Cheoung Ek Killing Fields, a memorial stupa now marks the site of dozens of mass graves.

Above: Phnom Penh extends over 678.46 km^2 (262 sq. miles) and until recently has been an almost completely low-rise city.

Opposite: Completed in 2009, the 32-storey Canadia Bank Tower (pictured) was one of the first high-rise buildings in Phnom Penh. In 2013, the 188-m (618-ft), 39-floor, Vattanac Capital Tower opened, and many other projects are underway.

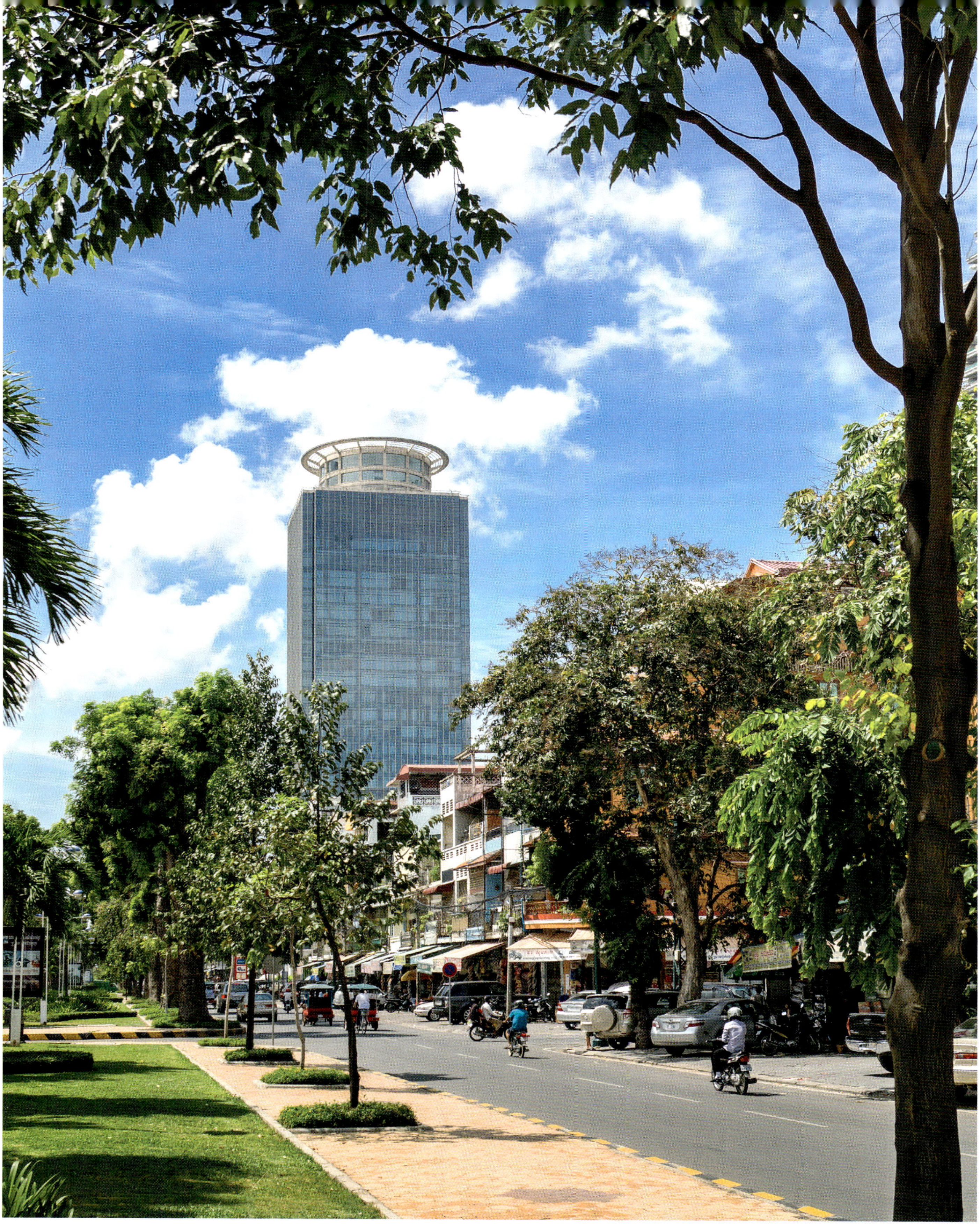

Right: Constructed in 1964, the Olympic Stadium in Phnom Penh never actually hosted the Olympics. It is, however, a popular place in the early evening for mass aerobic sessions and regularly hosts popular football matches.

Opposite top: Phnom Penh is a fascinating city to explore on foot, especially in the early morning as it begins to awake and the air is cooler. Within its network of streets and alleys, there are peaceful temples, chaotic markets and many other treasures to be discovered.

Opposite below: Pigeons take flight as Buddhists monks, shading themselves from the midday sun with umbrellas, walk past the Royal Palace.

Below: Light trails from cars driving along Phnom Penh's riverfront are evidence of the city's somewhat erratic driving style. In recent years, traffic has boomed and congestion at rush hour is now a fact of life in the burgeoning and increasingly wealthy city.

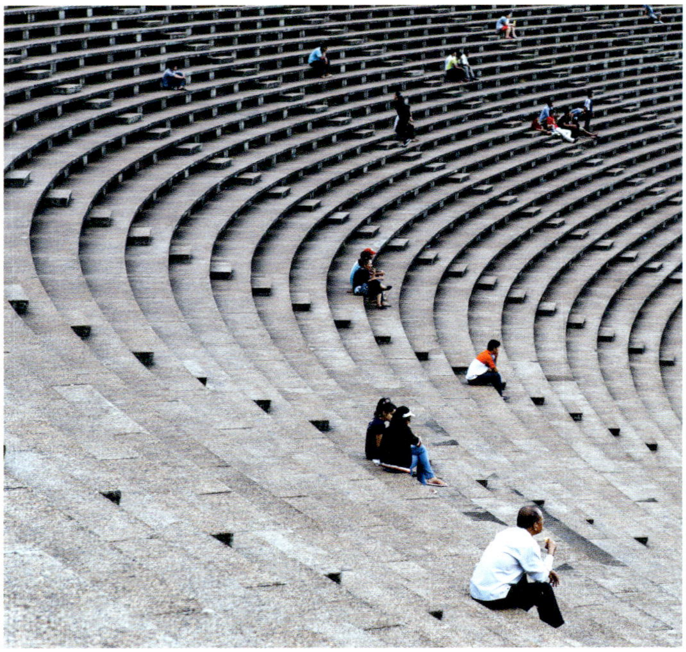

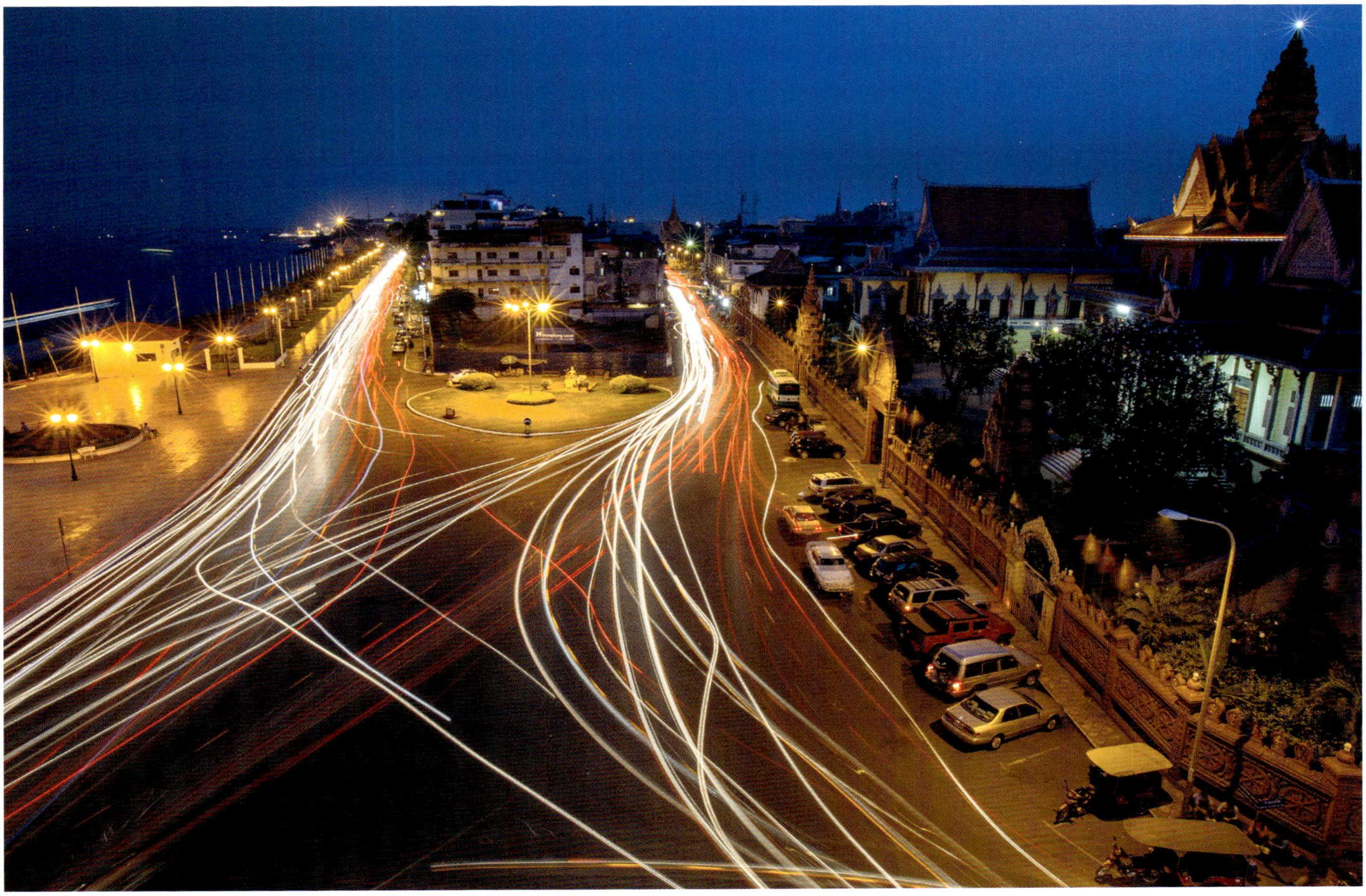

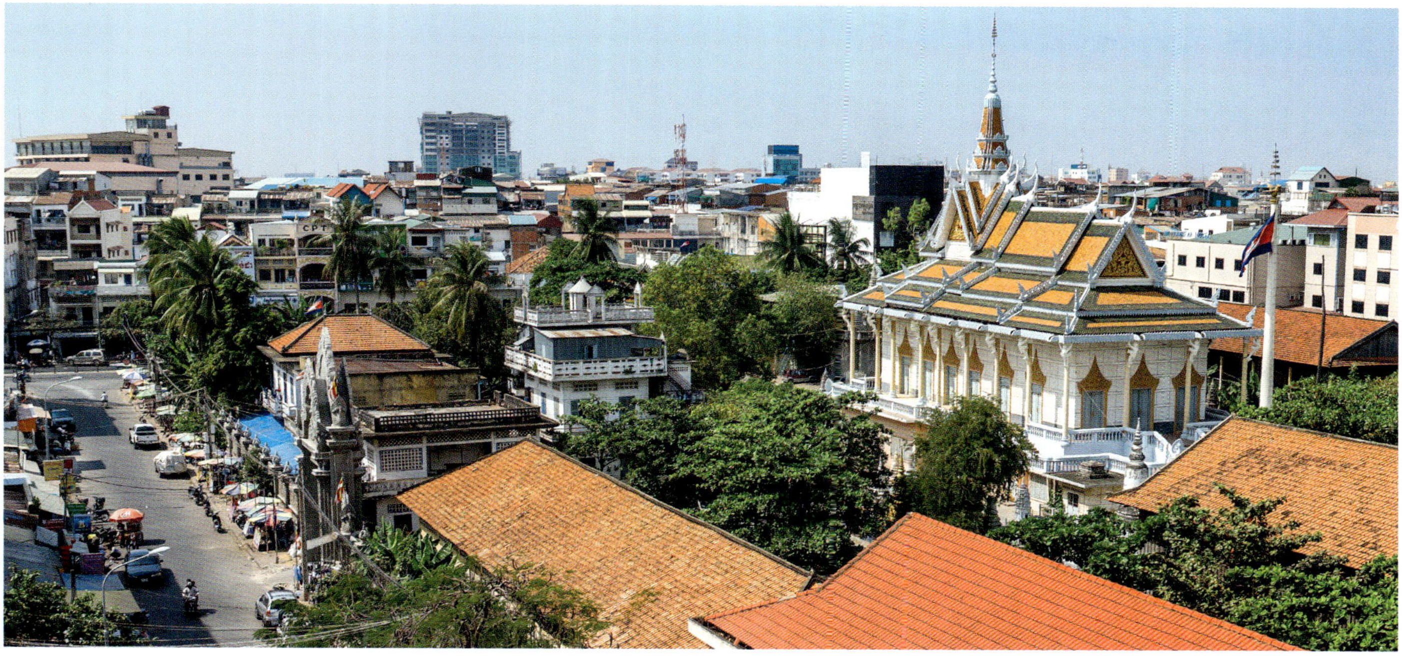

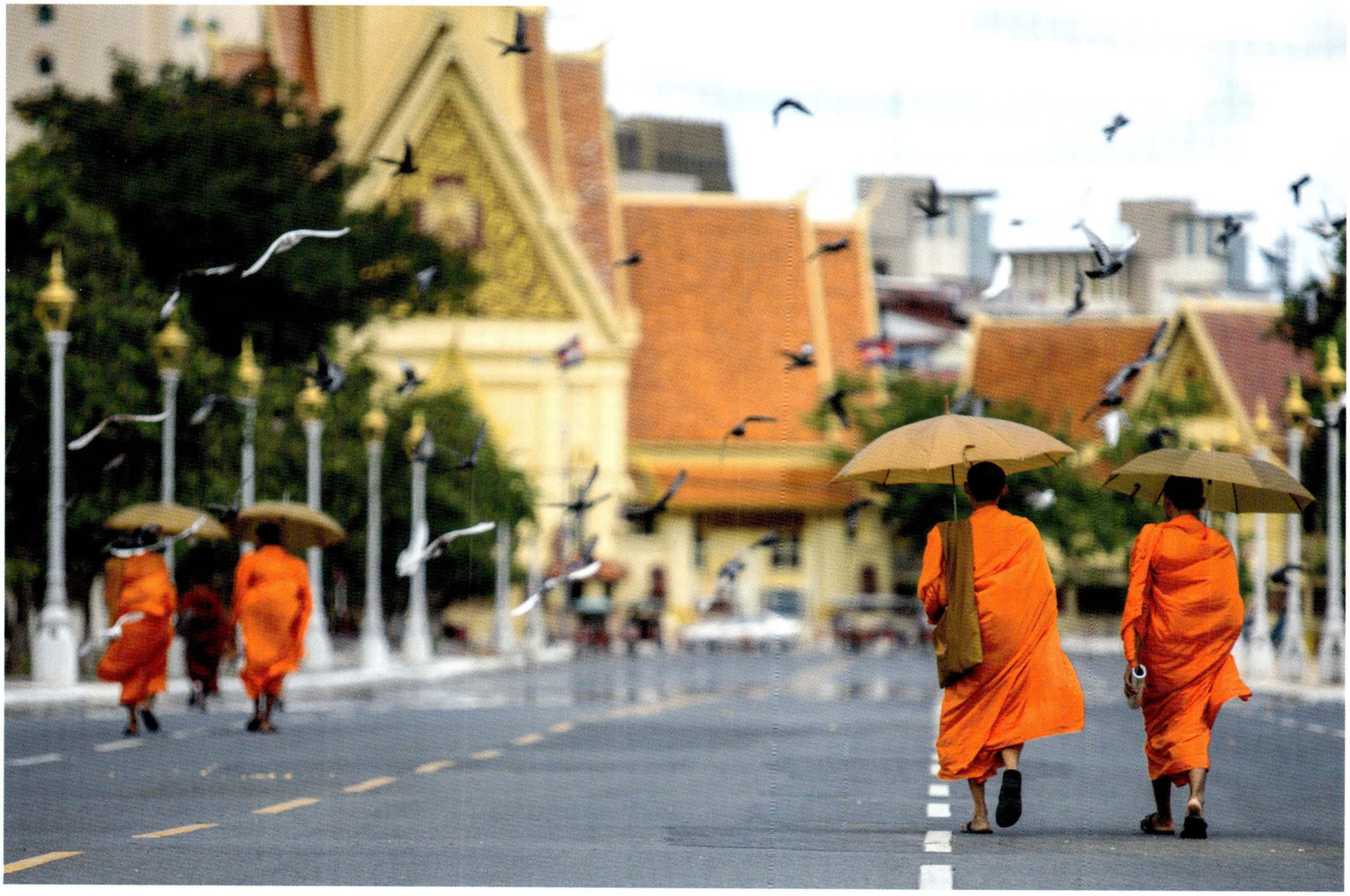

In the evenings, Phnom Penh locals and foreigners alike gravitate towards the riverfront. For health-conscious women, the expansive promenade is the venue for a daily aerobic workout. For the princely sum of 1,000 riel ($0.25) they join exercise classes and dance to a mix of Khmer tunes and hip hop blaring from oversized speakers. Similar classes are held all over the city, including at the Olympic Stadium. On the other side of the road, the scene is more relaxed. As the light fades, tourists and expats enjoy ice-cold Angkor beer at riverfront bars and restaurants, including the renowned Foreign Correspondents' Club. Once a watering hole for jaded journos, it now welcomes all-comers and is one of the city's most popular hangouts.

Phnom Penh's energy is palpable. The city's soundtrack is composed of the buzz of motorcycles, the whir of angle grinders and a chorus of vendors' chatter. Youthful, exuberant and forward looking, Phnom Penh is a city with many charms and a brave new future.

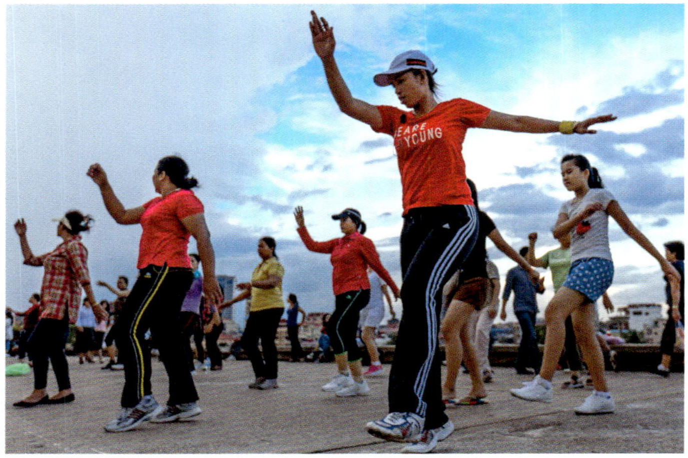

Above: Khmer women love to exercise in public. Aerobic sessions are held along the riverfront, in parks and at the Olympic Stadium.
Below: The Foreign Correspondents' Club or FCC on the riverfront is a popular bar and restaurant.

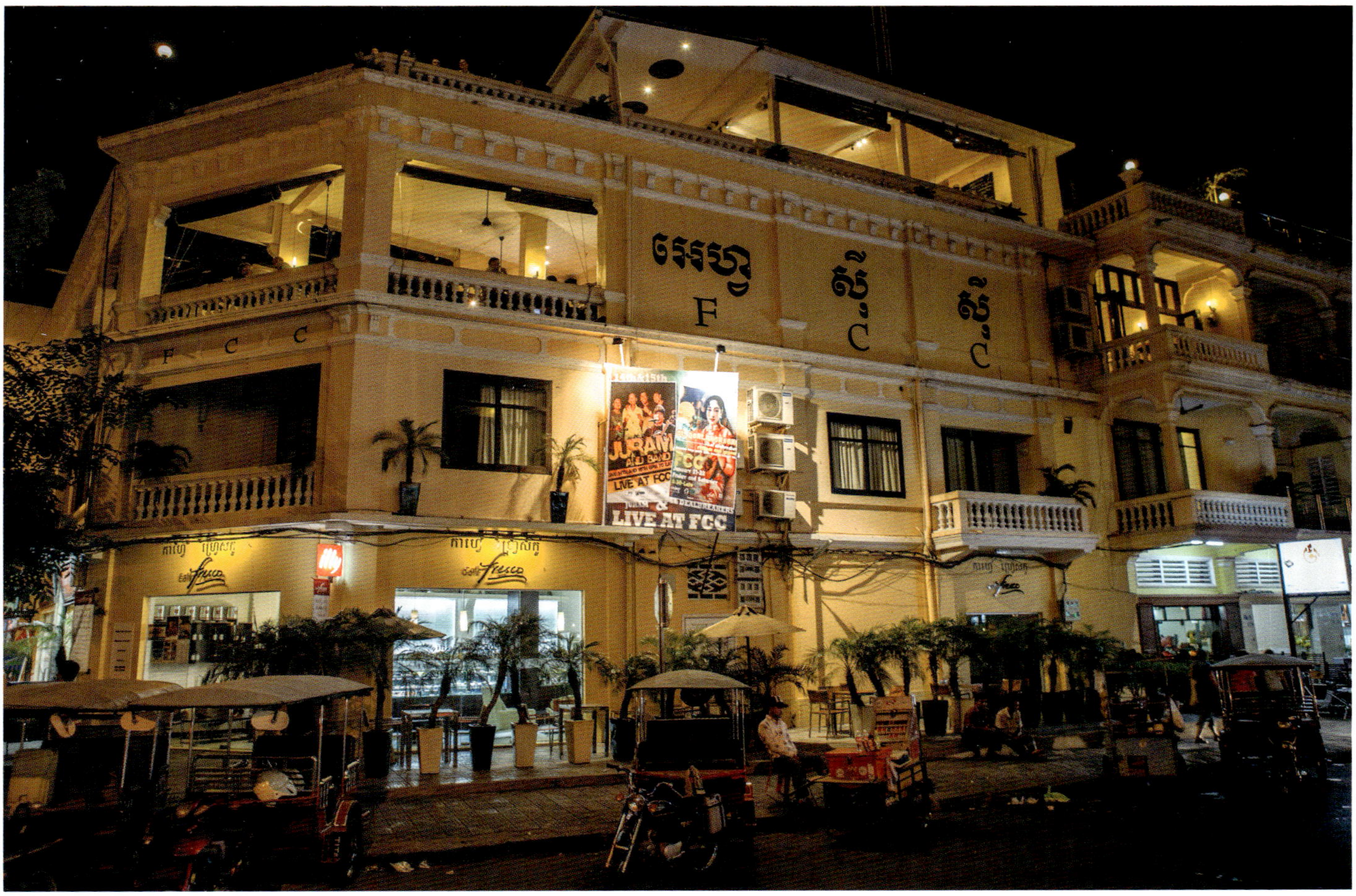

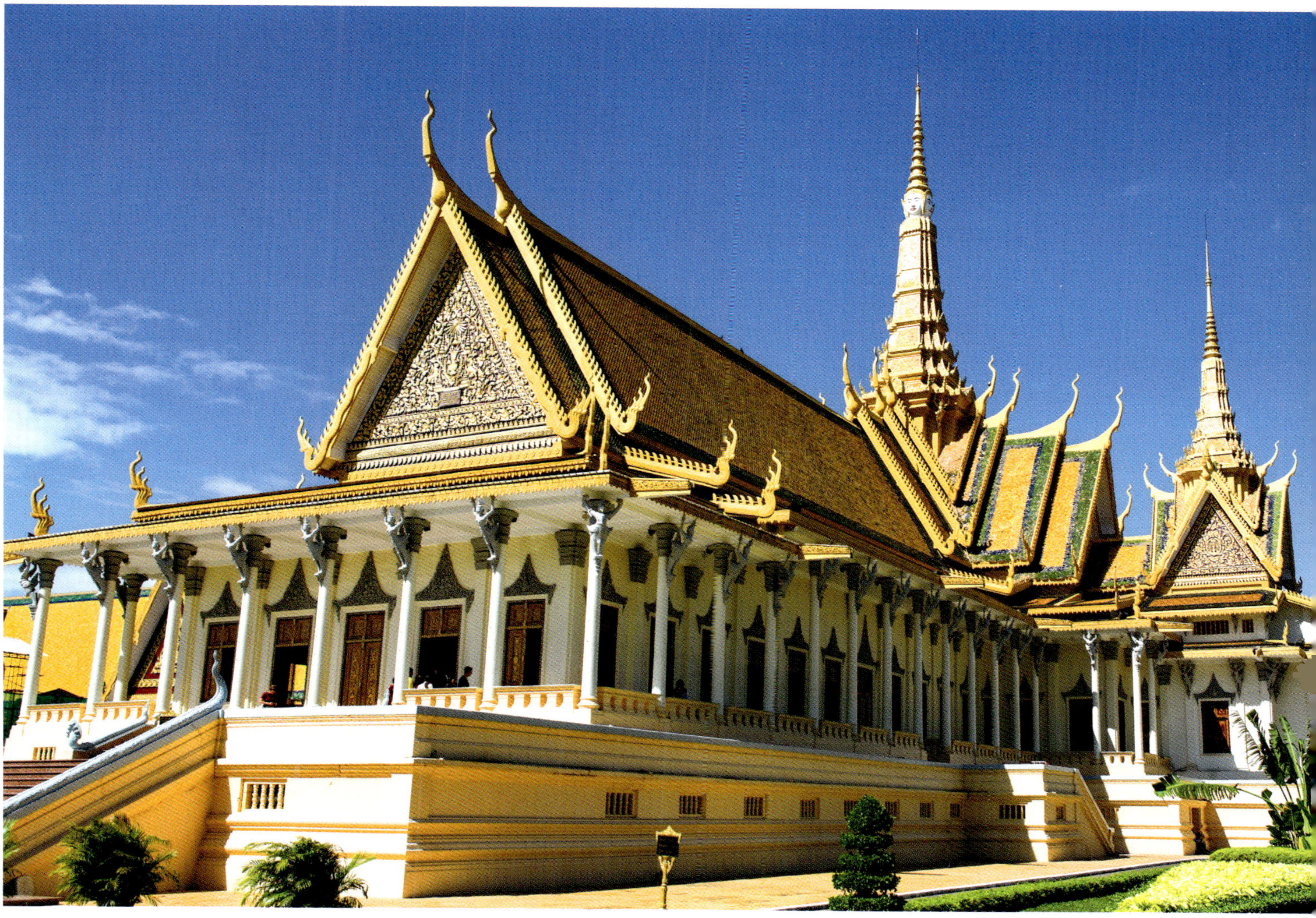

The jewels in Phnom Penh's historic crown are The Royal Palace and the Silver Pagoda. Within an expansive walled compound, parts of the Royal Palace complex date from 1866. Here buildings house Buddha statues, including an emerald Buddha encrusted with precious stones, as well as other religious and royal artefacts. Built for King Norodom I, the Royal Palace breaks the skyline with sweeping tiled roofs and stupa spires. It is fronted on Samdech Sothearos Boulevard by the Chan Chaya Pavilion which was constructed in 1913 to replace an earlier wooden pavilion. Often referred to as the Moonlight Pavilion, it was used once used for royal banquets and dance performances.

Until his death in 2012, the Royal Palace was still the official home of His Majesty King Norodom Sihanouk, King of Cambodia, although he had actually lived in self-imposed exile in North Korea and China from 2004. As a royal residence, sections of the compound are off-limits to visitors but many of its highlights can still be enjoyed. On entering the palace compound, visitors first come to the Throne Hall or Preah Timeang Tevea Vinicchay. Like Chan Chaya Pavilion, this is the second structure to serve as a throne hall and dates from 1917. It was here that King Sisowath was crowned in 1919. The striking building features a 59-m (194-ft) spire with a four-faced head representing Brahma, the Hindu god of creation. Inside, the beautiful ceiling is decorated with scenes from the *Reamker*.

Above: The Throne Hall at the Royal Palace was once used for coronations and formal events with international dignitaries. Today the public can admire the impressive architecture and frescoes.

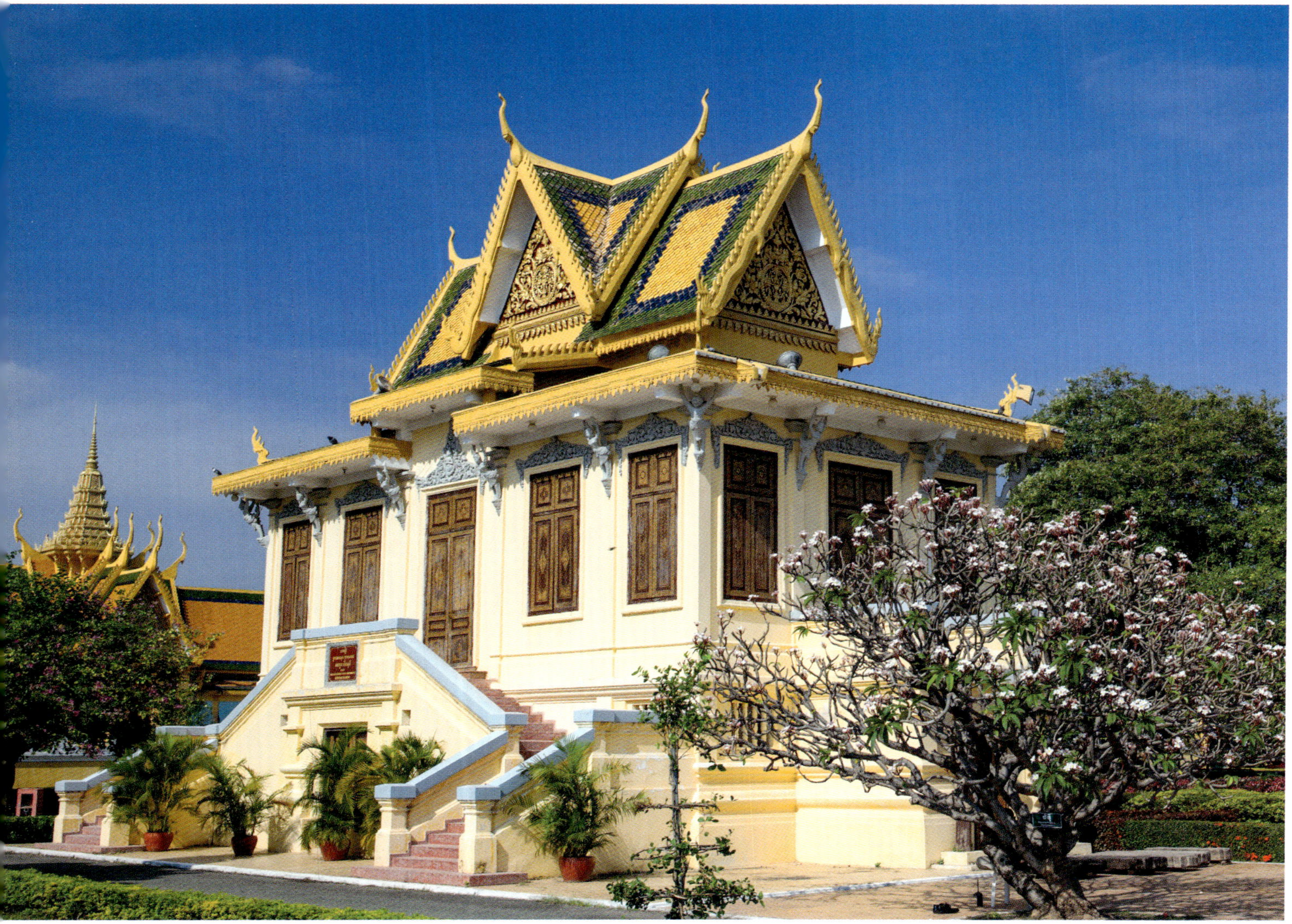

Above: Hor Samran Phirun is one of four similar structures within the grounds of the Royal Palace. Constructed in 1917, it is said that former kings would mount and dismount elephants from a platform here.

Opposite: Within the grounds of the Silver Pagoda is an ornate stupa containing the ashes of King Ang Doung (1796–1860), the great-great-grandfather of the late King Sihanouk. There are three other similar stupas in the grounds dedicated to former royalty including King Norodom I (1834–1904) and King Suramarit (1896–1960).

Wat Preah Keo Morakot or the Temple of the Emerald Buddha is located within a separate compound. It is more commonly referred to as the Silver Pagoda because of the more than 5,000 silver tiles that cover the floor. The opulent temple was originally used by the royal family for prayer and listening to sermons given by monks. Guests enter by a stairway hewn from Italian marble. Within the temple sits the diminutive Emerald Buddha and a tall, gold, standing Buddha weighing in at 90 kg (660 lb) and encrusted with thousands of diamonds. Other highlights in the compound of the Silver Pagoda include time-faded frescoes depicting scenes from the *Reamker* painted along the walls of the courtyard. There are also several stupas containing the ashes of former kings and queens.

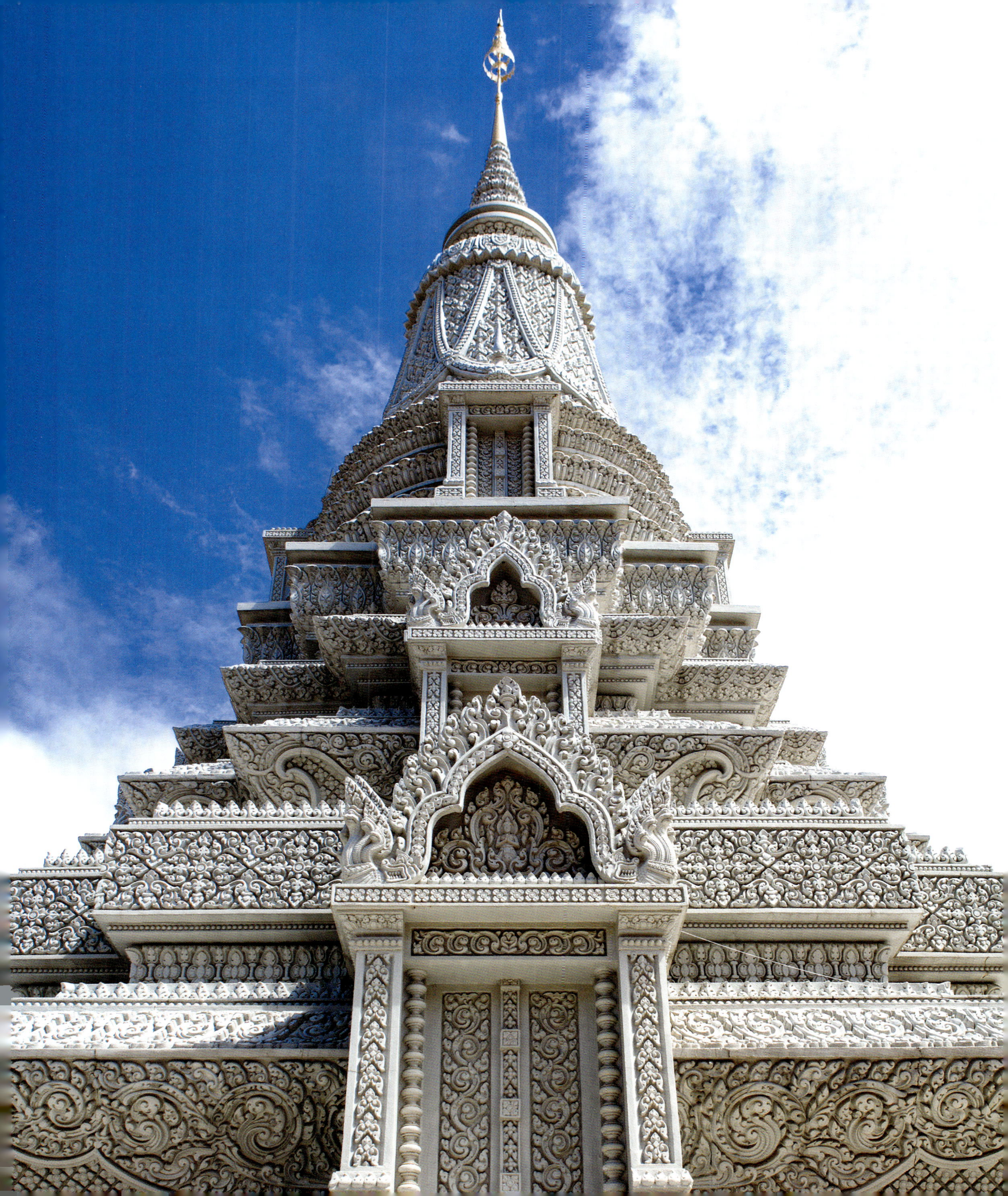

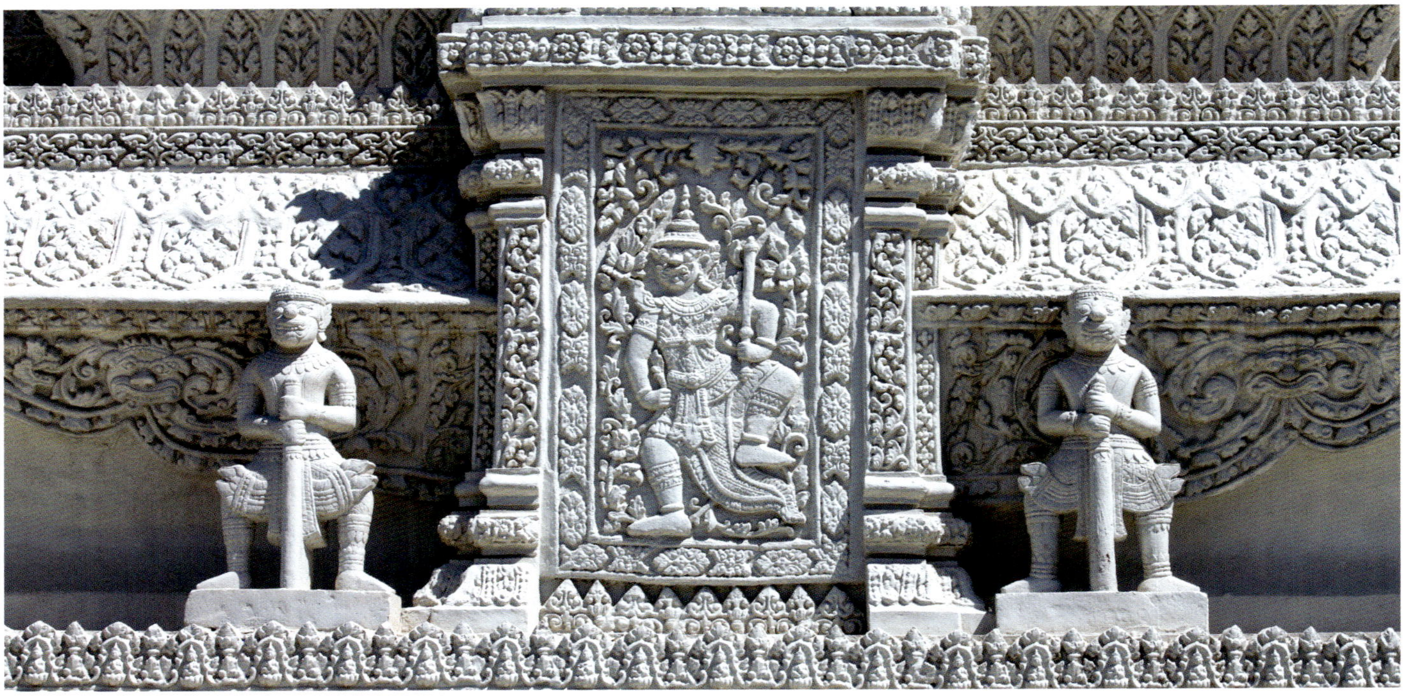

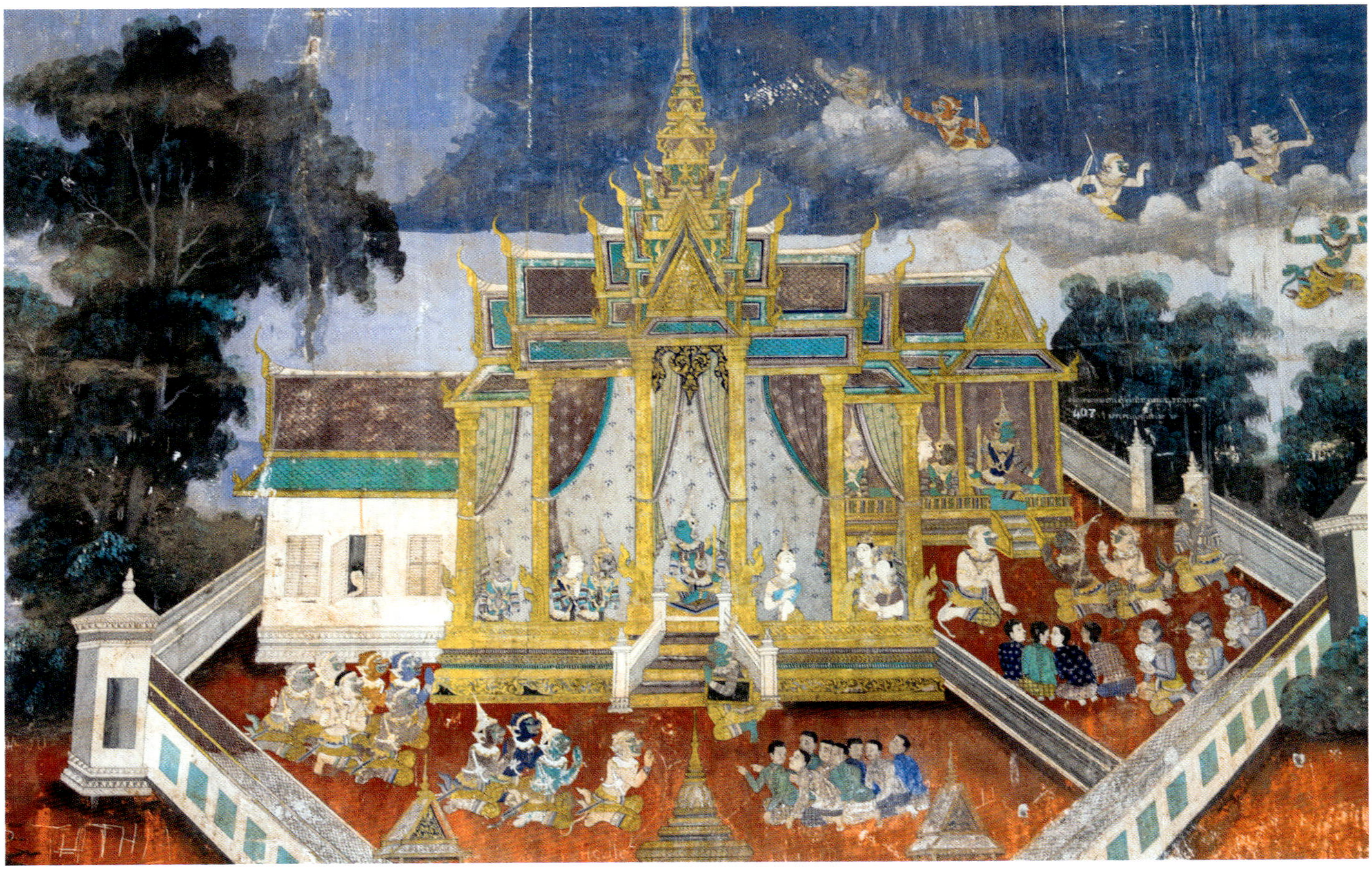

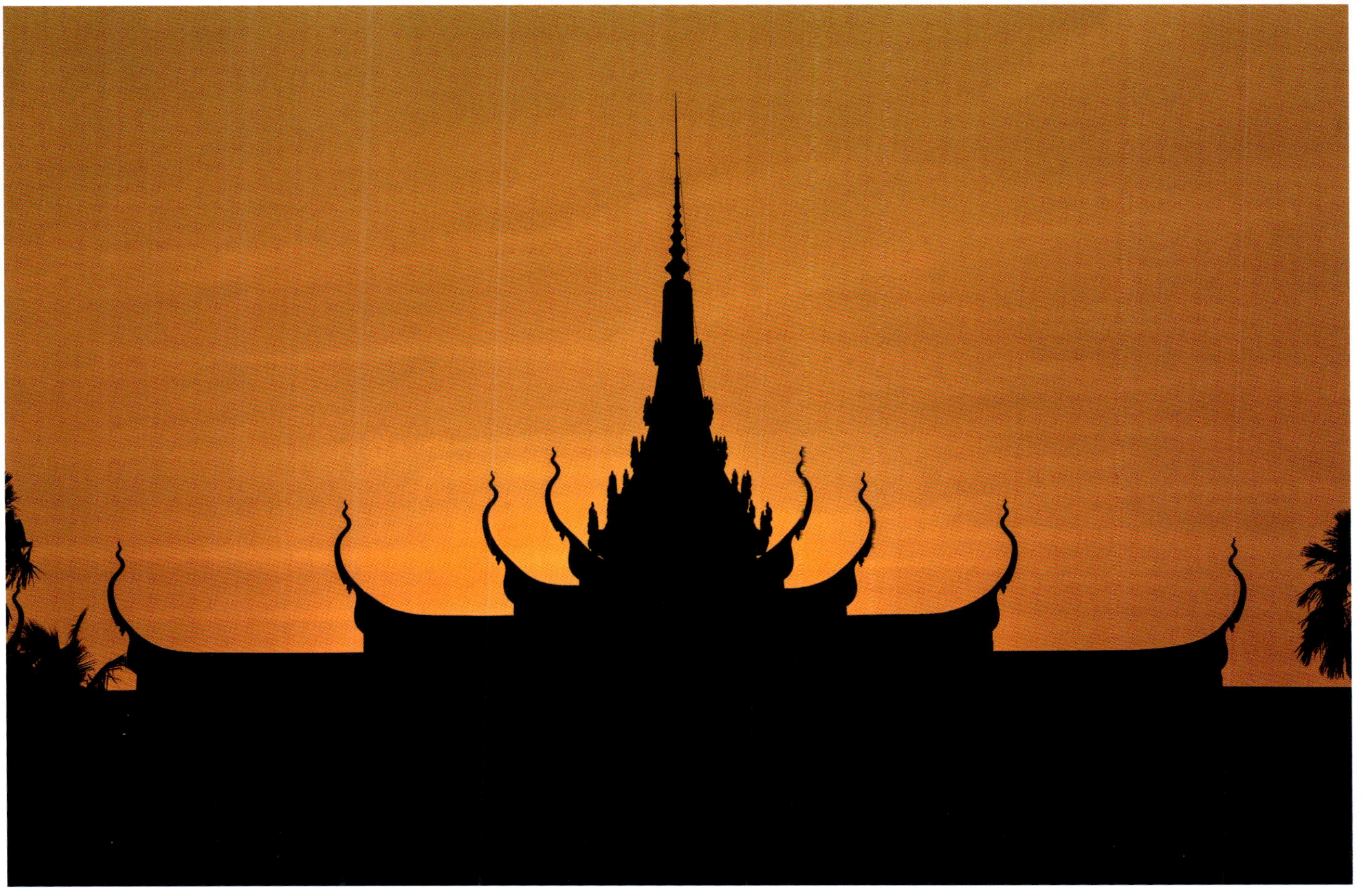

There can be few sights that encapsulate the essence of Asian exoticism more than the silhouette of Phnom Penh's National Museum at sunset. Yet this quintessentially Khmer structure was actually designed by the French artist, author, historian, educator and ethnologist, George Groslier (1887-1945).

The first French child to be born in Cambodia, Groslier was educated in France but returned to the land of his birth in 1910. In 1917, the Governor General of Indochina, Albert Sarraut, invited Groslier to write a proposal for a School of Applied Arts in Phnom Penh. However, in the course of his research the young Frenchman reached the conclusion that traditional Khmer arts were in danger of disappearing. In addition to the art school he also proposed building a museum and the creation of an organization dedicated to preserving craft knowledge.

Groslier's vision was soon realized, and the Musée Albert Sarraut was officially opened on the Khmer New Year, 14 April 1920, by H.M. King Sisowath and Groslier himself who was also appointed the museum's Director of Cambodian Arts and Conservation. Over the years, the building was extended with the addition of new wings. Following independence in 1953, control of the museum and the collection Groslier had catalogued was handed over to the Cambodians. However, the museum still employed a French director. It was not until 1966 that the first Cambodian was appointed as Director of the National Museum and Dean of a newly created Department of Archaeology at the Royal University of Fine Arts.

Above: The National Museum houses a collection of beautiful stone carvings, many of which have been removed from their original locations to prevent theft.

Opposite top: A detail from one of the stupas in the grounds of the Silver Pagoda that contains the ashes of royalty.

Opposite below: Beautiful but faded frescoes on the cloister walls in the grounds of the Silver Pagoda.

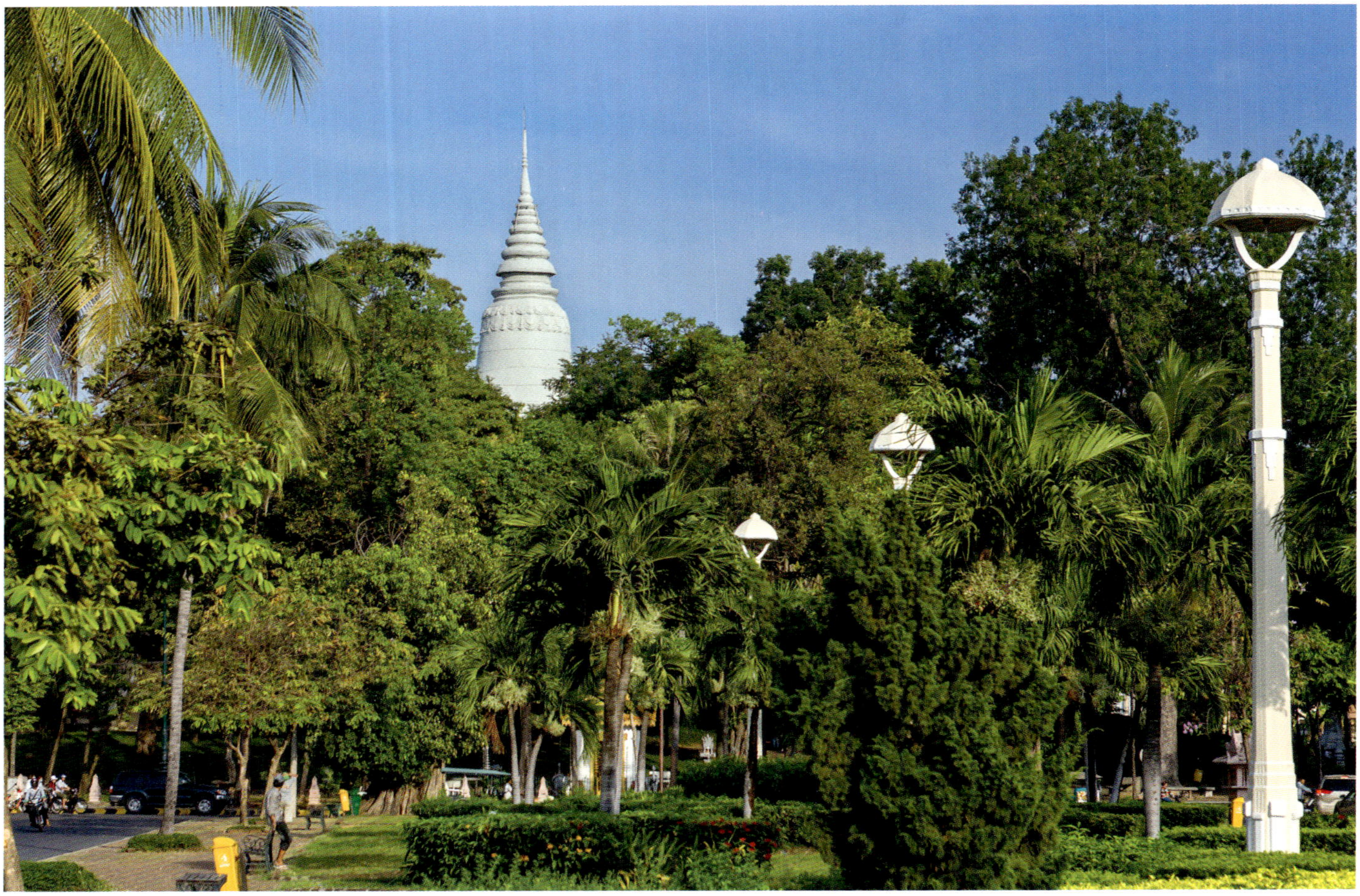

Phnom Penh takes its name from Wat Phnom which crowns a 27-m (88-ft) man-made hill at the end of Norodom Boulevard, a short distance from the Tonlé Sap River. Local legend has it that a wealthy widow called Daun Penh discovered four Buddha images inside a hollow of a tree and established a shrine on the hill to house them. More likely is an account that attributes it to the ruler Preah Ponhea Yat, who is said to have built the temple when he fled Angkor and created a new capital in Phnom Penh. The stairway that leads to Wat Phnom's landmark stupa is lined with images of *naga* or great snakes, guardians and lions, all of which are recent additions. In fact, the entire complex has been changed or renovated many times over the centuries. The dull grey stupa that tops the hill is less than impressive but within the *vihara* or monastery is a huge bronze Buddha which makes ascending the staircase worthwhile. The image is seated among dozens of smaller ones and often surrounded by flowers and lotus blossoms left by worshippers. The colourful walls and ceiling are painted with scenes from the life of Buddha and the *Reamker*. Between the *vihara* and the stupa there is also a popular shrine dedicated to the Daun Penh of the legend.

Above: Wat Phnom sits atop a small hill in a district once known as the French Quarter. Today, this popular tourist attraction also acts as a busy traffic island.

Opposite top left: The stupa at Wat Phnom is rather plain by Khmer standards but is said to contain the ashes of Preah Ponhea Yat (1393–1463).

Opposite top right: Ornate roof finials of Wat Phnom's main hall.

Opposite below: The large Buddha image in Wat Phnom's main hall is surrounded by smaller images, flower offerings, candles and other items of worship. There are also many more shrines within the temple grounds and in the gardens that surround the hill. The gardens were designed by the French in the late 19th century.

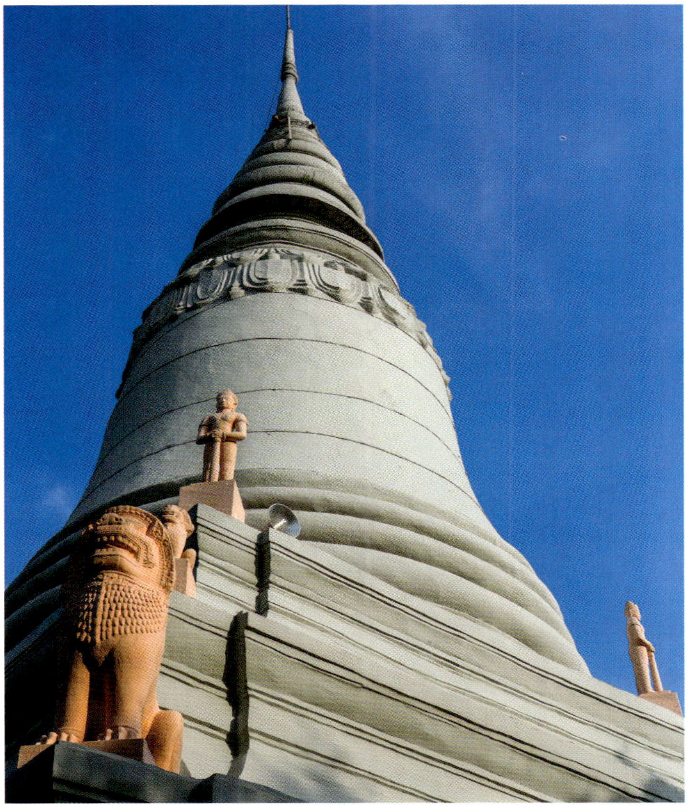

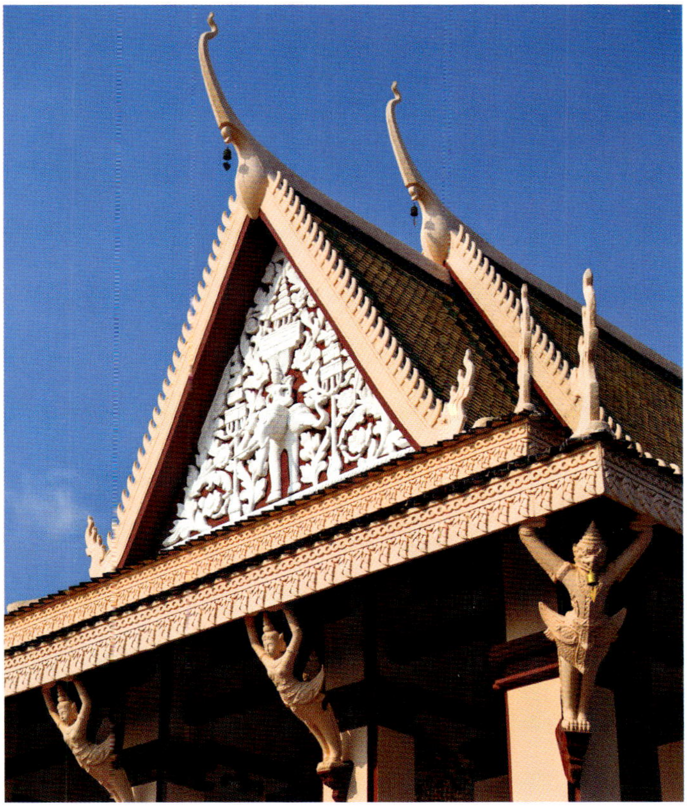

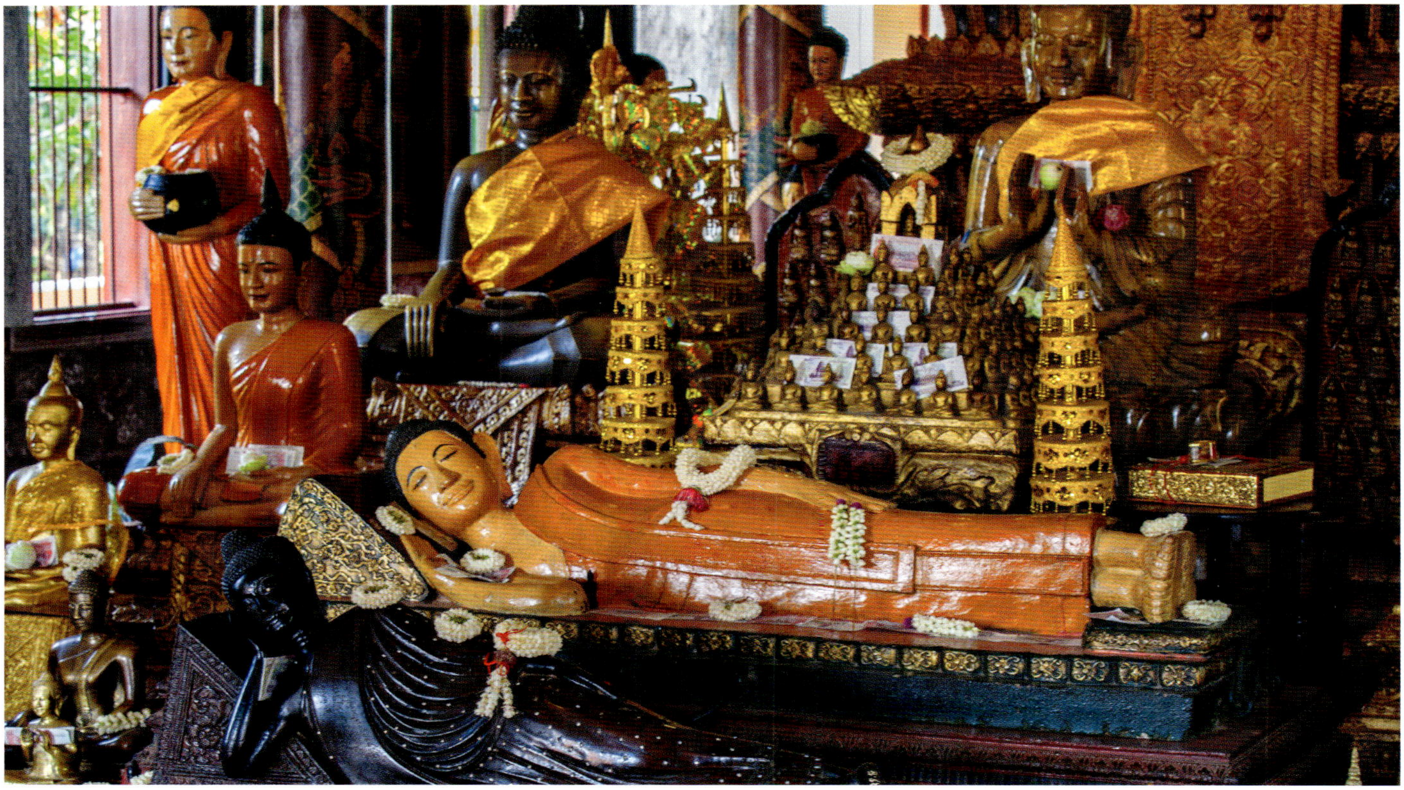

COLONIAL-ERA ARCHITECTURE

Cambodia's rich history and culture have bestowed it with a diverse collection of visually striking buildings. Like all colonizers, the French imposed their architectural style on Cambodia and it is these villas, markets, shophouses and local administration buildings that make the biggest impression on visitors. Many have been lost or are almost beyond saving; some are simply in need of a little sympathetic restoration, while others have already been returned to their former grandeur. There are architectural gems in all states of repair in provincial towns across the country but some of the most impressive can be found in the capital city, Phnom Penh. Walking tours that take in all the highlights are a great way of discovering the city and its history.

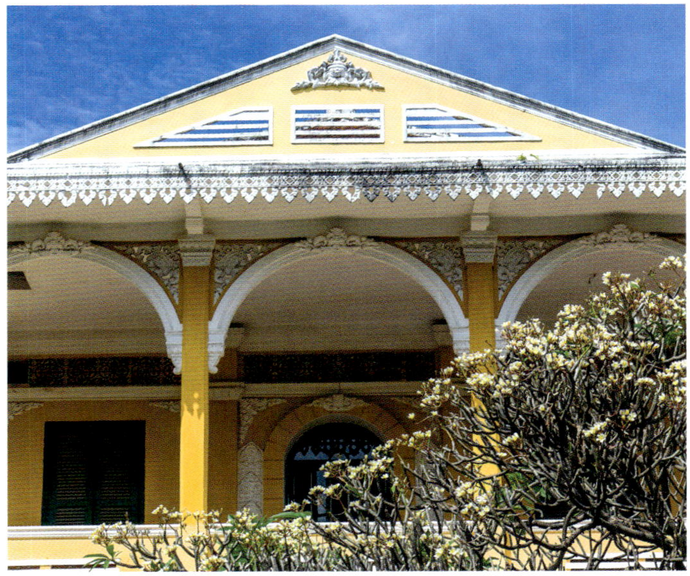

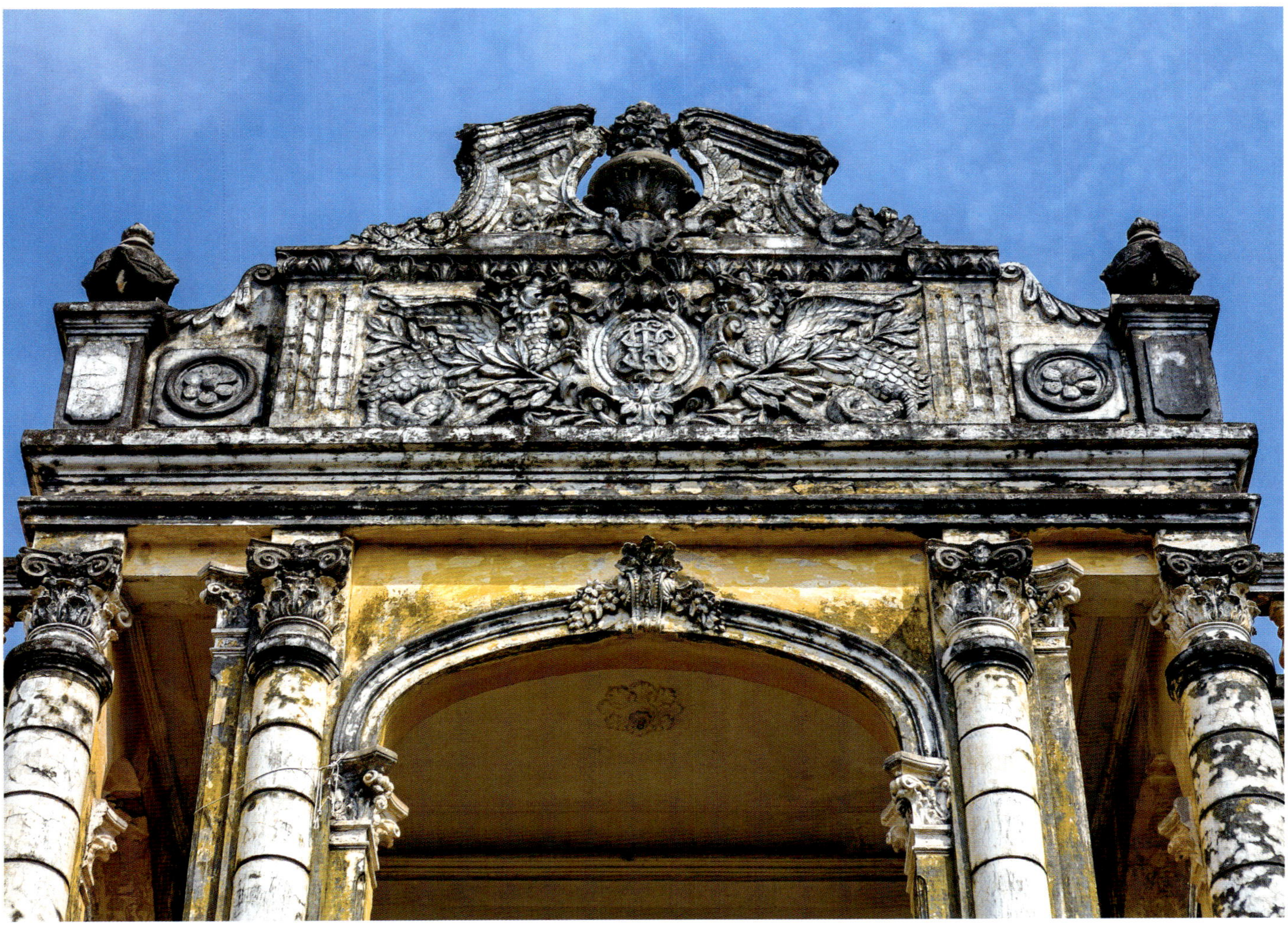

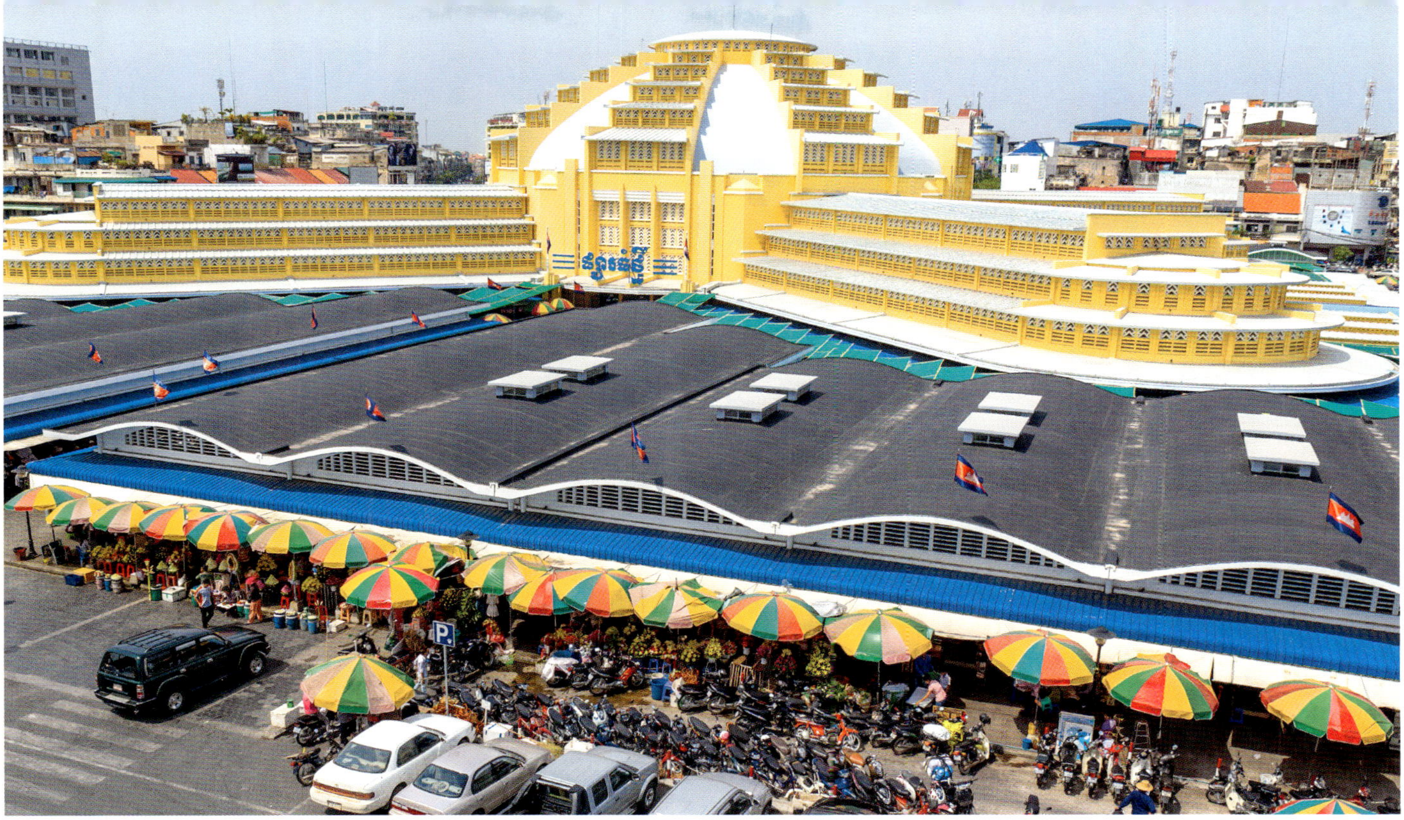

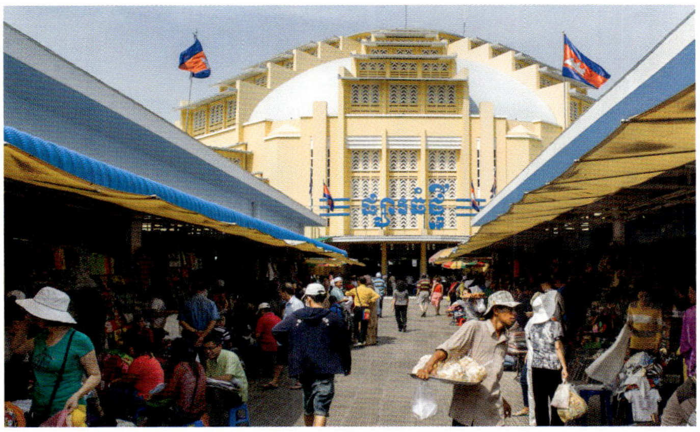

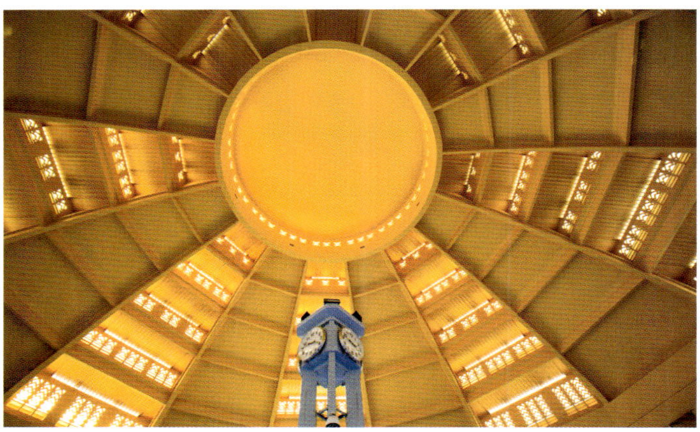

Psar Thmei, more commonly known as the Central Market, is a city landmark and one of the finest Art Deco period buildings in Southeast Asia.

At the site where the market now stands there was once a lake formed when earth was excavated to build the hill on which Wat Phnom stands. When plans for the market were drawn up by the architect Jean Desbois, the French drained and filled the lake. Construction of the market began in 1935 and was completed just two years later. Cleverly designed to be light, airy and cool, the market features four covered wings that lead to a central 26-m (85-ft) high and 30-m (98-ft) wide dome. The market, which houses gold traders, clothing vendors, food stalls, flowers sellers and a fresh food market, was renovated in 2011.

This page Phnom Penh's Central Market, or Psar Thmei (literally 'new market'), is one of the city's most striking buildings. The Art Deco structure and the newer wings added in 2011 are crowded with shoppers daily from 5 a.m. to 5 p.m.

Opposite top: An old royal villa on Street 178, opposite the University of Fine Arts. It was built around 1910.

Opposite below: Phnom Penh has some of the most beautiful, colonial-era buildings in Southeast Asia, unfortunately, many are in a dilapidated state like the 19th century Villa Picturesque.

The Post Office in Phnom Penh dates from 1895 and is one of the city's finest surviving colonial-era buildings. Situated in the heart of a district once known as the French Quarter, it was designed by Daniel Fabre. It benefitted from extensive renovations in 2004 and still serves its original purpose as a post office. Other grand buildings in the surrounding area include the former police headquarters, believed to have been built in 1925, and the former Bank of Indochina, which has been transformed into an upmarket European restaurant.

The restored UNESCO building was constructed between 1910 and 1920 and was once the residential villa of a wealthy Chinese merchant. Located on Samdech Sothearos Boulevard facing Mount Meru Square in front of the National Museum, it is one of several colonial-era villas in the area and was a family home until the Khmer Rouge marched into Phnom Penh in 1975. From 1979 until 1989 it came under the control of the Vietnamese Military City Police who used it as their headquarters before eventually opening as the UNESCO office at the end of 1991.

Built in 1932, the Art Deco architectural style of the Royal Railway Station reflects that of the Central Market. The station was originally built to serve passengers travelling to Battambang. Cambodia's railway was abandoned many years ago but is currently being modernized. It is said that following the fall of Phnom Penh in 1975 to the Khmer Rouge, the leadership held a meeting here and made the decision to evacuate the city.

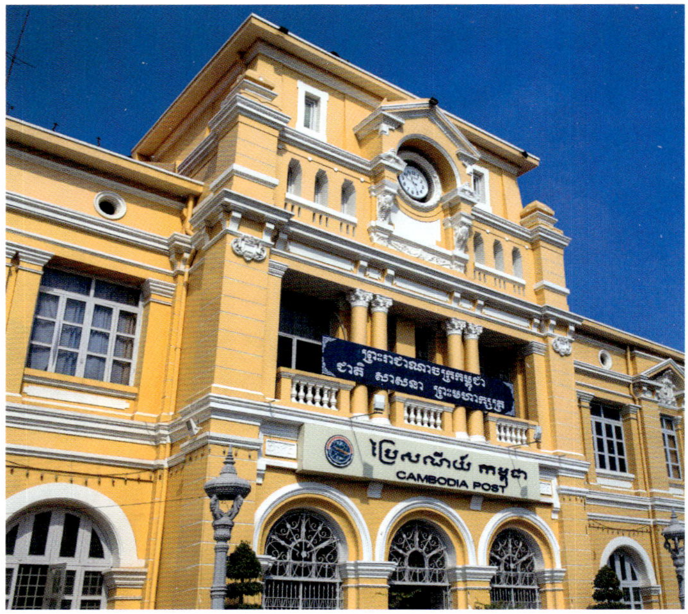

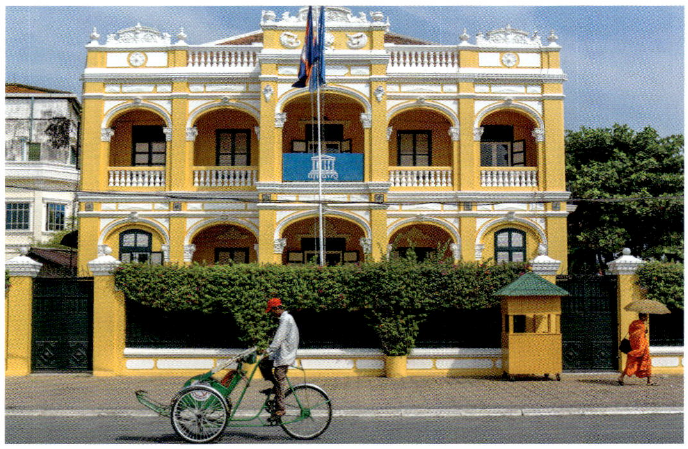

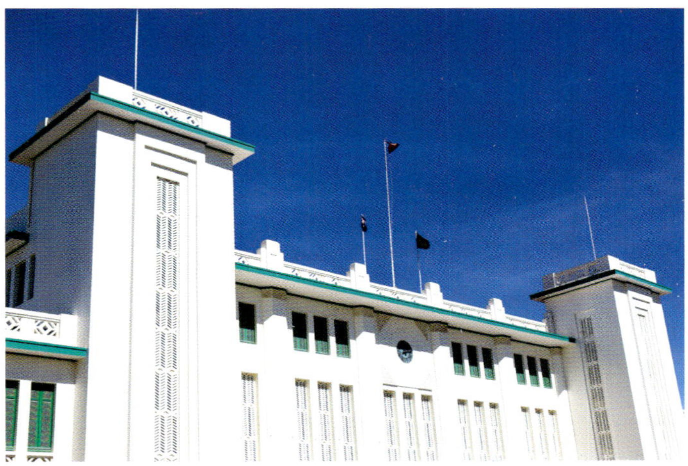

Above right: An interesting morning can be spent walking around Phnom Penh looking at the colonial-era buildings, such as the Post Office which dates from 1895. Most hotels can provide a route map for a walking tour.

Centre right: The UNESCO headquarters on Sothearos Boulevard is one old building that has benefited from careful restoration. The work was carried out in 2008.

Right: It has been many years since trains pulled into Phnom Penh's Art Deco station but the building has been restored.

Opposite: The Raffles Hctel Le Royal was built in 1929 but over the years many additions have been made. The stately old building fell into disrepair during the Khmer Rouge years but careful restoration in recent years has made it one of the city's finest hotels.

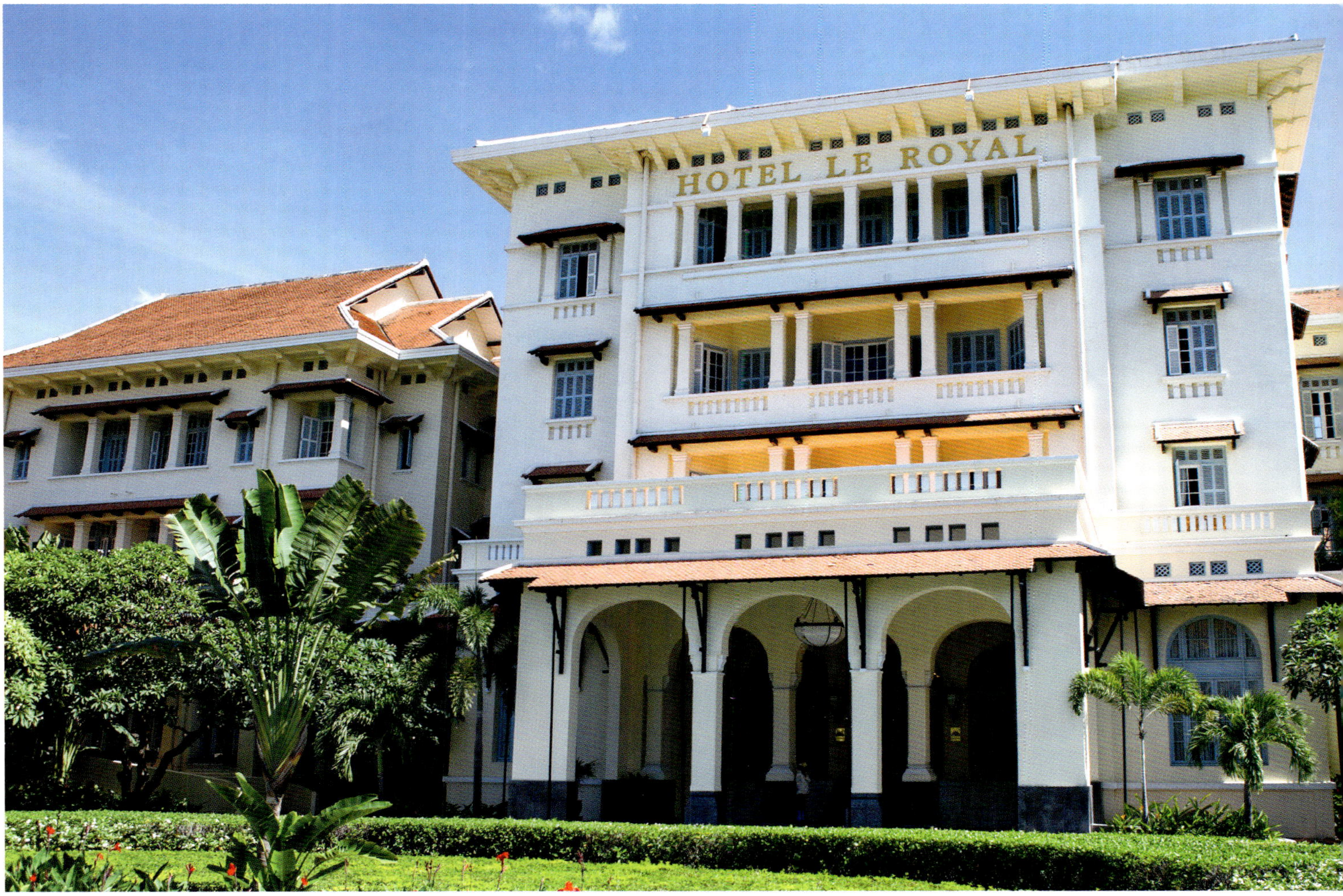

The Raffles Hotel is one of Asia's most venerable and prestigious properties. The original plan for a hotel to be known as Le Royal was proposed in 1923 while Cambodia was under French occupation. The architect, Ernest Hébrard, who also worked on city plans for Phnom Penh, designed the 54-room Le Royal, along with a sister hotel in Siem Reap to accommodate visitors to Angkor, and another property in Vietnam's historic town of Hué.

Construction began on a small parcel of land at the corner of Avenue du Maréchal Joffre (now known as Rukhak Vithei Daun Penh or Street 92) in the then-fashionable European Quarter of the city and close to the famous landmark of Wat Phnom. At the time the area was bordered by canals on three sides but these were filled in during the 1920s as part of Hébrard's ambitious plans. The project also included the creation of the tree-lined avenue that fronts the hotel and leads to Wat Phnom, and the construction of Psar Thmei, the extraordinary Art Deco central market, both of which remain today and continue to give the city its special character.

Hébrard had designed Le Royal with four floors, making it the tallest and most imposing building in Phnom Penh at the time. However, unlike fellow architect Georges Groslier who had drawn inspiration from traditional Khmer style structures to create the Musée Albert Sarraut, Hébrard's grand design was a showcase for new, bold and distinctly French, colonial-era architecture. The impressive building was constructed with Cambodia's balmy climate in mind and featured wide corridors and high ceilings, shuttered windows and shady walkways. The original Le Royal had 54 guestrooms, four of which shared communal bathrooms.

Le Royal officially opened on 20 November 1929 with a decadent party attended by His Majesty Sisowath Monivong and leading dignitaries from the expatriate community who enjoyed a buffet, dance and music from an orchestra brought in from Saigon to mark the occasion.

During the 1930s and 40s, Le Royal was at the heart of Southeast Asia, then known as French Indochina, and Phnom Penh was a popular destination for the rich and famous. Visitors were able to sail from Singapore to Bangkok before continuing on to Phnom Penh by road or rail. It was also possible to travel from Saigon by road. One of Le Royal's most distinguished guests at the time was Charlie Chaplin. In April 1936 he stayed at the hotel with Paulette Goddard, his co-star in the movie, *Modern Times*, before heading to Siem Reap where he visited the temples of Angkor.

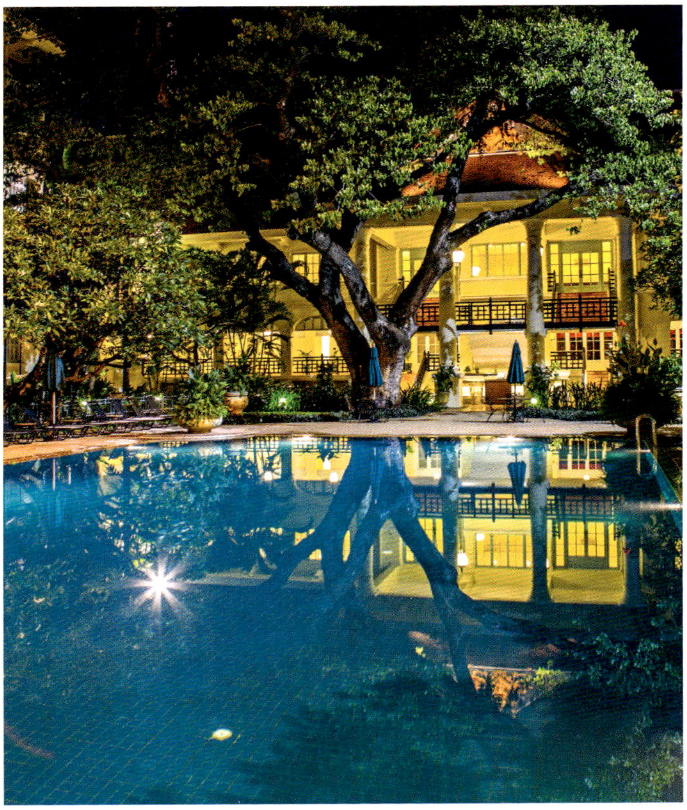

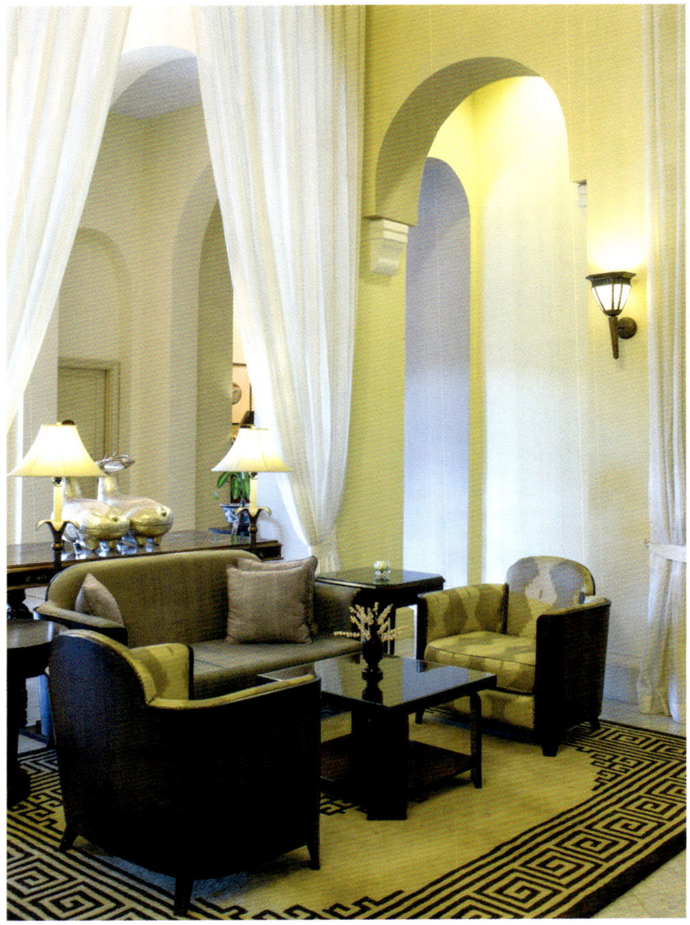

Above: The pool and garden within the Raffles Hotel Le Royal is a sanctuary where guests can escape the hustle and bustle of the city.
Above right: The lobby has been tastefully restored and reflects the classic style of a bygone era.

During the late 50s, architect Henri Chatel was responsible for the hotel's expansion. He added bungalows, the alfresco restaurant, Le Cyrène, a swimming pool and terrace, and renovated the lobby. From 1970 to 1975, the hotel name was changed to Le Phnom. During the rise of the Khmer Rouge and the subsequent bombardment of the city, the Red Cross declared the hotel a neutral zone and medical teams even established an operating theatre in the bungalows. However, as the brutal invaders tightened their grip and the city fell to Khmer Rouge forces on 17 April 1975, the hotel was abandoned altogether. From 1975 to 1979, it was used by members of the Pol Pot regime for offices, storage and accommodation. In 1980 when the Khmer Rouge were ousted, the property housed international aid agencies and once again changed its name, this time to Hotel Samakki or Solidarity Hotel, a name that remained until Sihanouk was reinstated as King in 1993 and its name reverted to Le Royal.

THE ELEPHANT BAR

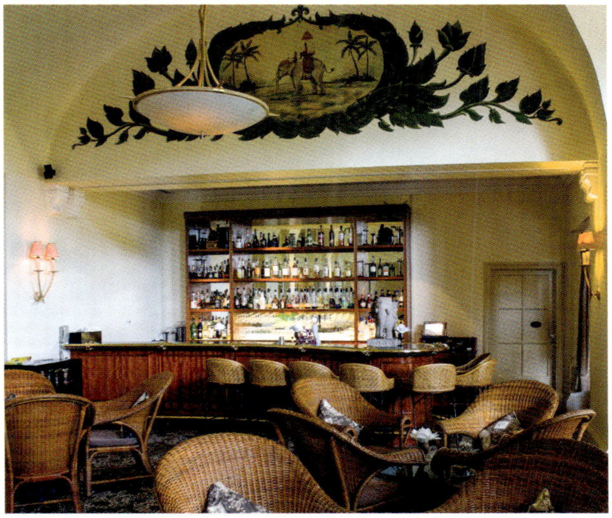

The nightly Happy Hour at Raffles Hotel Le Royal's renowned Elephant Bar is an institution among the expatriate community in Phnom Penh, particularly on a Friday evening. It's also an experience loved by hotel guests and other visitors who come to enjoy the special ambience of the historic bar. Comfortable wicker chairs, lazy ceiling fans, period décor and a pianist create the perfect setting for a memorable evening of classic cocktails, fine wines or chilled local beers. The Elephant Bar's signature cocktail celebrates the visit of Jackie Kennedy in 1967, en route to Angkor. It is said that when the hotel was being renovated, the glass from which she drank a Champagne cocktail was found, still with her lipstick on it. Hence, the 'Femme Fatale' was created using an enticing blend of Champagne, Crème de Fraise Sauvage and a splash of Cognac.

In 1996 under the supervision of Raffles International Limited, the hotel was extended, and, while retaining much of the charm of a bygone era, refurbished to meet the needs of discerning travellers. Today, following the construction of three new courtyard wings and further refurbishment in 2011, the hotel offers 170 beautiful period guestrooms and suites, each enhanced by Khmer works of art. Now known as Raffles Hotel Le Royal, the luxurious Phnom Penh hotel is an essential experience for visitors to the city.

The Monument of Independence or Vimean Ekareach not only commemorates independence from the French which was granted on 9 November 1953, but is also a memorial to Cambodia's war dead. The impressive 20-m (65-ft) high structure stands proudly at the centre of one of Phnom Penh's busiest intersections, the junction of Sihanouk and Norodom Boulevards. It was designed by Cambodia's most celebrated architect, Vann Molyvann, and completed five years after independence in 1958. Vann Molyvann drew on the heritage of Angkor to create what is surely one of the world's most potent and assertive statements of independence. Built from red sandstone, the design is in the form of a stylized lotus bud embellished with more than one hundred heads of the mythical *naga* snake.

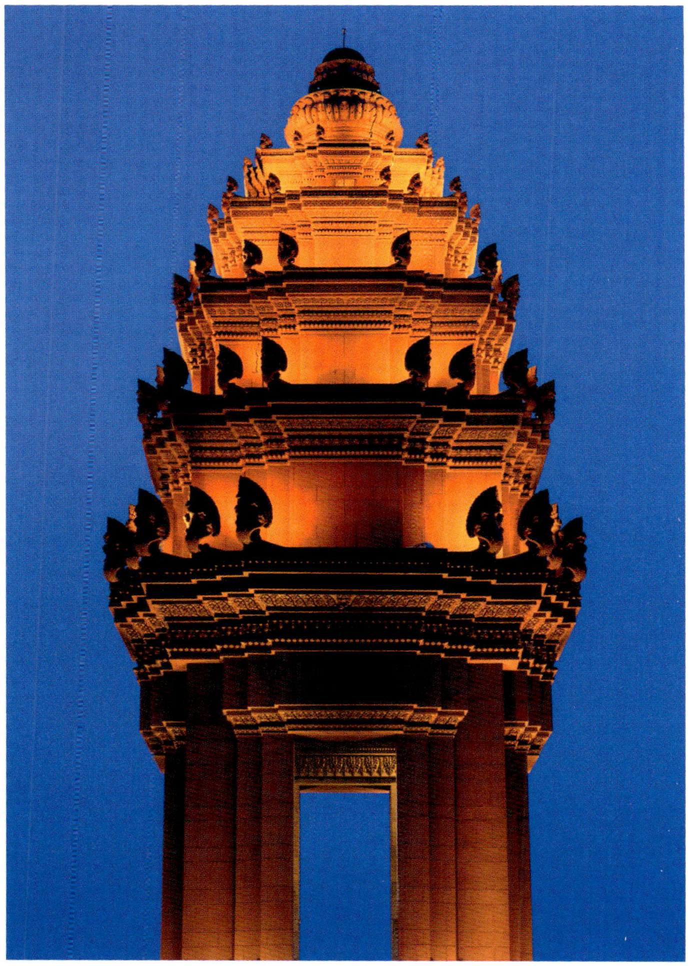

Above: Lit up at night, the Independence Monument is a beautiful sight. The structure benefited from restoration work in 2013.

CITY MARKETS

At the heart of every Khmer kitchen is produce bought from the local market, or psar. The freshness of fish, meat and vegetables is considered extremely important to home cooks and visits to the markets are often made twice daily, once in the early morning and again in the late afternoon.

Typically, morning markets open before daybreak and fizzle out at about 10 a.m. while evening markets kick off at about 4 p.m. and often trade until after dark. In Phnom Penh there are many sprawling markets to explore. Colourful, chaotic and definitely not for the squeamish, they are an assault on the senses and a delight to explore. Highlights include Psar Chas, also known as the Old Market, and Psar Kandal, both of which are open in the morning and in the evening. Across the Monivong Bridge is the vibrant Psar Chhbar Ampoeu.

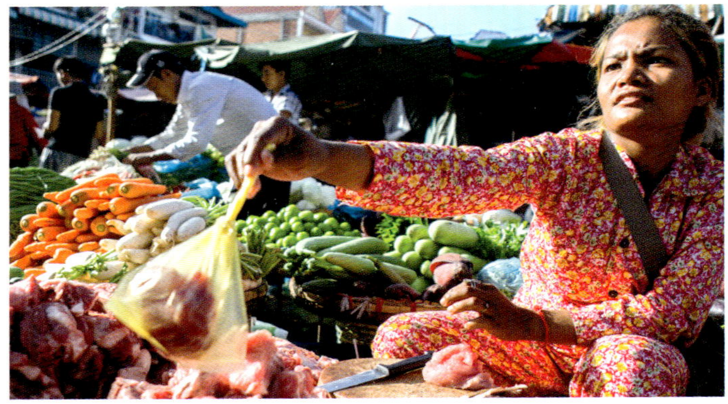

Above: A vendor selling pork in one of Phnom Penh's many fresh food markets. By daybreak, most markets are crowded with shoppers eager to buy the best produce.

Below: A stall at Psar Chhbar Ampoeu with a wide variety of herbs and vegetables.

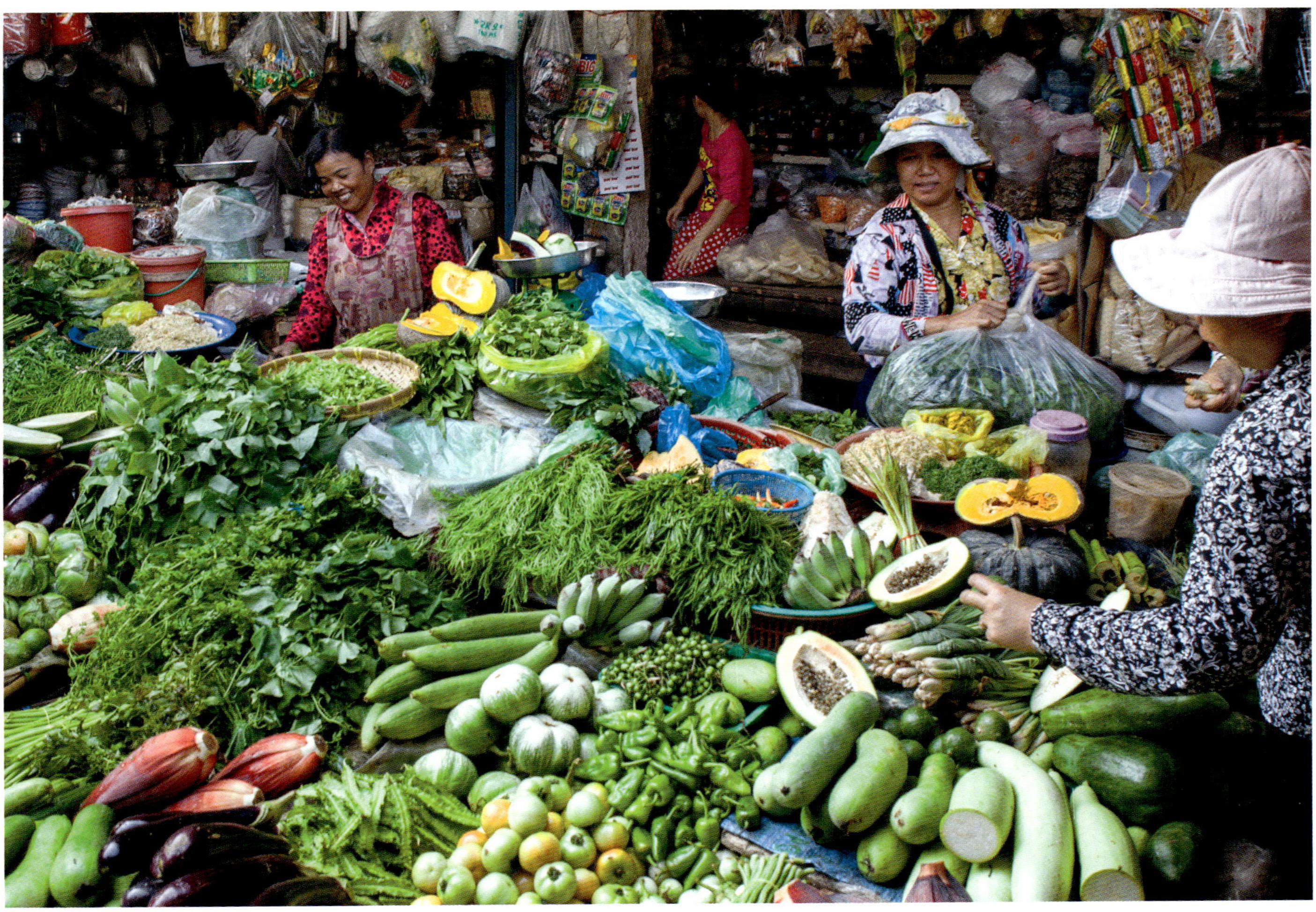

THE RUSSIAN MARKET

The Russian Market acquired its name in the 1980s when it was frequented by Russians. Today it is one of the most popular destinations for tourists looking to pick up gifts and souvenirs. The crowded market is packed with stalls selling anything from Buddha images to ceramic bowls, copy DVDs and CDs, jewellery and silks. There is also a large section selling slight seconds of clothing from the many textile factories in and around Phnom Penh, making it a great place to buy brand names at a fraction of the price back home.

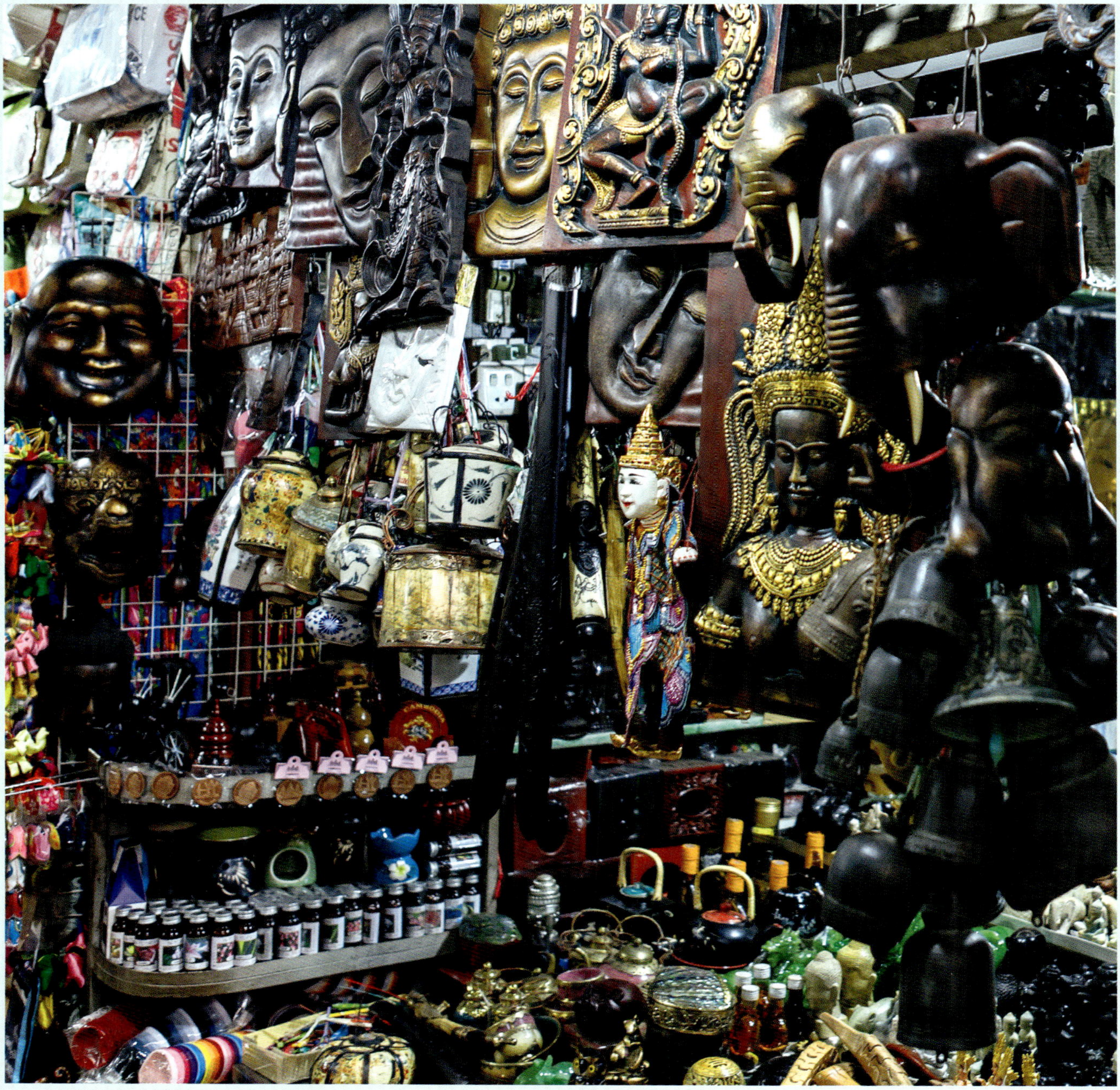

A BRUTAL PAST

It is impossible to mention Cambodia without calling to mind the brutal Khmer Rouge regime. Two of the most visited places in Phnom Penh are the Tuol Sleng Genocide Museum that was once Chao Ponhea Yat High School, and Camp Choeung Ek, one of many infamous killing field sites scattered around the country where victims were tortured and their bodies dumped in mass graves. To ensure that Tuol Sleng Genocide Museum and the Killing Fields do not cast a shadow over a trip to Cambodia, it is essential to appreciate just how far the country and its people have come in the three decades since these appalling atrocities were committed.

Visitors to the Tuol Sleng Genocide Museum must prepare themselves for an emotionally harrowing experience. From a distance you could be forgiven for thinking this is just an ordinary low-rise school. But then the barbed wire in front of the classrooms becomes visible – and a gallows.

During the Khmer Rouge era, the school was known simply as S-21. Created on the orders of Pol Pot as a detention and interrogation centre, it is thought that as many as 20,000 citizens passed through the doors to be tortured and murdered by the Khmer Rouge. At the museum, classrooms on the ground floor have been left as they were found. In rooms once filled with the laughter and inquisitive questioning of children, there is an eerie silence and the chilling sight of leg irons and metal beds where torture was carried out. On the upper floors claustrophobic numbered cells are stained with blood. One of the most haunting experiences, however, is the thousands of black-and-white images of victims displayed on boards throughout the building. Like all regimes that have committed genocide, the Khmer Rouge was perversely meticulous in documenting those it killed. The Tuol Sleng Genocide Museum opened to the public on 19 August 1979 to expose the truth about the inhumanity of the Khmer Rouge.

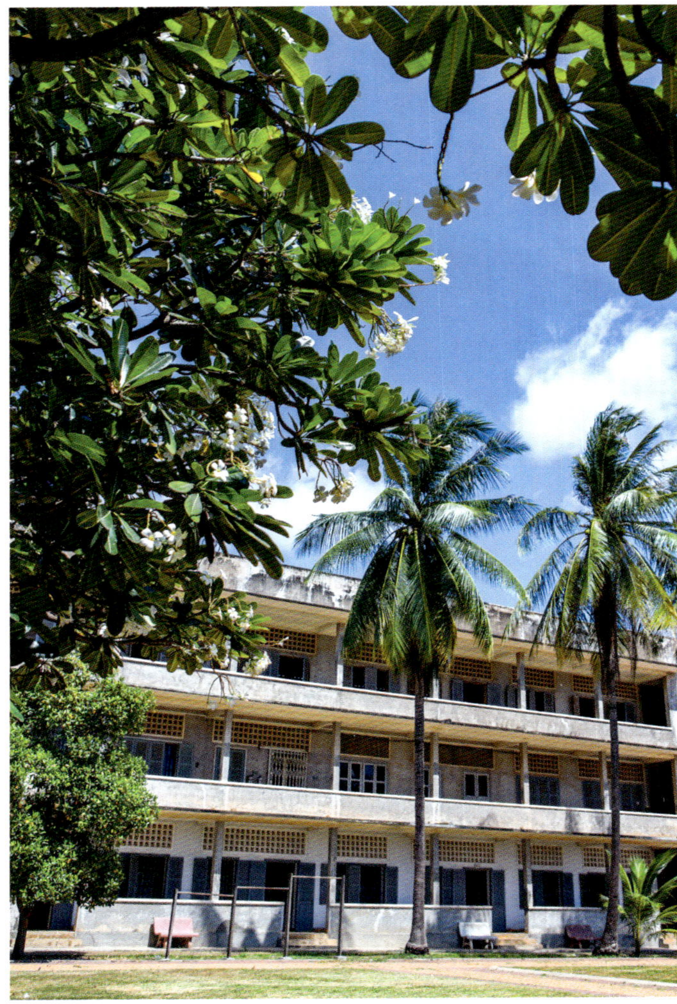

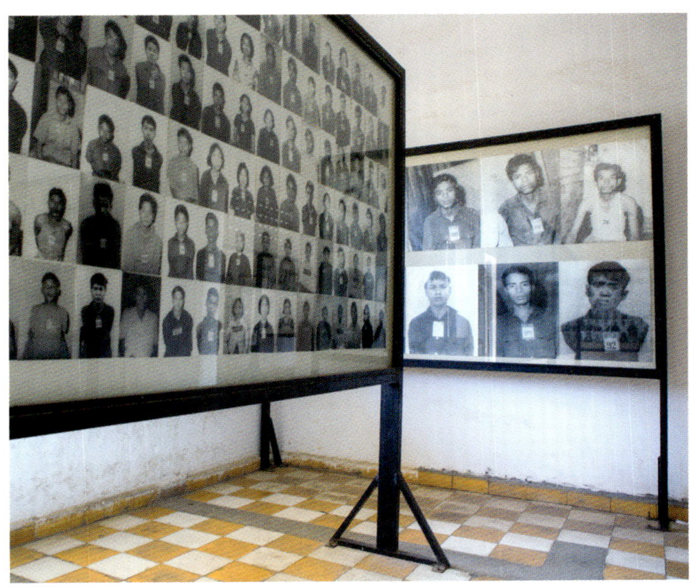

Top right: Once a place of laughter and learning, Chao Ponhea Yat High School was taken over by the Khmer Rouge and used as a place of torture. Today, it is Tuol Sleng Genocide Museum, a haunting but necessary reminder of the past.
Right: Hundreds of photographs of Khmer Rouge victims are on display at the Tuol Sleng Genocide Museum.

CHUM MANH – A SUVIVOR OF TUOL SLENG

Seventy-eight year old Chum Manh spends the remaining years of his life helping to ensure Cambodia never forgets its terrible past. The elderly man is one of just 14 people who survived Tuol Sleng and lived to see his torturers stand trial. The former car mechanic can often be seen at the museum where he makes a living selling a magazine called *Searching for the Truth*.

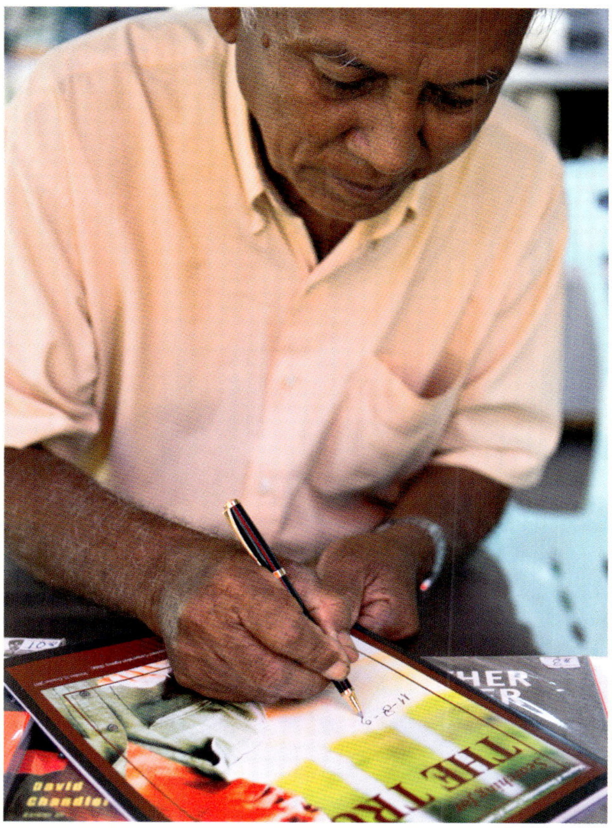

Choeung Ek is one of more than 300 known Killing Field sites scattered across Cambodia. Located on the site of an old orchard 15 km (9 miles) from the capital, it is here that the remains of almost 9,000 Cambodians were discovered in mass graves. The centre is now one of the country's biggest tourist draws and, although it is a disturbing experience, it has been thoughtfully managed and, through the use of an informative and often chilling audio tour, an exhibition and movie, presents the truth about what happened between 1975 and 1979.

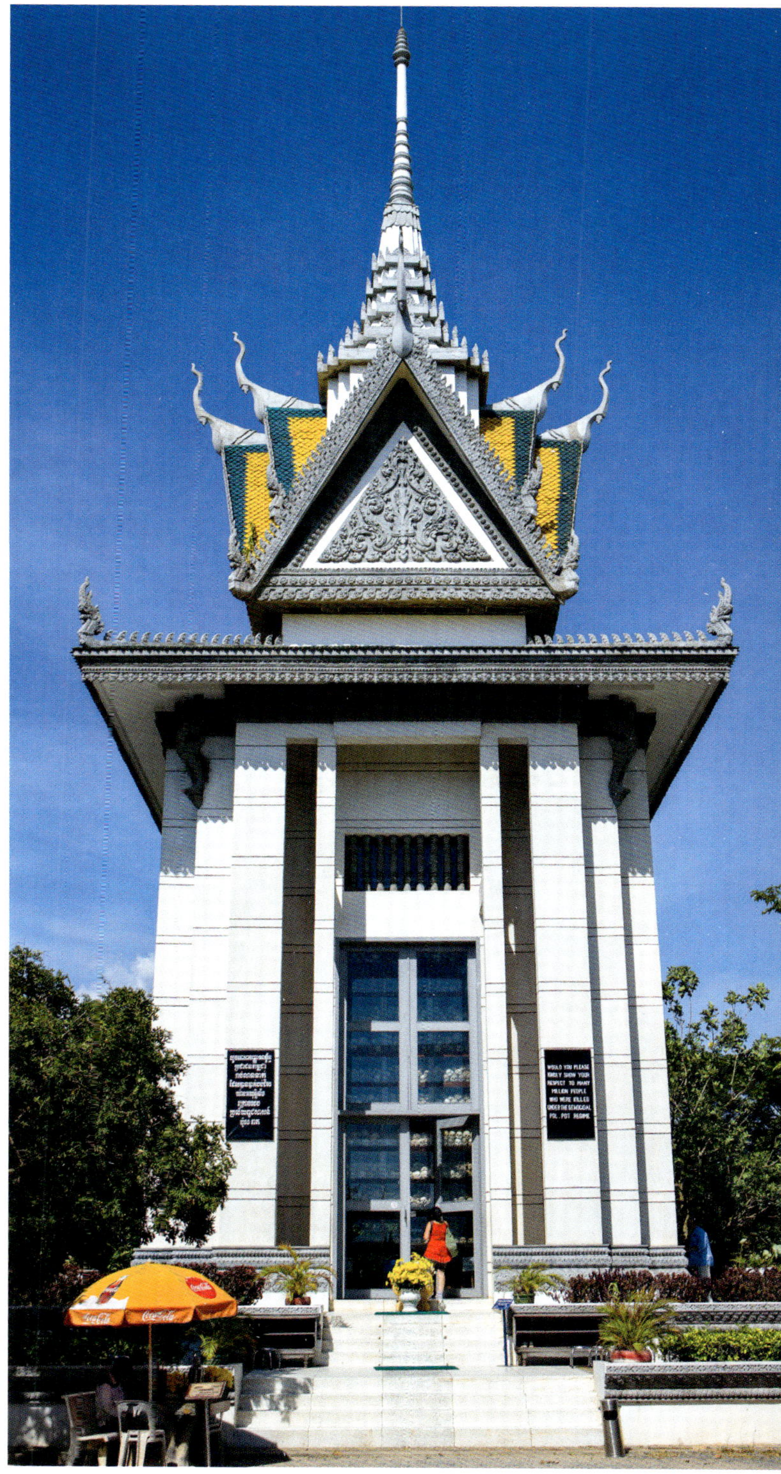

Above The main feature of the Choeung Ek Genocidal Centre is the memorial stupa which contains the skulls of 8,000 men, women and children, all clearly visible through glass panels.

AROUND PHNOM PENH

Forty kilometres (25 miles) north-west of Phnom Penh, a visit to Oudong, the site of one of Cambodia's former capitals, is an interesting day-trip. At the weekend, hordes of Phnom Penhites descend on Oudong to enjoy dining at makeshift restaurants at the foot of the mountain, to pay their respects at the temples and take in the panoramic views from the summit.

Originally known as Oudong Meanchey or 'noble victory', it became the stronghold of a succession of Khmer kings until 1866 when King Norodom moved the capital to Phnom Penh (see page 58). Clearly chosen for its defensive capabilities, Oudong is on a mountain ridge that rises above the rice fields, snaking its way south-east to north-east. The ridge is topped by several stupas and temples which can be reached by way of two stairways, one at each end of the ridge. One of the most interesting is the yellow, four-faced stupa of Chet Dey Mak Proum that contains the ashes of King Monivong (1927-41). The tradition of erecting stupas on the ridge continues today and the latest, known as Sanchak Mony Chedei, was built to house bone relics of the Buddha and was consecrated by King Norodom Sihanouk in 2002 during a ceremony that attracted hundreds of thousands of worshippers. Beneath the intricate 42-m (138-ft) stupa is a room containing several thousand images of Buddha. The view from the platform surrounding the stupa is spectacular and stretches across the plains as far as the eye can see.

Opposite and below: It's a steep climb up the stairway to the stupas that crown the hill at Oudong but the view is ample reward. The landscape of rice fields, villages and temples stretches to the horizon. The Tonlé Sap River can also be seen in the far distance, winding its way to Phnom Penh.

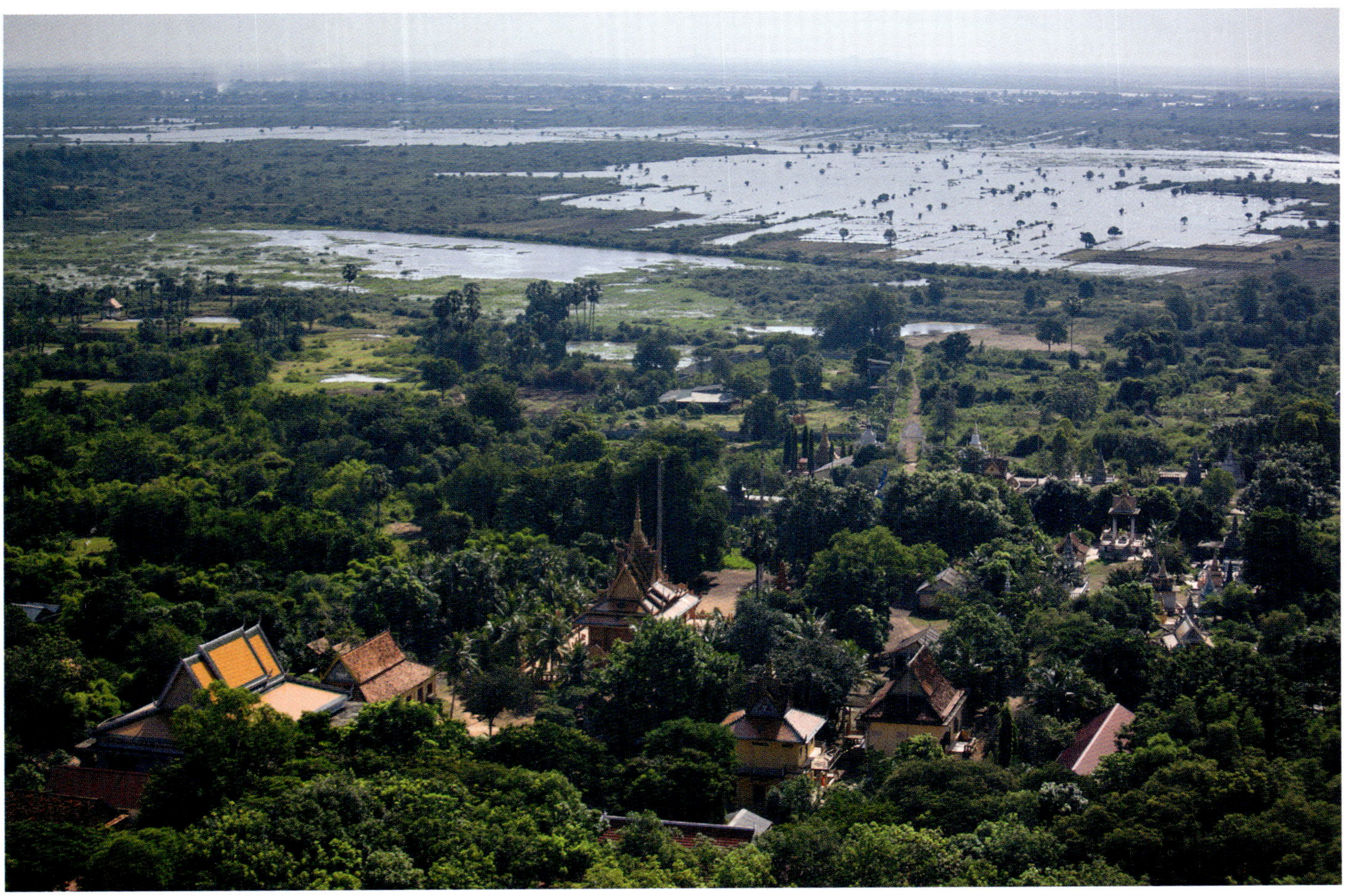

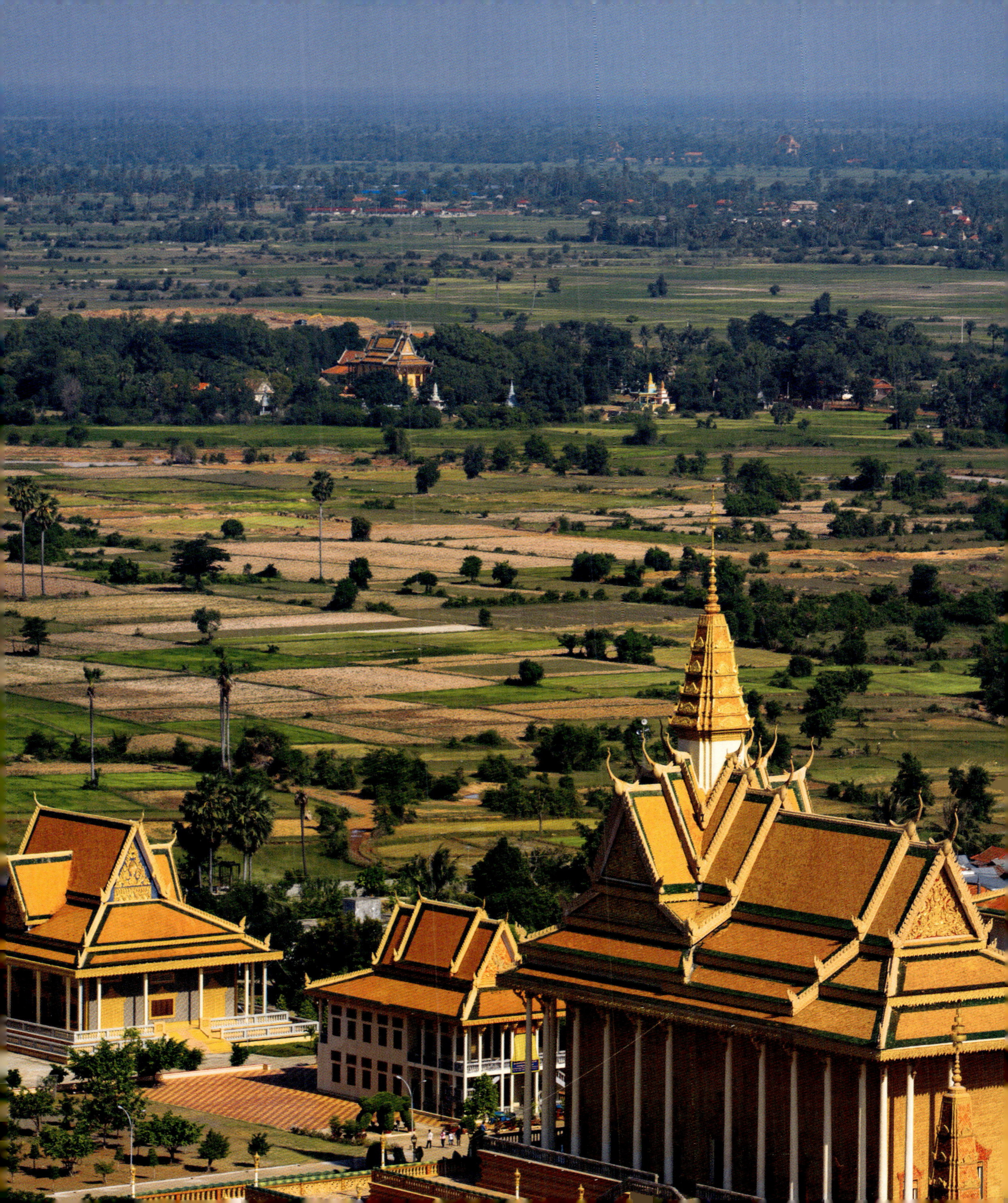

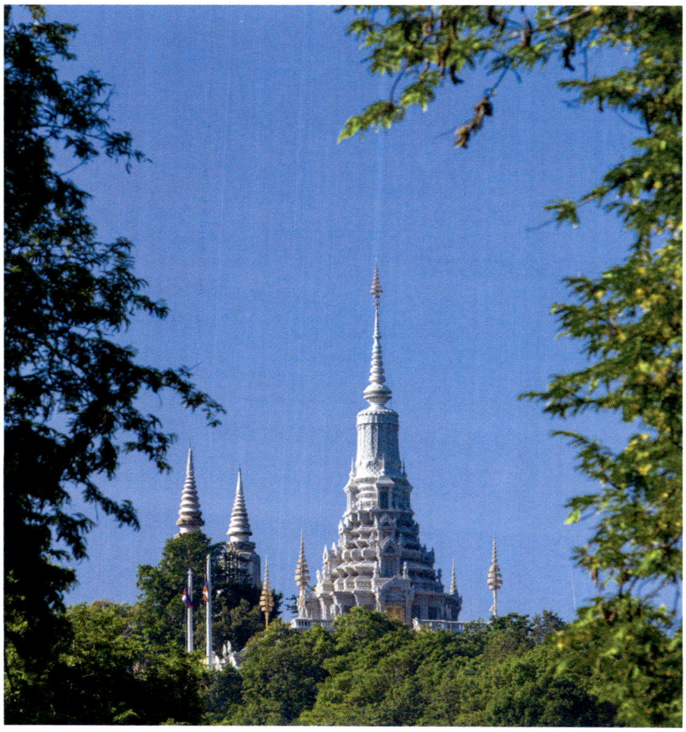

Above and right: The mountain ridge at Oudong is lined with several stupas, the latest of which is Sanchak Mony Chedei. It was built in 2002 to house Buddha relics donated by Sri Lanka.
Below right: The enormous seated Buddha within Oudong's Wat Arthross, also known as the Temple of Eight Points, was recently restored. It's a popular place of pilgrimage.
Below: The steps leading to Wat Arthross are lined with donation baskets, each placed in front of a sign telling fortunes related to a person's year of birth.

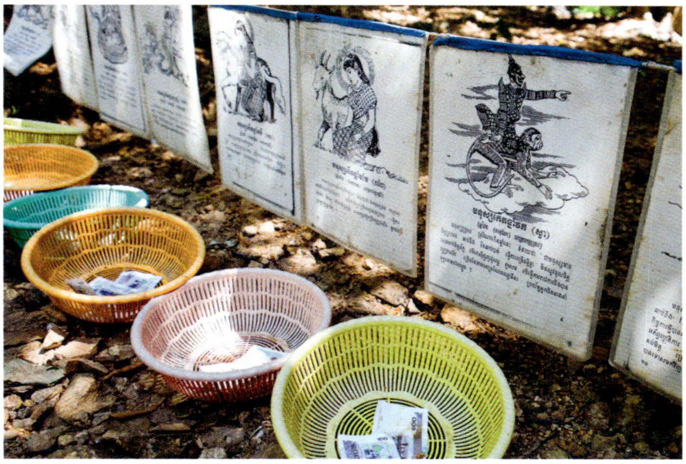

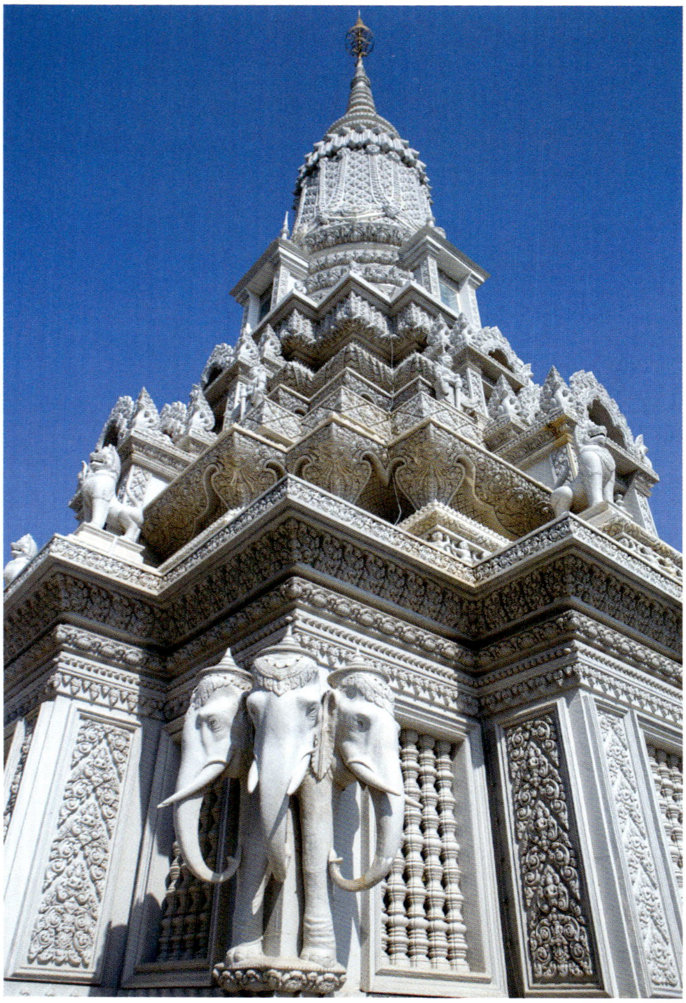

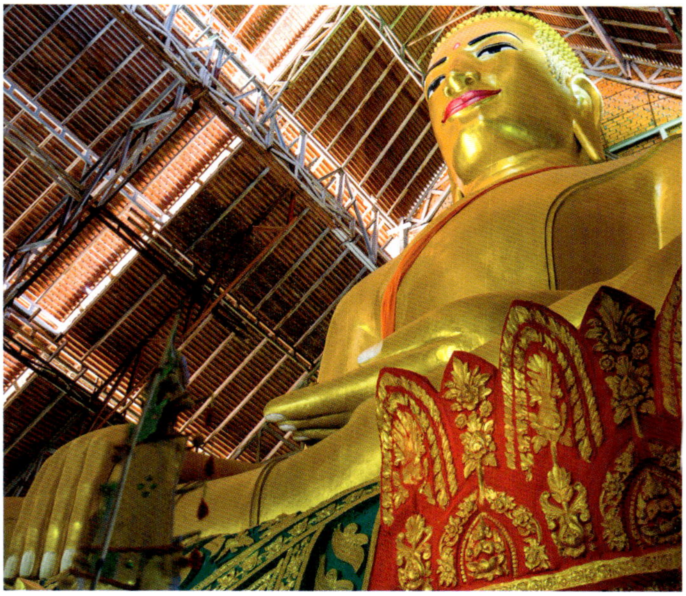

PICNICS AT KIEN SVAY

There is nothing that Cambodians like to do more in their spare time than join together with friends and family for a leisurely day of food and drink. Kien Svay is one of the most popular places to escape to at the weekends from the increasingly chaotic Phnom Penh. Just 15 km (9 miles) east of the capital on a scenic tributary of the Mekong River, Kien Svay is a collection of stilted bamboo and thatch huts that stretch out along the water's edge. Huts can be rented by the hour for a small fee. Friends bring their own food and drink, buy it from the nearby market, or order from restaurants. Vendors in boats also pull up at the hut moorings selling snacks and fruit. It is possible to hire a boat and boatman for a pleasurable afternoon trip down the river.

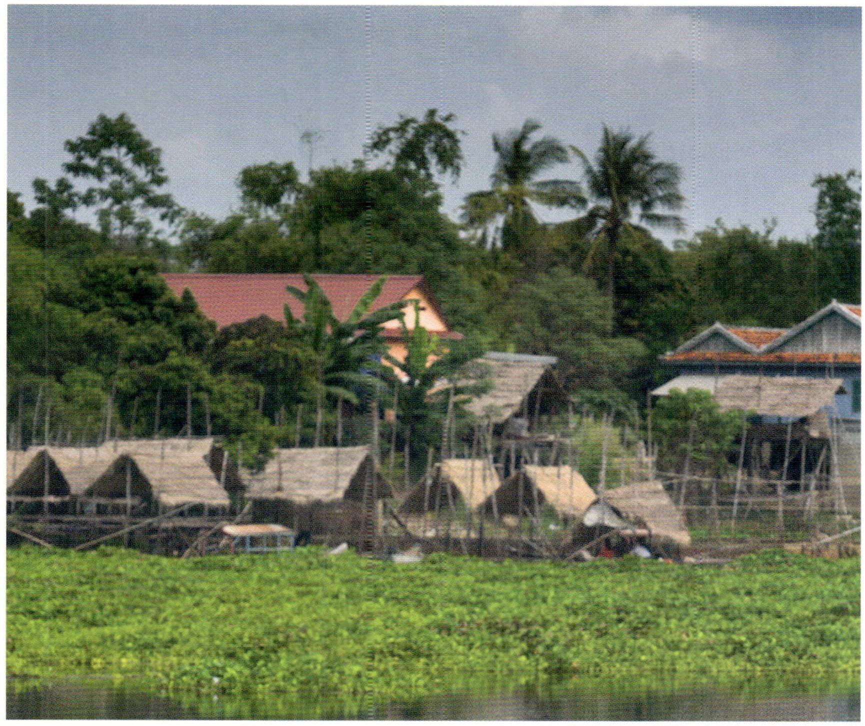

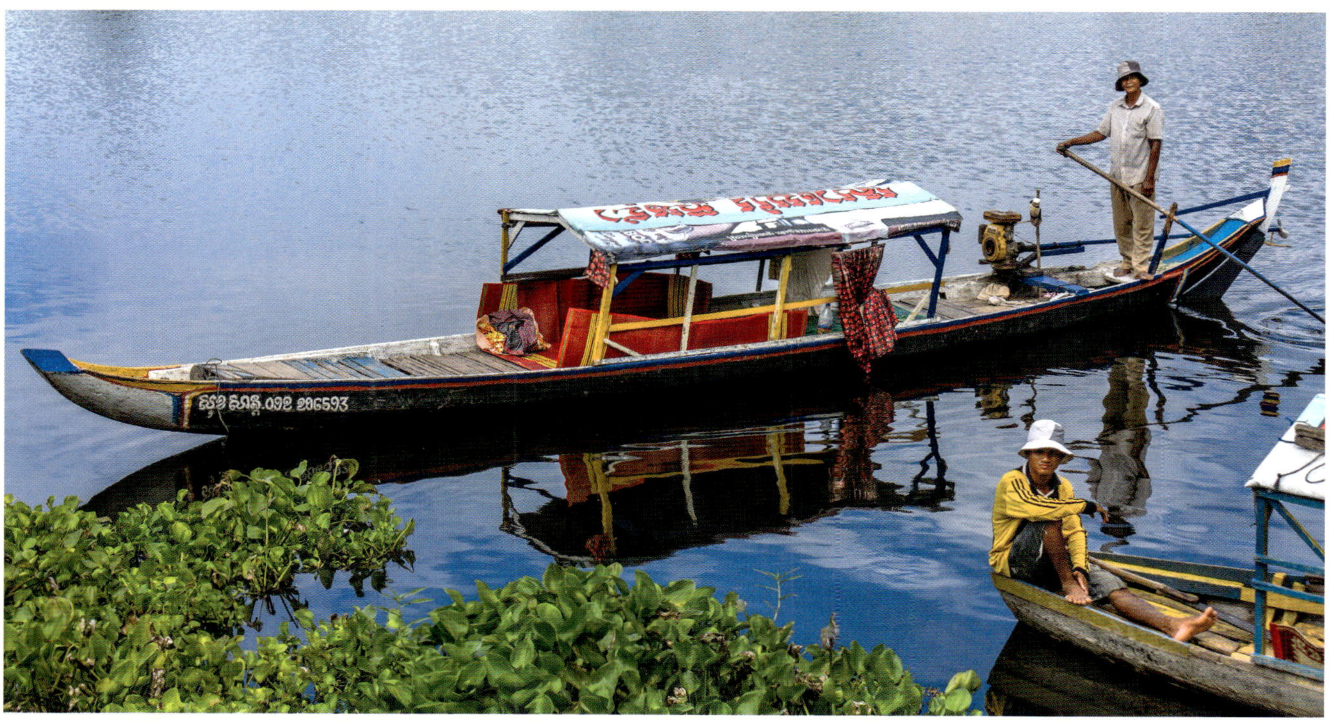

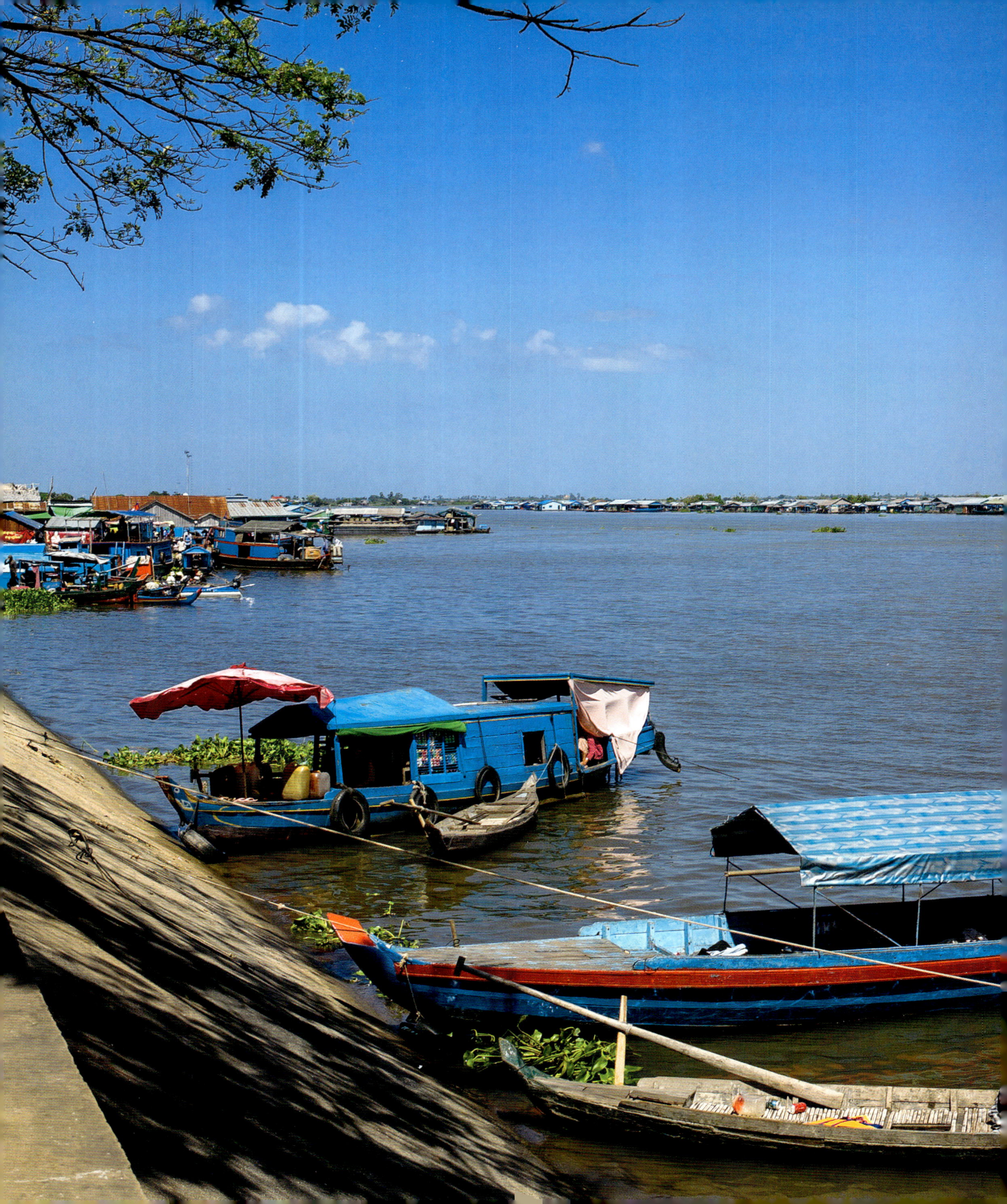

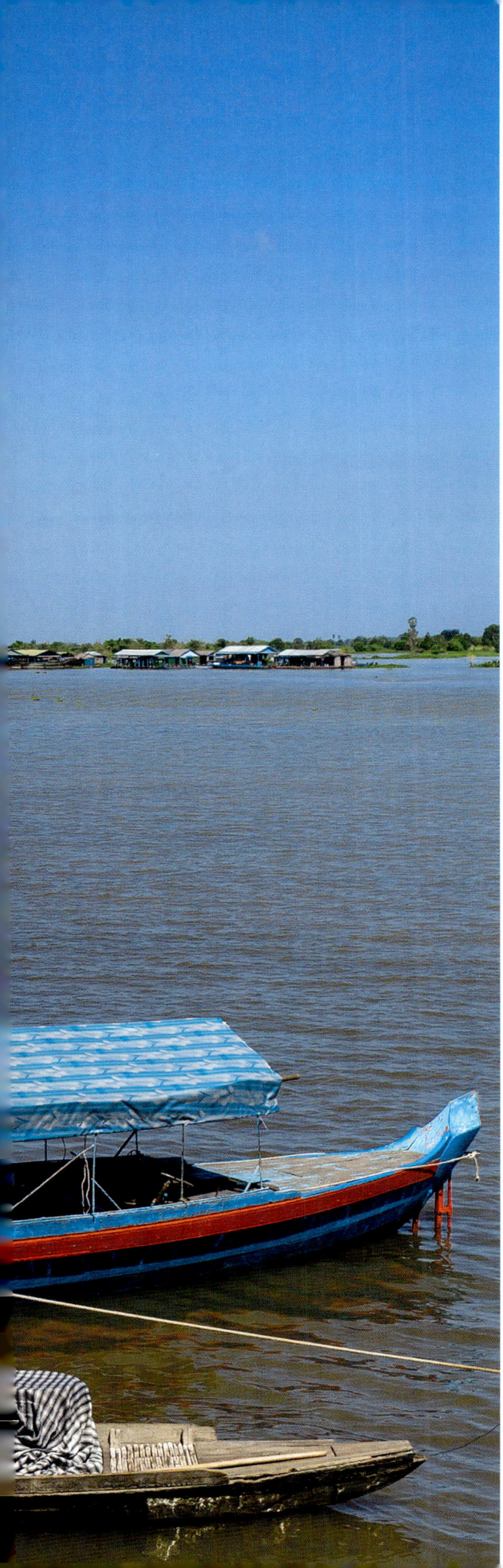

CHAPTER III

The NORTH-WEST

Exploring the Mountains

At the centre of north-west Cambodia is the Tonlé Sap and dozens of villages that rely on its bountiful supply of fish for their livelihood. Exploring some of the less touristy stilted and floating villages allows a glimpse into an almost other-worldly, waterborne existence. Further west is the delightful town of Battambang. Renowned for its splendid collection of colonial-era shophouses and villas, the charming town has enough to hold visitors for several days and is surrounded by beautiful countryside. To the north, an historic journey leads to the sacred Phnom Kulen and the mysterious jungle temple of Beng Mealea, on to Anlong Veng, a former Khmer Rouge stronghold and resting place of Pol Pot, and finally to the mountain-top Prasat Preah Vihear, a controversial ancient monument on the Cambodian-Thai border that still stirs nationalistic rivalries reminiscent of days gone by.

Left: Just 90 km (56 miles) from Phnom Penh, the floating villages around Kompong Chhnang make an interesting day-trip from the city. Visitors can enjoy a pleasant hour or two exploring them by boat.

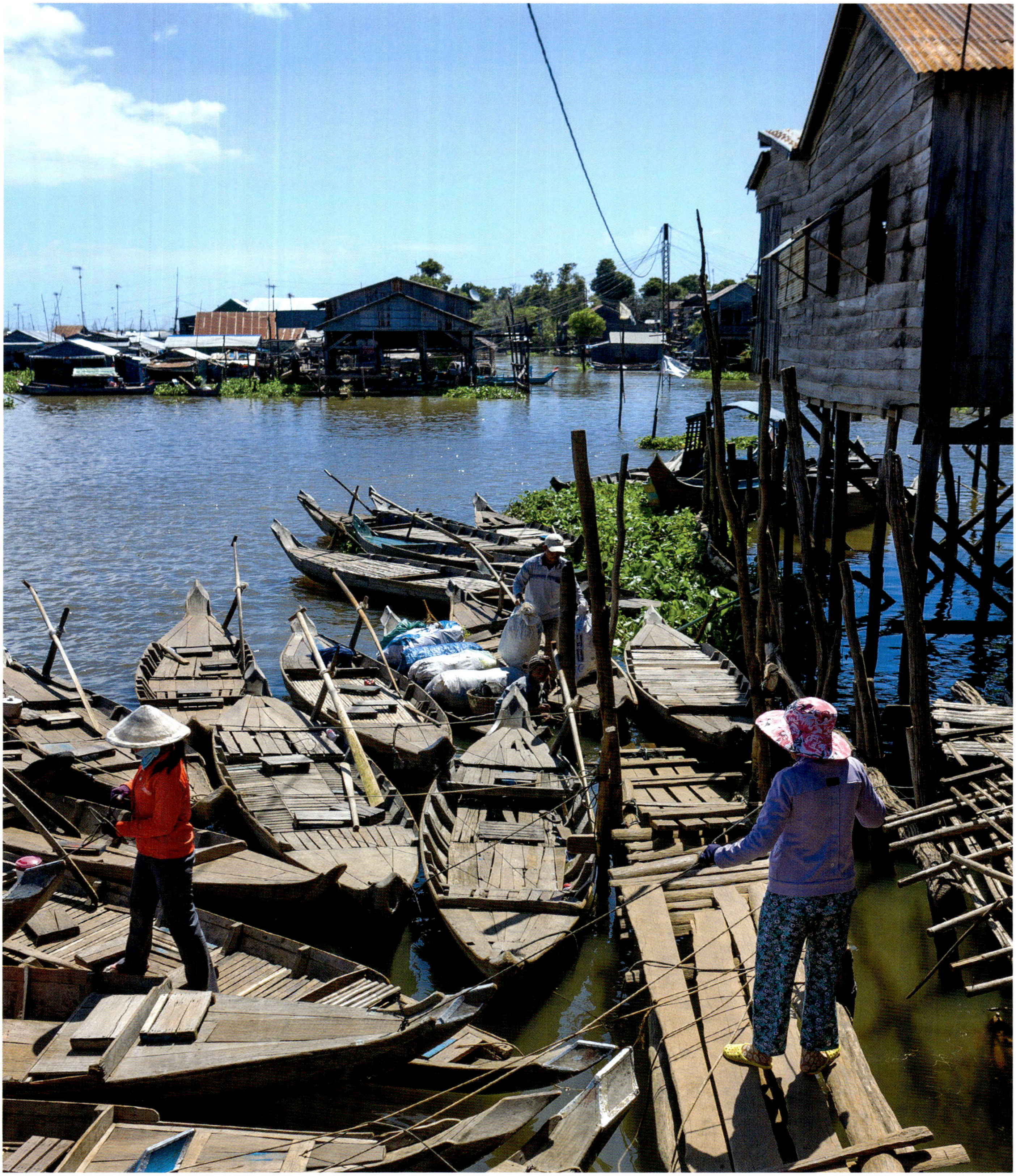

The province of Kompong Chhnang and its namesake capital are well worth exploring and are easily reached by car or bus on a day-trip from Phnom Penh or en route to Battambang.

Much of the earthenware pottery produced in Cambodia comes from this province. Meaning 'pottery port', the aptly named town of Kompong Chhnang skirts the banks of the Tonlé Sap, 90 km (56 miles) from Phnom Penh. The Vietnamese traders who inhabit the outer fringes of the town sit patiently in front of their simple roadside stores and await customers eager to haggle for fruit and vegetables, woks and cooking utensils, fish traps, pungent dried shrimps and stacks of dust-covered, glazed bowls imported from their homeland. Along the quayside, feisty Vietnamese girls quickly descend on tourists, offering them boat rides that explore the nearby floating villages of Phoum Kandal and Chong Kos. The flatbed teak sculls are rowed standing up by a pair of girls, gently skimming the water and providing an experience that is far preferable to the large tour boats that are also available. Out on the lake, clusters of houses are perched high above the water on gangly wooden legs and enormous, elaborately constructed fish traps tell of the welcome catch which will accompany the Tonlé Sap's annual deluge. The boat trip is a fascinating voyage that opens a window onto a unique way of life.

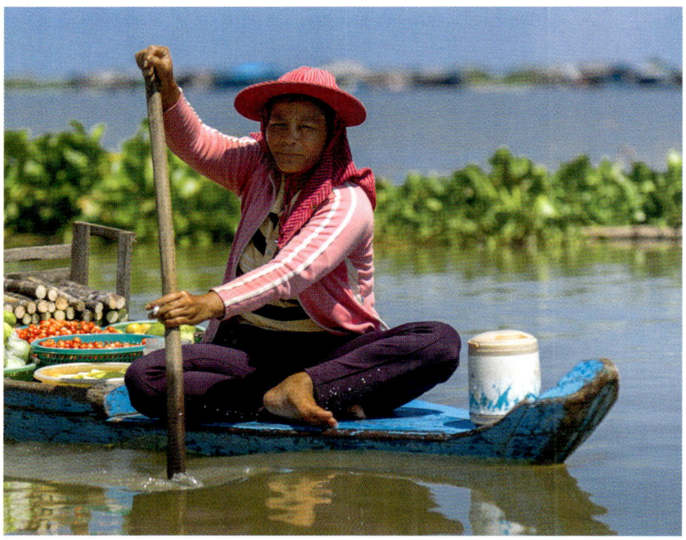

Above and opposite: The floating villages at Kompong Chhnang are inhabited by Vietnamese who make their living fishing and fish farming, and by selling fruits and vegetables from paddle boats.

ONDOUNG ROSSEY POTTERY VILLAGE

A short distance from Kompong Chhnang, the pottery village of Ondoung Rossey sits surrounded by the chessboard patterns of rice fields. Many women in this peaceful farming community produce simple functional earthenware pots made from locally sourced clay: water jars, cooking pots and charcoal burning stoves. They make the pots without using a potter's wheel. Instead they use an ancient technique known as 'paddle and anvil', whereby a cylinder of clay is supported on the inside with a stone – the anvil – and beaten on the outside with a wooden paddle to thin and shape the pot, before it is dried and fired in a pyre fuelled by rice straw. It's a highly skilled technique unchanged for centuries. The busiest time in Cambodia for pottery production is between November and June. During this time bullock carts led by itinerant pottery salesmen and loaded high with pots can be seen travelling around the country at a sedate pace.

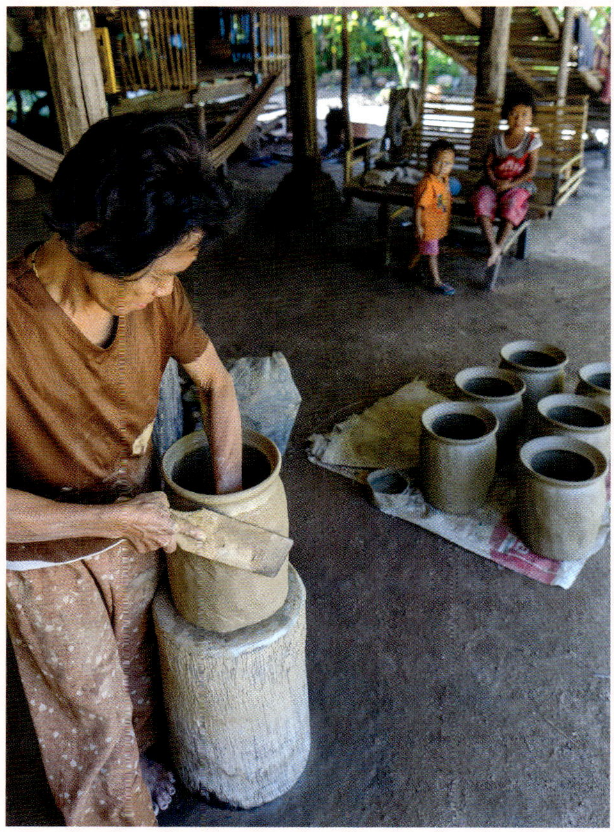

Once an important administrative centre for the French, today Battambang (which is actually pronounced *Battam-bong*) is Cambodia's second city yet only has a population of around 150,000. Easily reached by a good road from Phnom Penh or Siem Reap, the town's easygoing charm and its treasure trove of historic buildings have seen it enjoy a sharp rise in visitors. Bicycle tours are also available for those who wish to explore the surrounding villages and countryside.

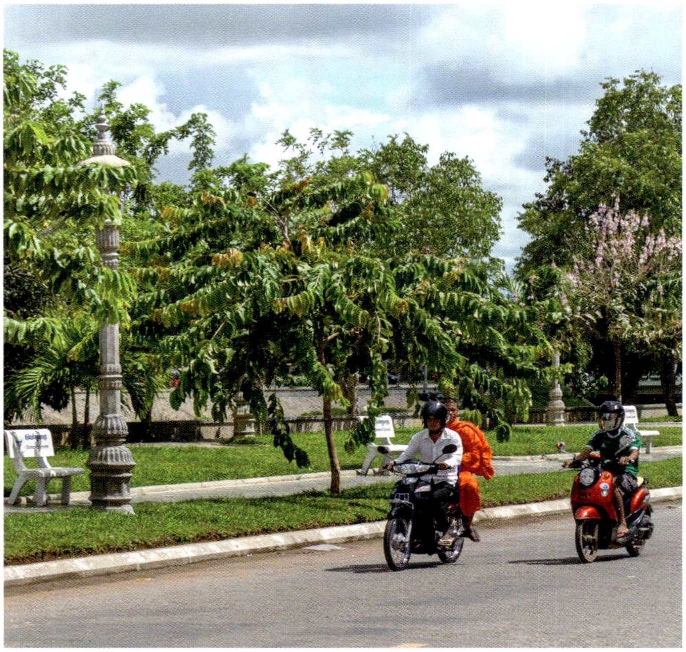

Battambang takes its name from the legend of the lost stick or *bat dambong* which tells the story of a peasant famer who found a magic stick that he used it to overthrow the king and take the throne himself. The town is pushed up against Sangker River. Here, the road that runs parallel to it is lined with classic shophouses (buildings that serve as both a business premise and a house) with shuttered windows that were built during the French protectorate. It was during this period that the town's population boomed and it grew into a bustling centre for trade and commerce. This was due to the introduction of an urban development plan that included an orderly grid layout of streets, and bridges spanning the Sangker River. A railway line linking Battambang with Phnom Penh also boosted business.

Many of the town's fine buildings have a dishevelled appearance but, thanks to a recent Cambodian-German project, they are once again being valued and some slowly restored. To aid the town's re-gentrification, Battambang Municipality and the German Development Service, the DED, launched a joint initiative called "Our City – Our Heritage". The inspirational project is committed to maintaining the town's special identity and historical character through preservation and education. But it is an on-going struggle. The lack of enforceable regulations and a general disinterest in preserving the past from a population that is keen to look forward not back, mean that buildings are often altered without consideration for the original structure, covered with unsightly modern signage, or left to fall into a seriously dilapidated condition. With the aid of a map produced by the organization, visitors can enjoy a self-guided walking tour of the town's many architectural highlights. Within the central area, there are 800 heritage buildings that date from the French era and the period immediately after independence.

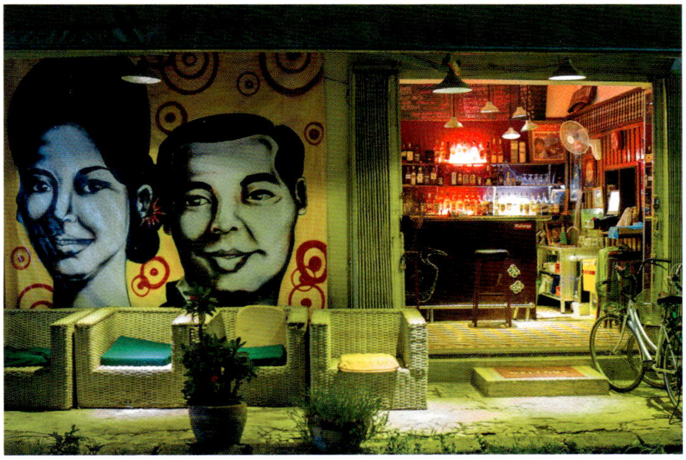

Highlights that have benefitted from restoration include the Sala Khaet, the Governor's Mansion. Its construction was started by the town's last hereditary governor, Chhum Aphaiwong, who employed an Italian architect to create an opulent residence. Inspired by European designs, it features five-metre (16-ft) high ceilings, mosaic floor tiles and grand staircases. Another classic building lovingly restored is a former residential villa located on Battambang's riverfront and now owned by the Bank of Cambodia.

The town is also home to several attractive Buddhist temples and historic Khmer-style wooden houses. A short distance from the riverfront is Psar Nath, an Art Deco local market headed by a clock tower, where locals shop for fresh produce and a myriad household goods.

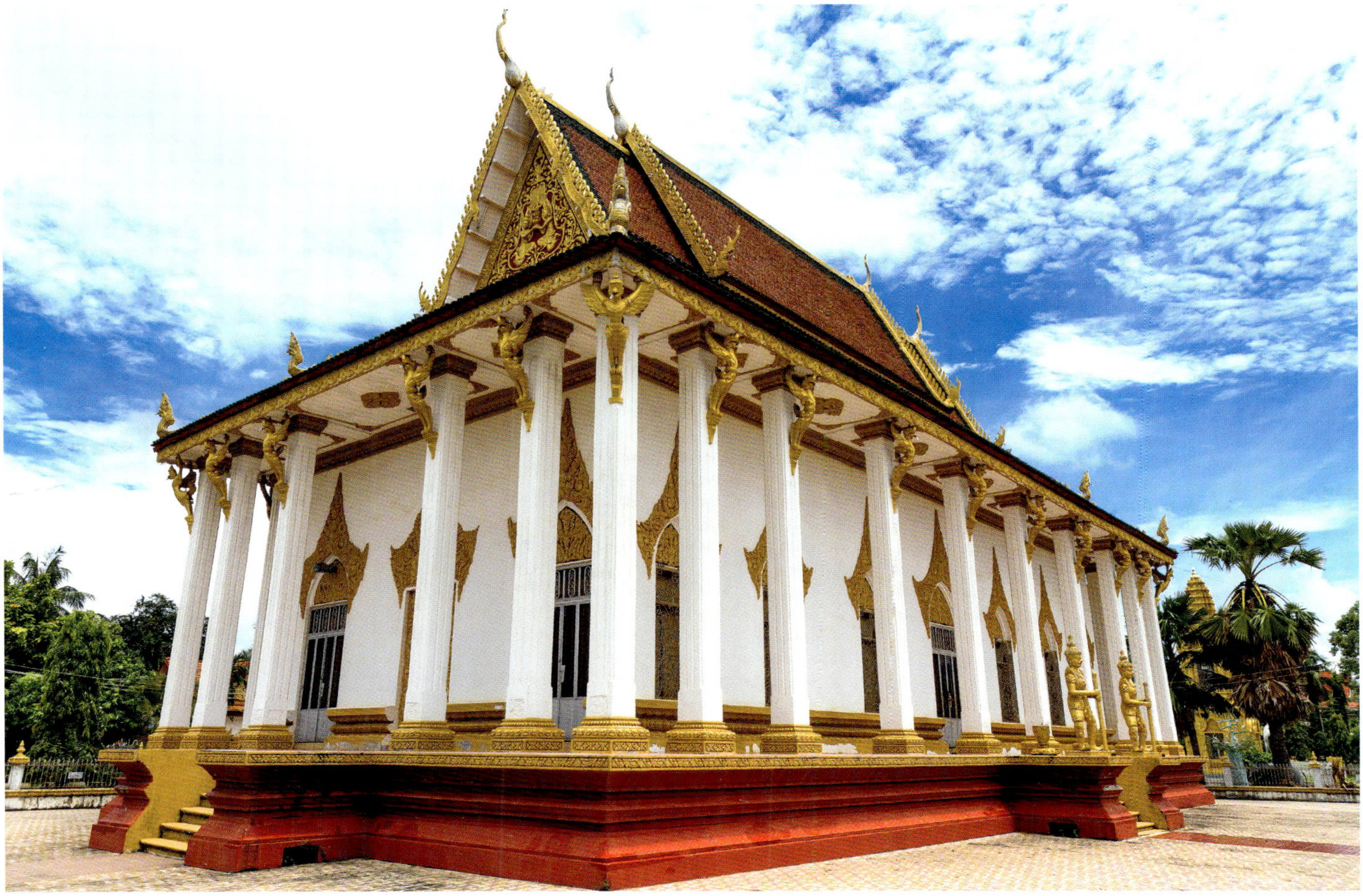

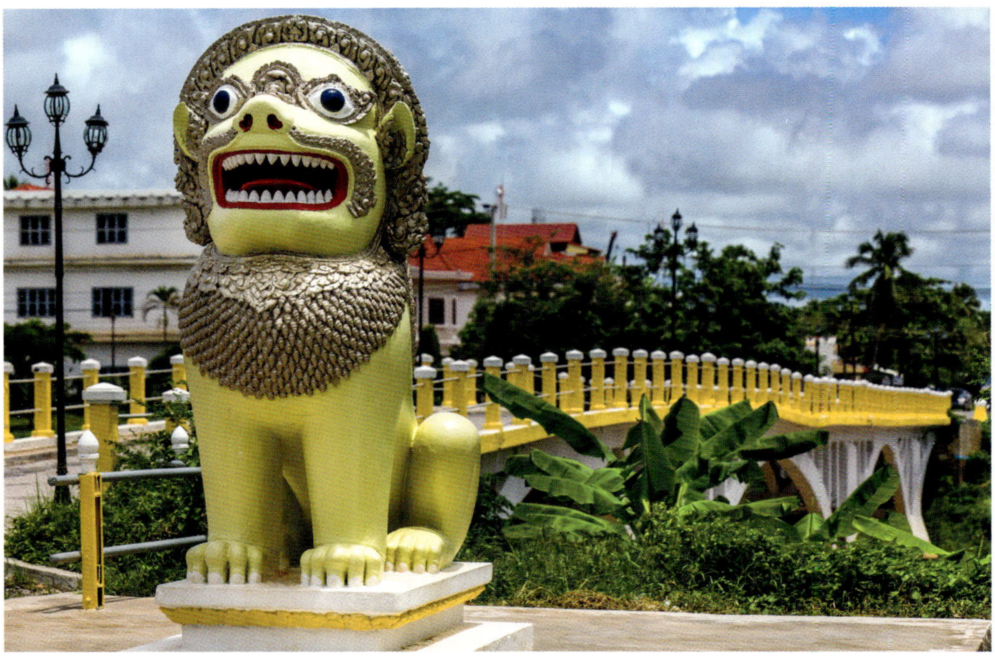

Above: There are many interesting temples to explore in the centre of Battambang including Wat Kampaeng and many temple ruins in the surrounding countryside.

Left: Built by the French in 1916, the old bridge in Battambang is guarded by huge lions.

Opposite top: The riverfront road in Battambang also features a leafy promenade where locals like to take an early evening stroll.

Opposite below: Battambang is enjoying renewed interest from international tourists and many trendy bars and restaurants have opened in the last few years.

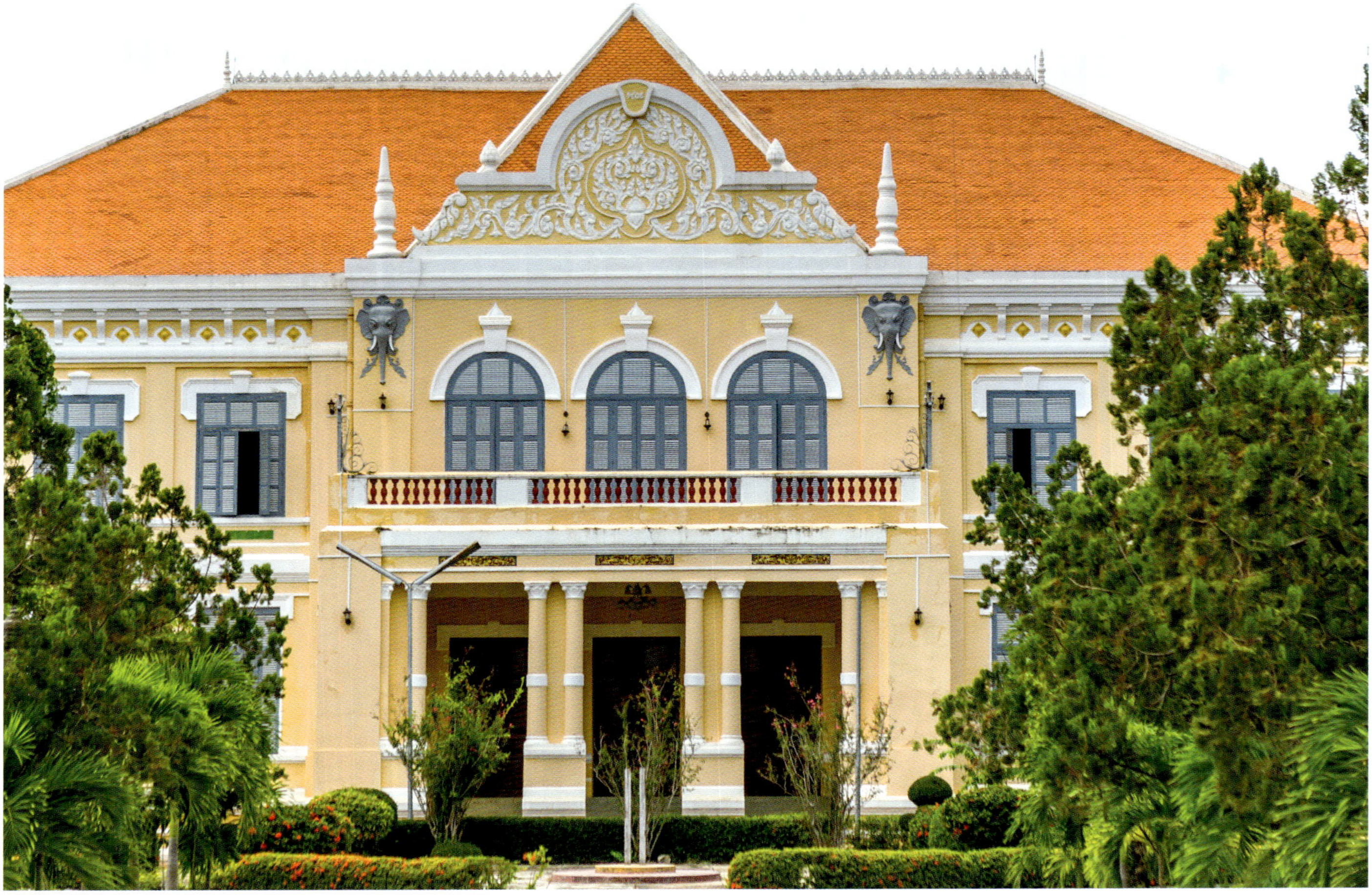

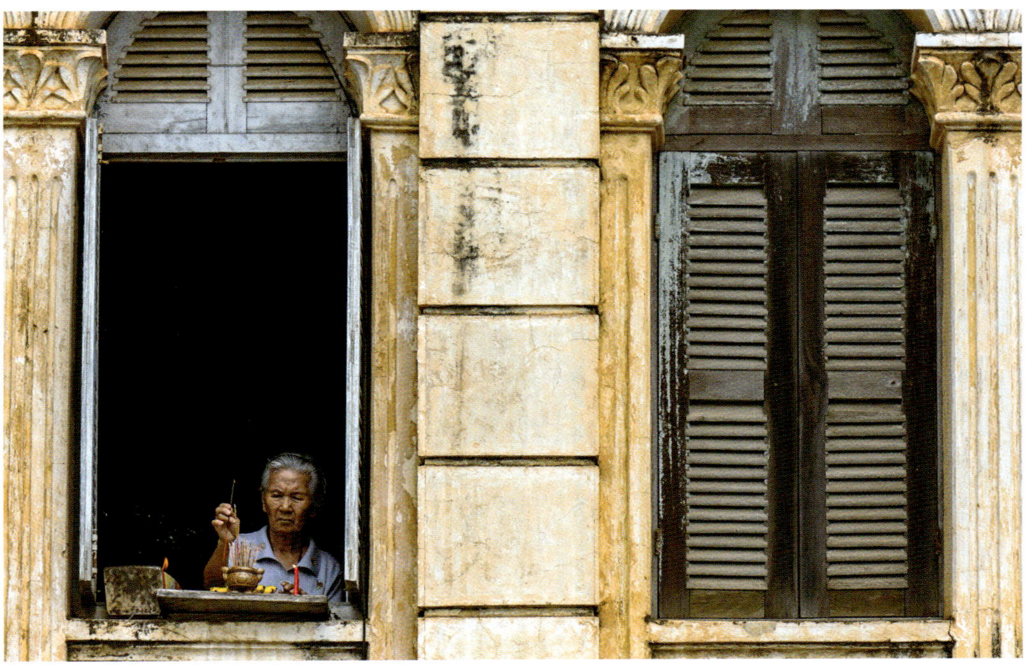

Above: Sala Khaet, the Governor's Mansion, is one of the grandest of Battambang's many French colonial-era buildings. It sits directly at the end of the road leading from the old town bridge.
Left: An old lady lighting incense and making an offering at her shrine in one of Battambang's old riverfront shophouses.
Opposite: One of Battambang's old villas on the riverfront road now serves as the National Bank of Cambodia.

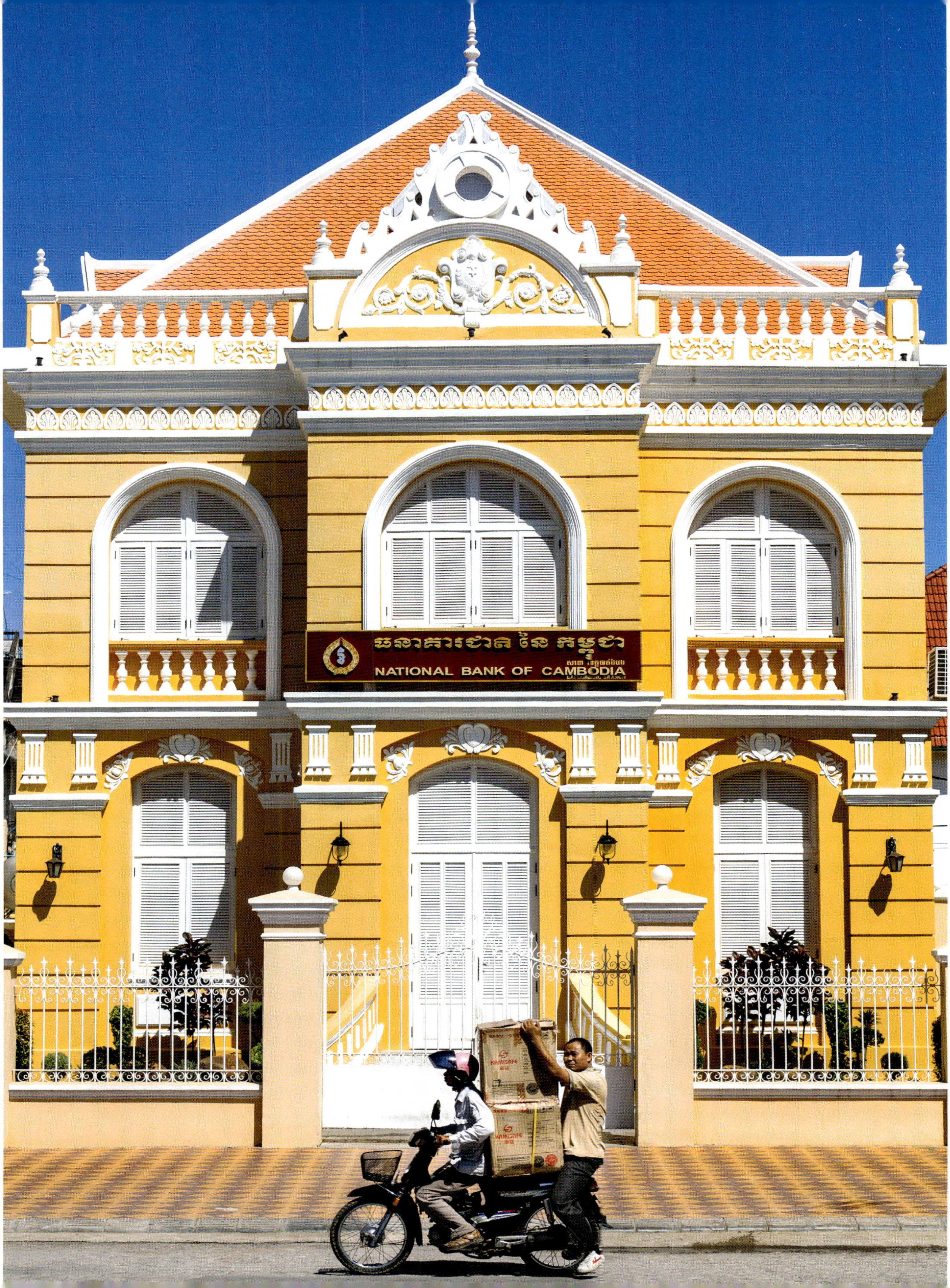
NATIONAL BANK OF CAMBODIA

A CALL TO ALMS

The daily giving of alms to monks is an important merit-making ritual for Buddhists and takes place all over Cambodia. Each morning at around 9 a.m., monks leave the temples to process around the streets, stopping at homes and shops were they wait in silence for donations of food including rice and home-cooked dishes. In Battambang, centrally located temples and the grid of narrow streets make it an excellent place to watch almsgiving. After they have completed their rounds, the monks take the donations of food back to the temple where a simple meal is prepared and served at around 11.30 a.m., their last until daybreak.

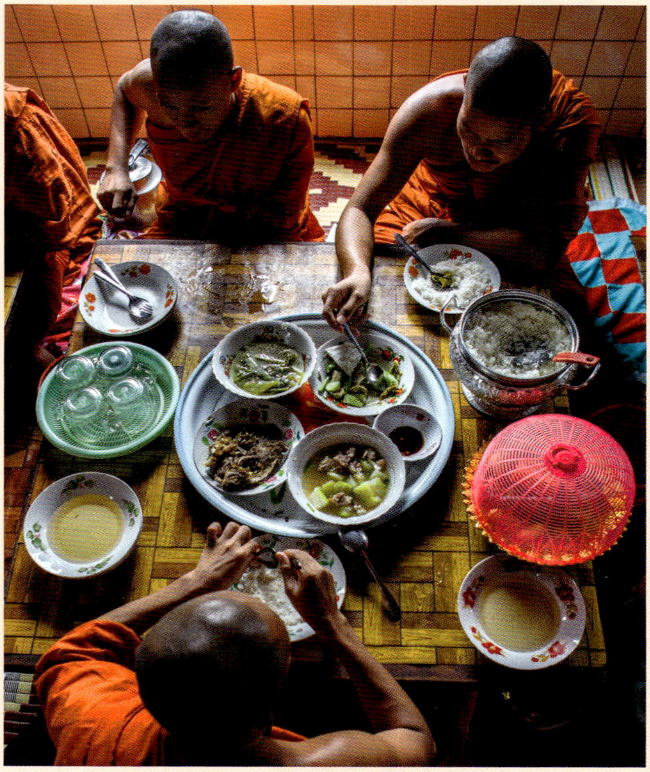

Right: After their midday meal, monks fast until sunrise. Typically, they dine together, seated at a long communal table. **Below:** For many visitors, watching dozens of Buddhist monks collecting alms is a fascinating sight. Lines of monks in their saffron robes walk barefoot through the narrow streets, stopping at shops and houses where they receive donations and give a blessing in return.

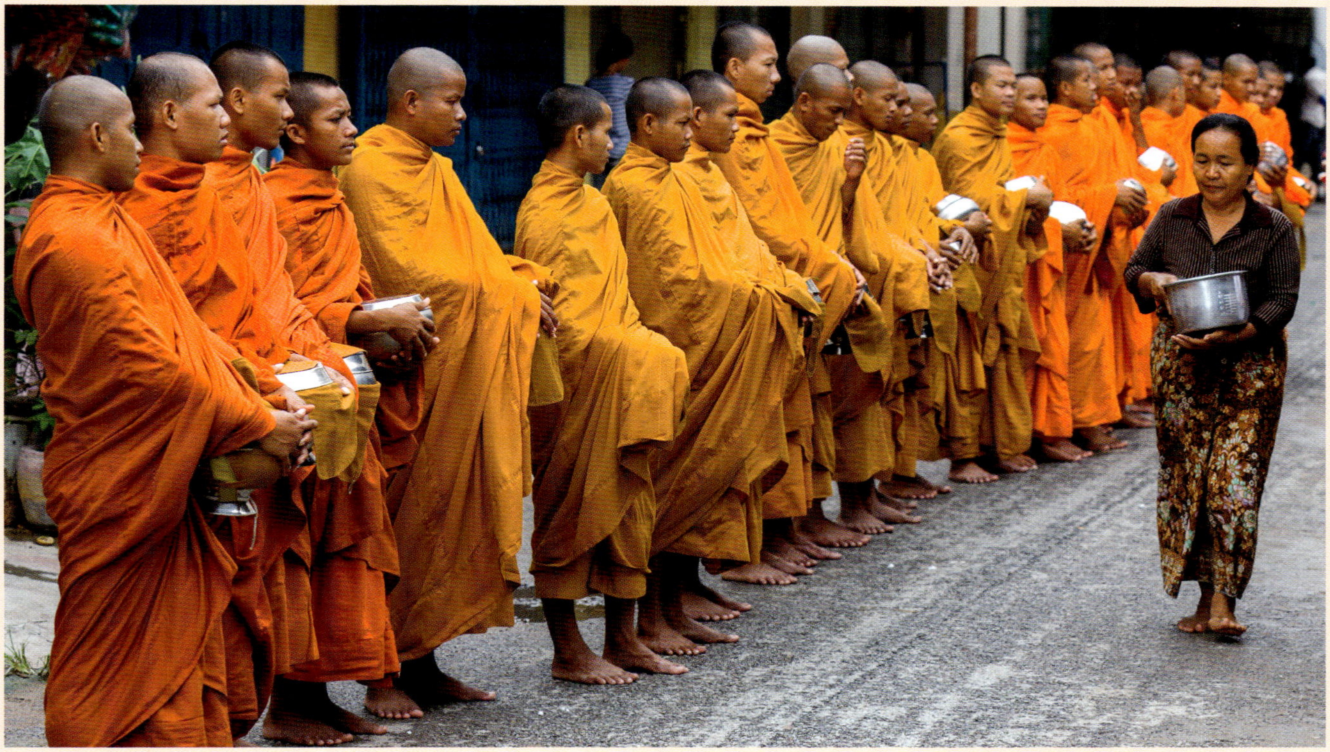

Once known as Mount Mahendraparvata, Phnom Kulen is regarded as a sacred mountain by many Cambodians. The 500-m (1,640-ft) hill stretches for 12 km (7½ miles) across a fertile plain, just over an hour north-east of Siem Reap. The site was the pre-Angkor capital founded by Jayavarman II during the ninth century and, according to ancient inscriptions, this is where he declared himself universal ruler in 802. It's a very popular place for locals from Siem Reap who come here by *tuk-tuk* to enjoy picnics beside waterfalls, and visit temples and shrines. The road up the mountain is too steep for *tuk-tuks* to manage but motorcycles waiting at the bottom will take pillion passengers on the scenic journey through dense forest. One of the highlights at the summit is the reclining Buddha at the temple of Preah Ang Thom. Hewn from sandstone, the 17-m (55-ft) image is believed to date from the 16th century.

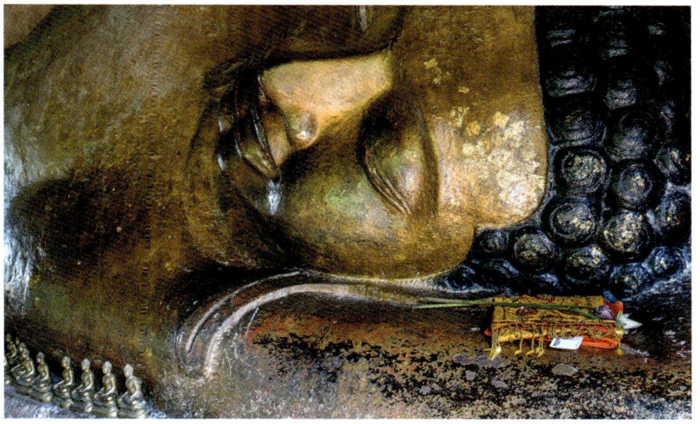

Above: The stone Buddha image at Preah Ang Thom, Phnom Kulen.

Below: A monk's shrine at Preah Ang Thom. Buddhists visit the monk to hear his sage advice and receive blessings.

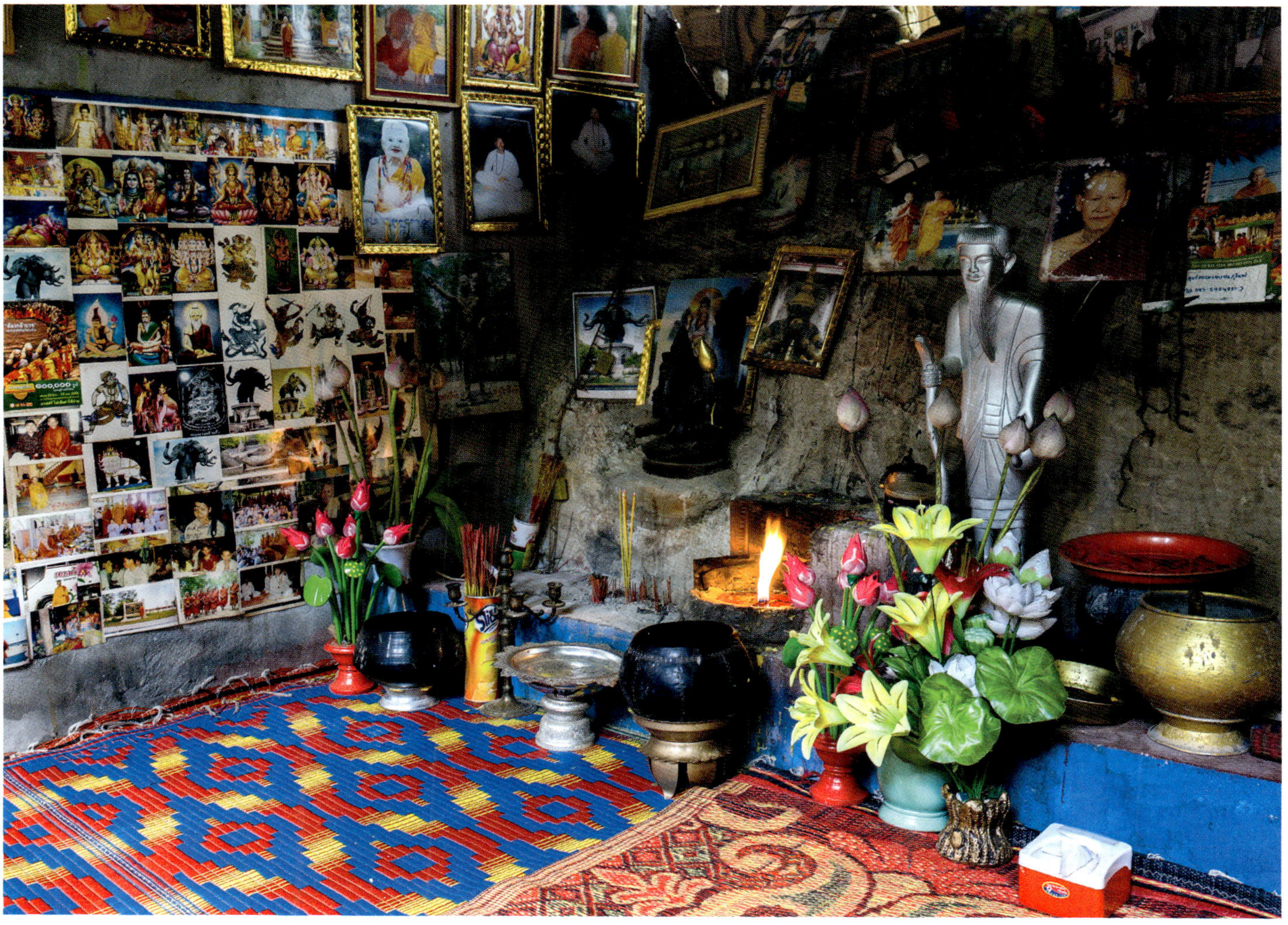

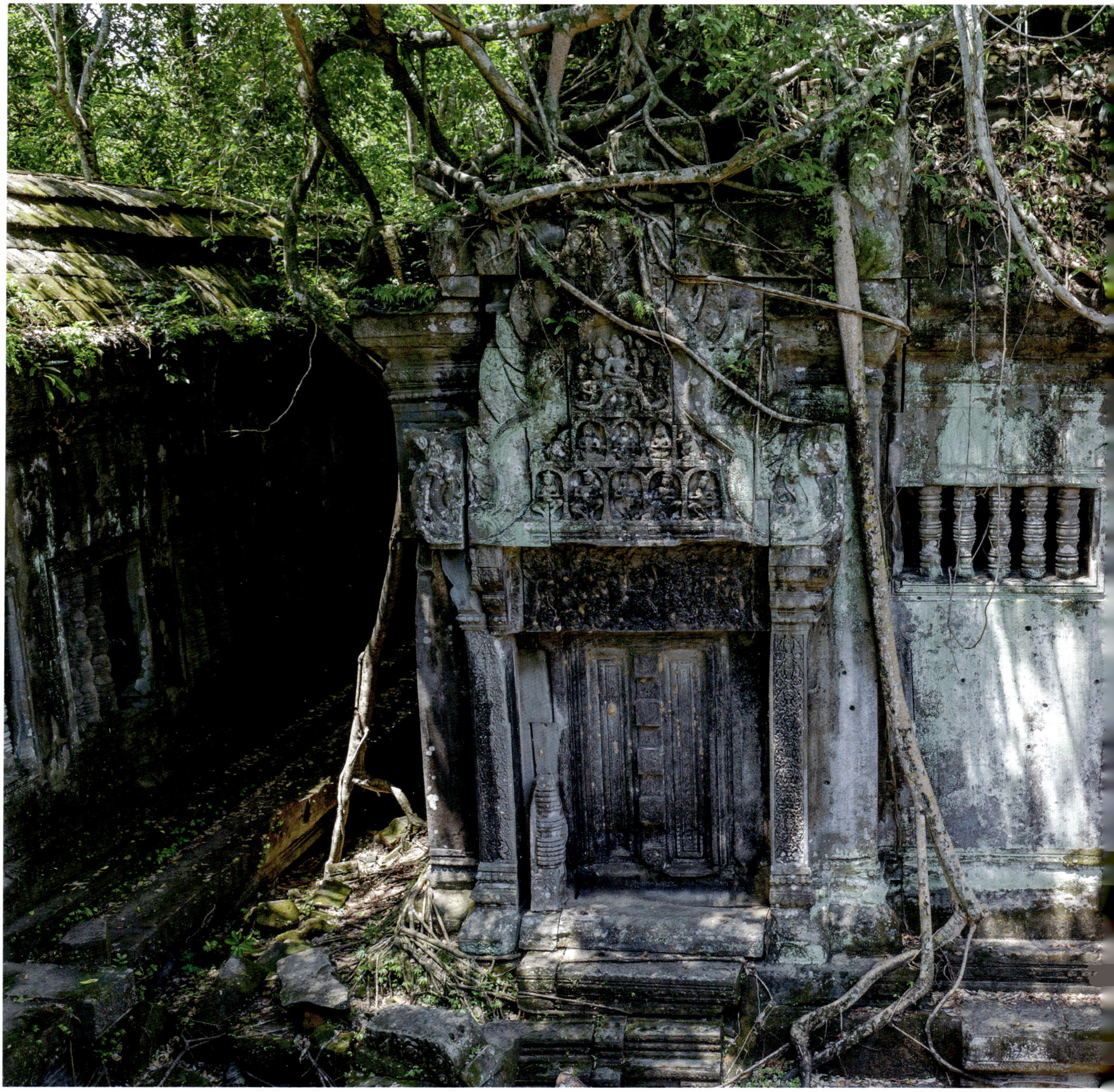

Above: Beng Mealea is one of Cambodia's most atmospheric temples. Over the years, it has been almost completely taken over by the slowly advancing forest.

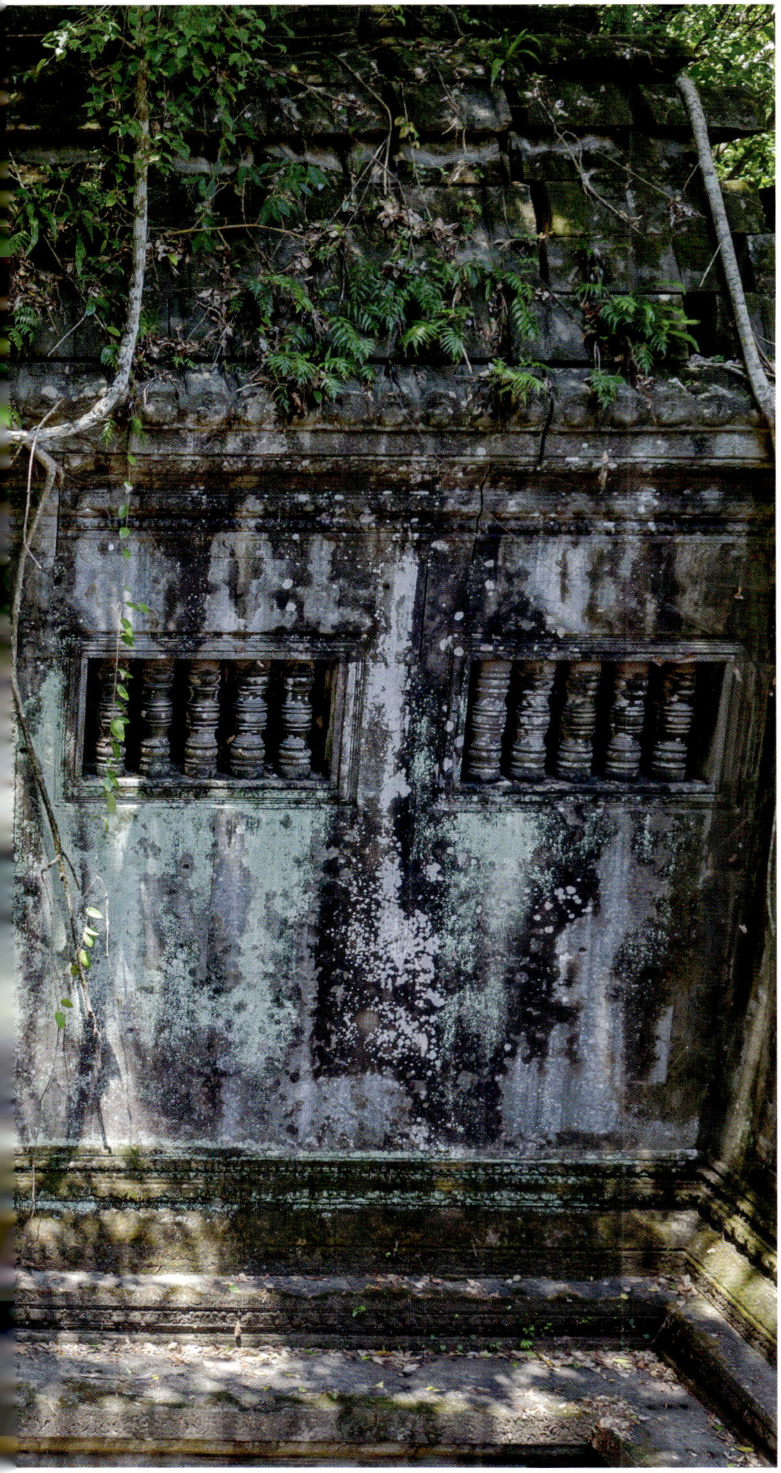

Seven kilometres (four miles) south-east of Phnom Kulen is the eerily atmospheric temple, Beng Mealea. More than any of the Angkorian temples, it has almost completely surrendered to the encroaching jungle and, unlike Ta Prohm, which was made famous by the movie *Tomb Raider*, it welcomes considerably fewer visitors. This is mainly due to the fact that it takes a little effort to get there and although it can be comfortably be taken in on a day-trip from Siem Reap, it is often part of itineraries heading north to Koh Ker and Preah Vihear.

The construction of Beng Mealea was ordered by Suryavarman II in the early 12th century and is encircled by a broad, lotus-filled moat. It was one of the largest temples in the Khmer Empire and was designed with three covered galleries around a central tower, long since collapsed. Many sections of the galleries have also yielded to the ravages of time so that gaining access to the inner area requires the agility of a mountain goat, clambering over mountains of massive sandstone blocks and into darkened passageways. Fortunately a raised wooden platform has been erected for the benefit of the less sure-footed. It's a treasure worth exploring. There are exquisite carvings carpeted with delicate lichens, huge trees straddling defensive walls with ease and entire walls covered with a capillary-like network of roots that seem to breathe new life into the ancient stone.

Further north is Koh Ker (pronounced *Koh Kay*), a former capital of the Angkor Kingdom. It was established in 928 by Jayavarman IV who reigned from 928 to 944 AD. Several massive stone sculptures were removed from Koh Ker to protect them from looters and are on display at Phnom Penh's National Museum.

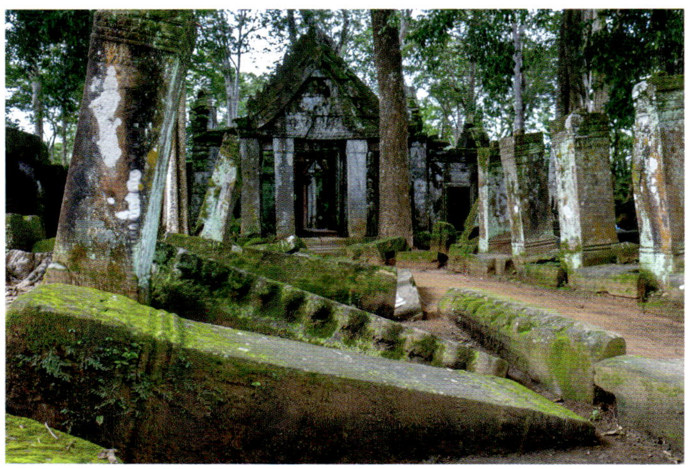

Right: Koh Ker, 120 km (75 miles) from Siem Reap, can be taken in en route north to Preah Vihear on the Cambodia-Thailand border.

ANLONG VENG

Anlong Veng is a dusty, nondescript town, close to the Thai border in the north-western province of Oddar Meanchey. Ordinarily it wouldn't receive even a cursory mention in the most detailed of guidebooks. Its notoriety comes from the fact that for more than a decade it was the last stronghold of the Khmer Rouge. Until it was taken by government forces in April 1998, it was also home to Pol Pot and other Khmer Rouge leaders, namely Nuon Chea, one of its chief ideologists and known as Brother Number Two, and Ta Mok, who was nicknamed the Butcher. Just outside the town is Ta Mok's former home, now partially derelict and open as a museum.

Below left: Pol Pot died in Anlong Veng on 15 April 1998. He was cremated and his ashes scattered in a nearby forest.
Below: The former home of Ta Mok is now a poorly maintained museum that attracts few visitors.

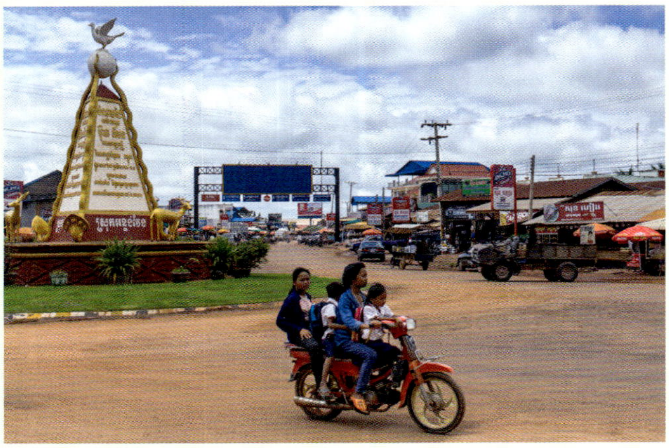

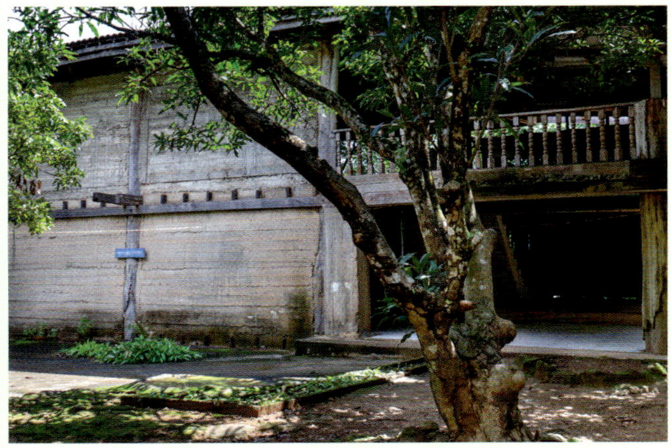

The temple of Preah Vihear is located in Cambodia's Dangkrek Mountains, where, from its stunning 625-m (2,050-ft) high plateau, it overlooks neighbouring Thailand. It was built in the first half of the 11th century to honour the Hindu deity, Shiva, but there is evidence that the plateau was used as a religious site as early as the ninth century.

In 2008, the temple was ratified as Cambodia's second UNESCO World Heritage Site, a move that acknowledged it as a masterpiece of Khmer architecture. When announcing the decision, UNESCO stated that Preah Vihear was "pure both in the plan and detail of its decoration and in its relationship to the spectacular landscape environment". The statement went on to say that the "site is exceptional for the quality of its architecture...as well as for the exceptional quality of its carved stone ornamentation". Those who have explored the many temples of Angkor will immediately recognize that it is indeed a unique structure.

Preah Vihear comprises a series of sanctuaries stretching north to south for 800 m (2,625 ft) on the elevated plateau, each linked by pavements and staircases that lead towards the main sanctuary. It is this elongated layout clearly created for the mountain environment that makes it so unusual. The temple includes a particularly beautiful depiction of the Churning of the Sea of Milk (see page 116), and images of Shiva manifesting as Sri Sikharesvara, the supreme god of the mountain, carved into pediments and lintels.

Preah Vihear's past may have been glorious but has also been the focus of a passionate and often heated debate between Cambodia and Thailand. The dispute dates from 1902 when then Siam and France, who were controlling Cambodia at the time, signed an agreement to establish lines of demarcation. A map drawn at the time was said to show the border following the line of the Dangkrek Mountains and placing Preah Vihear in Thai territory. In 1954, the Thai military occupied the site until

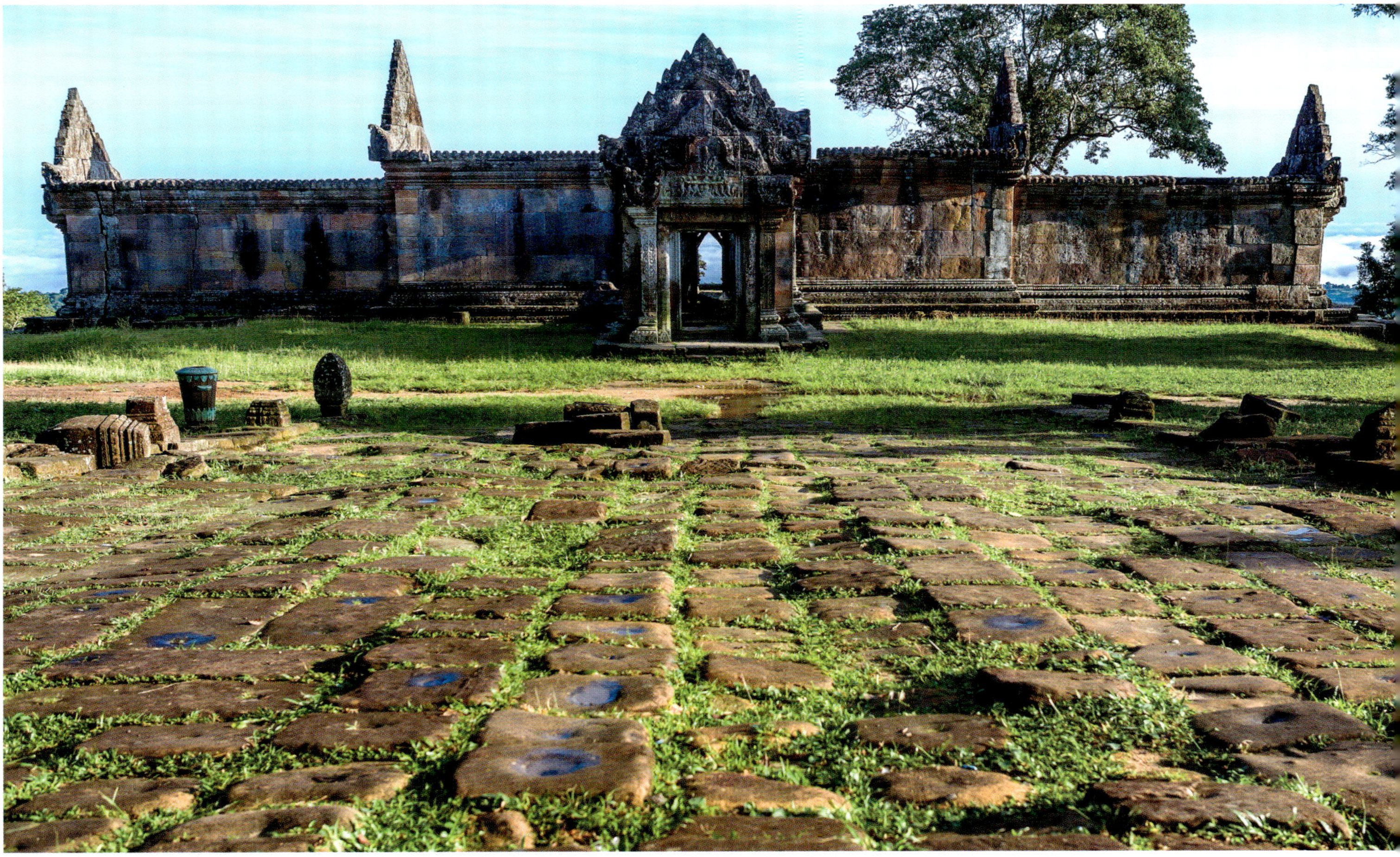

in 1962 the International Criminal Court of Justice (ICCJ) ruled in favour of Cambodia and the map presented to the ICCJ showed the temple sitting squarely in Cambodia. The decision in 2008 by UNESCO to list it as a World Heritage Site and a "masterpiece of Khmer architecture" reignited the debate and there have been several skirmishes in the area, fuelled by Thai politicians who often use the issue to create nationalist fervour at home.

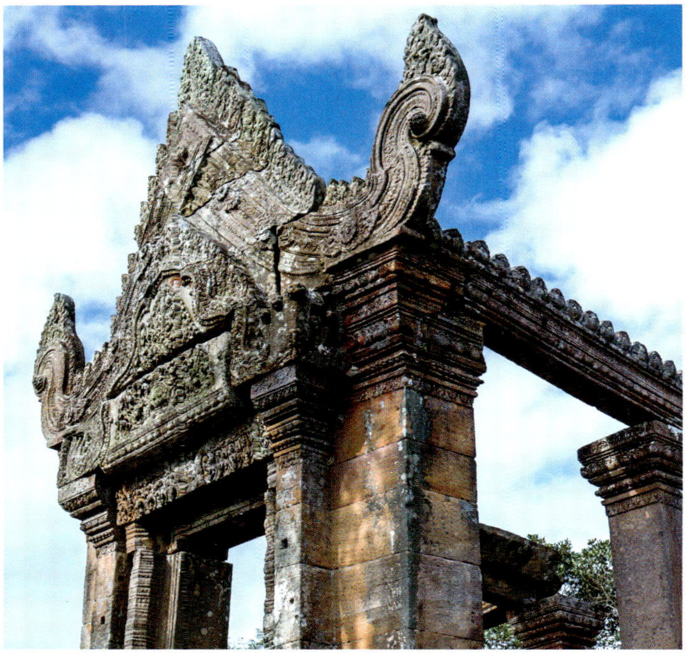

Above: From Siem Reap, it takes considerable effort and an overnight stay to visit Preah Vihear temple but it is worth the trip. The unique structure sits atop an elongated plateau and offers fabulous views of Cambodia and Thailand.

Right: Preah Vihear temple is considered to be the crowning achievement among the many jewels of Khmer architecture but it is also the cause of heated, often violent clashes between Cambodia and Thailand.

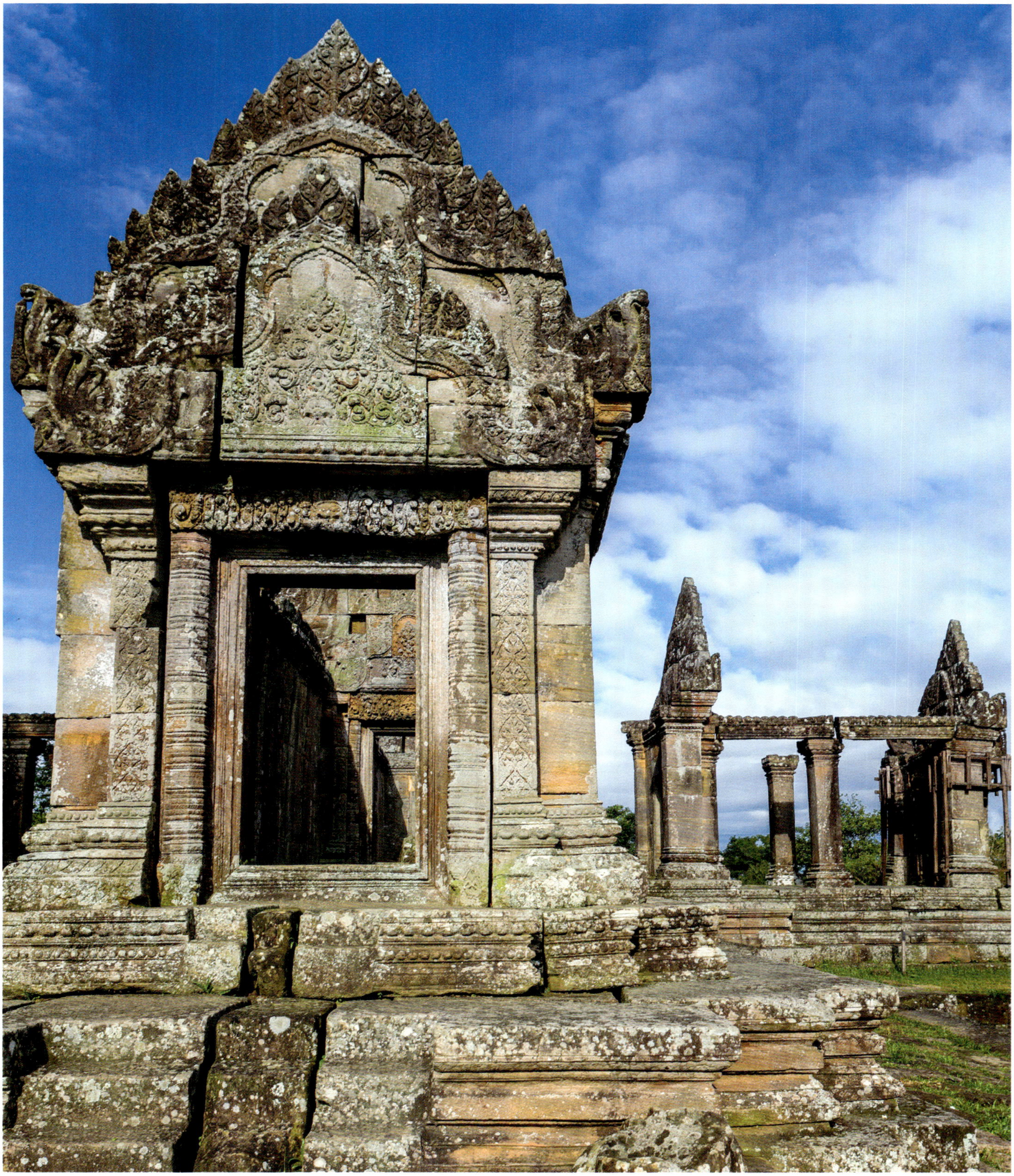

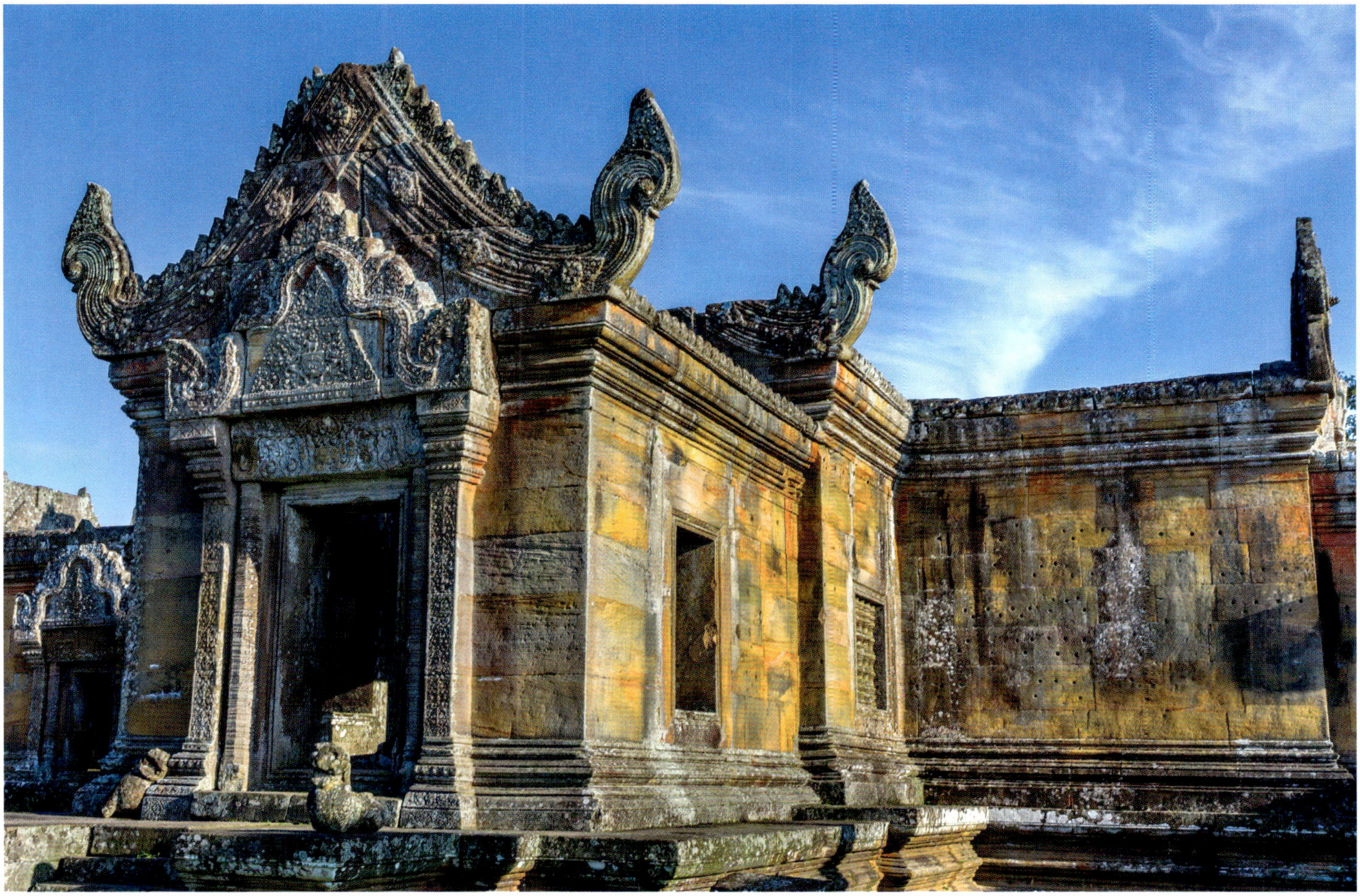

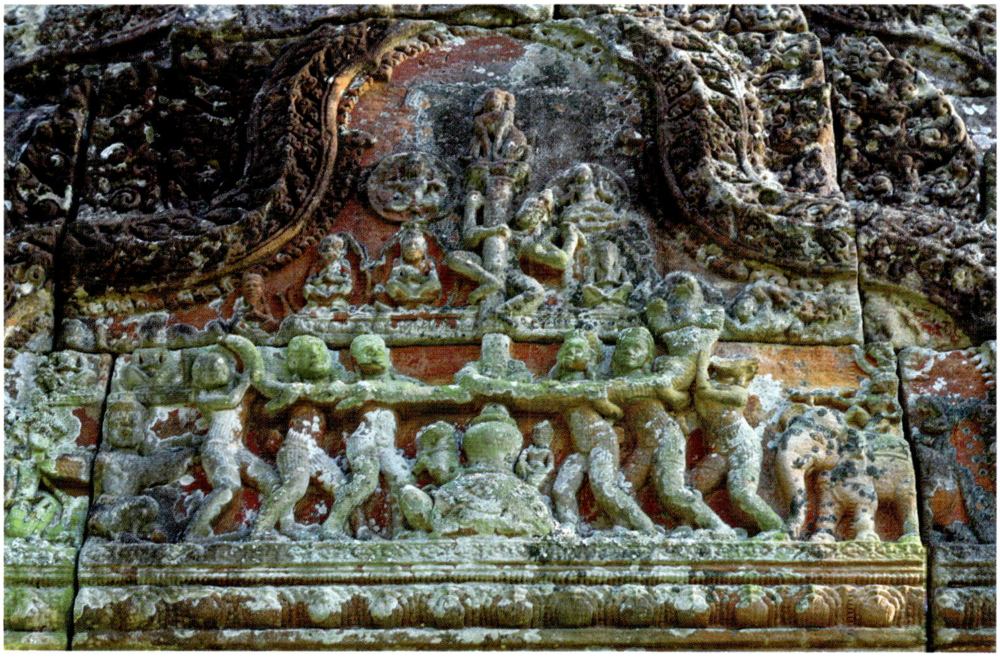

Above: When the temple was constructed in the ninth century it was dedicated to the Hindu god, Shiva. The famous monument lends its name to Preah Vihear Province.
Left: Preah Vihear features a truly beautiful interpretation of the Churning of the Sea of Milk (see page 116) on one of five *gopuras*, or arched entranceways.
Opposite: The elevated location of Preah Vihear is stunning but it is the form and decoration of the ancient structure that really impresses lovers of Khmer architecture. The temple is strikingly different from the temples of Angkor.

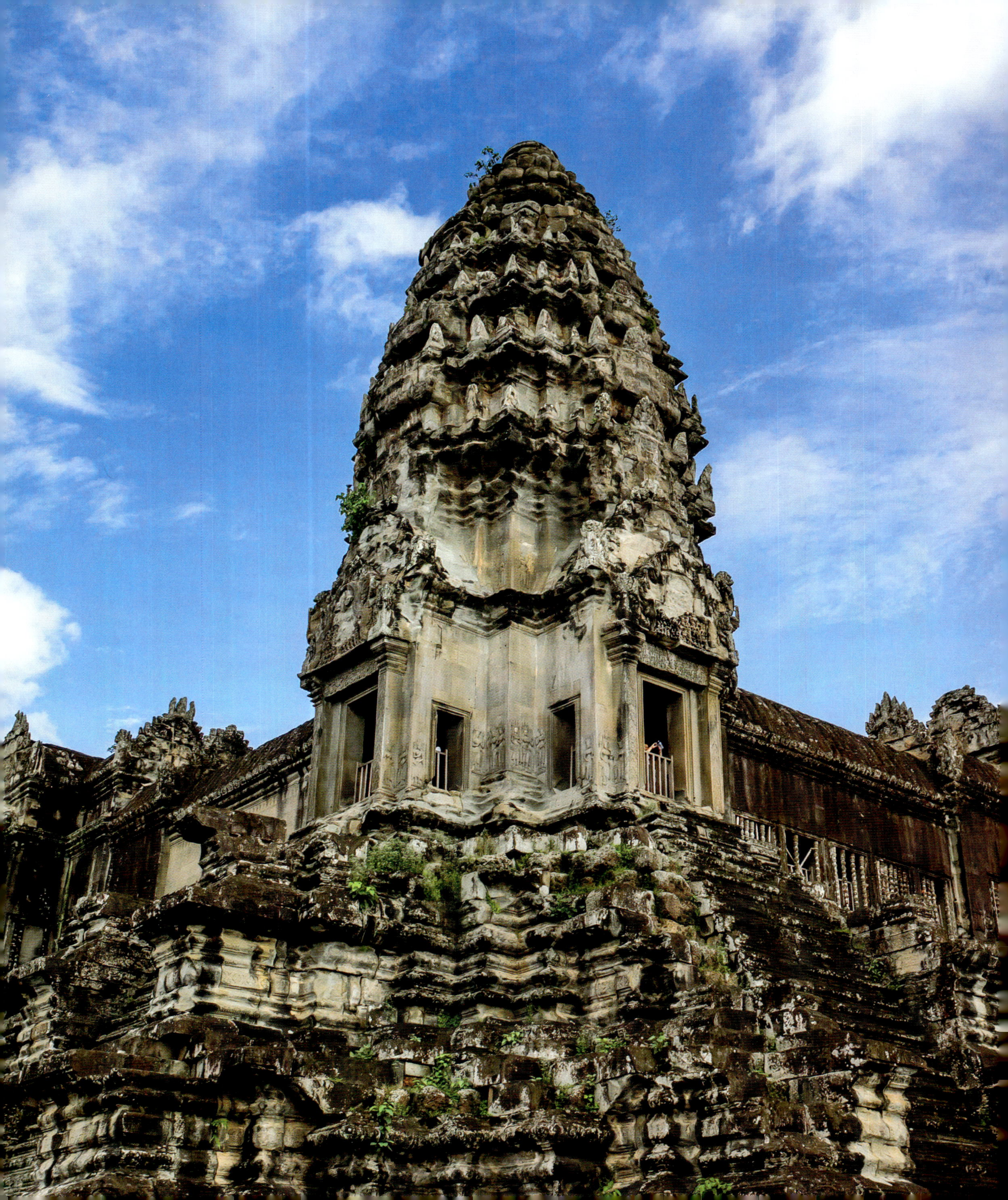

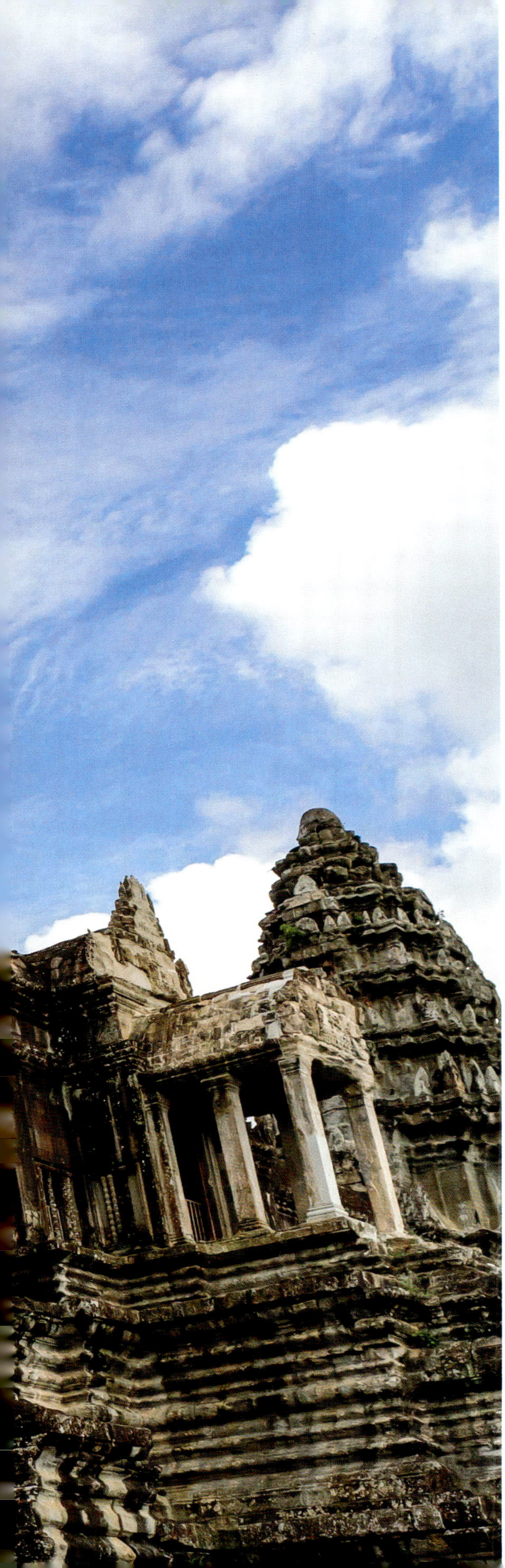

CHAPTER IV

SIEM REAP *and* ANGKOR

The Glories of the Past

Siem Reap is just eight kilometres (five miles) from the nearest of Angkor's many ancient sites and because of this it is Cambodia's most visited destination. The town's development began in the early 1900s when the French were excavating and documenting the temples. With the opening of the Grand Hotel d'Angkor in 1929, the town was placed firmly on the map of wealthy and adventurous travellers. A visit to the Angkor National Museum in Siem Reap is an excellent and informative precursor to a trip to the ruins. It explains the history of Angkor in a clear and concise manner, and includes a stunning collection of over 1,000 Buddha images.

Left: Angkor is one of Southeast Asia's most visited sites, and Angkor Wat is considered the finest of all its many temples. The temple is built on three levels and reaches a height of 65 m (213 ft). The upper or third level, shown here, features five central towers from where visitors can enjoy a panoramic view of the entire complex in all its glory and of the surrounding countryside.

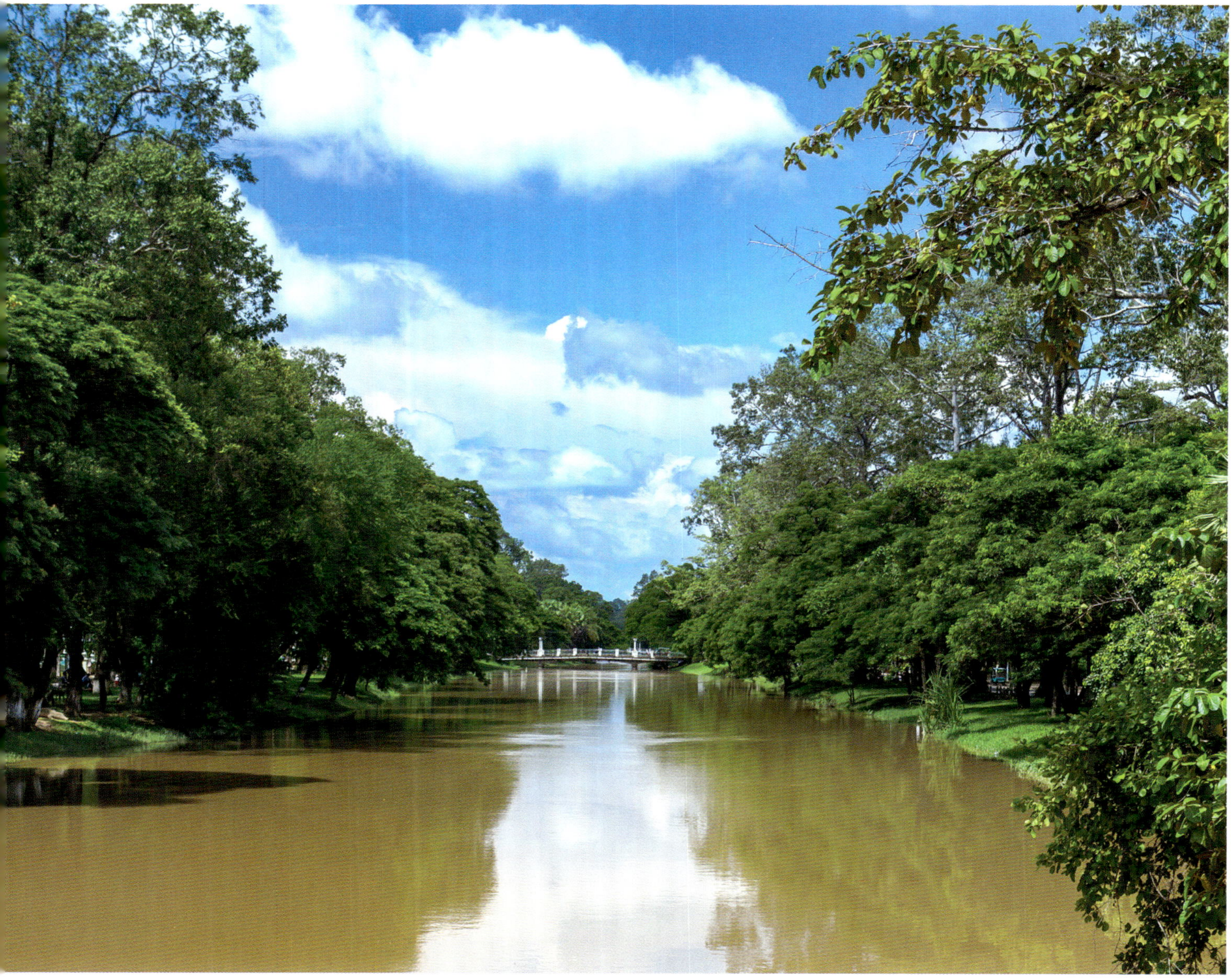

SIEM REAP

Siem Reap is enjoying a period of unprecedented and sustained development as it tries to cater to the more than three million visitors who come to see Angkor every year. Its many boutiques, restaurants and bars in Pub Street, cookery schools, craft workshops, night markets, and much more, provide a welcome break from exploring the ancient monuments. Despite the surge of development and new buildings, Siem Reap is not without considerable charm. Spread out along its namesake river which flows into the Tonlé Sap, there are old neighbourhoods to discover and pleasant walks to enjoy. In the centre of town is a covered market, Psar Leu, which in part is given over to selling gifts and souvenirs but also at its heart still daily serves the local community with an array of fresh produce and steaming bowls of noodles.

Above: Siem Reap River runs through the centre of town and is bordered by tree-lined paths. There are also many hotels and restaurants along the riverside.

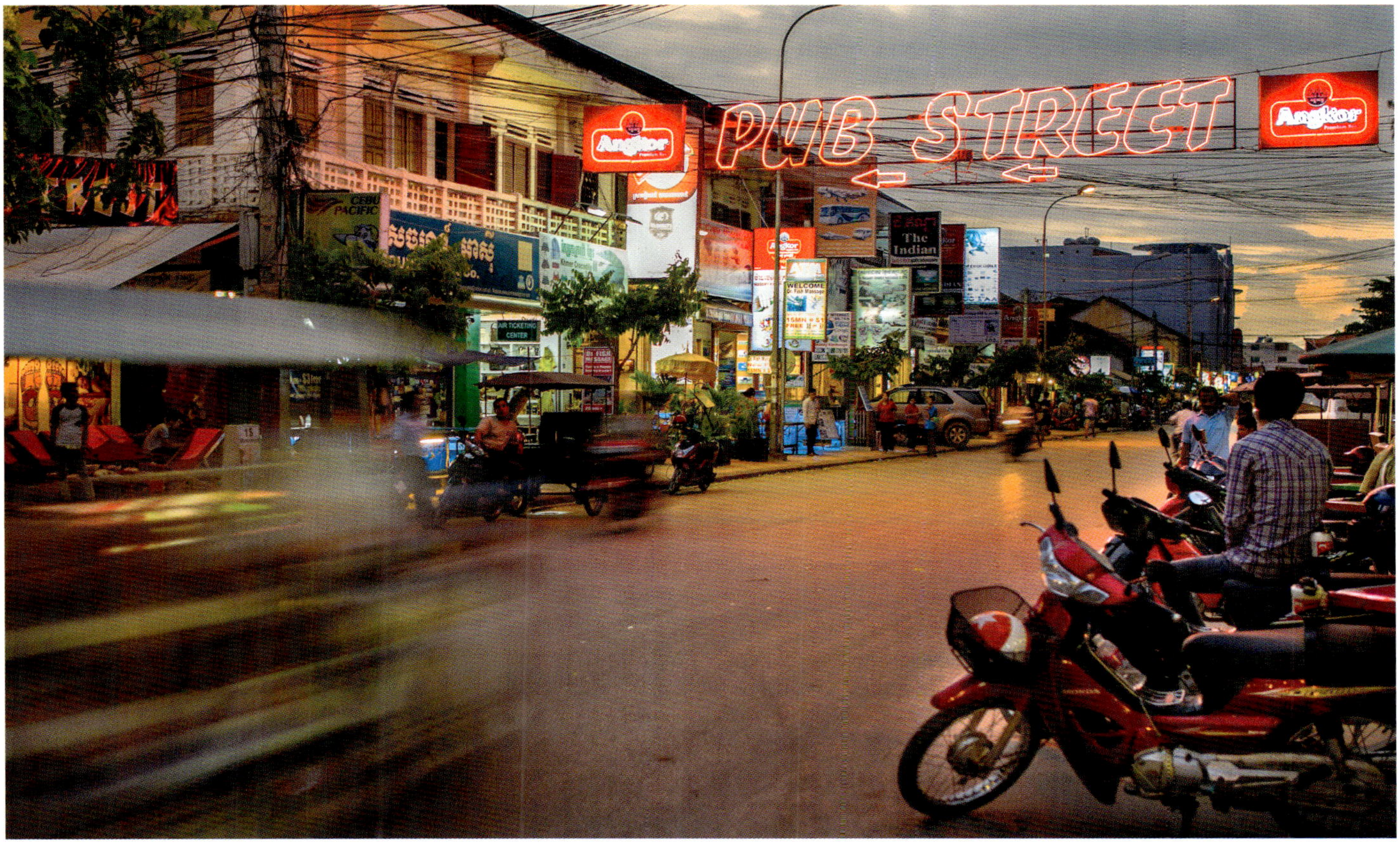

Above: Pub Street is the heart of Siem Reap's night scene and home to dozens of bars and restaurants.

Right: In the Pub Street area there are many alleys with cafés, chic boutiques and gift shops, open night and day.

Below: A painter training at *Artisans Angkor* working on a scene from a nearby floating village.

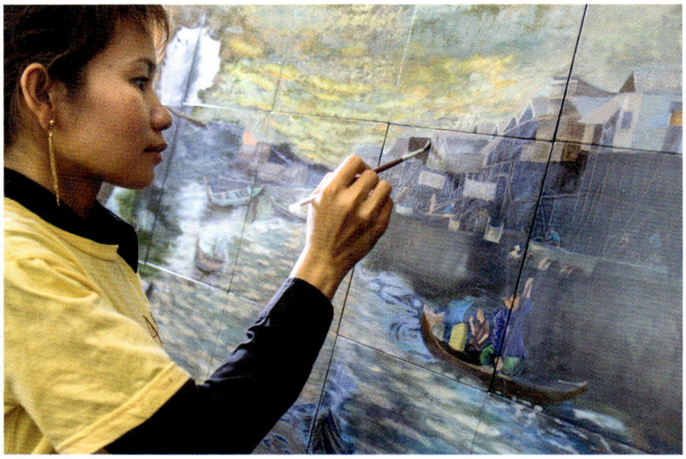

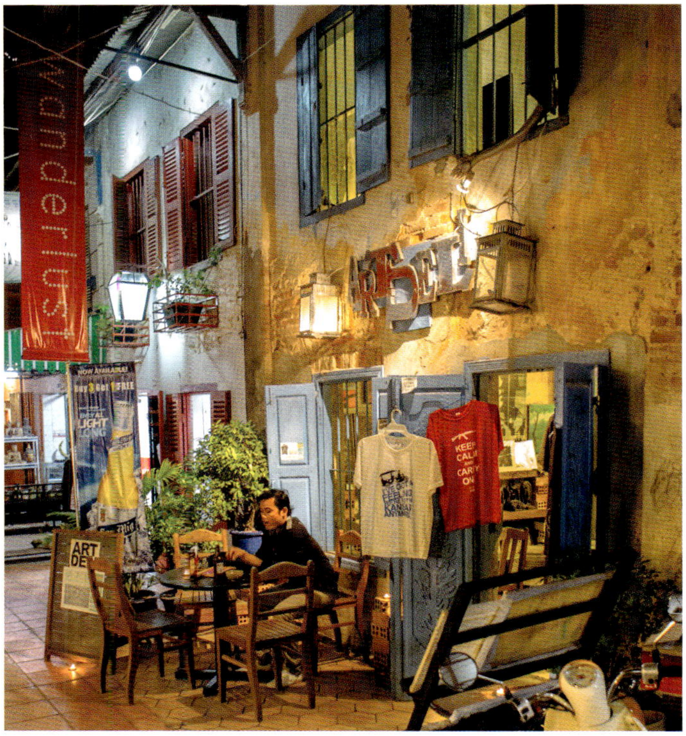

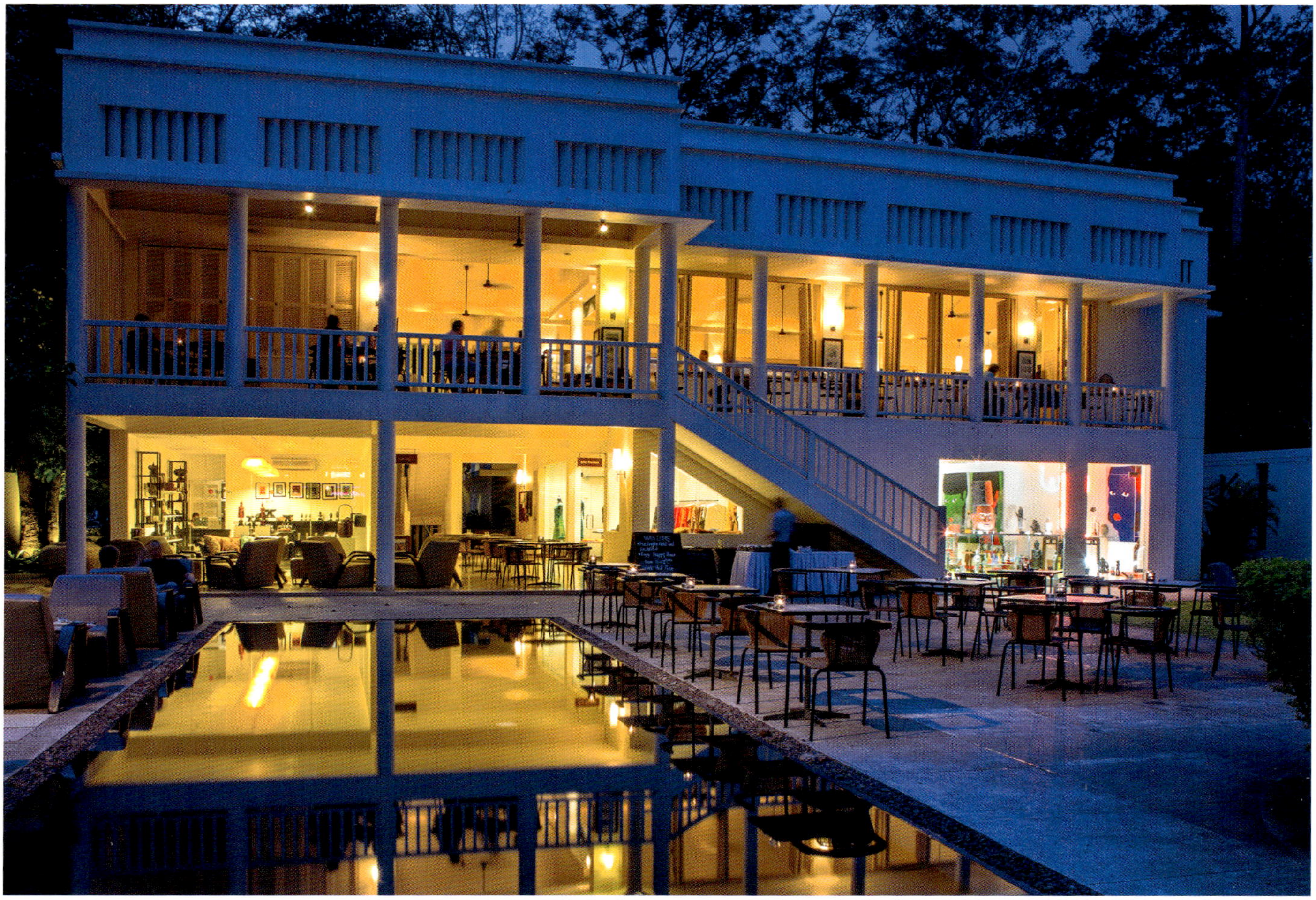

Above: The Foreign Correspondents' Club in Siem Reap is the perfect place for a pre-dinner drink.

Below: Spicy soup with prawns, one of the cookery-school dishes.

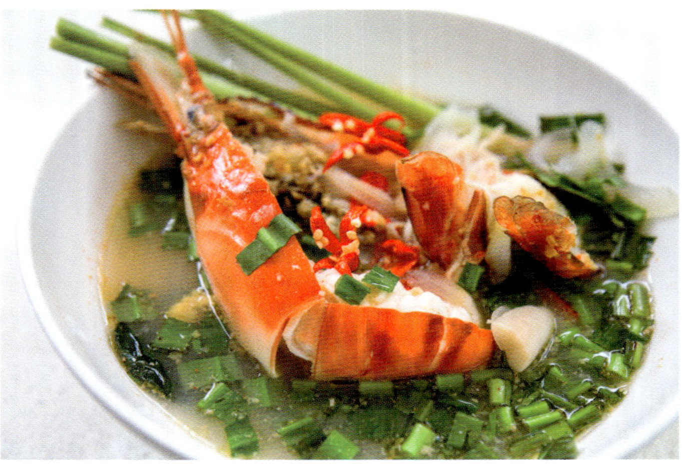

Visitors to Cambodia are always impressed by the cuisine and a number of cookery schools based in hotels now ensure that it is possible to have a hands-on experience of making the traditional dishes. At La Résidence d'Angkor by Orient-Express, chefs offer an exquisite menu called 'Khmer Discovery'. An excellent way to become acquainted with Cambodian flavours, the aptly named Bayon, Banteay Srei and Angkor Wat Tower set menus feature exotic temptations, such as Mekong lobster with ginger and Kampot green peppercorn, sun-dried fish salad with green mango and Khmer basil, and fishcakes with kaffir lime leaves and tamarind sauce, each beautifully seasoned and presented with artistic flair. At La Résidence d'Angkor guests can also join an excellent cooking class which includes a trip to the market to get familiar with local ingredients and instruction from a top chef who divulges the secrets and techniques of Cambodian cuisine, including how to make *amok* (see page 44).

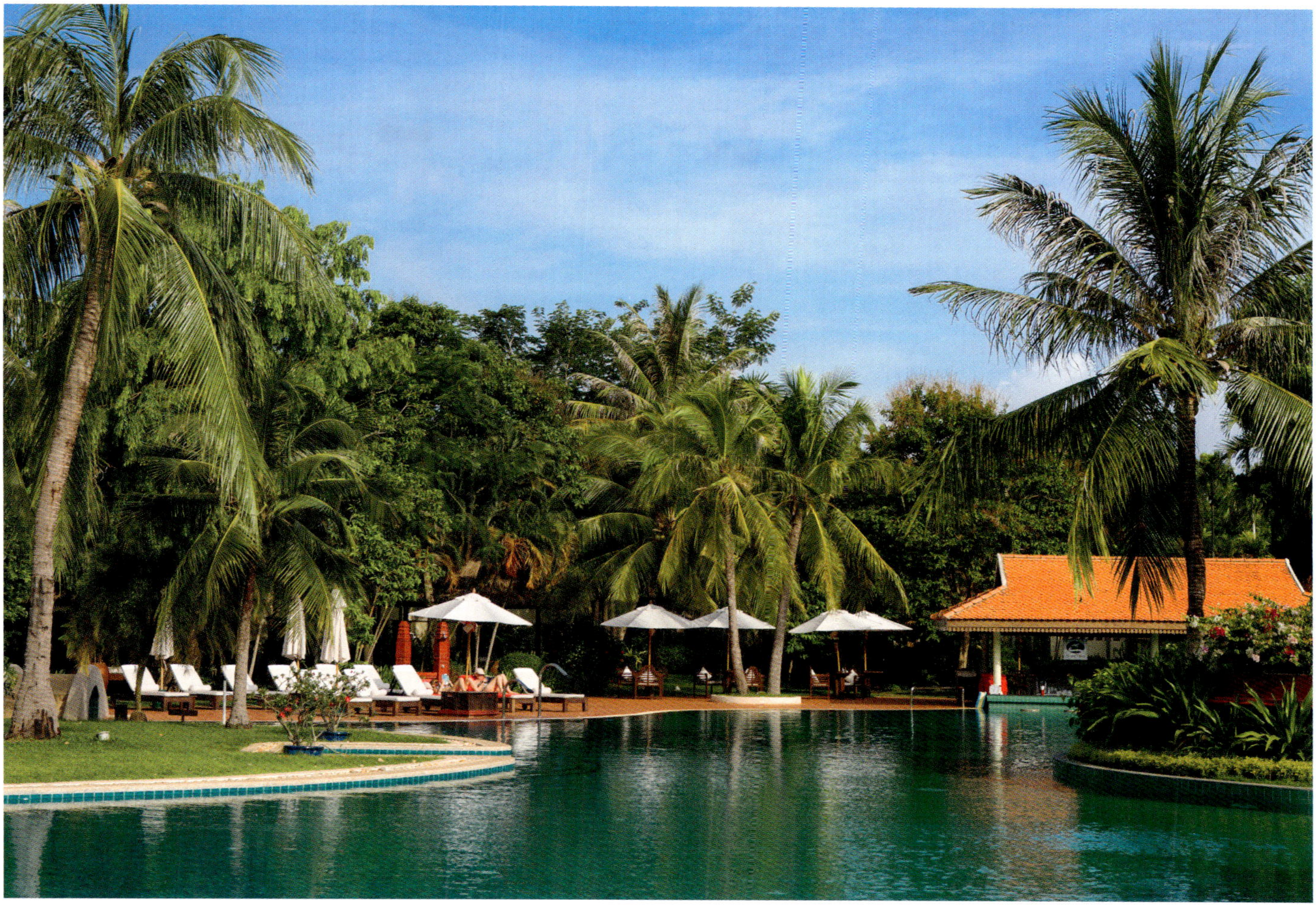

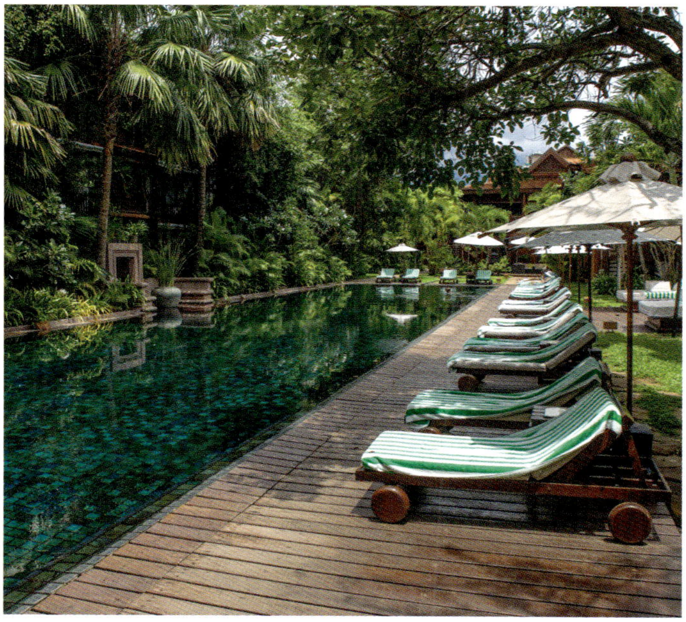

Above: Sofitel Angkor Phokeethra Golf & Spa Resort offers five-star luxury just a ten-minute drive from Angkor Wat.
Left: Poolside relaxation at La Résidence d'Angkor by Orient-Express, a tranquil oasis close to the centre of Siem Reap.

GOLF

Cambodia's first golf club opened in December 1996 but there are now five courses near Phnom Penh and three in Siem Reap. Managed by the Sofitel Phokeethra Royal Angkor Resort & Spa, the Phokeethra Country Club is ranked as one of the best The world-class, 18-hole course is set within beautiful natural and landscaped surroundings 20 km (12 miles) from the resort but served by a regular shuttle service.

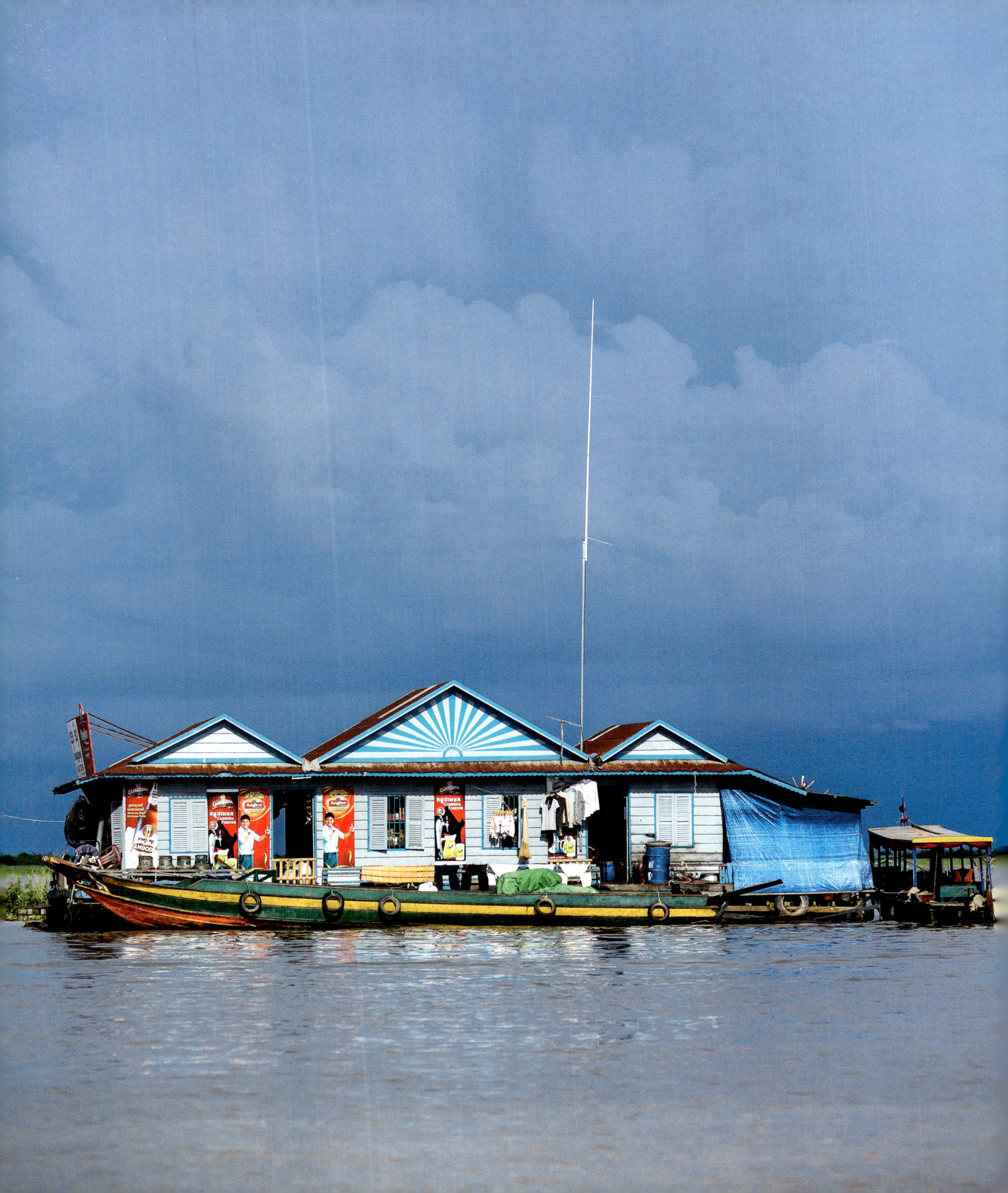

CAMBODIA
CAMBODIA
CAMBODIA
CAMBODIA FOREVER
Angkor
Angkor
CAMBODIA
CAMBODIA FOREVER

There are several floating villages and stilted communities on the Tonlé Sap within easy reach of Siem Reap, namely Chong Kneas, Kompong Phluk, home to the Flooded Forest (see page 20), and Kompong Khleang. The closest to town, Chong Kneas, is now managed by a Korean enterprise and attracts a constant flow of tour buses. The boats at Kompong Phluk are also managed by a company but it is a preferable experience with markedly fewer visitors. In the drier months, stilted houses here tower ten metres (33 ft) above a narrow waterway but in the rainy season visitors can paddle past doorways and through the forest. The most interesting villages are located at Kompong Khleang, 55 km (34 miles) from Siem Reap. This is the largest stilted community on the lake and receives the fewest visitors, especially in the low season months from March to October.

These pages: As the floating village closest to Siem Reap, Chong Kneas is the most commercial and attracts boat-loads of tourists throughout the day. Those in search of a more authentic experience will have to travel much further afield.

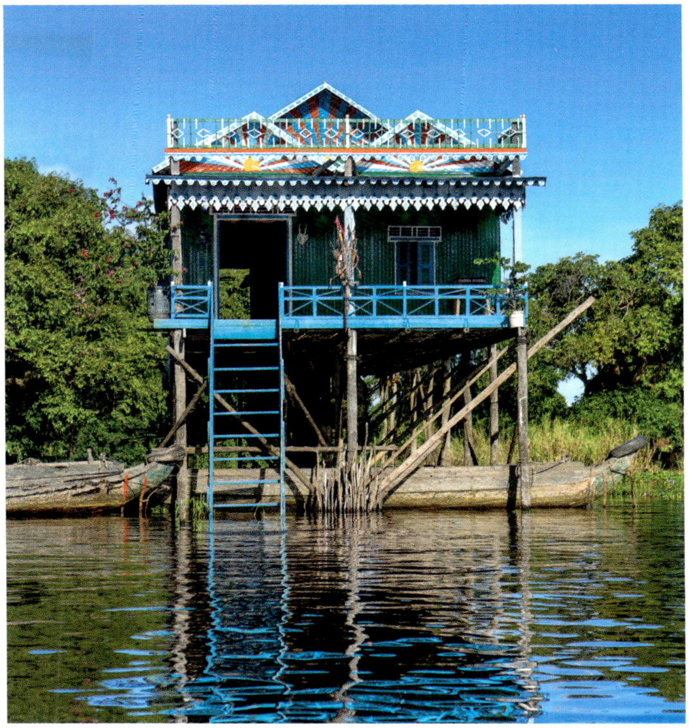

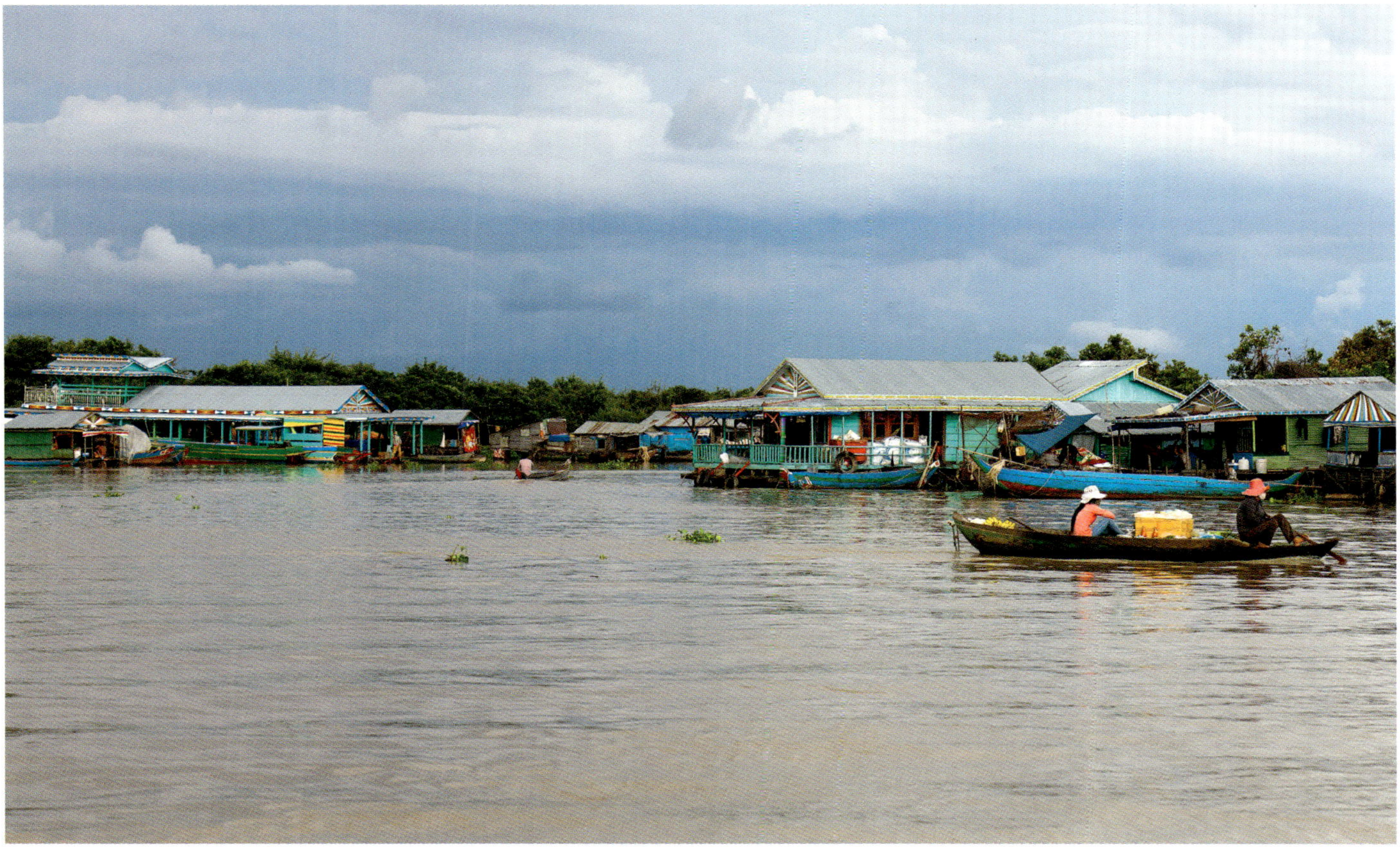

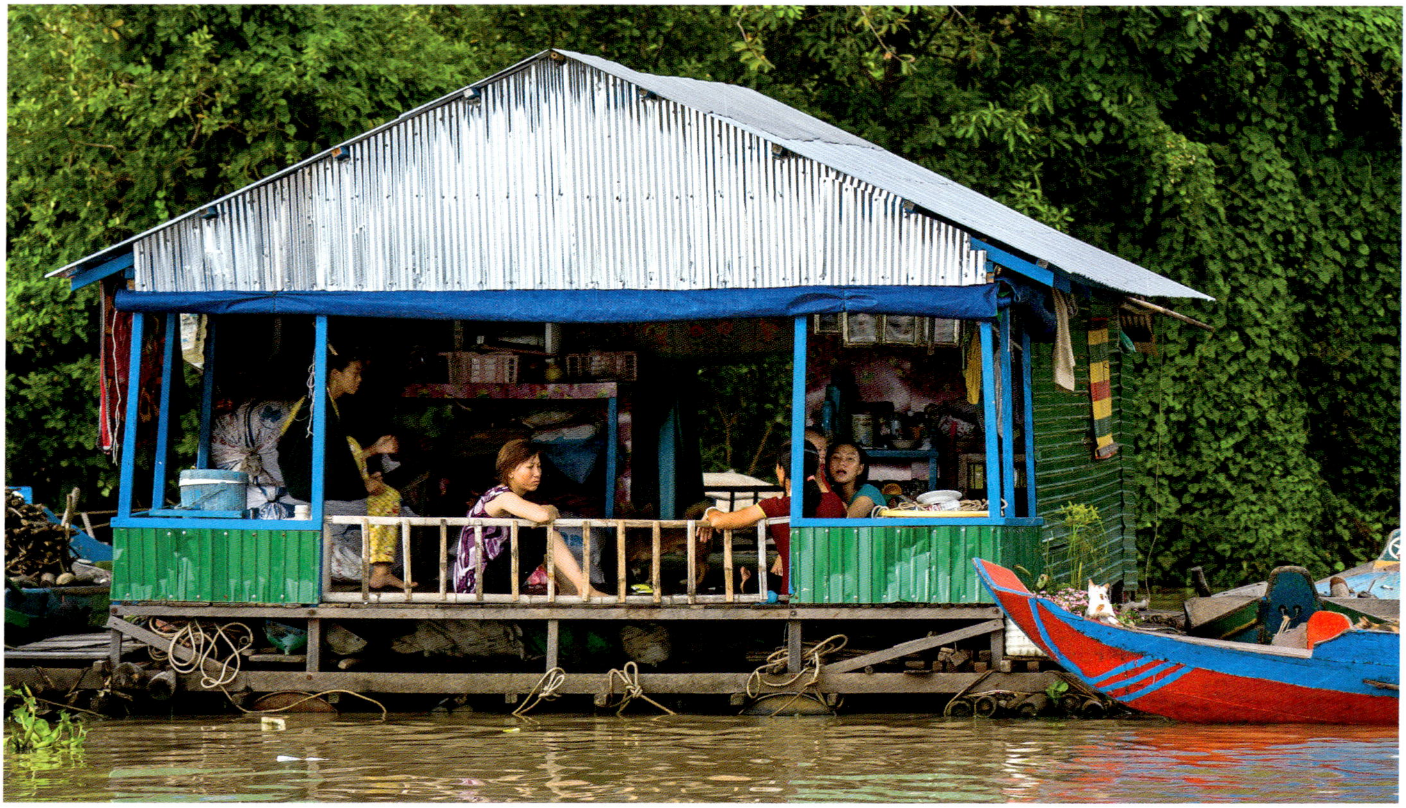

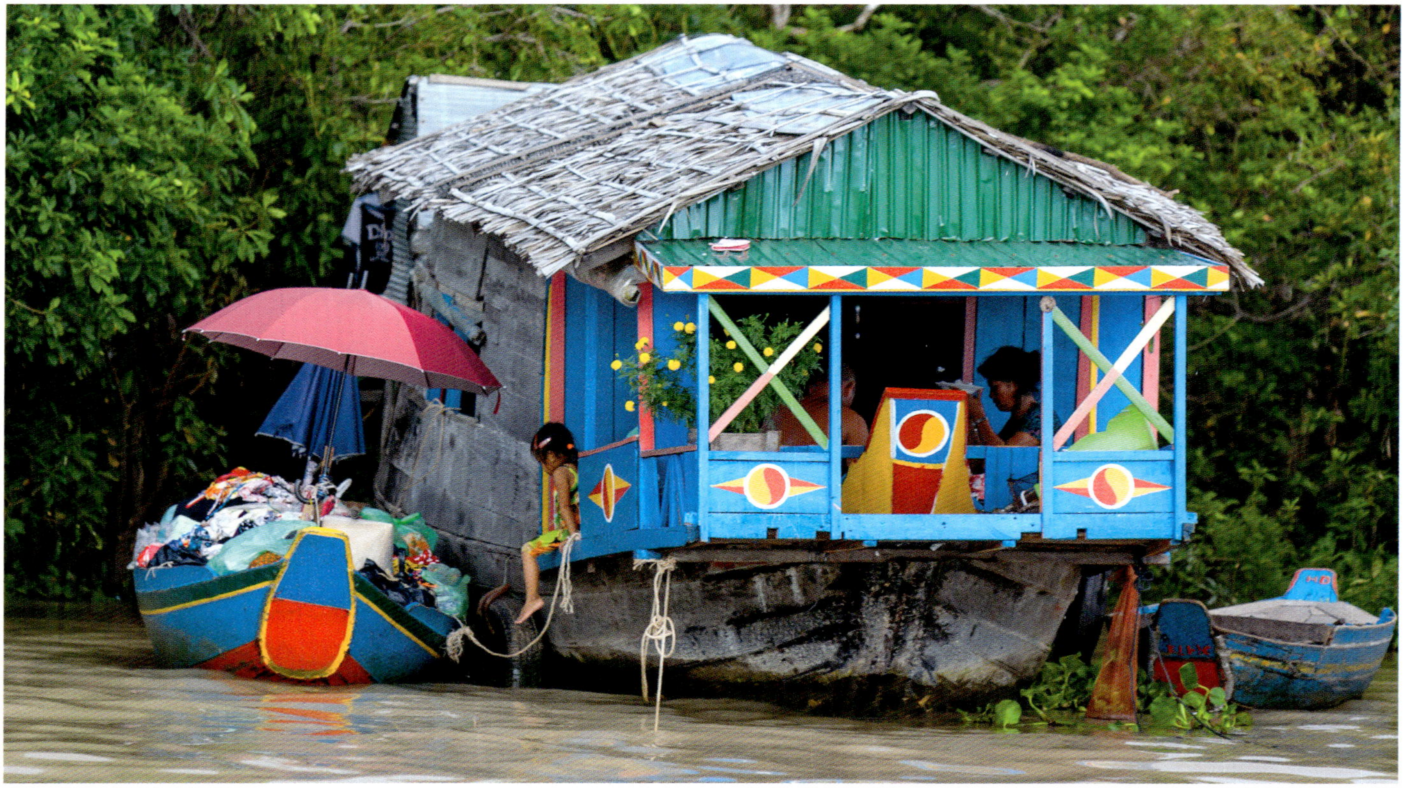

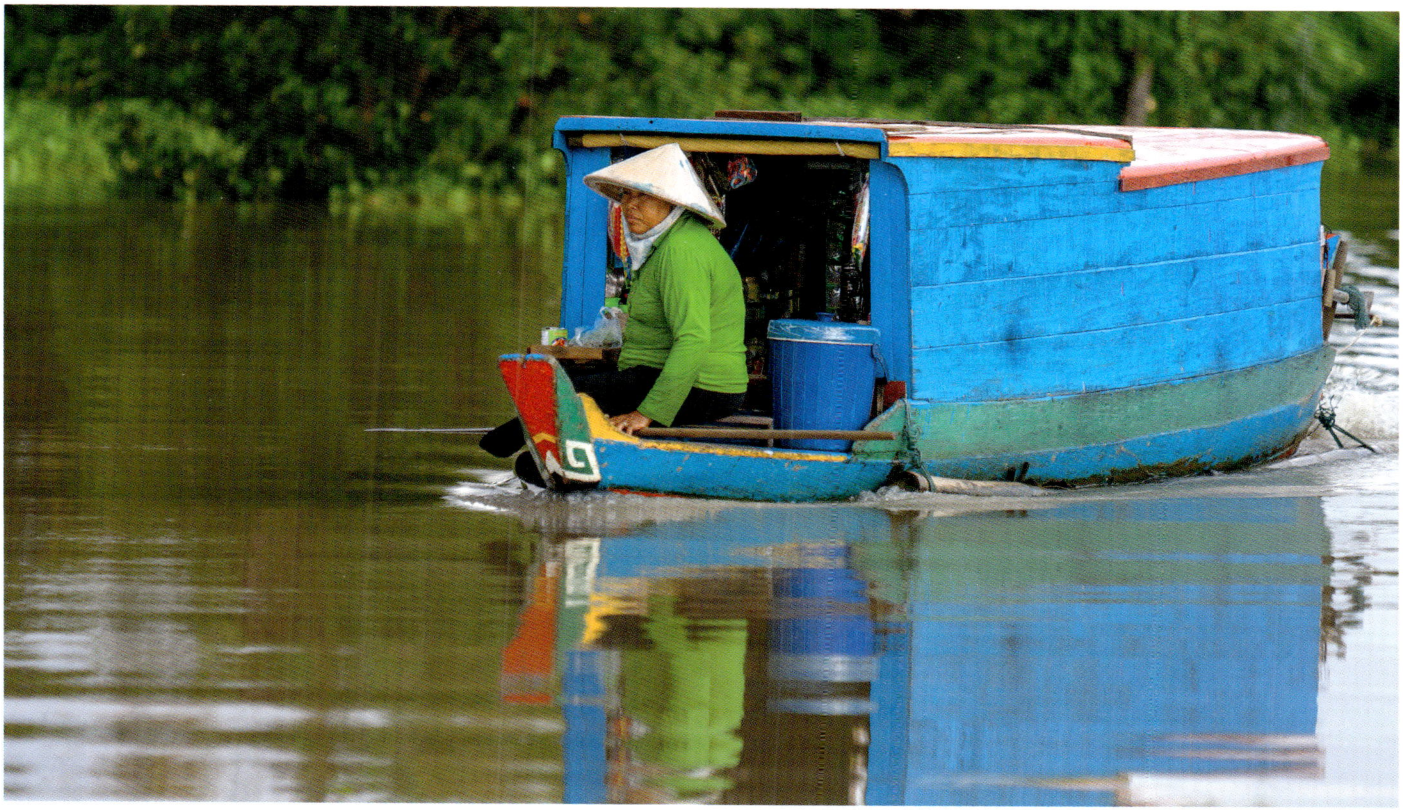

Above: A Vietnamese woman at Chong Kneas doing the rounds in her boat which also doubles as a floating shop.

Below and right: Salted fish hung out to dry on the side of a floating house, and a boy netting freshwater shrimps in the shallows of the Tonlé Sap.

Opposite: The floating houses at Chong Kneas are moved with the seasonal rise and fall of the Tonlé Sap.

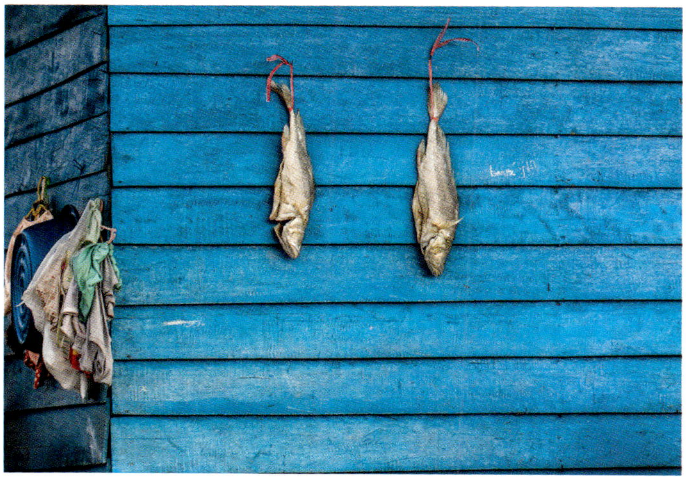

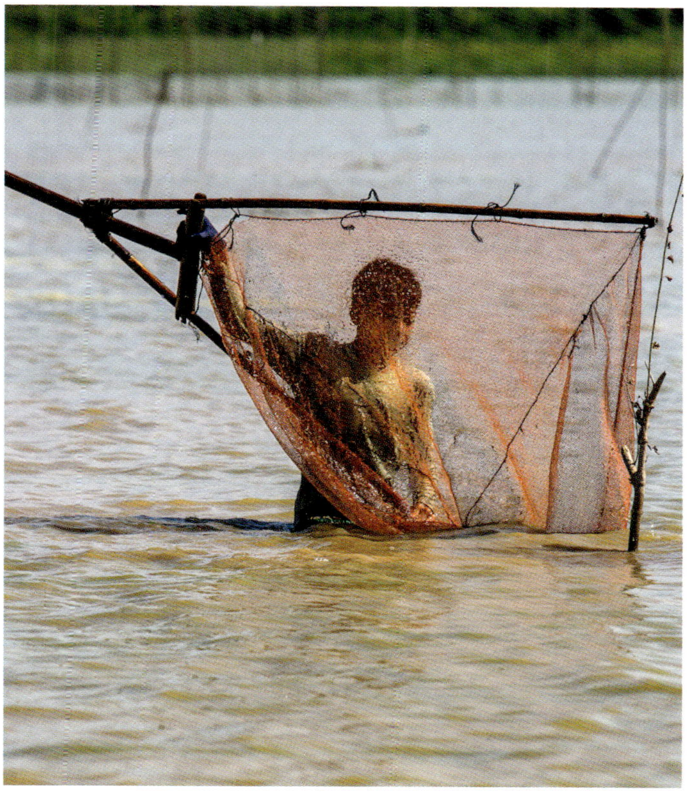

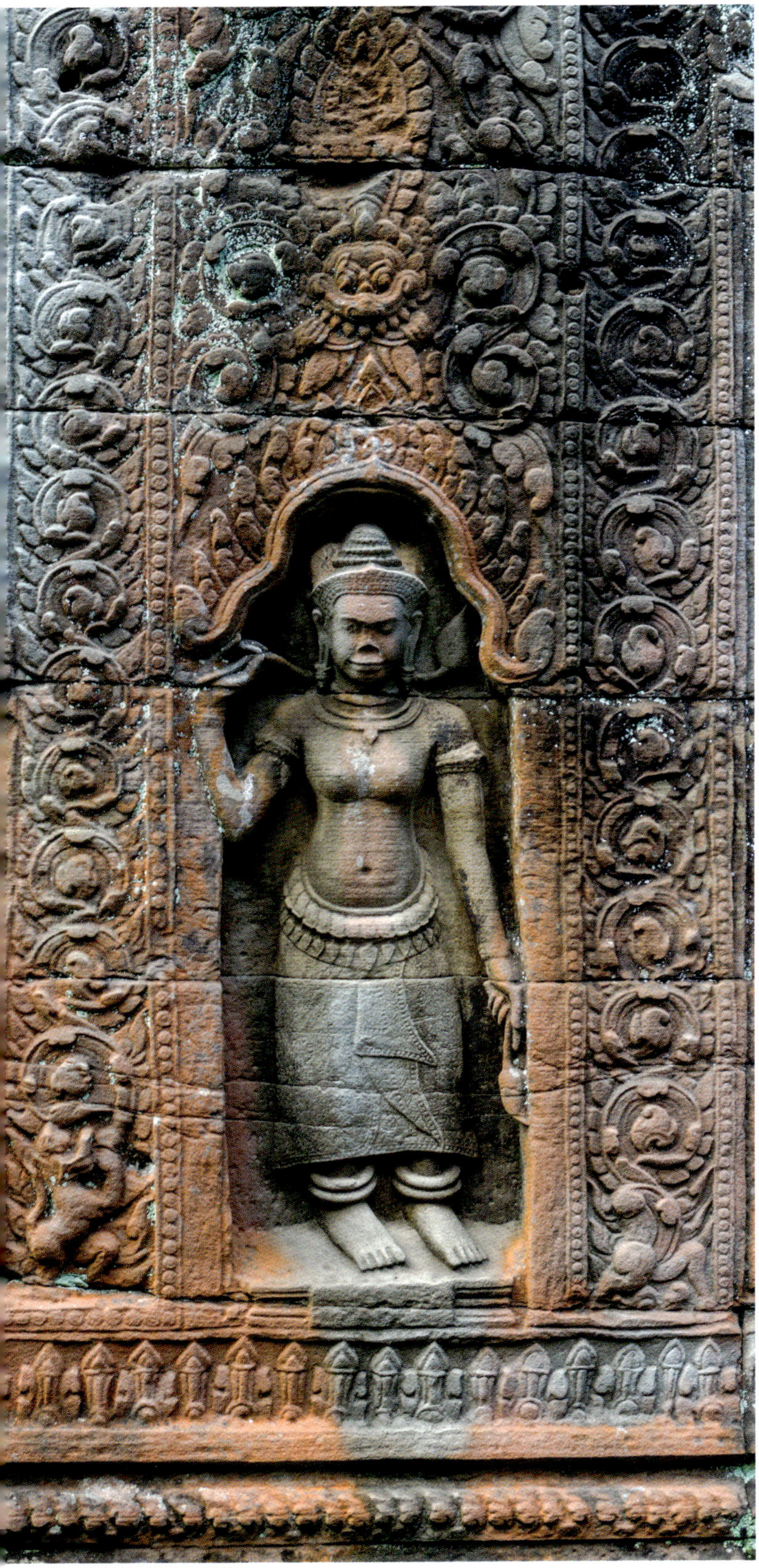

ANGKOR ARCHAEOLOGICAL PARK

In 1296, Zhou Daguan, a Chinese emissary who spent a year in Cambodia documenting the life and customs of the Khmer, gazed upon Angkor Thom and described it thus:

> *At the centre of the Kingdom rises a Golden Tower (Bayon) flanked by more than twenty lesser towers and several hundred stone chambers. On the eastern side is a golden bridge guarded by two lions of gold, one on each side, with eight golden Buddhas spaced along the stone chambers. North of the Golden Tower rises the Tower of Bronze (Baphuon), higher even than the Golden Tower: a truly astonishing spectacle with more than ten chambers at its base. A quarter of a mile further north is the residence of the king. Rising above his private apartments is another tower of gold. These are the monuments which have caused merchants from overseas to speak so often of "Cambodia the rich and noble".*

Today, seven centuries later, the splendours of Angkor Thom and another 90 temple sites within the Angkor Archaeological Park are still looked upon with astonishment by over one million visitors each year.

In December 1992, long before the large numbers of tourists began to arrive, Angkor's importance to mankind was officially recognized when it was inscribed as a UNESCO World Heritage Site. The global organization stated that Angkor was a masterpiece of creative genius representing a unique artistic achievement, and was an exceptional testimony to a lost civilization.

Covering an area of 401 km² (155 sq. miles), the vast and inspiring park requires several days to explore but is an essential part of any travel itinerary in Southeast Asia. Angkor Wat itself encompasses one square kilometre (a third of a square mile), and comprises three levels, a central tower and exquisite bas-reliefs. Other highlights include Bayon, the magnificent temple at the heart of Angkor Thom, featuring 54 towers, each with four enormous carved stone faces that are undoubtedly the most enigmatic and recognizable images in the world.

Left: Angkor's stone carvings are exquisite in design and detail.
Opposite: Dating from 961, Preah Rup temple is a representation of the mythical Mount Meru from Hindu mythology. Visitors enter from the east and have to ascend a steep stone staircase.

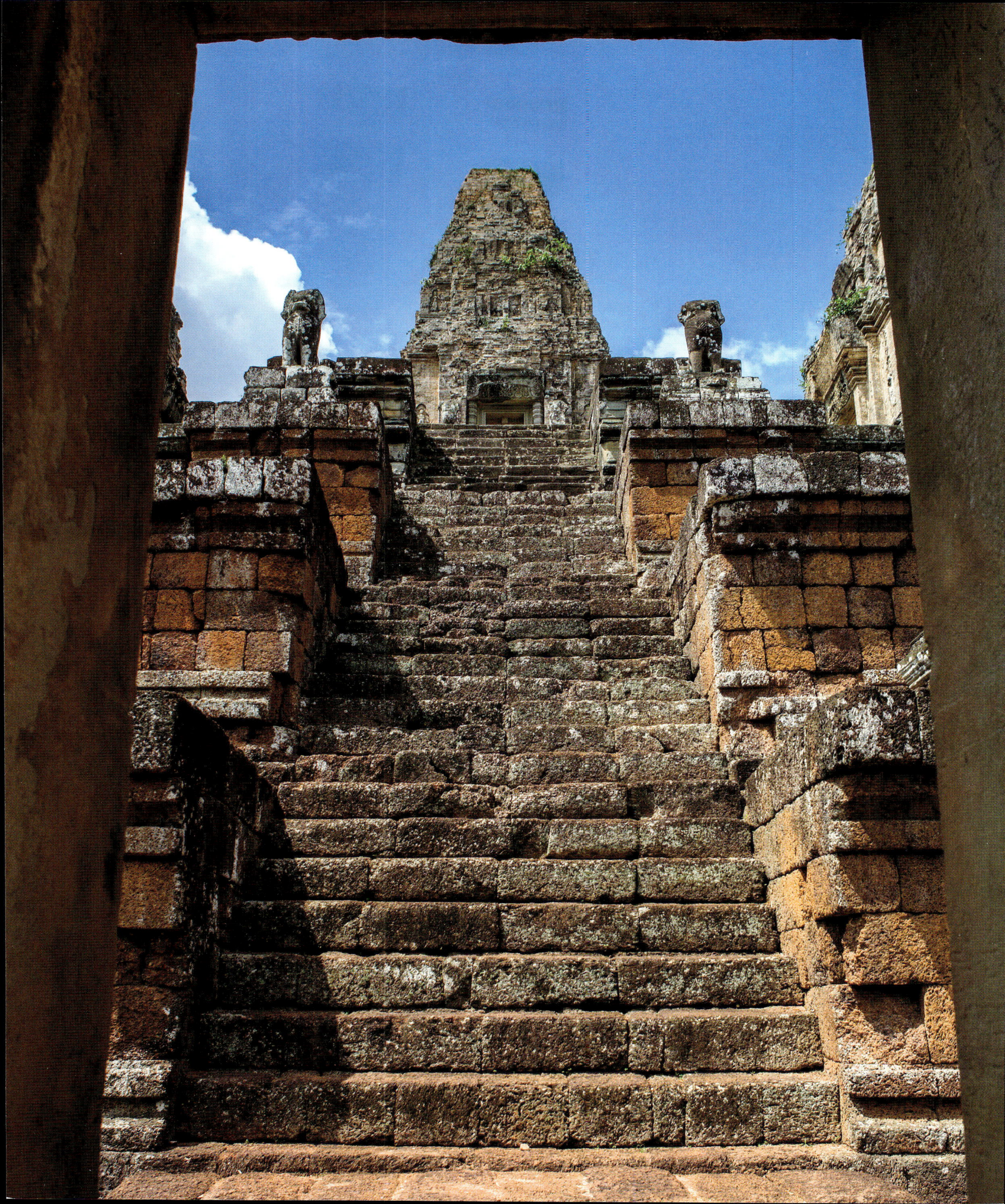

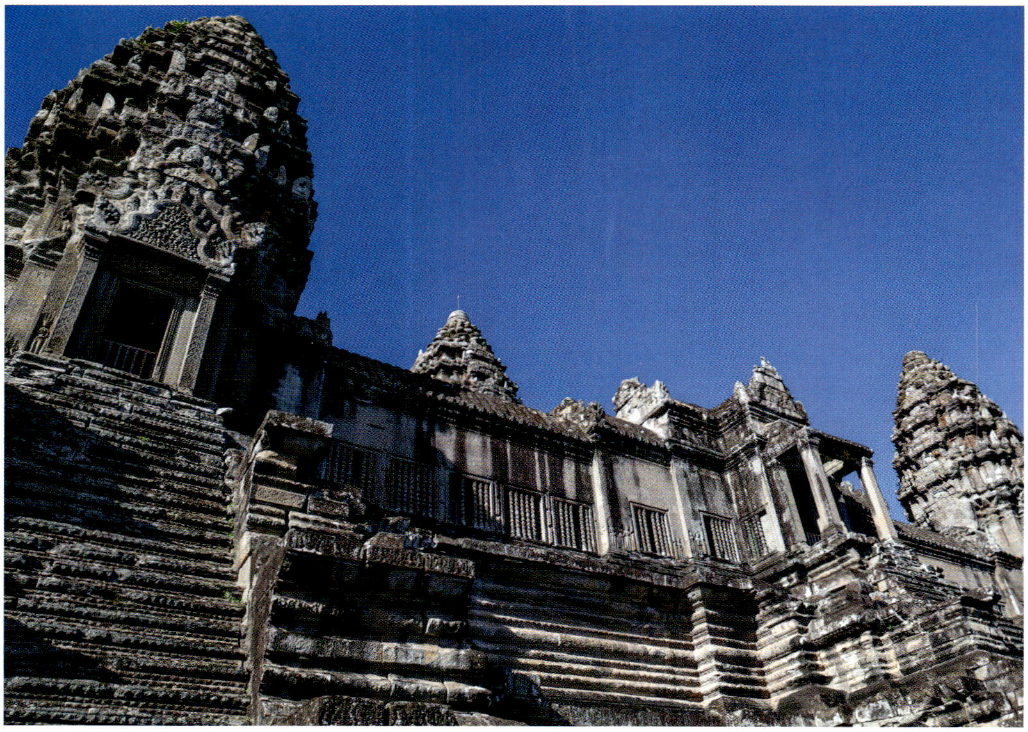

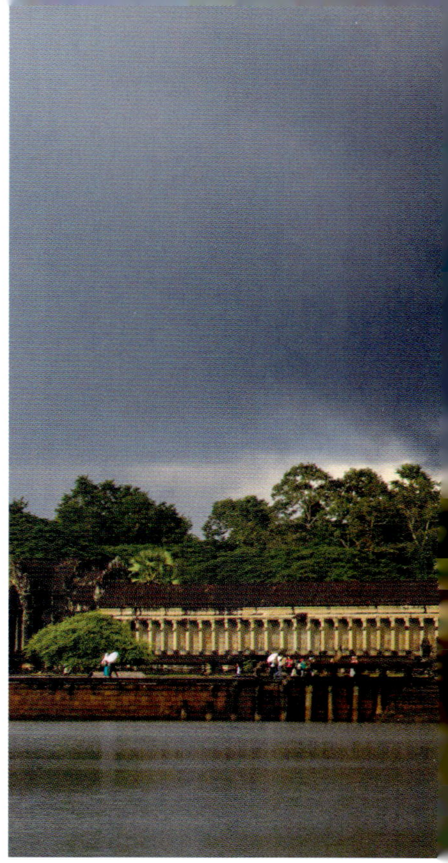

ANGKOR WAT

Of Angkor's many treasures, its finest is Angkor Wat, a truly magnificent and monumental temple which is without doubt one of the architectural wonders of the world. In her book *Angkor*, Asian art historian and scholar, Dawn Rooney said it displays "...perfection in composition, balance, proportions, reliefs and sculpture. This temple is an expression of Khmer art at its highest point of development". The complex extends over more than one square kilometre (a third of a square mile), and is made up of three levels and a central tower. Inscriptions bearing the name of Suryavarman II have led scholars to assert that construction started at the beginning of his rule in 1135 AD but was completed long after his death (thought to be around 1145–1150 AD). Angkor Wat took 30 years to complete.

Unlike other temples at Angkor that have entrances facing east, the orientation of Angkor Wat is to the west, a symbolic reference to the setting sun and death. The exquisite bas-reliefs within galleries also run from left to right as is commonly the case in Hindu tombs. Yet the design of Angkor Wat is clearly that of a temple. This has sparked debate among scholars as to whether it was constructed as a temple or a tomb. The answer is probably both; that it was a place of worship but also used as a mausoleum following the king's death.

Angkor Wat's three levels contain numerous galleries, courtyards and chambers. It is approached by a lengthy causeway across a broad moat leading to three entry towers and its façade. The entire complex is enclosed by a laterite wall. The causeway continues through the entrance and on to the Terrace of Honour where ritual dances are said to have been performed.

It is in the Gallery of Bas-reliefs that the true artistic majesty of Angkor Wat is revealed. The four covered walkways are open to the elements on one side and feature stunning carvings in a two-metre (6½-ft) band running left to right that tell tales of warfare and Indian myths and cover 1,200 m² (12,920 sq. ft) in total. The detail is simply exquisite. The west gallery recounts a mythical battle from the Hindu epic, the *Mahahbharata*, with images of rivals fighting fiercely on chariots and elephants. In the south-west corner is a scene from the *Reamker*, while the southern gallery documents an historical event showing Suryavarman II's army victorious in battle. This section also shows a rather gruesome depiction of hell and above it celestial Apsaras in heaven. It is the eastern gallery, however, that features Angkor Wat's masterpiece; a visually arresting interpretation of the Churning of the Sea of Milk (see page 116).

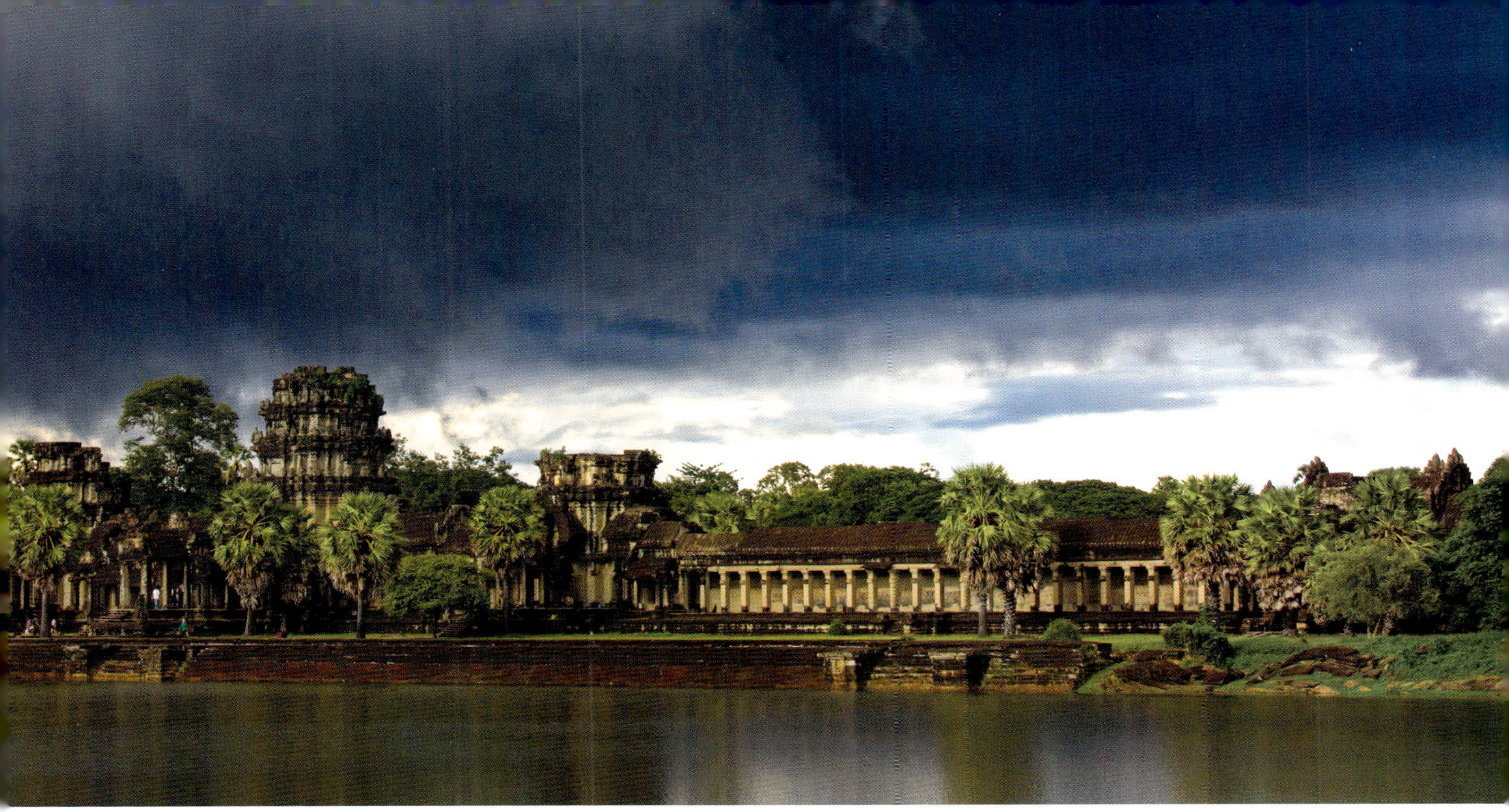

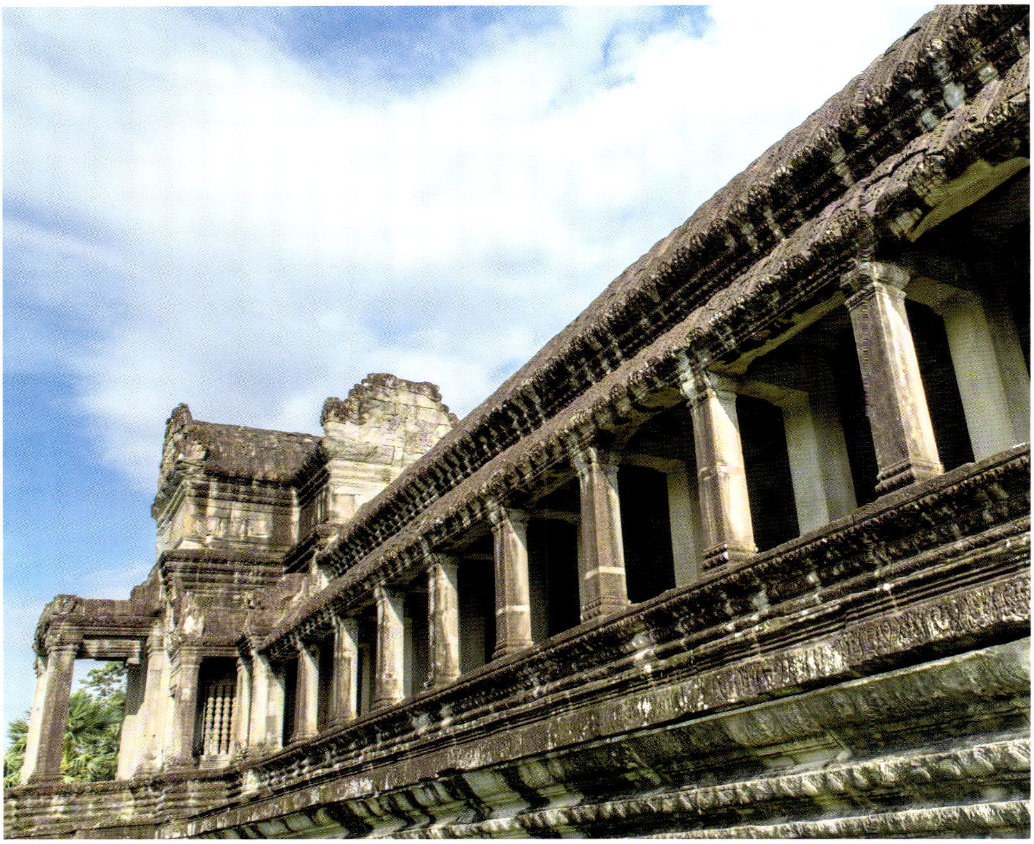

Above: The entranceway to Angkor Wat beneath a threatening sky. There are fewer visitors during the rainy season but the brief and heavy downpours do not spoil the experience.

Left: One side of the open pavilion that houses the Gallery of Bas-reliefs, home to some of the world's most accomplished stone carvings.

Opposite: The third level of Angkor Wat is crowned by five towers, one of which contains a revered Buddha image.

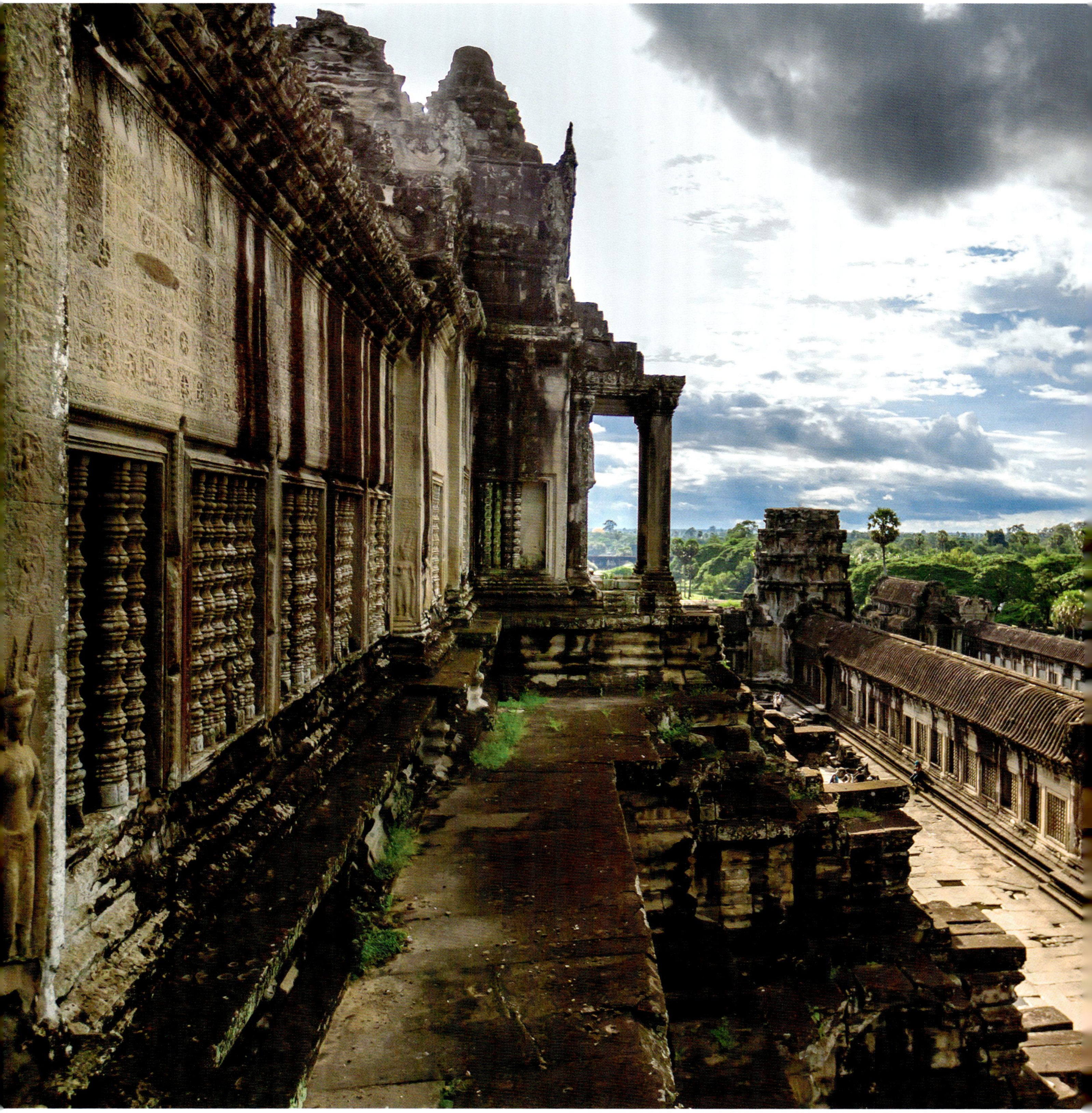

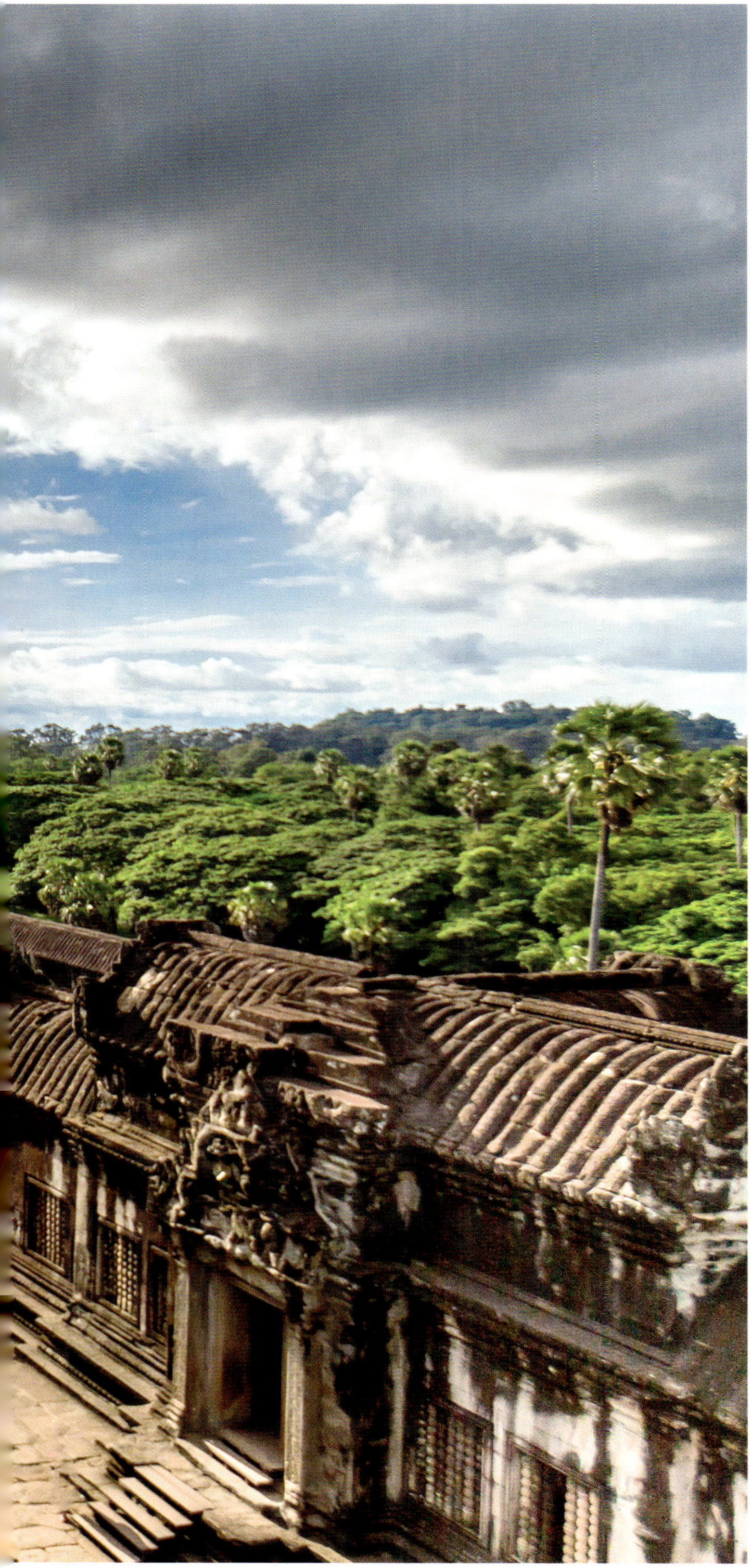

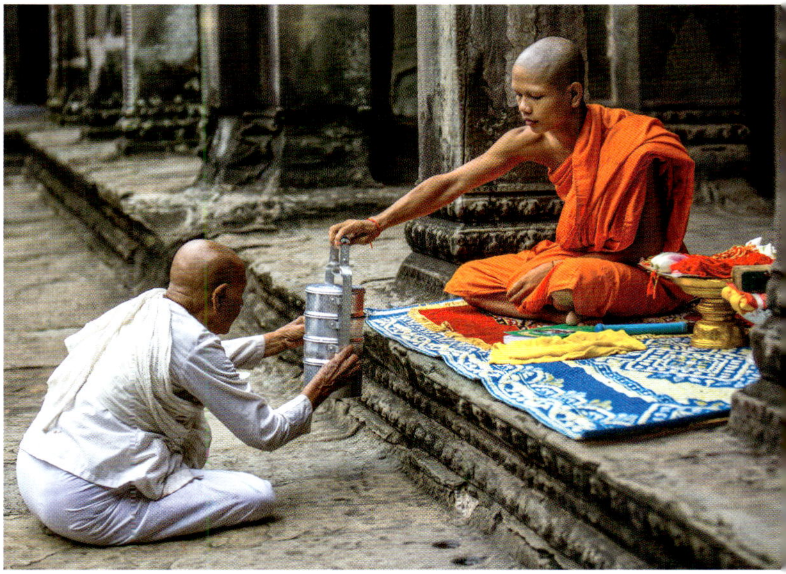

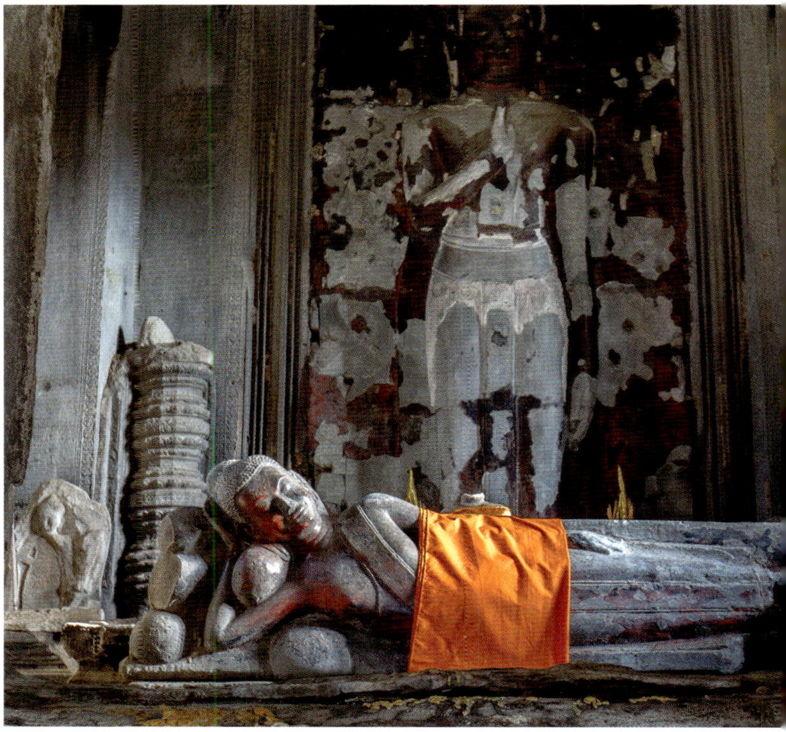

Above: A shrine within one of Angkor Wat's five towers on the third level houses an image of a reclining Buddha.

Top: A young Buddhist monk sitting within a gallery of Angkor Wat's second level collecting alms from an elderly nun.

Left: Looking out from the third level of Angkor Wat with the galleries of the second level visible below.

THE CHURNING OF THE SEA OF MILK

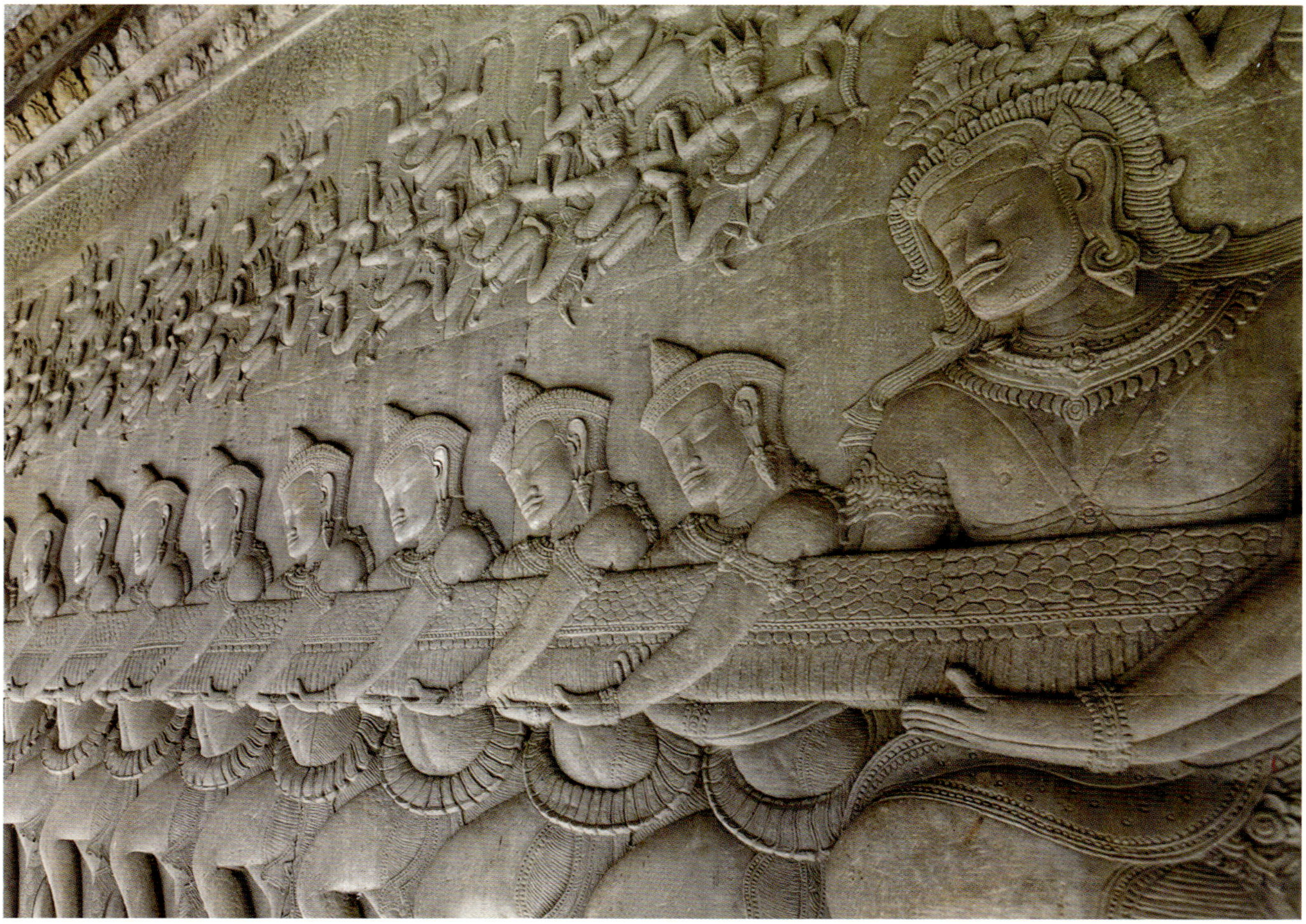

A highlight of Angkor Wat is the bas-relief of the Churning of the Sea of Milk, a stunning depiction of the Hindu myth of creation. The intricate 70-m (230-ft) panel runs the entire length of the temple's east gallery and is regarded as the one of the world's most exquisite stone carvings.

Divided into three sections running horizontally along the gallery, the centre of the scene depicts the serpent Vasuki being pulled to and fro by 92 demons at the head end while 88 gods, with the assistance of Hanuman, the monkey god, pull on the tail in an effort to produce the elixir of immortality, a task they endured for one thousand years. The lower section shows real and mythical aquatic creatures in the sea; above graceful flying Apsaras look down on the giant tug-of-war.

In the myth, Vasuki wraps himself around Mount Mandara which acts as a pivot but problems arise when the mount begins to sink and the constant churning causes the mighty serpent to spew his venom into the sea. To avert disaster and save the gods and demons, Shiva drinks the poison but it burns his throat and leaves a distinctive blue mark. Vishnu also intervenes in his reincarnation as a tortoise and uses his shell to prop up the mountain, and then appears in human form to oversee another one thousand years of churning.

Eventually, as shown in the middle section, the Sea of Milk gives forth *amrita*, the essence of life and immortality and other wonders including Airavata, the three-headed elephant, and the nymph-like Apsaras.

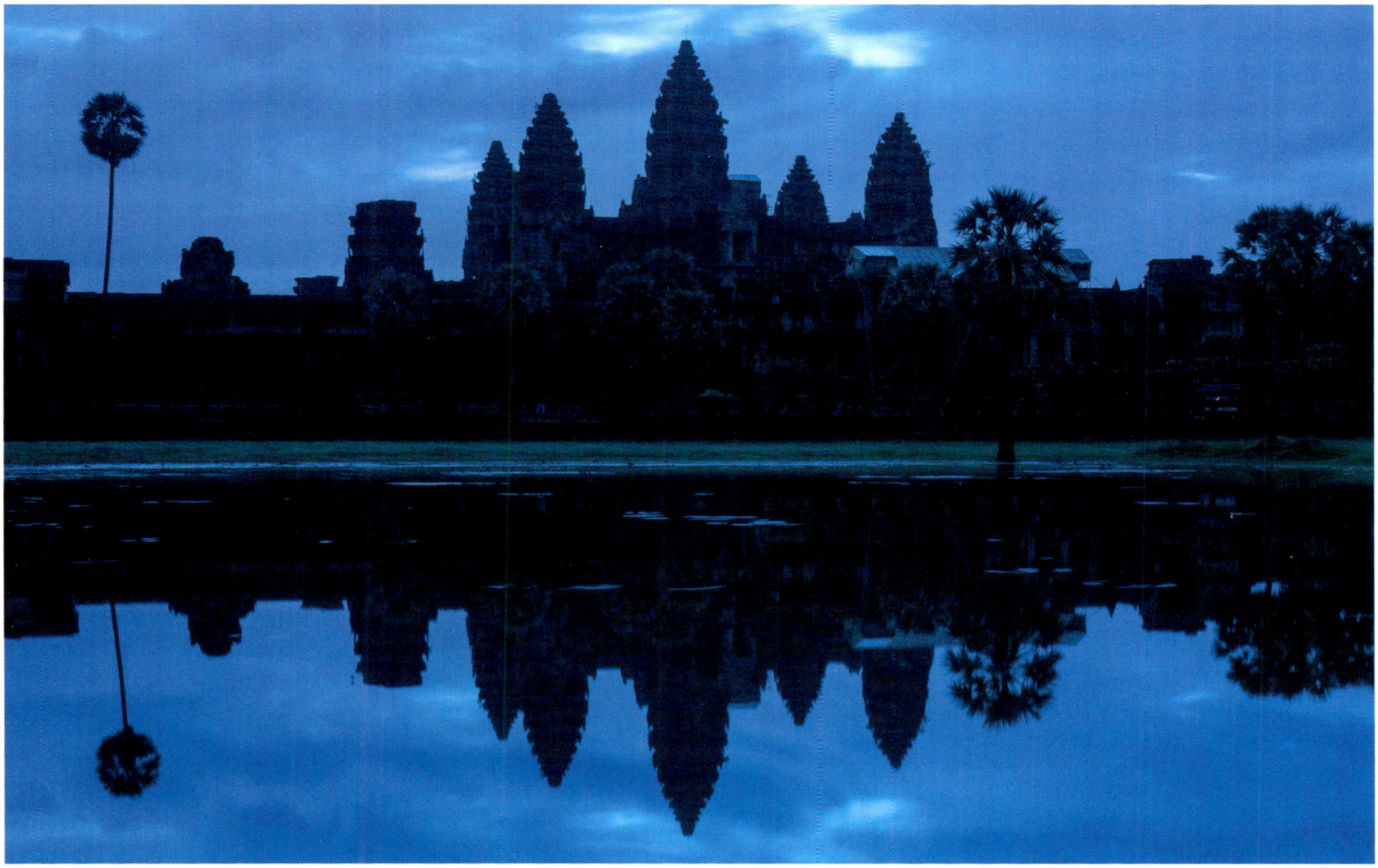

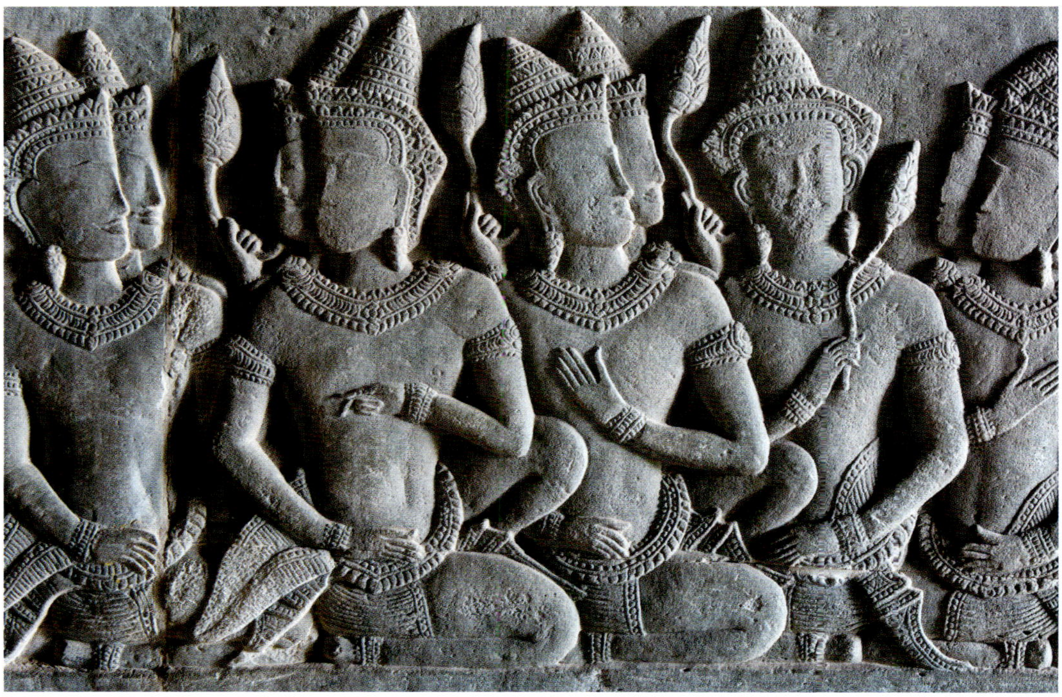

Above: The distinctive silhouette of Angkor Wat reflected in a pond at daybreak.

Left: Beautiful images carved in sandstone in the Gallery of Bas-reliefs. It is worthy of several visits at different times of day to see the carvings in light and shadow.

Overleaf top: Angkor Wat is always busy. Nothing has been done to limit the number of visitors, so that conservationists are increasingly concerned about the impact this is having on the temple.

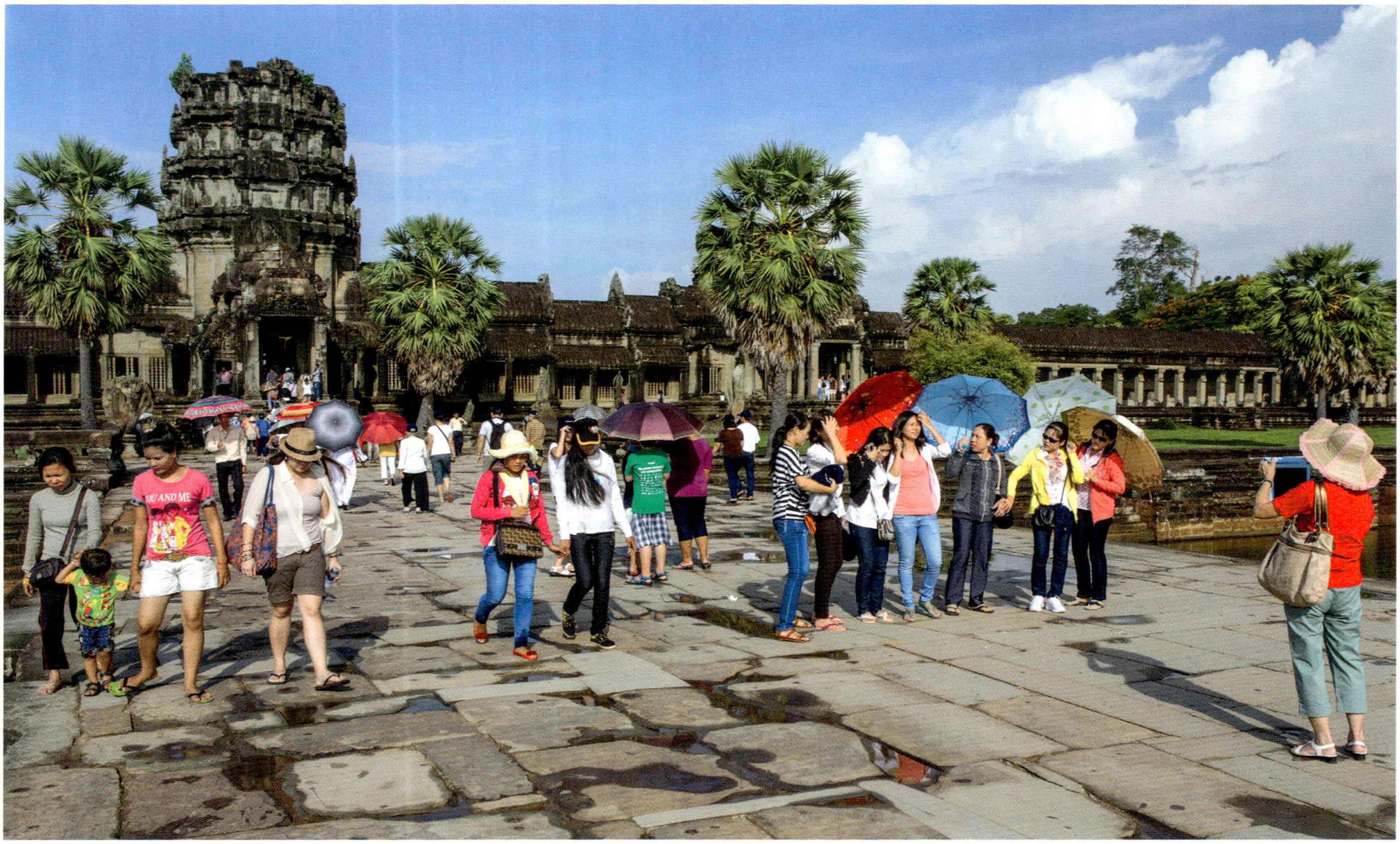

CHEEKY MONKEYS

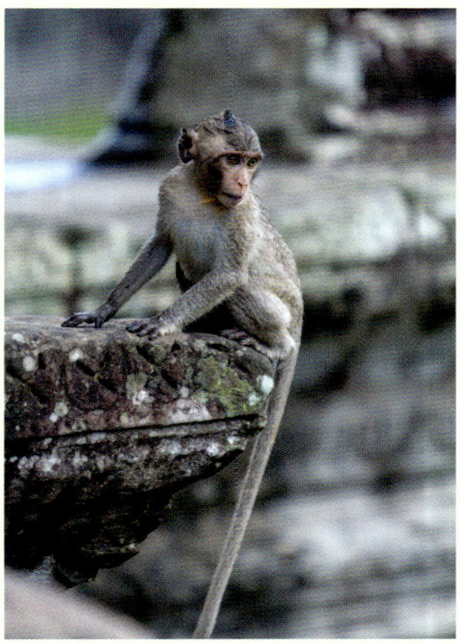

Visitors to Angkor Wat will see troupes of bright-eyed, long-tailed macaques that live in nearby trees. The females and their offspring are lead by a dominant male and spend the day clambering on temple walls and parading along galleries. Although they look delightful, be on guard. These cheeky monkeys are master criminals well practised in the art of hit-and-run theft. They will spot any opportunity to grab a bottle of water, fizzy drink or snacks from unsuspecting passersby. They are also very strong, fast and have extremely sharp teeth. Photographing Angkor's marauding macaques from a distance is advised.

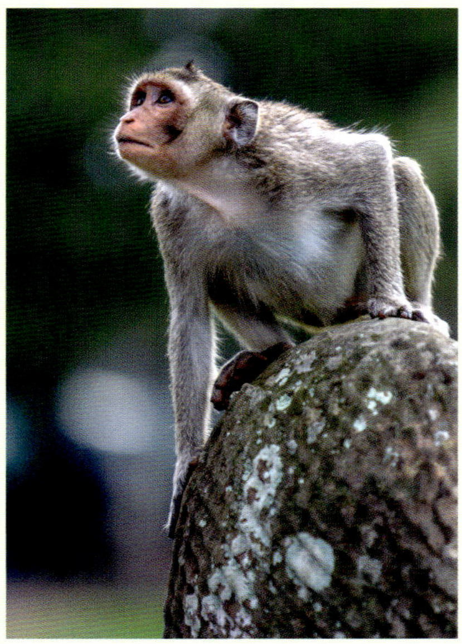

APSARAS AND DEVATAS – CAMBODIA'S CELESTIAL NYMPHS

Visitors to Cambodia soon add a new word to their vocabulary: Apsara. Often appropriated as a name for resorts, travel companies and restaurants, Apsaras are actually mythical female celestial dancers that graced the walls of Angkor-era temples as early as the eighth century AD.

Scholars of Khmer art and archaeology often differentiate between the sensual flying nymphs, or Apsaras, and the enigmatic standing figures, known as Devatas, which are thought to be guardians of the temple. Exquisite bas-reliefs of the highly stylized Apsara figures can be seen in abundance at Angkor Wat, where over 1,700 have been recorded, and at other ancient monuments of the UNESCO World Heritage Site.

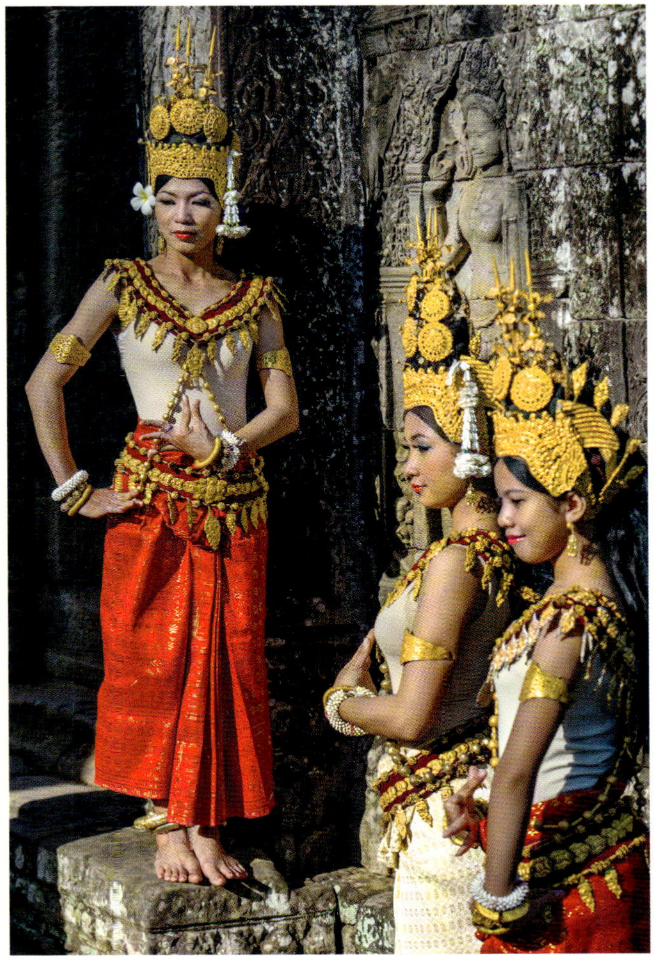

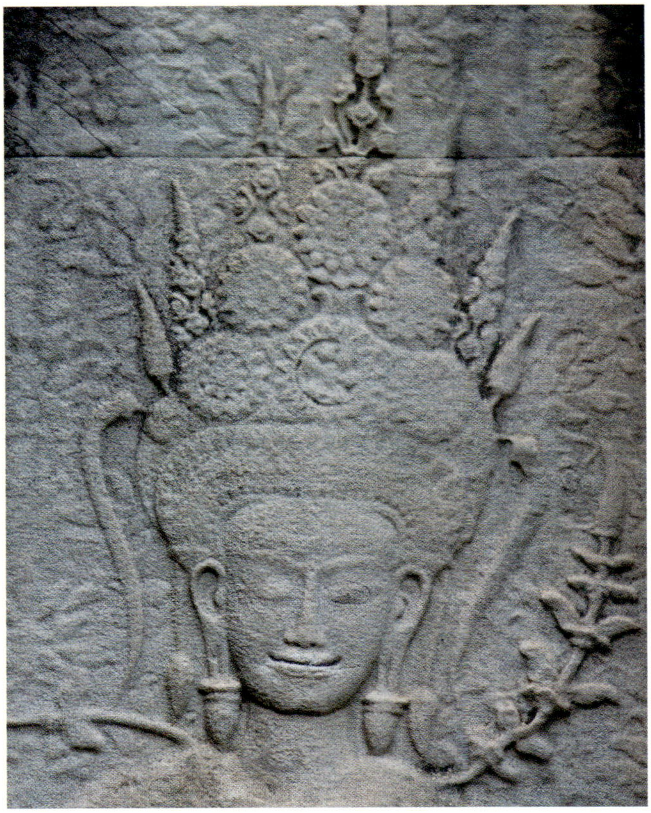

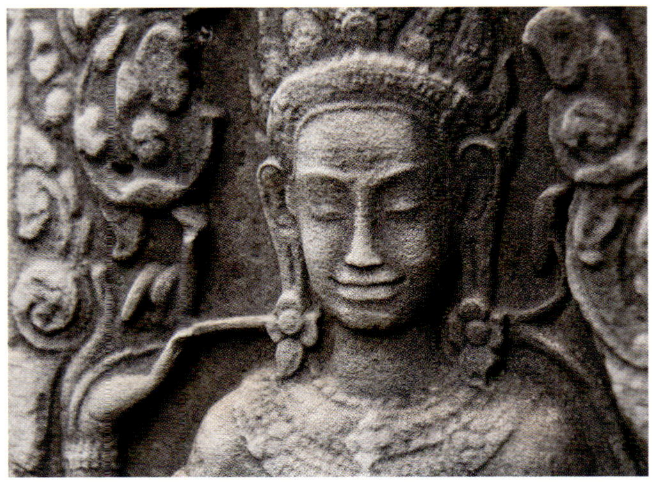

Above and below right: Although many of the Apsara images have faded with time, it seems only to have enhanced their astonishing beauty.

Above right: A trio of celestial nymphs bring the past to life.

ANGKOR THOM

Angkor Thom, or the Great City, was the last capital of Angkor. At its height, it is thought to have had a population of up to one million citizens, the majority of whom would have resided outside the city walls. The inner area would have been the domain of the king, his officials, priests and the military. Angkor Thom is approached across a causeway that spans an expansive moat. Lined with 54 grimacing, mythical demons on one side and 54 gods grasping nine-headed *naga* serpents on the other, it leads up to a grand 23-m (75-ft) *gopura*, an arched entranceway, topped with four massive stone heads facing north, east, south and west. There are five such gates providing access to Angkor Thom, one at each of the cardinal points plus at the Gate of Victory which also stands to the east. Once inside, Angkor Thom's treasures include the Royal Palace (of which little remains), the Terrace of Elephants, the Terrace of the Leper King, and most spectacular of all, the Bayon.

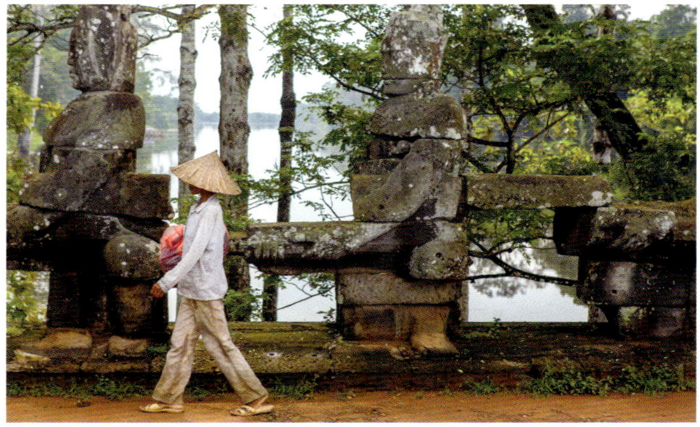

Above: A woman walking across the causeway leading to Angkor Thom. The huge balustrade features 108 stone image, 54 demons on one side and 54 gods on the other, all grasping *naga* serpents.
Below: The road through the grounds of Angkor Thom.
Opposite: Angkor Thom has five arched entranceways, or *gopuras*, each 23 m (75 ft) high and topped with four stone faces.

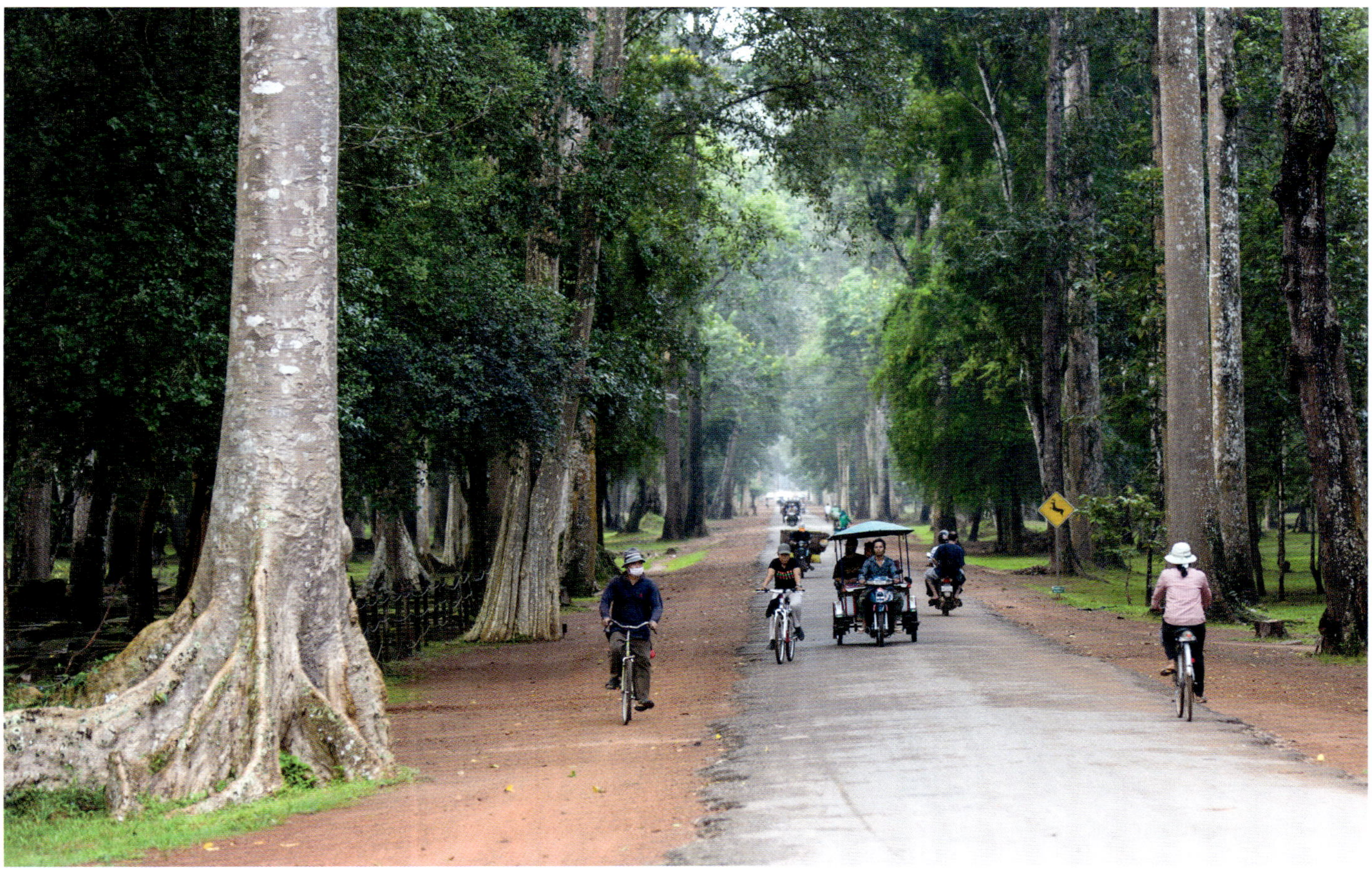

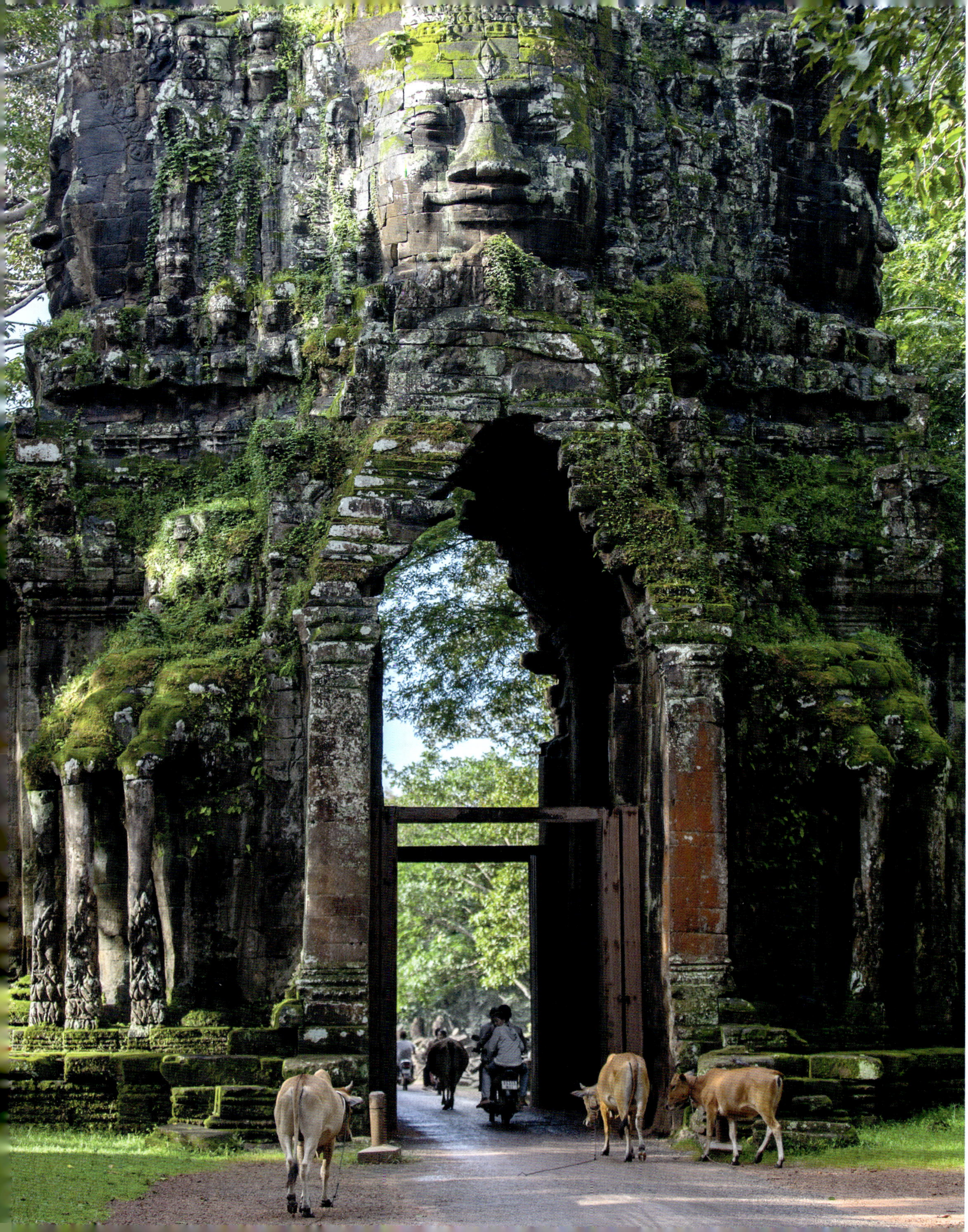

Located at the centre of Angkor Thom, Bayon is undoubtedly one of Angkor's most visually impressive temples. It was originally thought to be a Hindu temple dating from the ninth century but later, following the discovery of a Bodhisattva Avalokiteshvara image, was reclassified as Buddhist and dated to the late 12th century. Angkor Thom is rich with symbolism and its Bayon is said to be a link between heaven and earth.

Each of Bayon's 54 towers features four carved faces, over 200 in total, each believed to be a likeness of Jayavarman VII (1181–1220). Although the powerful imagery of the enigmatic carved faces is the magnet that draw visitors to the temple, the bas-reliefs on the gallery walls are exquisite and should not be overlooked. Providing insight into daily life, they include scenes of dancing, cooking, pottery making, fishing and hunting, all executed with superb craftsmanship and attention to detail.

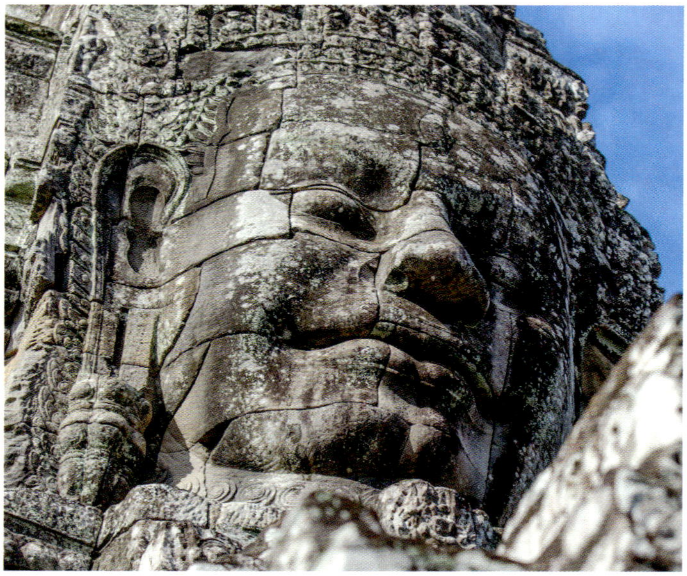

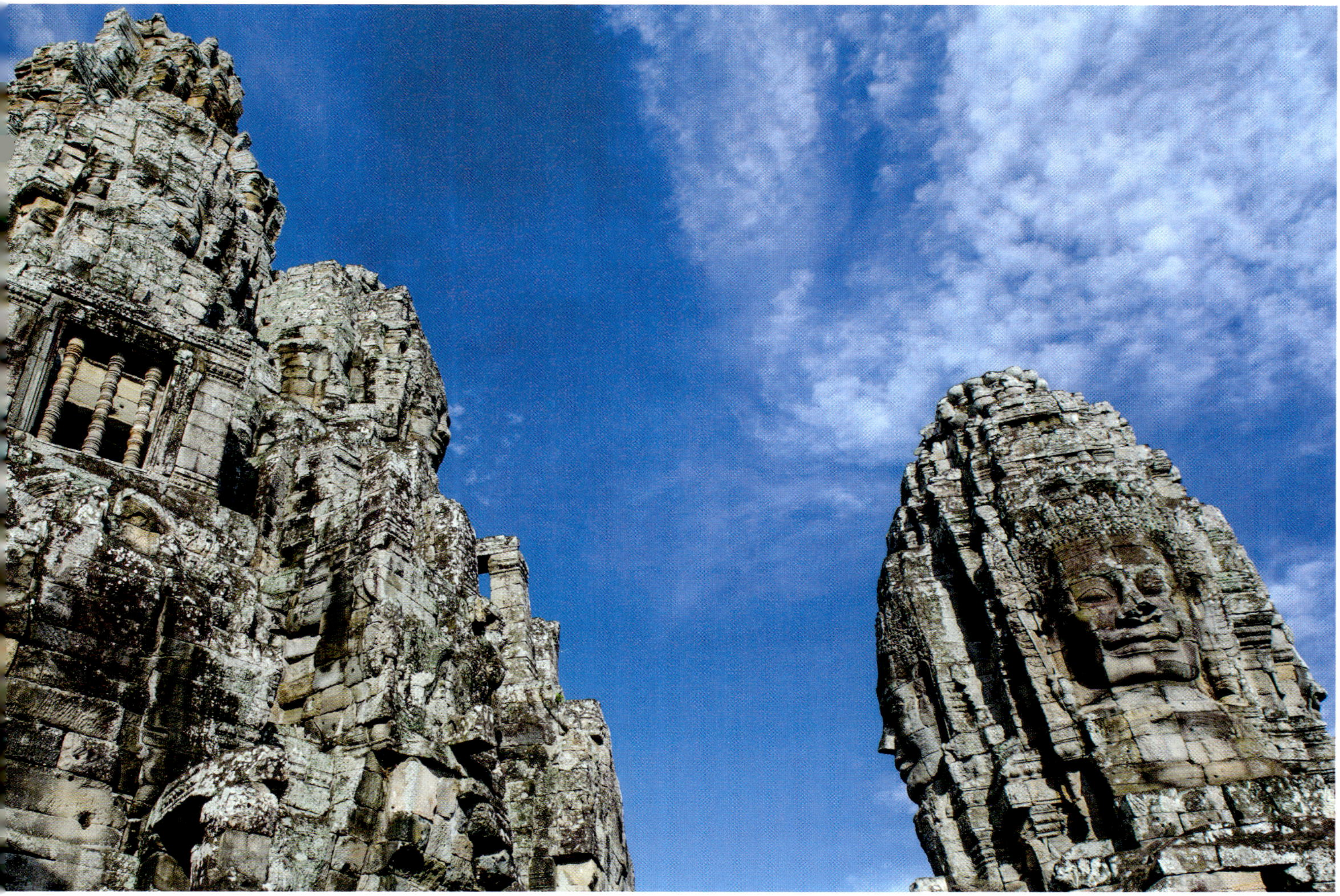

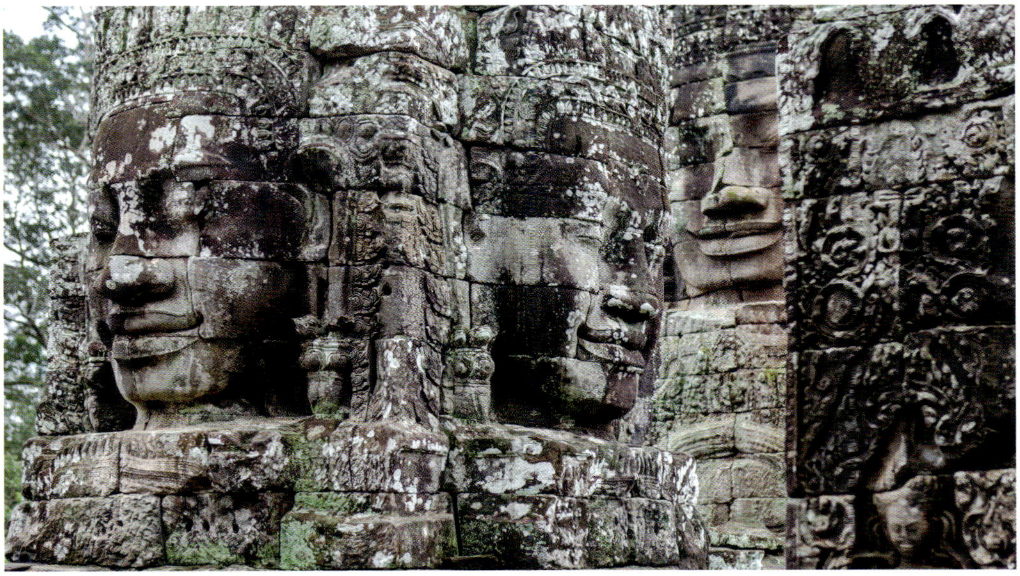

These pages: In 1296, the sight of Bayon left the Chinese emissary, Zhou Daguan, spellbound. Over 700 years later, its mysterious allure remains as powerful as ever.

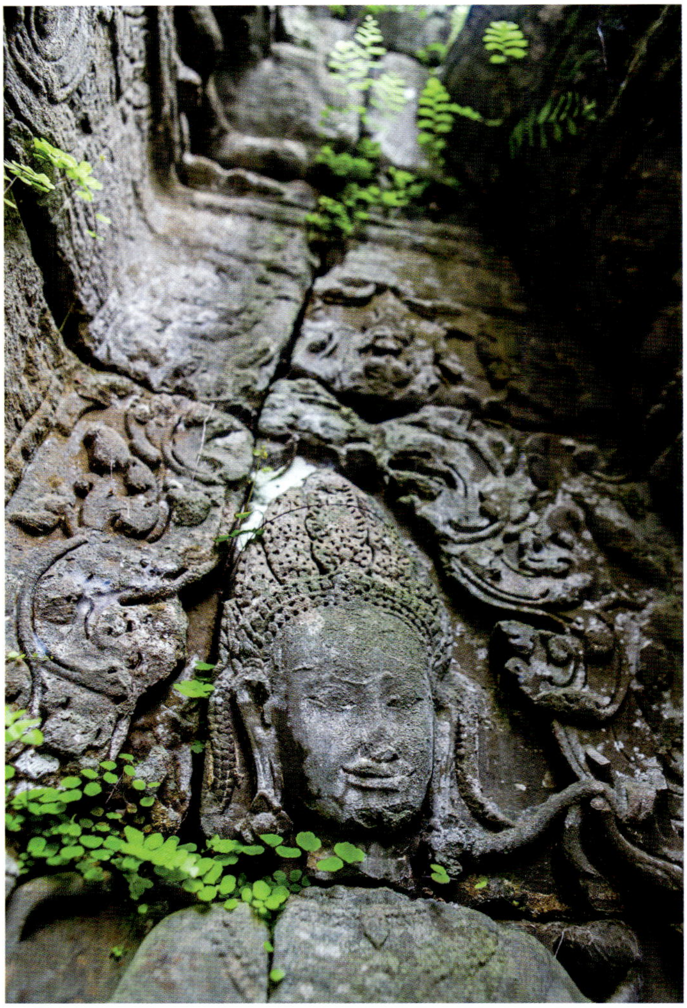

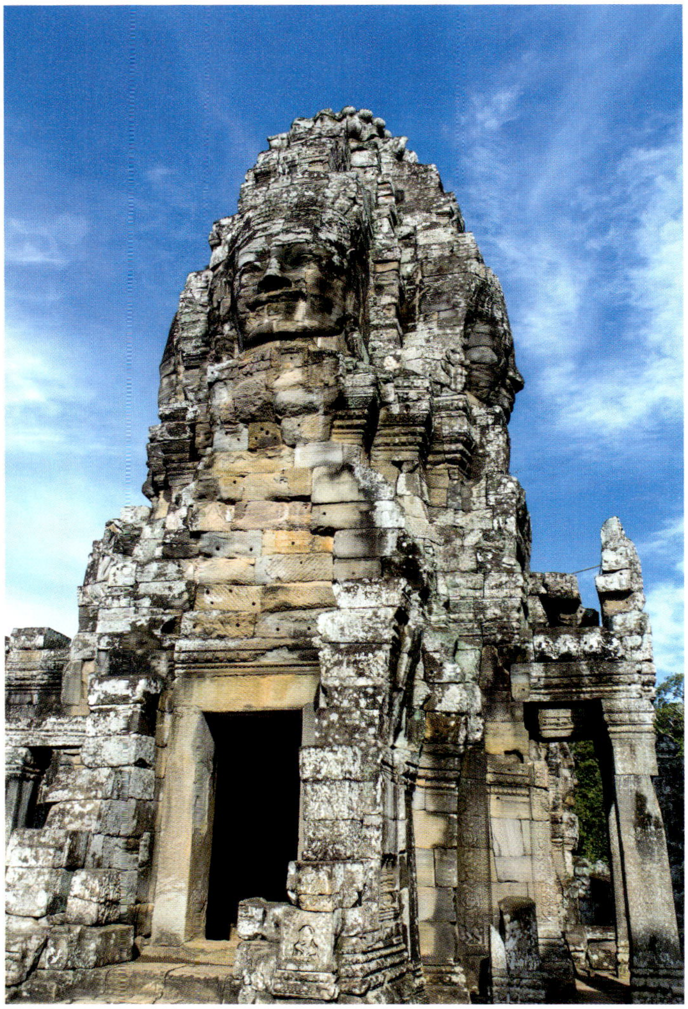

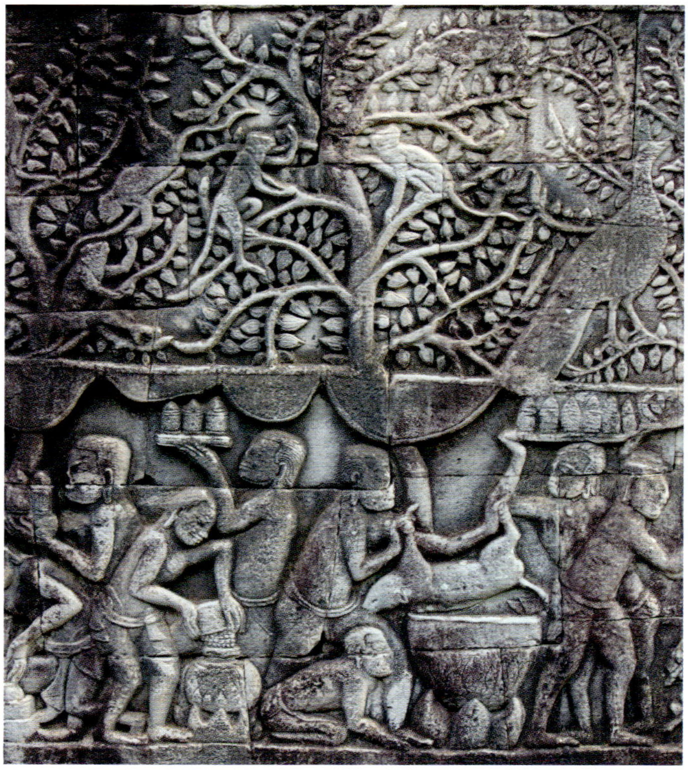

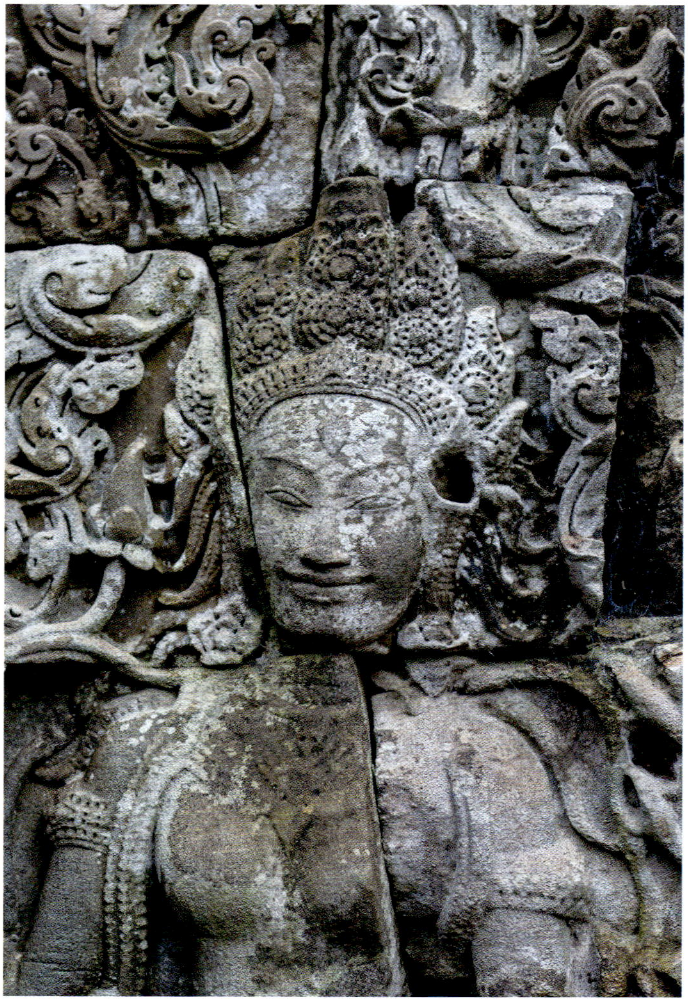

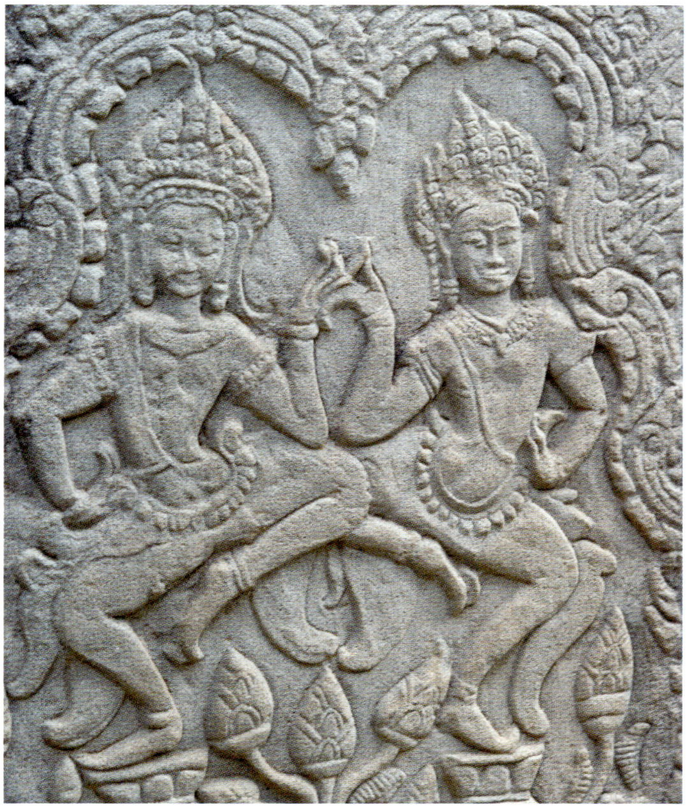

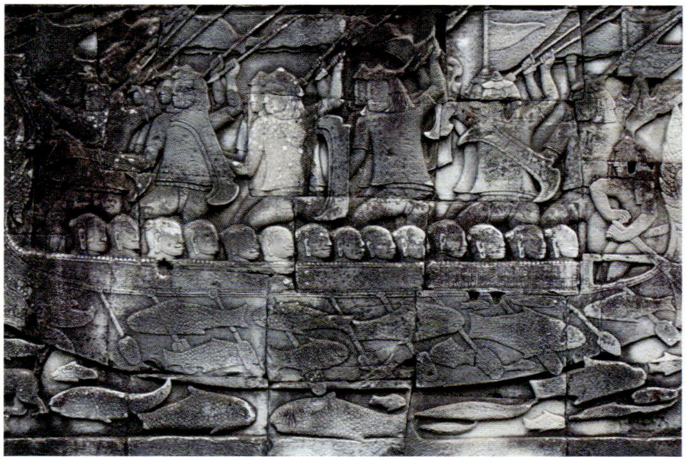

This page: Bayon's 54 towers dominate the temple but its outstanding stone carvings should not be overlooked.

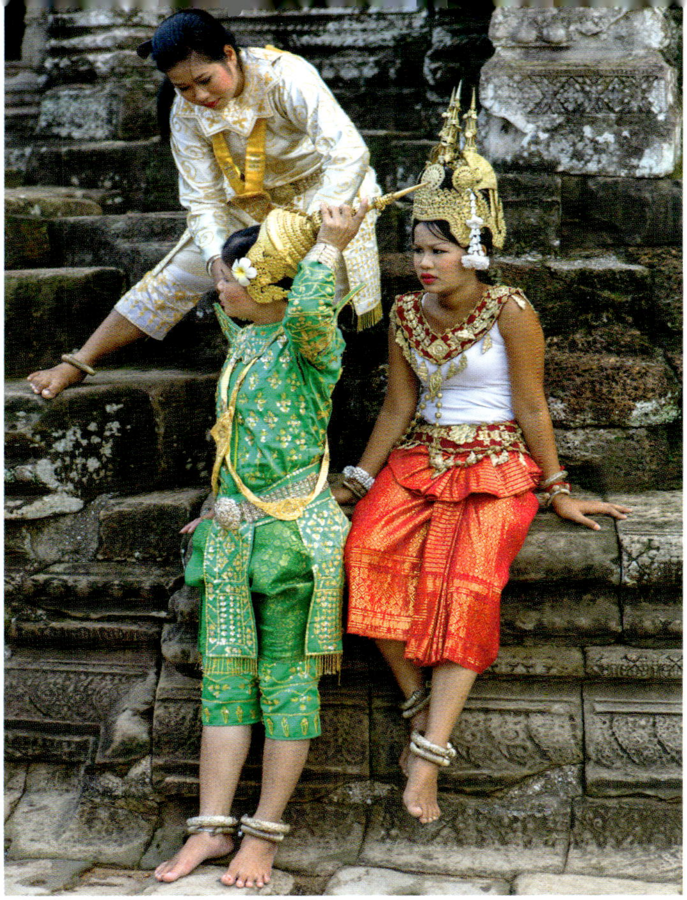

The Terrace of Elephants stretches for 300 m (985 ft) across the front of the Royal Palace. Lined with carvings of almost life-size pachyderms – *garudas* or mythical bird-like creatures – and scenes of hunting, it was built for Jayavarman VII but over the years it was altered and extended. The terrace, which was used for grand ceremonies and as a viewing platform for welcoming the returning army, can be approached by five stairways, one at each end and three at the front.

Immediately north is the Terrace of the Leper King. Also built during Jayavarman VII's reign, it features fabulous bas-reliefs along the exterior and interior walls. The terrace derives its name from a statue of the Leper King found here and is thought to represent either Kubera, the god of wealth, or Yasovarman I, both of whom suffered from leprosy. However, several other theories have been expressed including that the terrace was used as the site for a royal cremation and that the statue is the god of death. The image of the seated Leper King on the terrace is a copy – the original can be seen in the courtyard of the National Museum in Phnom Penh.

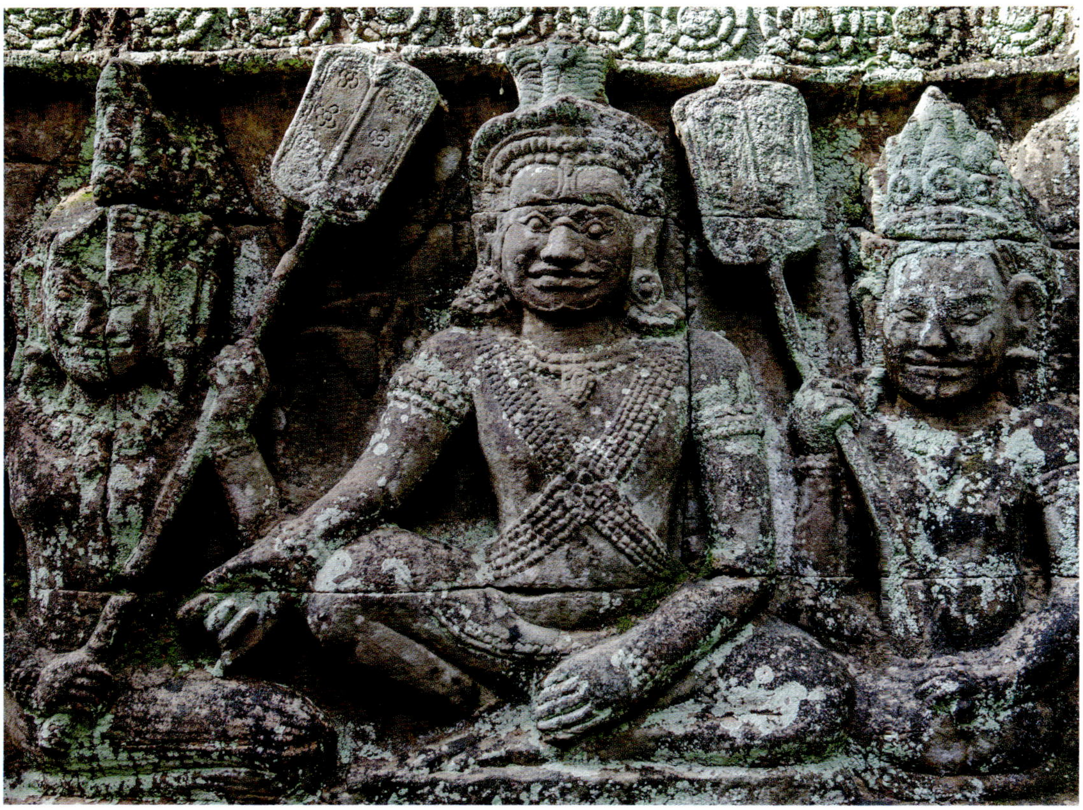

Above: As one of Angkor's most popular temples, Bayon is also a place to find reincarnations of Apsaras, each with the less-than-celestial aim of relieving tourists of their dollars in exchange for a hastily snapped photo.

Left: Bayon's extensive galleries and many niches feature religious and mythical imagery, as well as scenes from everyday life.

TA PROHM – THE *TOMB RAIDER* TEMPLE

Ta Prohm has become one of Angkor's most visited temples since it was used as a set in the Hollywood movie, *Tomb Raider,* starring Angelina Jolie as Lara Croft.

Ta Prohm lies to the east of Angkor Thom. It was constructed from the mid-12th century to the early 13th century during the reign of Jayavarman VII. Inscriptions found at the site but now removed for safekeeping to the National Museum in Phnom Penh state that Ta Prohm controlled 3,140 villages in the area. The entire site, at the heart of which sits one of the largest temple complexes in the area, is enclosed by a laterite wall. Once inside visitors can explore a network of galleries, passageways and inner sanctuaries.

When it was rediscovered by explorers in the 19th century, Ta Prohm had long since been enveloped by the slowly advancing forest. Seeds dropped from the canopy above had taken root in crevices and grown into towering trees, supported on a base of Angkorian stone. It was as if the entire temple had morphed into another life form. In the 1950s, the British travel writer Norman Lewis said in his book *A Dragon Apparent: Travels in Cambodia, Laos and Vietnam,* "Ta Prohm is an arrested cataclysm. In its invasion, the forest has not broken through it, but poured over the top, and the many courtyards have become cavities and holes in the forest's false bottom". And little has changed save for a little structural re-enforcement and restoration. The temple remains the domain of the forest and is one of Angkor's most extraordinary sights.

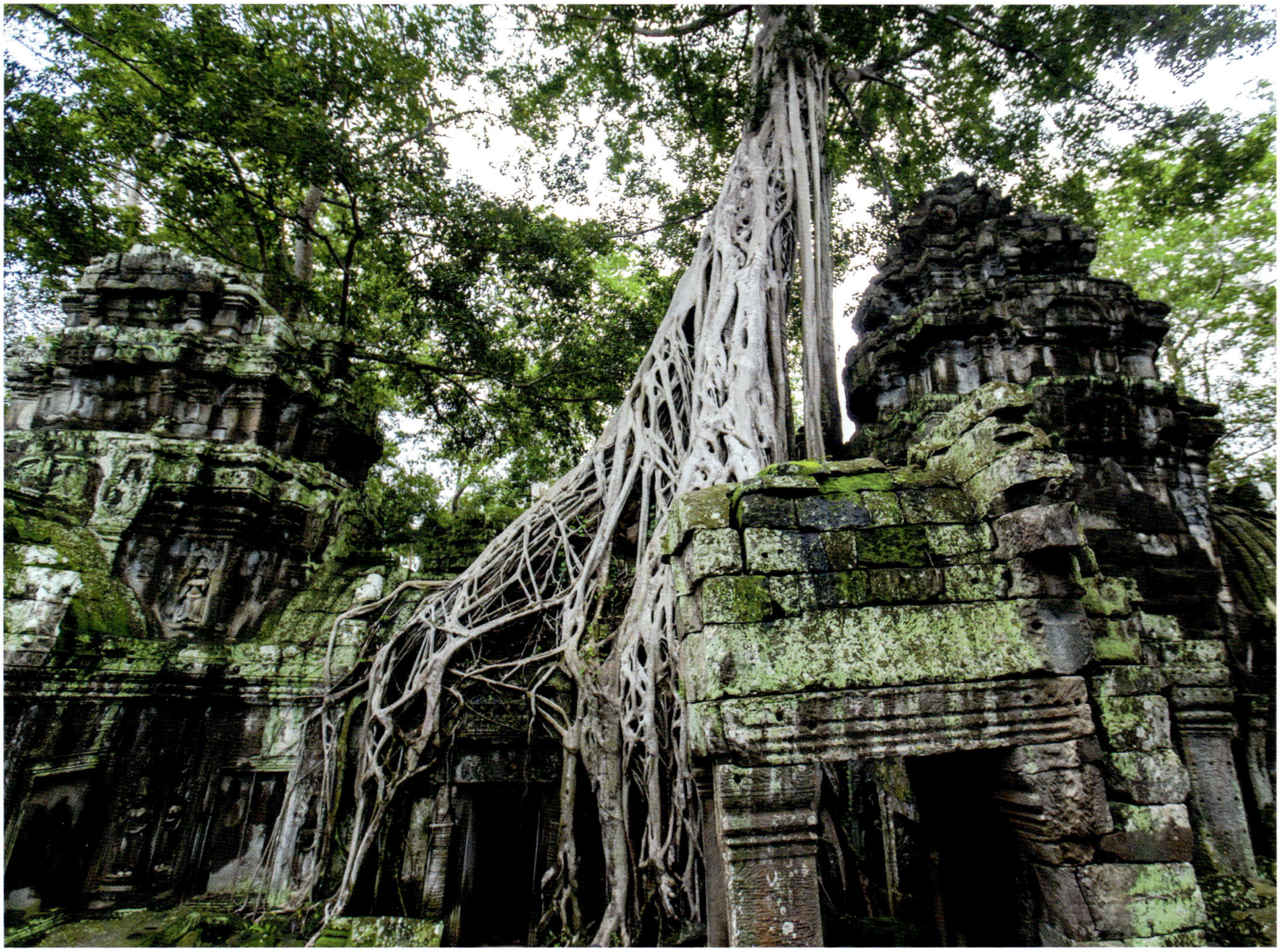

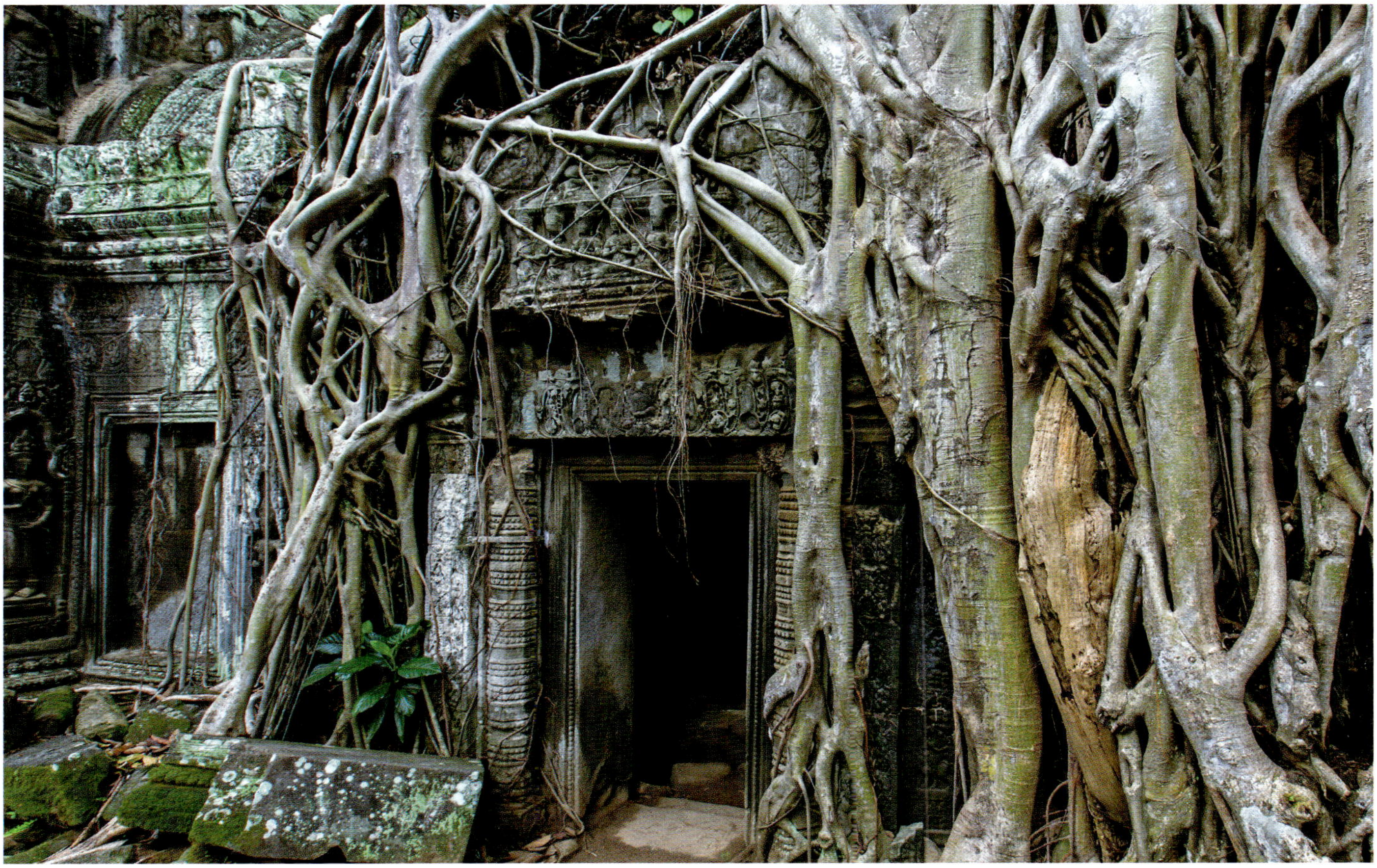

Above: After Ta Prohm was rediscovered in the 19th century, pathways were cleared so that it could be easily accessed and surveyed but all the major Kapok and Banyan trees that straddled the ruins were left in place.
Right: Images of Apsaras carved into a recess at Ta Prohm.
Opposite: In the mid-1930s, author H. W. Ponder wrote of Ta Prohm, "Everywhere around you, you see nature in its dual role of destroyer and consoler; strangling on the one hand, and healing on the other; no sooner splitting the carved stone asunder than she dresses their wounds with cool, velvety mosses...".

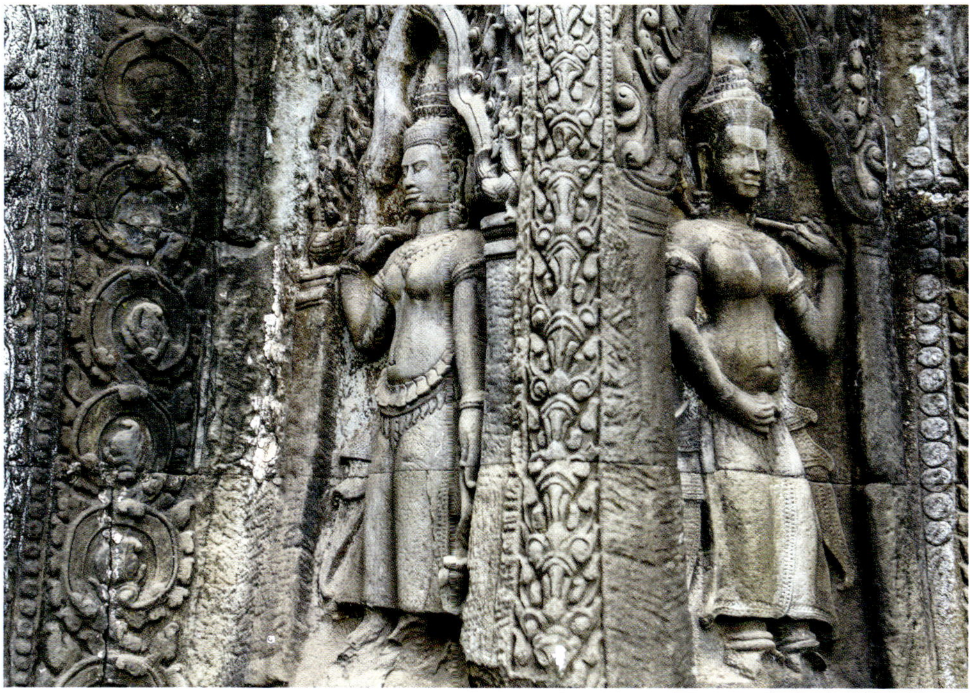

PREAH KHAN – THE CITY OF THE SACRED SWORD

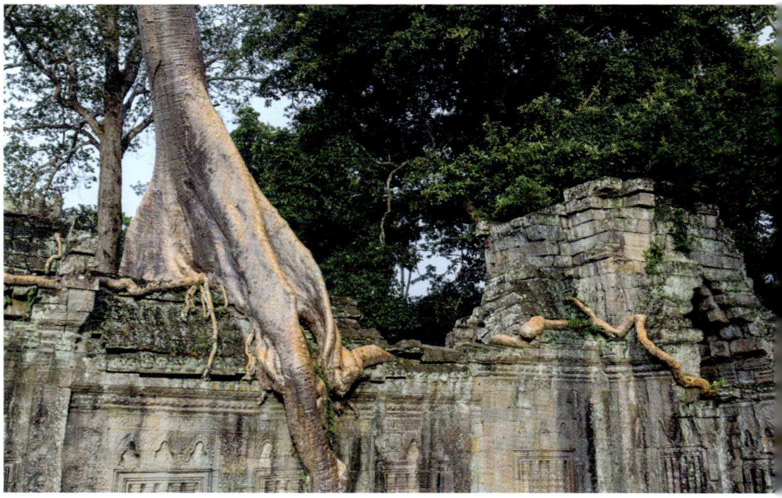

Preah Kahn, or The City of the Sacred Sword, is a reference to Jayavarman VII's victory over Cham invaders in 1191. The huge Buddhist complex was built on the battlefield. Like Ta Prohm, the 23-hectare (56-acre) site has been taken over by the forest. With its massive trees rooted in stone, dimly lit corridors and small courtyards to explore, it is one of the most atmospheric of Angkor's temples, particularly when bathed in the warm glow of late afternoon light. It is at this time of day that the images come to life and the true beauty of time-weathered stone is revealed.

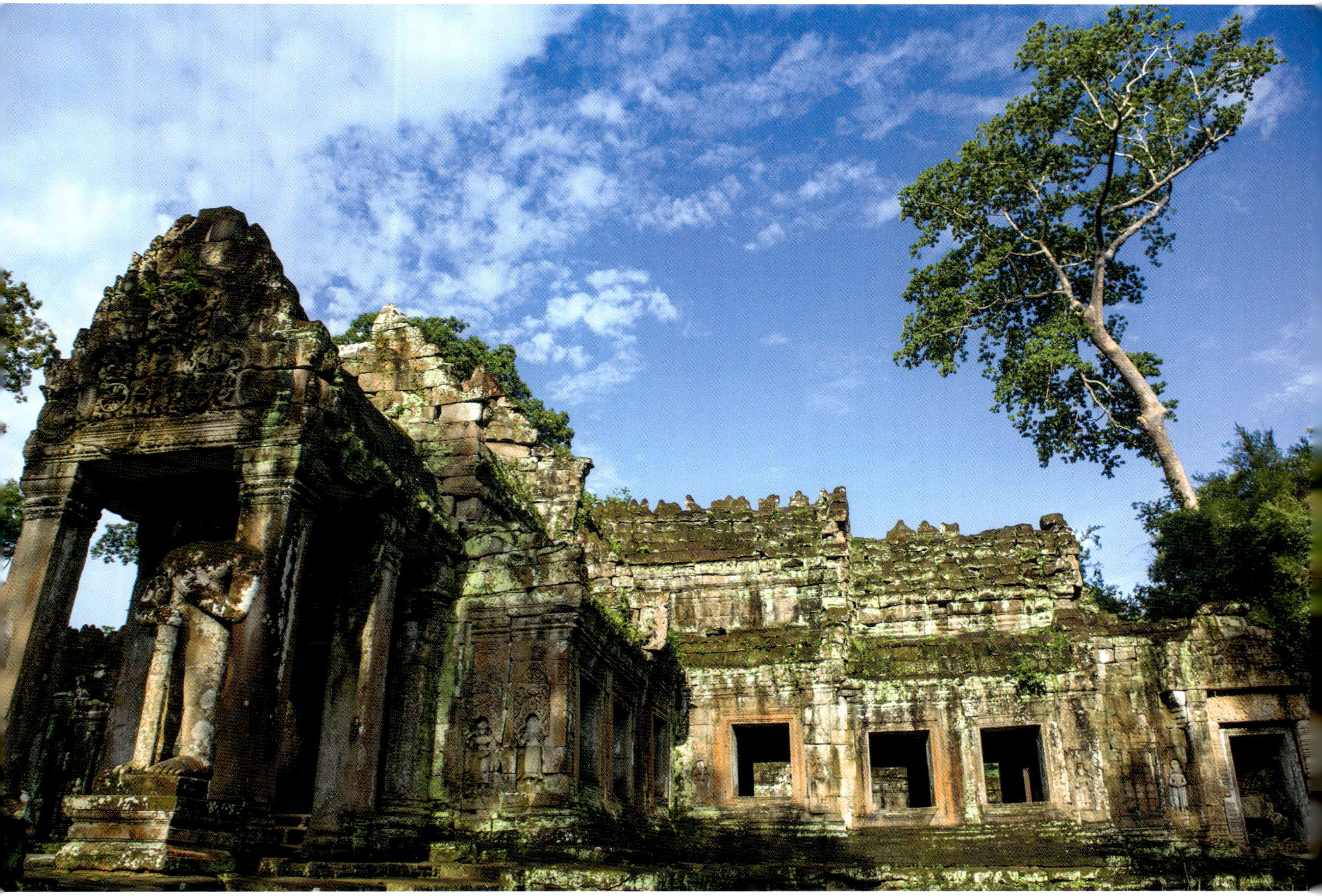

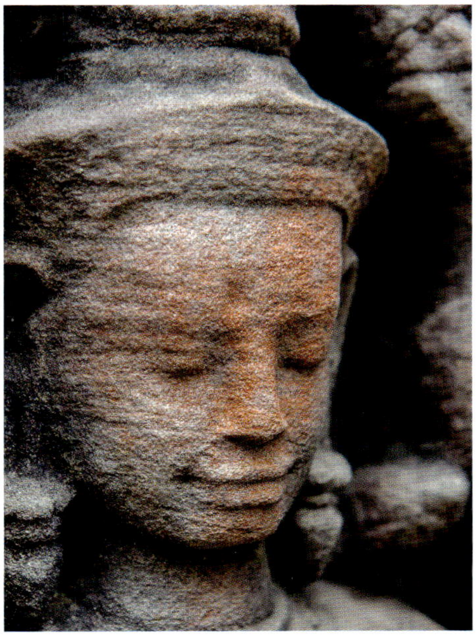

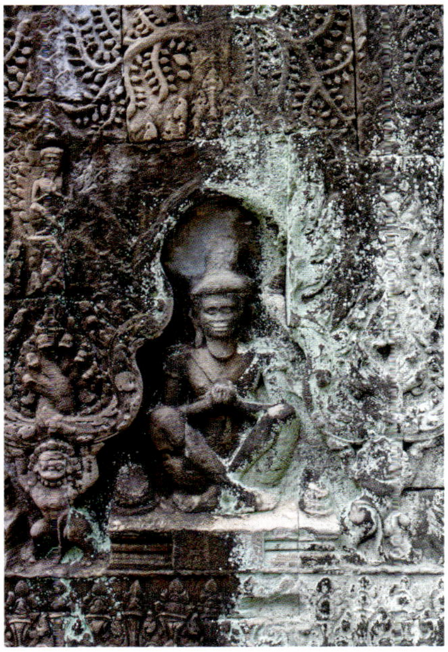

Left and far left: The courtyard walls at Preah Khan feature sandstone carvings of exceptional beauty.

Below: Preah Khan is an extremely atmospheric temple complex. Its network of corridors and courtyards, ceremonial spaces and shrines are a delight to explore.

Opposite page: When Preah Khan was rediscovered by the French in the 19th century, it was comprehensively documented by archaeclogists and art historians. Today, it is benefiting from ongoing conservation work.

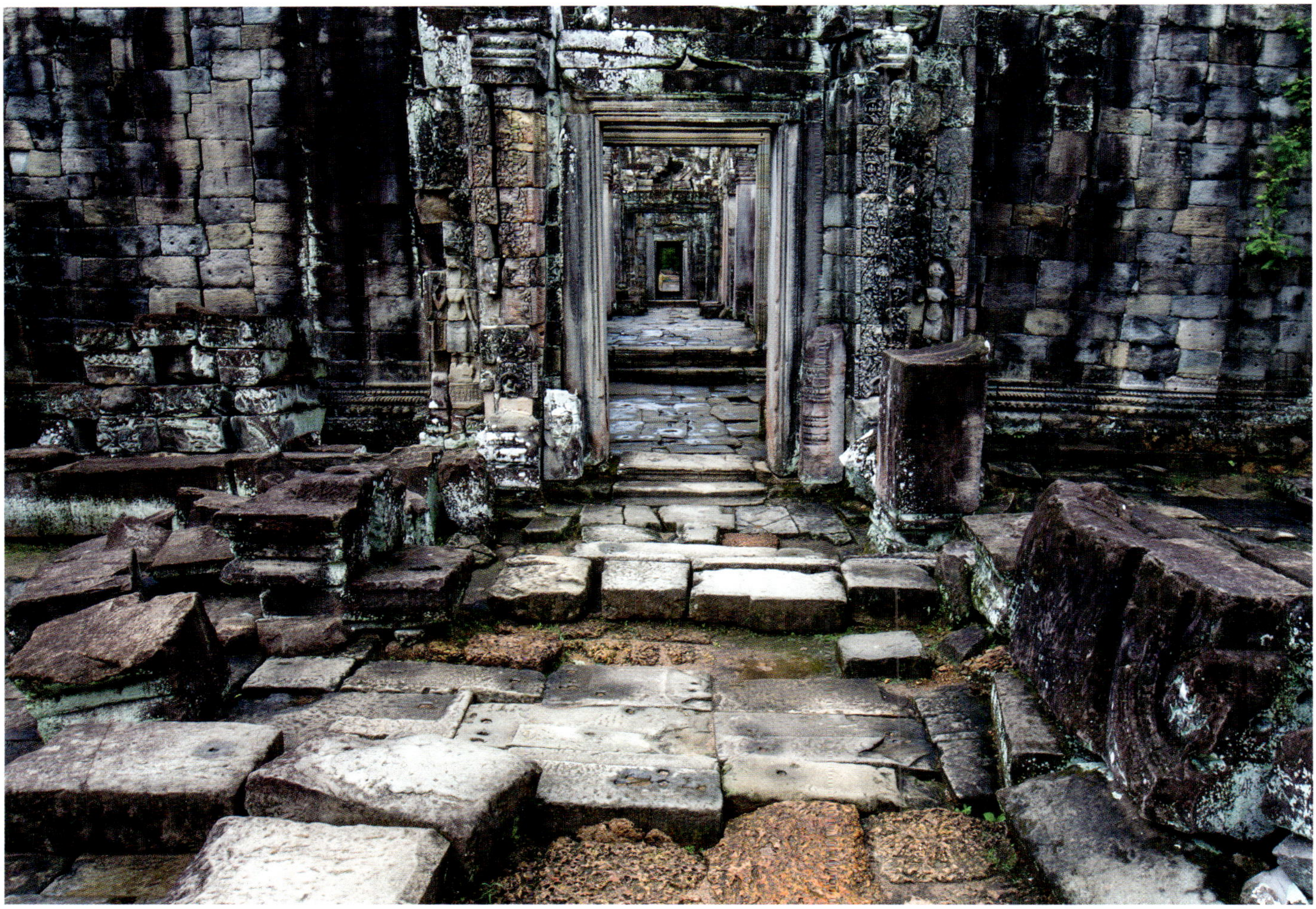

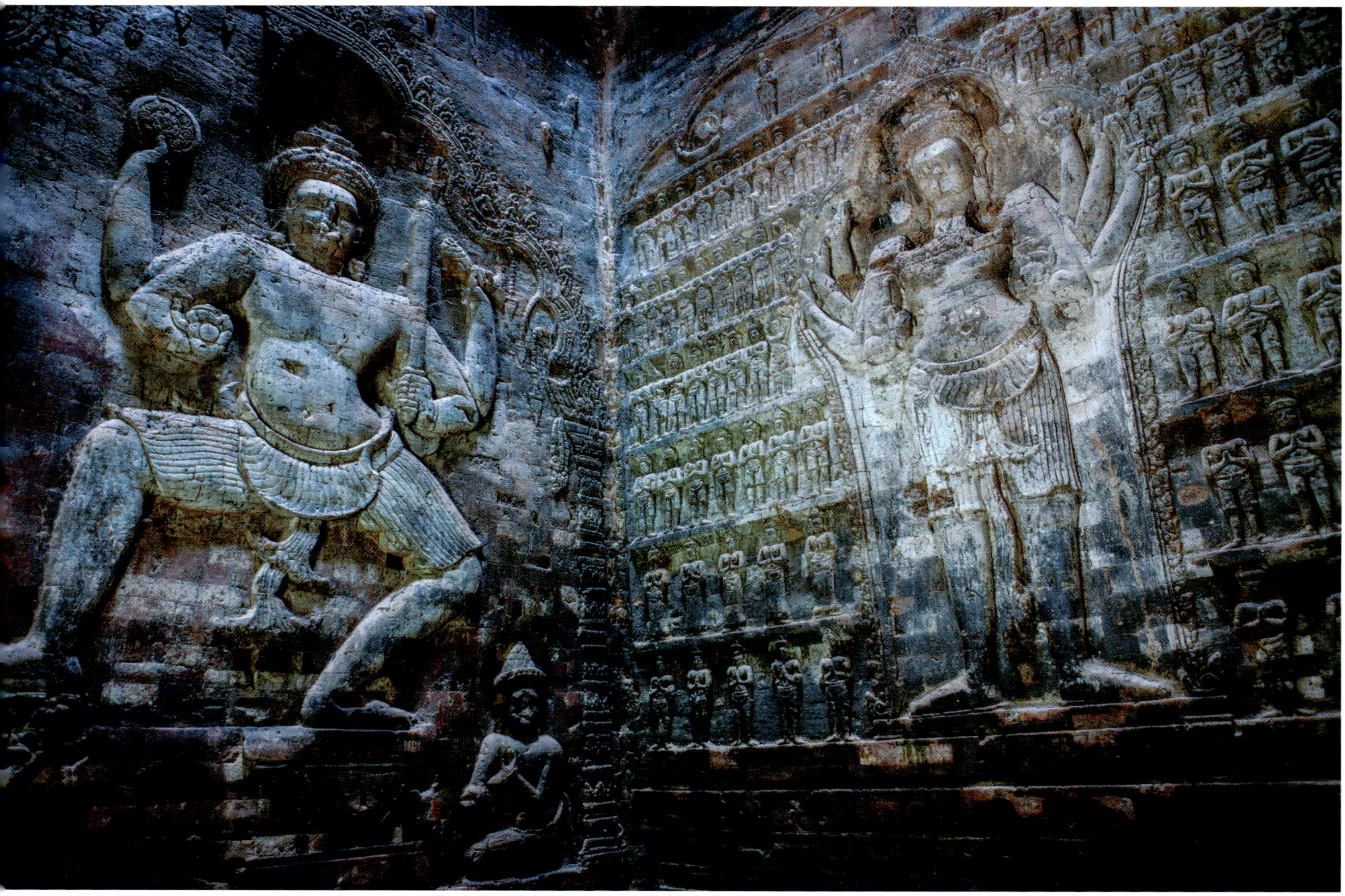

PRASAT KRAVAN – THE CARDAMOM SANCTUARY

From the outside, Prasat Kravan appears to be one of Angkor's least impressive structures. However, the central of the five towers that date from the early 10th century draws admirers of Khmer art. Inside, to the left of a central linga, the wall is decorated with an image of Vishnu striding the world to assert his domination. It's a truly sensational piece of beautifully preserved art that is complemented by similarly impressive images of Vishnu on the facing and right side walls.

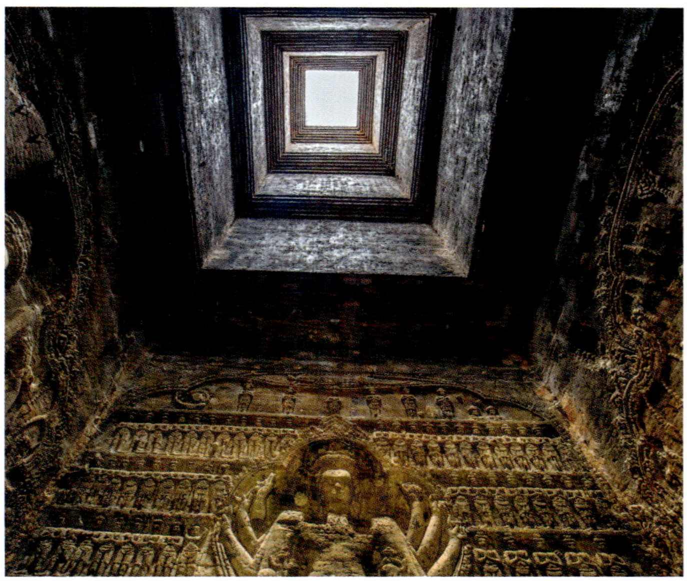

Above: Images of a four-armed Vishnu striding the universe and an eight-armed Vishnu surrounded by meditating devotees.
Right: Looking up to the heavens from within the central tower.

TA SOM

Diminutive but no less beautiful, Ta Som's location on the outer reaches of the Angkor site mean it can often be enjoyed in solitude. Dating from the end of the 12th century, the Buddhist temple's central sanctuary is enclosed by three concentric walls. The eastern *gopura*, or arched entranceway, is held in the inescapable grasp of ficus tree roots.

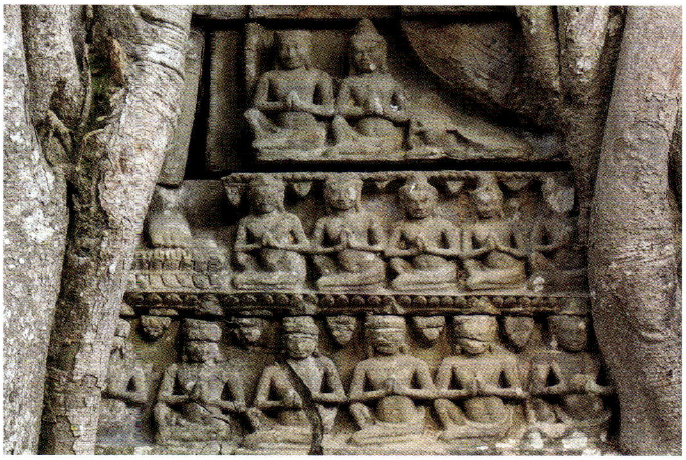

Right: Detailed stone carvings are visible between the tree roots.
Below: The *gopura* at the eastern side of Ta Som has yielded to the smothering embrace of an enormous Ficus tree.

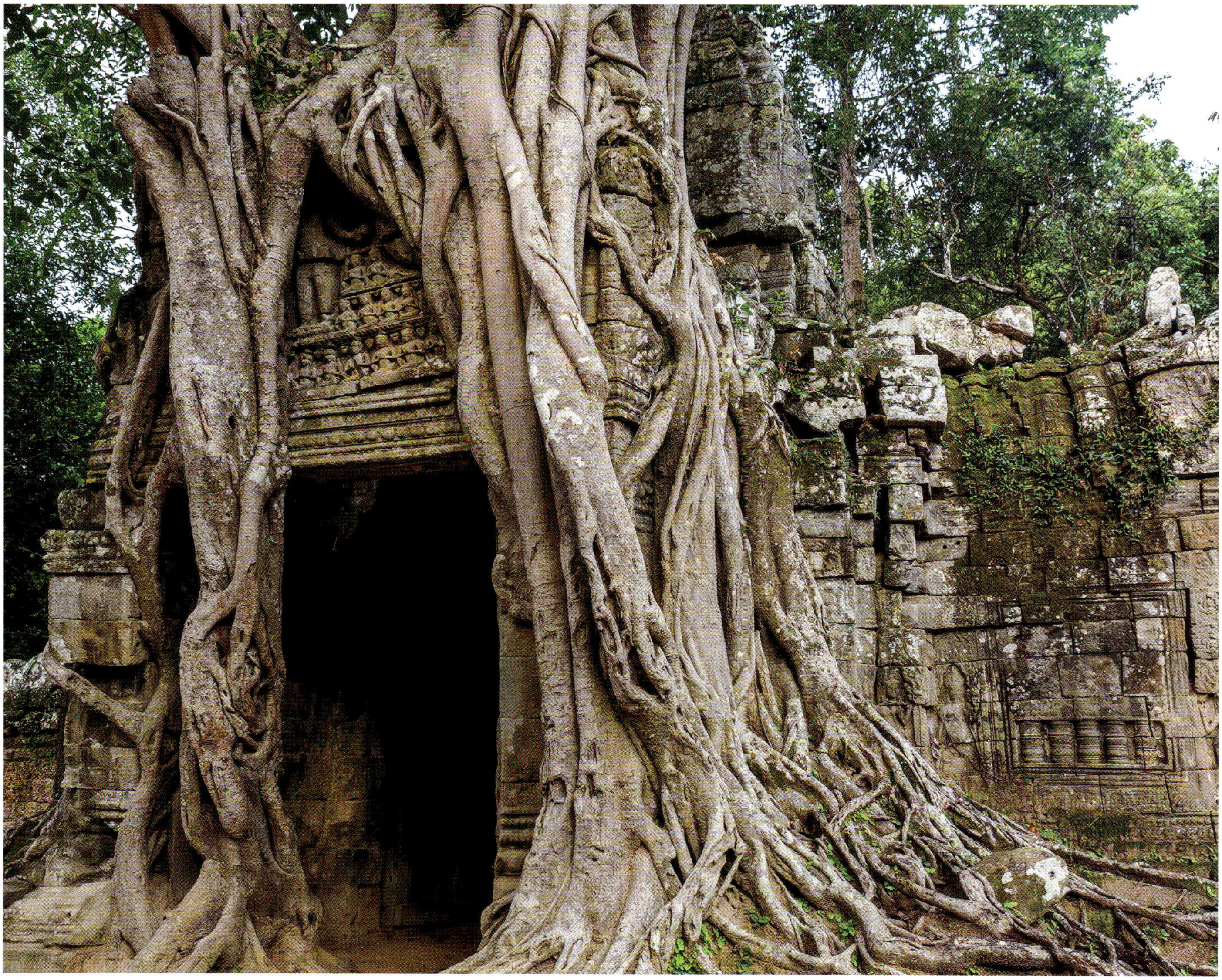

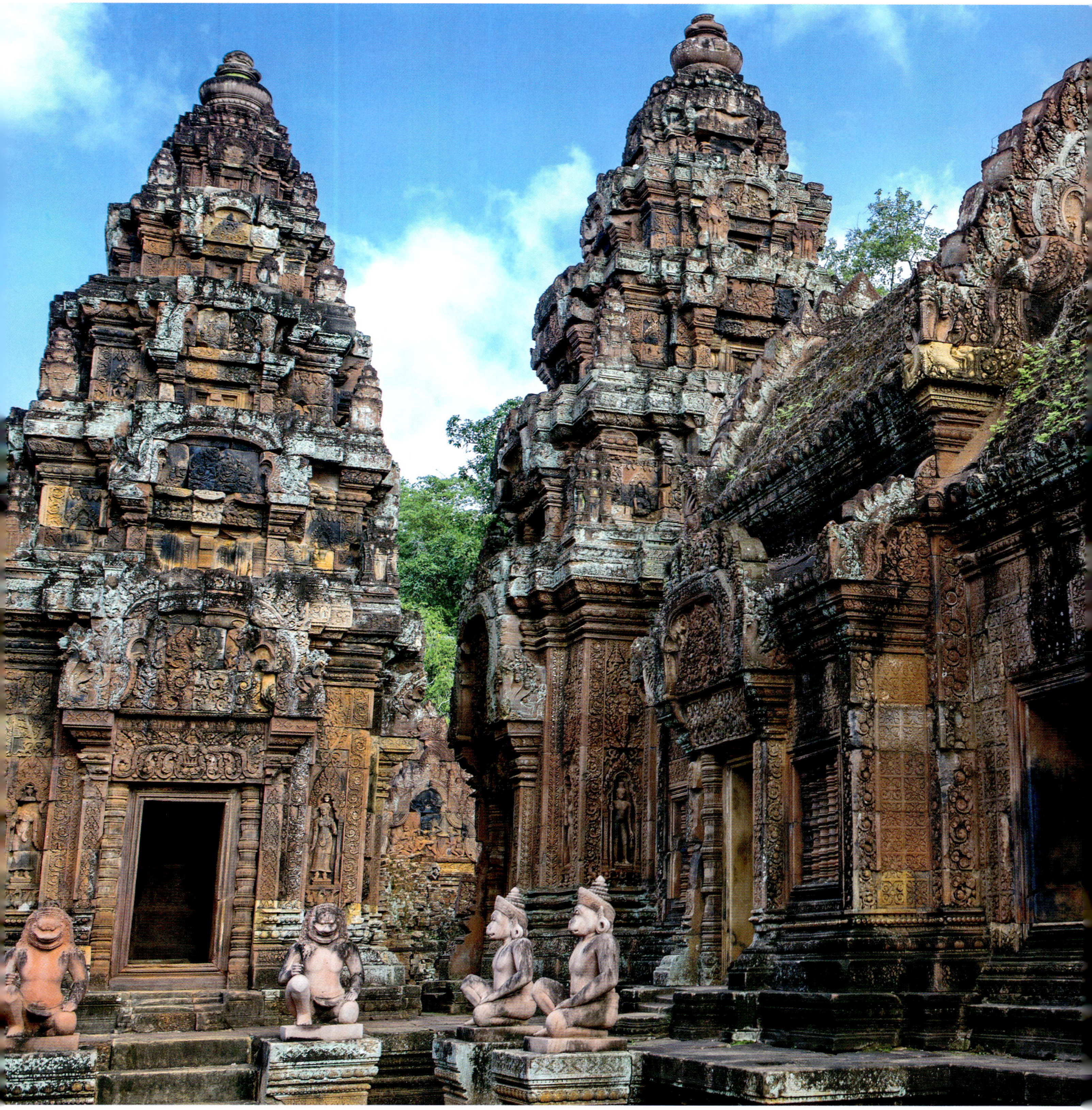

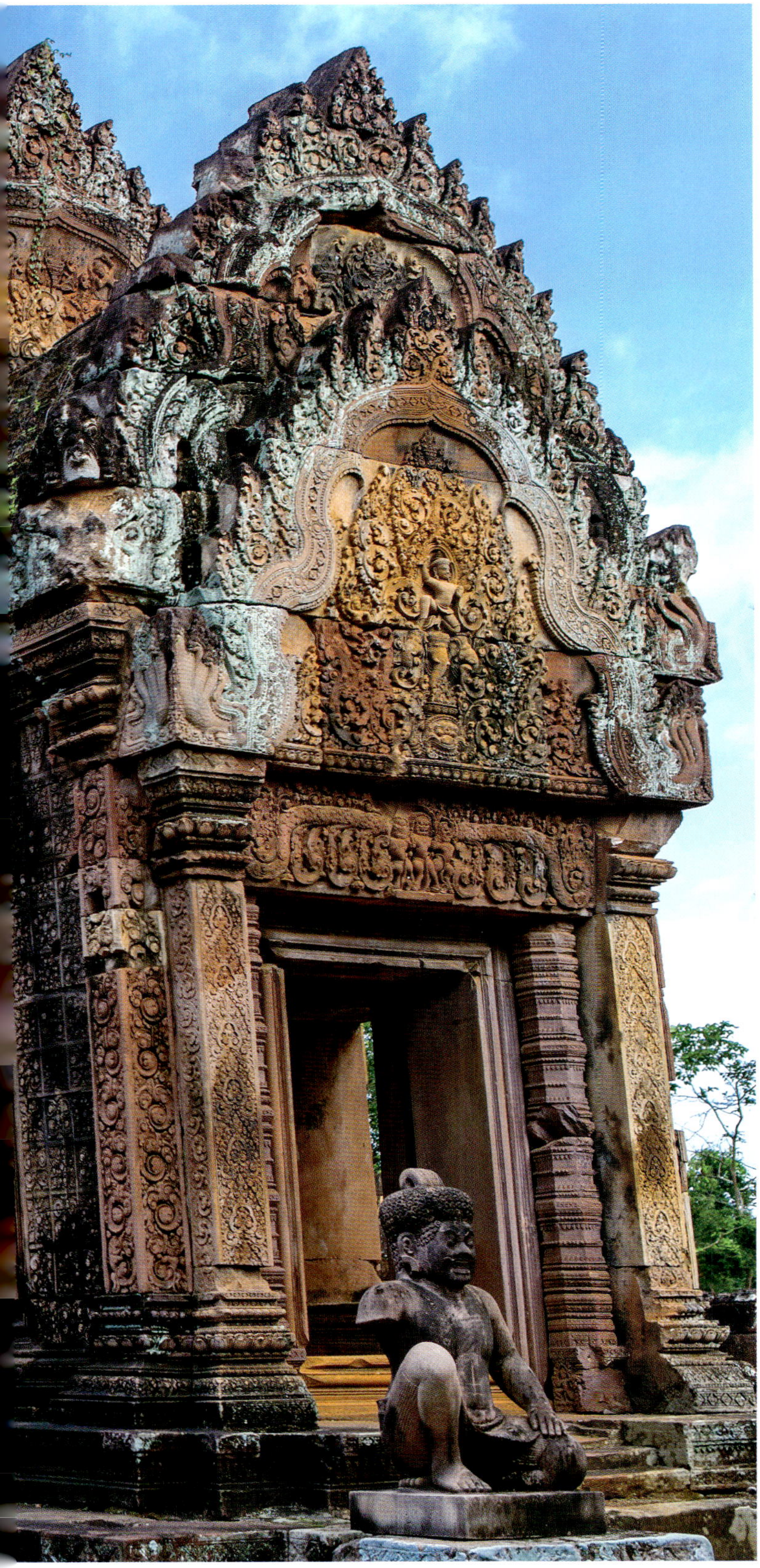

BANTEAY SREI

One of the finest temples beyond Angkor, and an essential feature of any itinerary, is Banteay Srei. Often referred to as the Citadel of Women or the Citadel of Beauty, it is 38 km (24 miles) from Siem Reap, and the journey there passes through some beautiful countryside. Constructed using sandstone of an orange and pinkish hue, Banteay Srei's intricately carved reliefs are renowned as some of the finest in Cambodia. Due to looting, the larger sculptures at the site are replicas, the originals of which can be seen at the National Museum. The temple dates from 967 AD and was dedicated to the Hindu deity, Shiva.

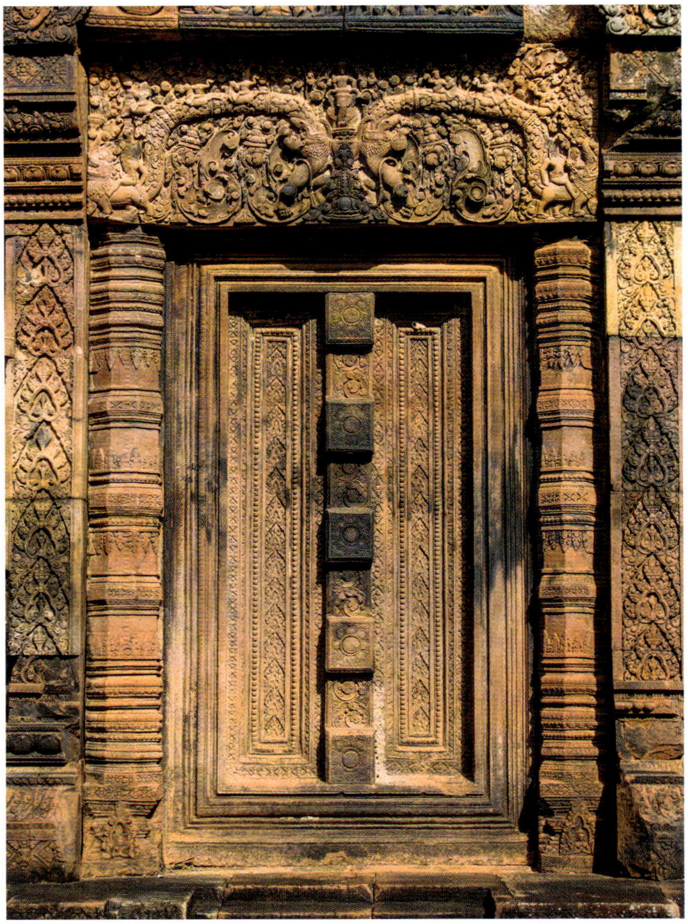

Above: The carvings at Banteay Srei use floral motifs and geometric designs with stunning effect.

Left: Banteay Srei is almost completely covered with intricate carvings which include scenes from the Indian epic, the *Ramayana*.

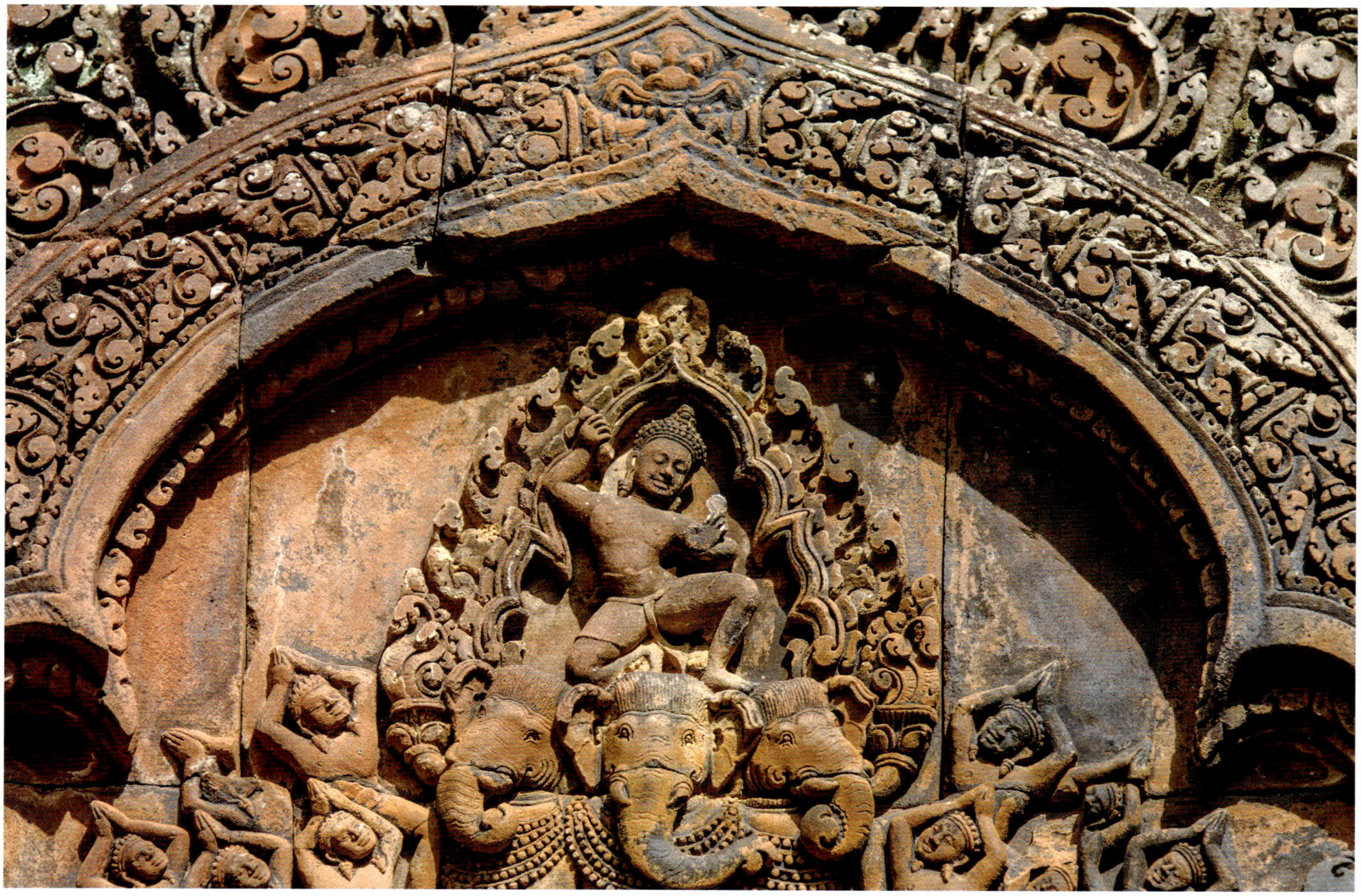

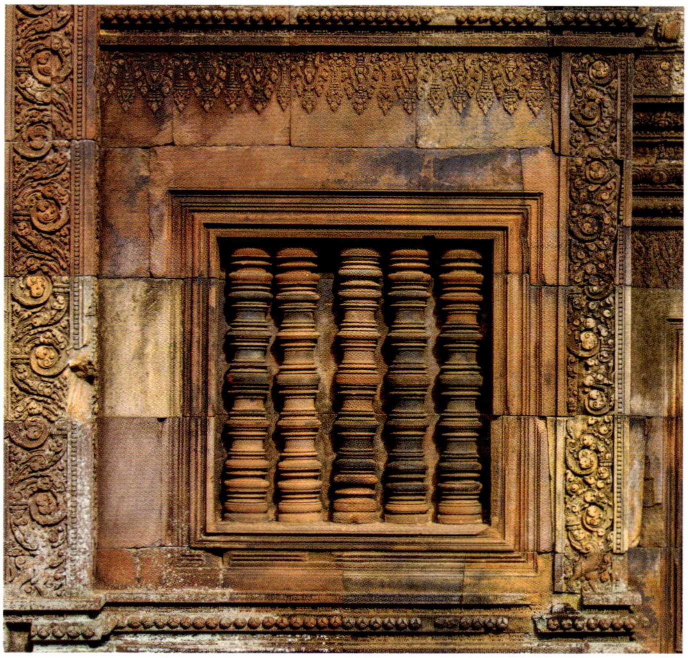

Above: The ancient carvings are remarkably well preserved.
Left: The hard sandstone, quartz arenite, is said to carve like wood, enabling craftsmen to create extremely delicate floral flourishes.

FERTILITY SYMBOLS

Twelve kilometres (7½ miles) beyond Banteay Srei is Kbal Spean, the site of a riverbed carved with over 1,000 *linga* that date from the 11th century. *Linga* are ancient fertility symbols representing the power of the Hindu god, Shiva, and often formed part of important religious rituals. They can be seen at many Angkorian temples in several different forms. Some stand within a square base called a *yoni* that represents the female genitals. Some temples at Koh Ker (see page 95) have particularly impressive examples of both *linga* and *yoni*.

PHNOM BAKHENG – THE SUNSET VIEWPOINT

The symmetrical Hindu temple that crowns Phnom Bakheng, or Bakheng Mountain, is one of the earlier Angkor period structures. Dating from the late ninth century, it was built during the reign of Yasovarman I who ascended the throne in 889 AD. It was built as a symbolic representation of Mount Meru, a sacred mountain that features in both Hindu and Buddhist cosmology. Originally, Phnom Bakheng's seven levels which recreate the seven heavens of Indra, were adorned with 108 towers, most long since collapsed. What remains is the central sanctuary on the upper terrace. From this 67-m (220-ft) vantage point, a spectacular view of Angkor Wat can be enjoyed just over one kilometre (⅔ mile) to the north-west, and on a clear day, as far as Phnom Kulen 30 km (18 miles) to the north.

Reached by an elephant ride or a twenty-minute walk up a steep trail, Phnom Bakheng's elevation has made it the location of choice to see an Angkor sunset. Like the sunrise in front of Angkor Wat, it attracts hundreds of visitors all vying for limited space.

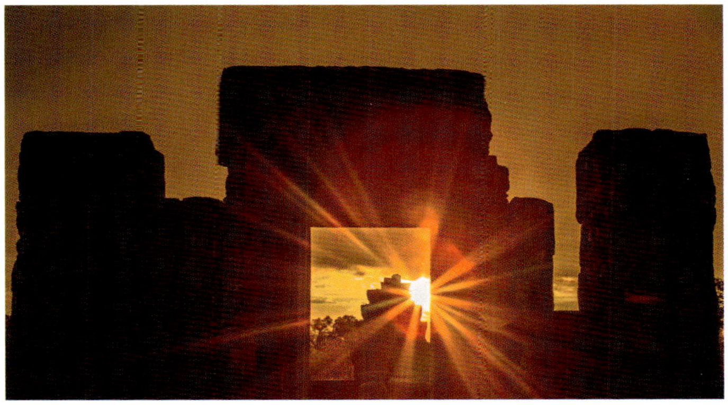

Above and below: To avoid the crowds and enjoy the panoramic view, Phnom Bakheng is best visited any time except sunset.

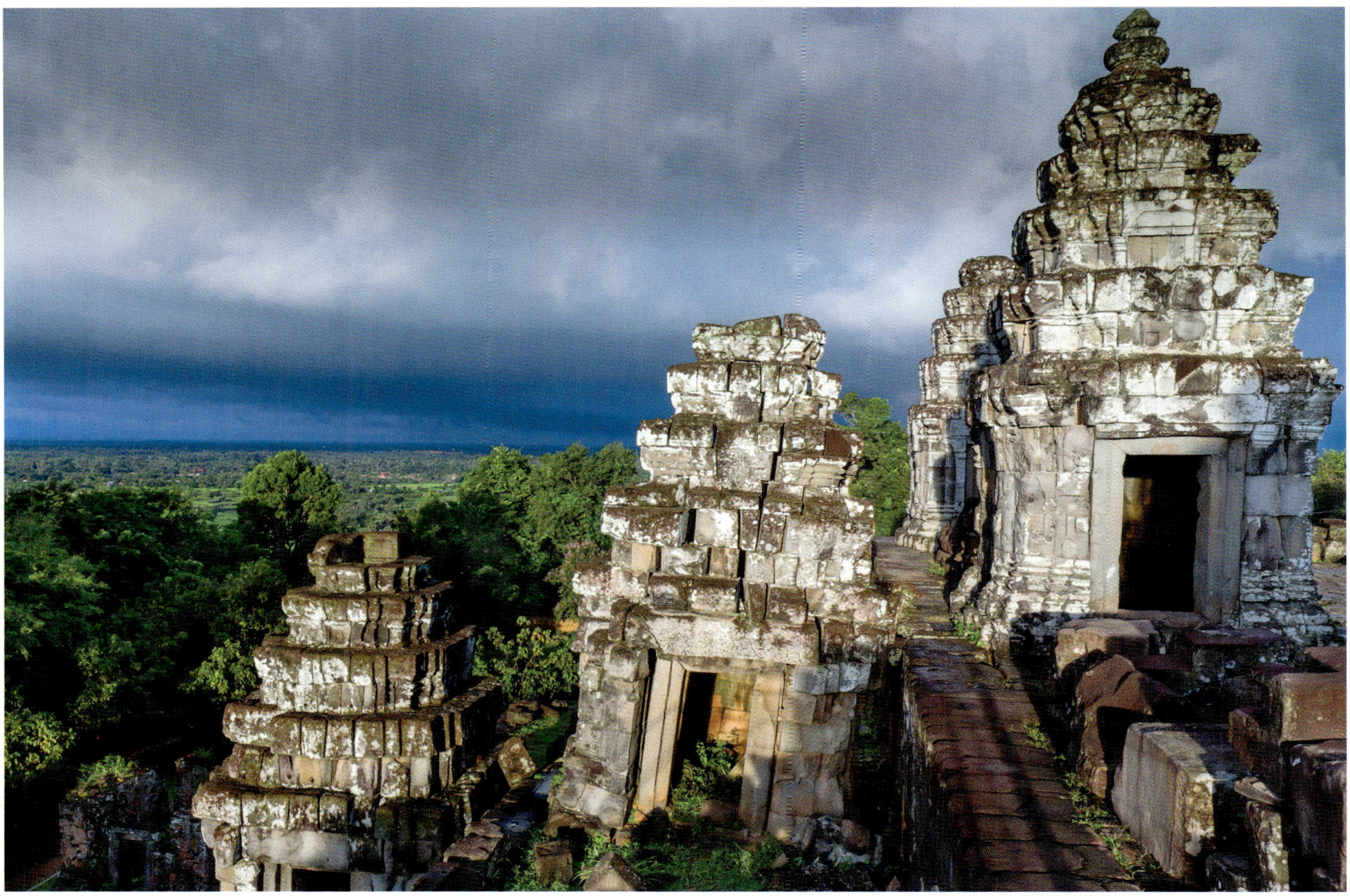

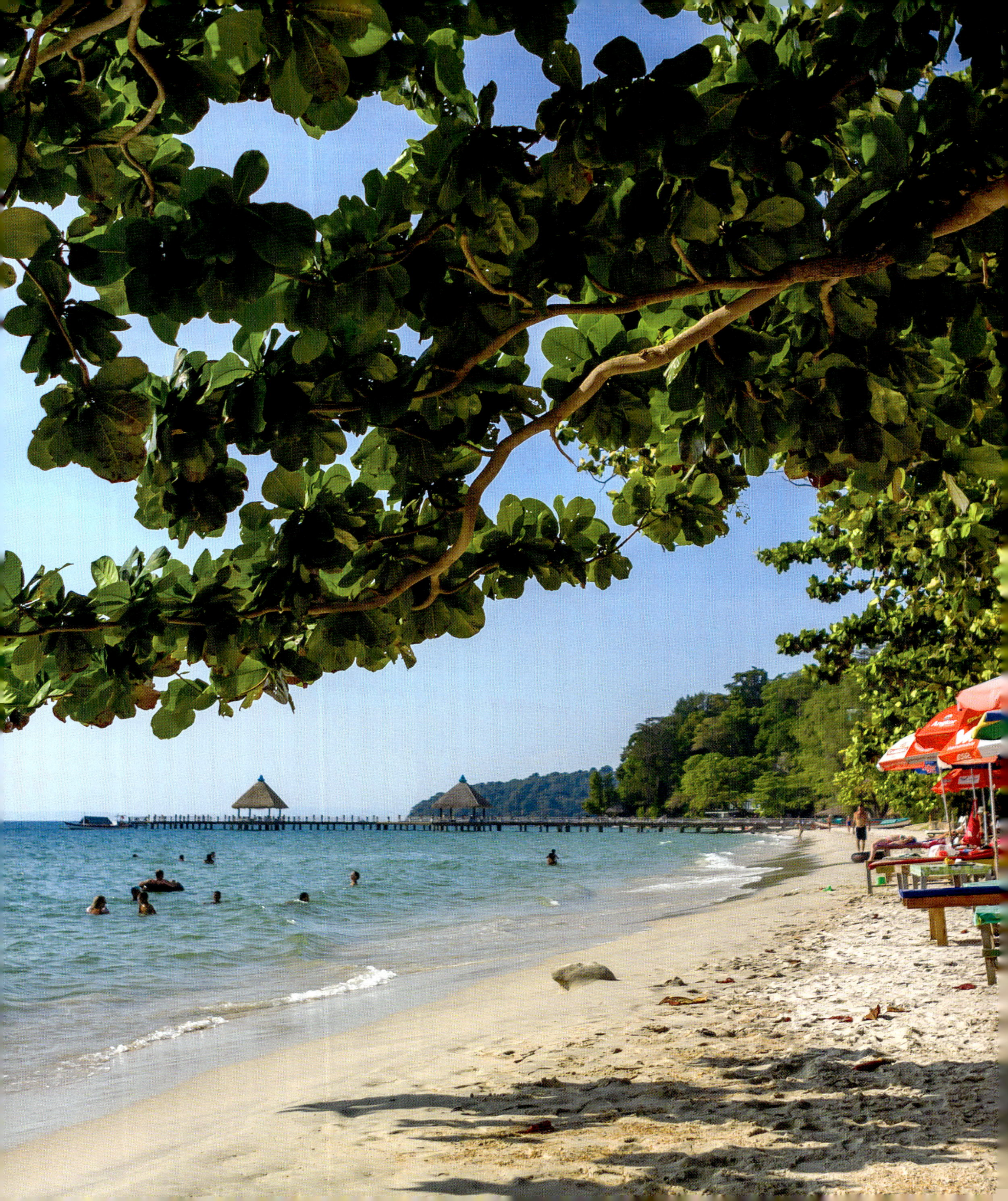

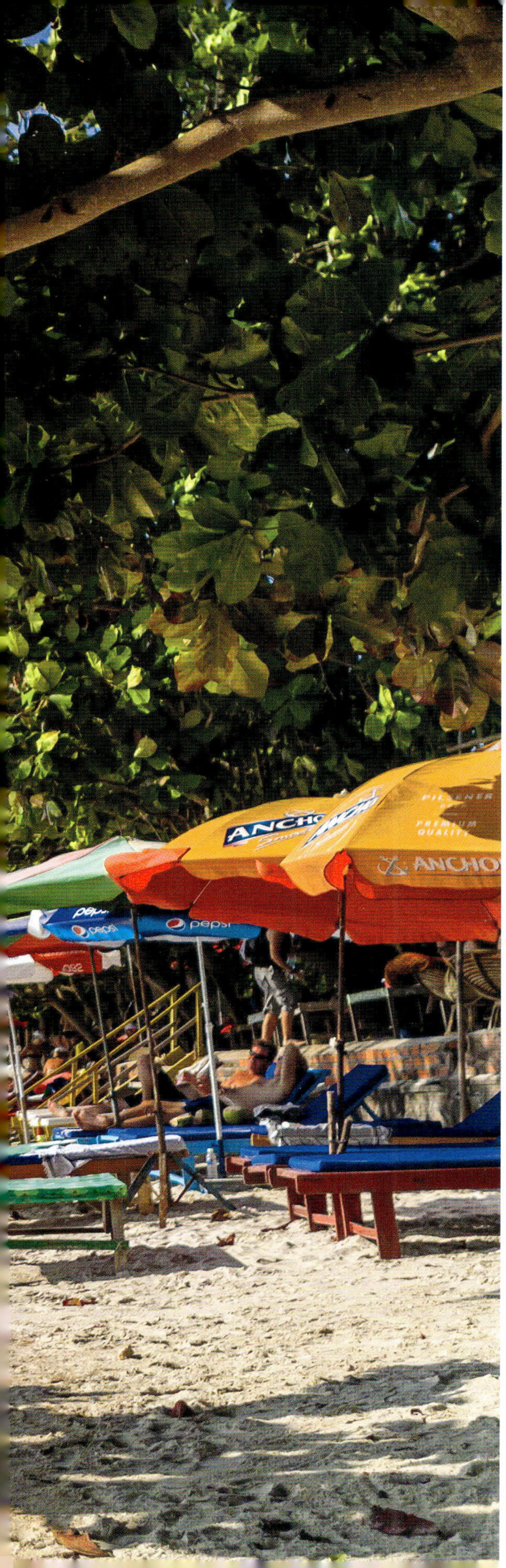

CHAPTER V

THE SOUTH COAST

Relaxing Beaches

Once the favoured getaway destination for administrative officials during the French occupation, the south coast of Cambodia has experienced a revival of interest and its many charms are now seducing Phnom Penh's growing middleclass and international travellers alike. And it's easy to see the attraction: here is a glorious 450-km (260-mile) stretch of coastline, lapped by crystal-clear waters, where lazy days can be spent soaking up the sun and evenings dining on freshly caught seafood.

Left: For many years, Cambodia's lovely beaches were almost deserted but they are now attracting increasing numbers of international and local holidaymakers. Despite this, they remain far less busy than those of neighbouring Thailand. Like all good things, however, development is coming so enjoy the tranquillity while it lasts.

Just a few hours' drive from the country's capital, the town of Sihanoukville, known to locals as Kompong Som, is the biggest town of the south and home to a busy commercial port, the popular Serendipity and Occheuteal beaches, and a dozen or so islands all within easy reach.

Further south lies the sleepy riverfront town of Kampot with many fine examples of colonial-era architecture, and, not far from the border with Vietnam, Kep, with its famed crab market, seafood restaurants and a beachfront promenade. Yet there is more to the south's allure than sun, sand and seafood. The coastline is backed by national parks, mountain ranges, wildlife sanctuaries and a conservation corridor, as well as ancient temples.

On the journey south, midway between Phnom Penh and Kep, travellers can stop off at Takeo, in itself an unassuming provincial town but the starting point for a 20-km (12½-mile) boat ride to the pre-Angkor-era archaeological site of Angkor Borei. Further south at the southern tip of the Elephant Mountains is Bokor Hill Station where visitors can explore atmospheric ruins that date from the 1920s and look out across the plains running toward the coast from a 1,000-m (3,280-ft) viewpoint. North-west of Sihanoukville, the Koh Kong Conservation Corridor embraces mangrove forests and the incredible biodiversity of the Cardamom Mountains, a spectacular range that includes Phnom Aural, Cambodia's highest mountain at 1,770 m (5,805 ft) and Southeast Asia's second largest expanse of primary rainforest (see page 21).

SIHANOUKVILLE

A 160-km (100-mile) sprint by car south-west of Phnom Penh is the port and resort town of Sihanoukville. In truth, it is a scrappy, litter-strewn town with haphazard development and a seedy image, but it does have many mostly quiet beaches, easy access to nearby islands and an abundance of fresh seafood dishes that can be sampled while lounging in deckchairs.

The town was named after King Norodom Sihanouk, and as Cambodia's only deepwater port, has flourished on the back of maritime trade. Sihanoukville is a new town, having been created only in 1960, five years after work on the port had begun. The town also gained notoriety as the site of the last

Opposite top: The view of Sihanoukville and nearby islands as seen from Wat Leu. The temple sits atop a forested hill two kilometres (one and a quarter miles) north-west of the town centre.

Opposite below left: The beachfront road at Sihanoukville's Hawaii Beach is lined with thatched-roof bars and restaurants. The town has seven main beaches, each with a distinctly different character.

Opposite below right: The monument at Sihanoukville's Independence Square was erected in 1985. It is located at the intersection of Ekareach Street and Mittapheap Kampuchea Soviet Street (Cambodia-Russia Friendship Street).

Below: Vimean Tao Meas, or the Golden Lions Monument, is Sihanoukville's most distinctive landmark. Constructed in 1996, it is situated on a traffic island and surrounded by gardens between Occheuteal and Sokha beaches.

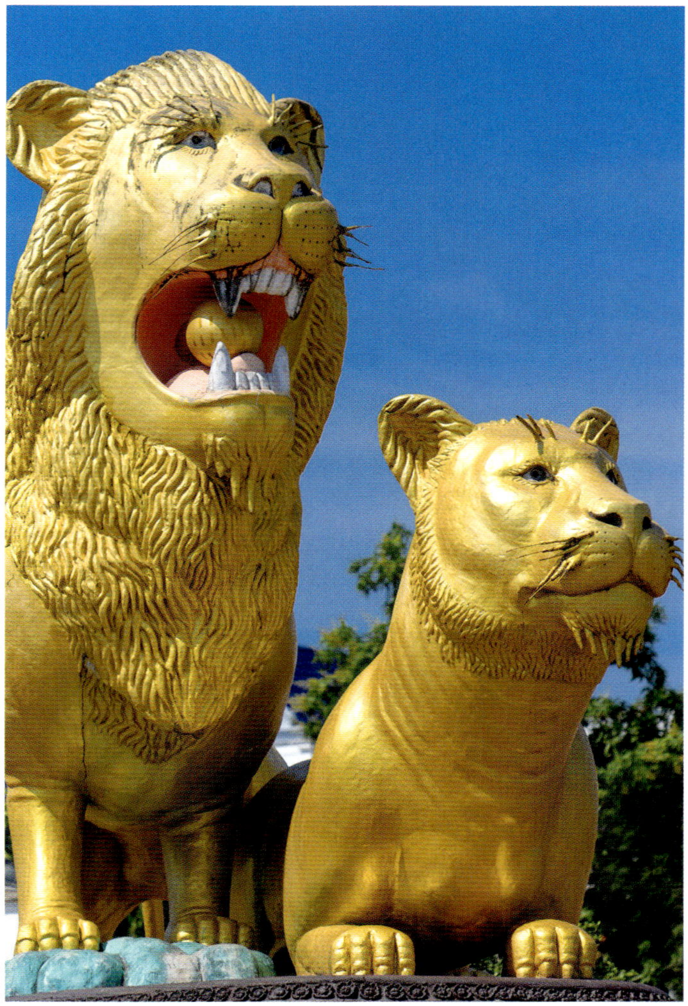

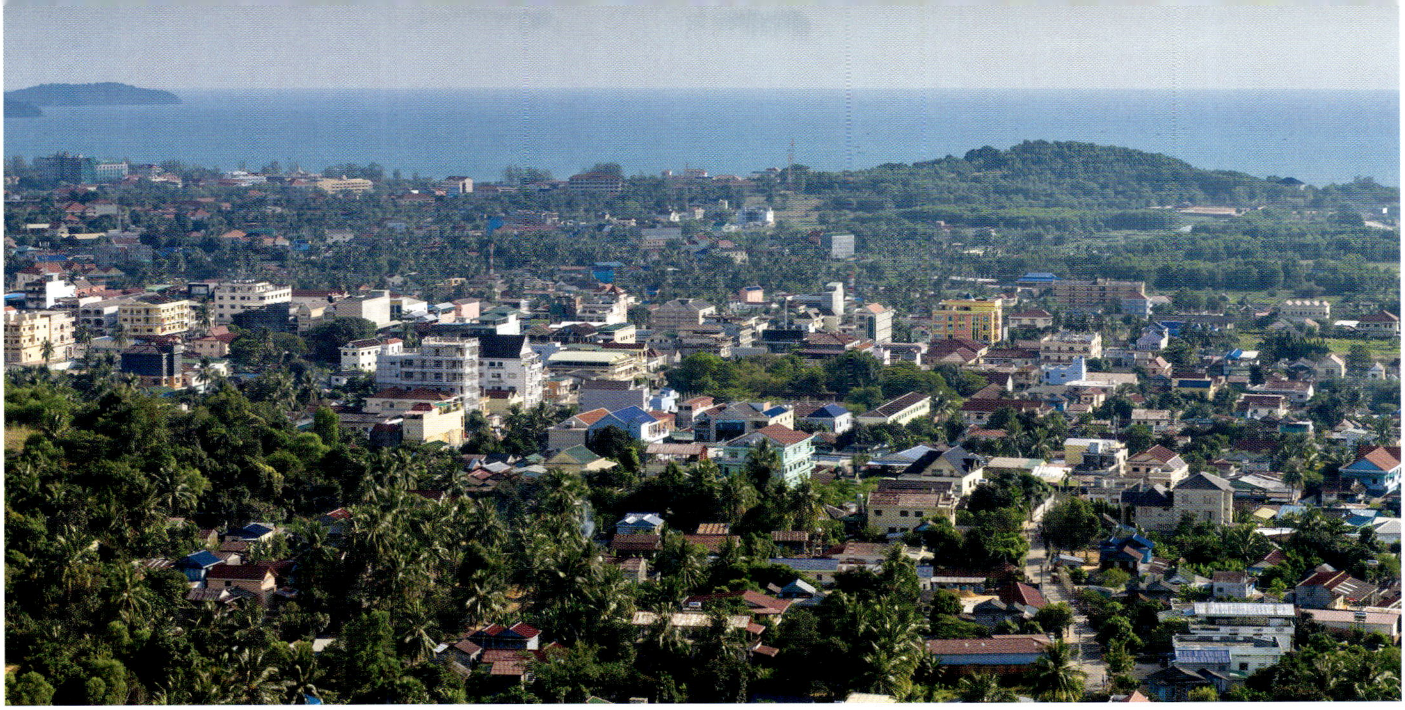

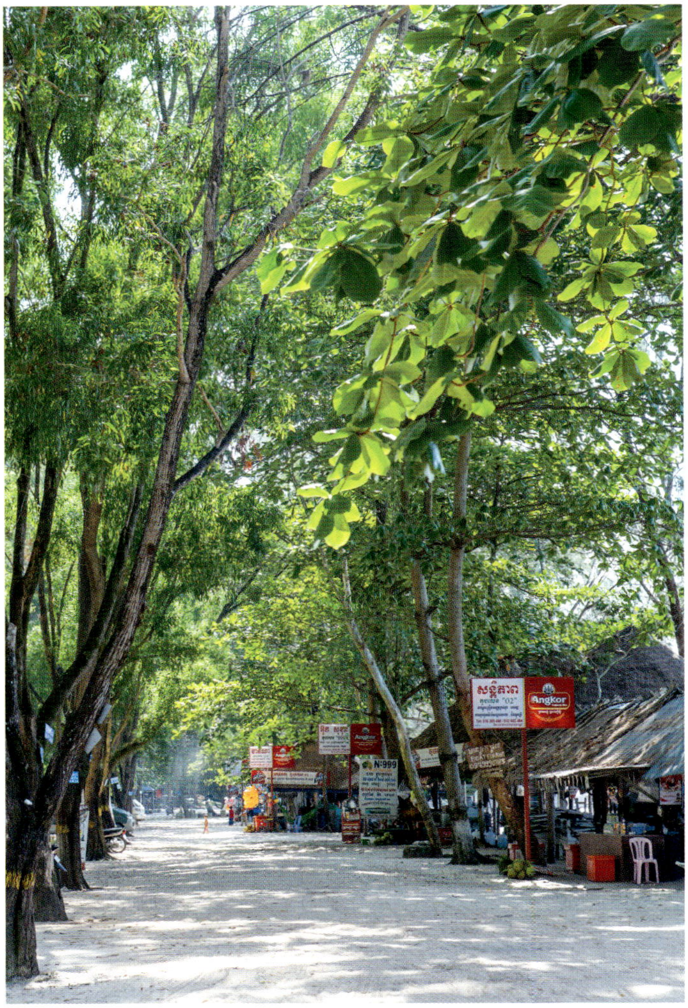
Angkor
N-999

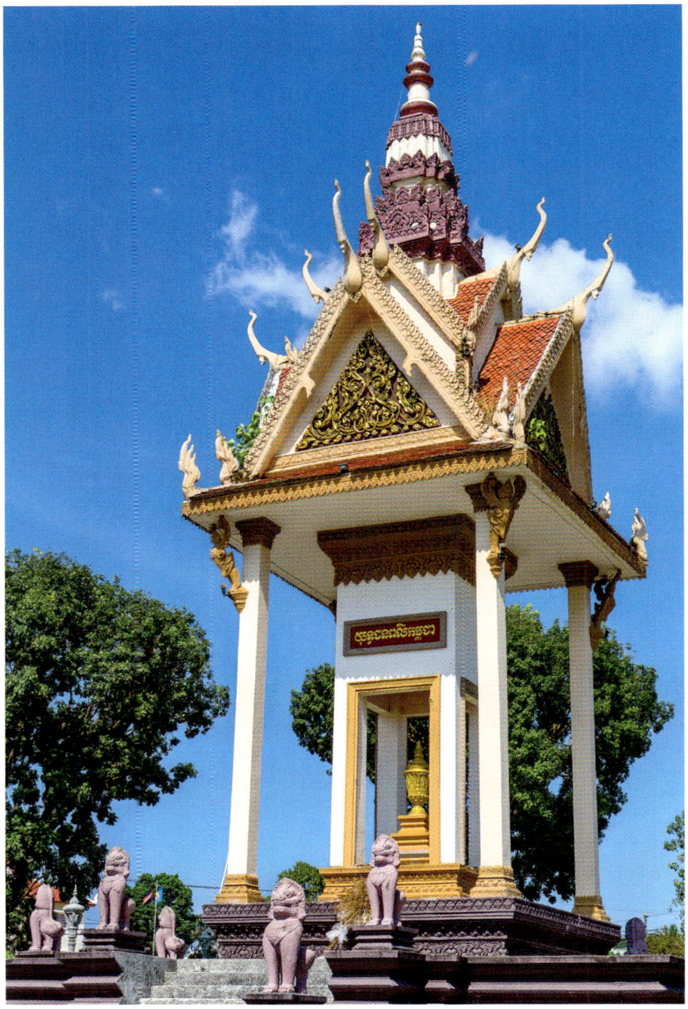

battle of America's war on Vietnam. Known as the Mayaguez incident, on 12 May 1975, just two weeks after Saigon had fallen to the People's Army of Vietnam, brazen Khmer Rouge forces captured an American merchant ship, the SS *Mayaguez*, 50 km (31 miles) off the coast near the island of Koh Tang. In response, America's President Gerald Ford ordered marines to storm the vessel. However, when they boarded the ship they found that it was deserted. Unknown to the Americans, the crew of the merchant ship, who were later found, had been released by the Khmer Rouge before the attack took place by being set adrift in fishing boats. The marines also attacked the island which was defended by 100 Khmer Rouge soldiers, suffered 18 casualties and lost several helicopters in the ensuing battle.

Sihanoukville's other not insignificant claim to fame is as the location for the factory of the country's national brew, Angkor Beer.

Sihanoukville has seven main beaches, namely Independence, Lamherkay, Occheuteal, Otres, Serendipity, Sokha and Victory. The most popular is Occheuteal Beach, a four-kilometre

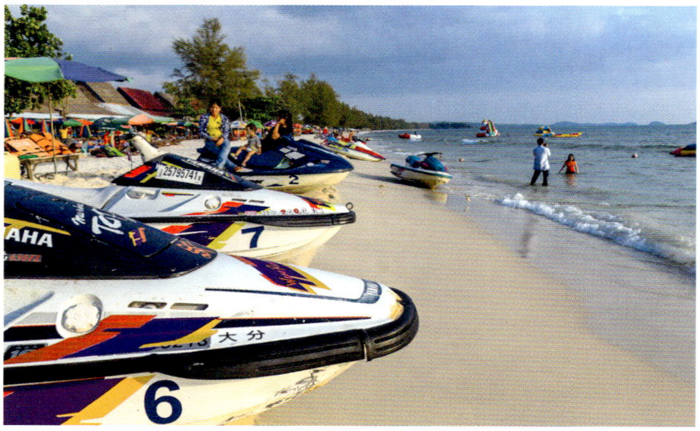

Above and below: Occheuteal Beach is one of Sihanoukville's most popular. In the early evening, tourists lounge in deckchairs enjoying seafood and beer while they wait for the sun to set. It's also a good place to hire jet skis and book fishing trips.

Opposite top: Victory Beach is one of the quieter beaches.

Opposite below: Tour boats also leave from the pier at Victory Beach for snorkelling trips to nearby islands.

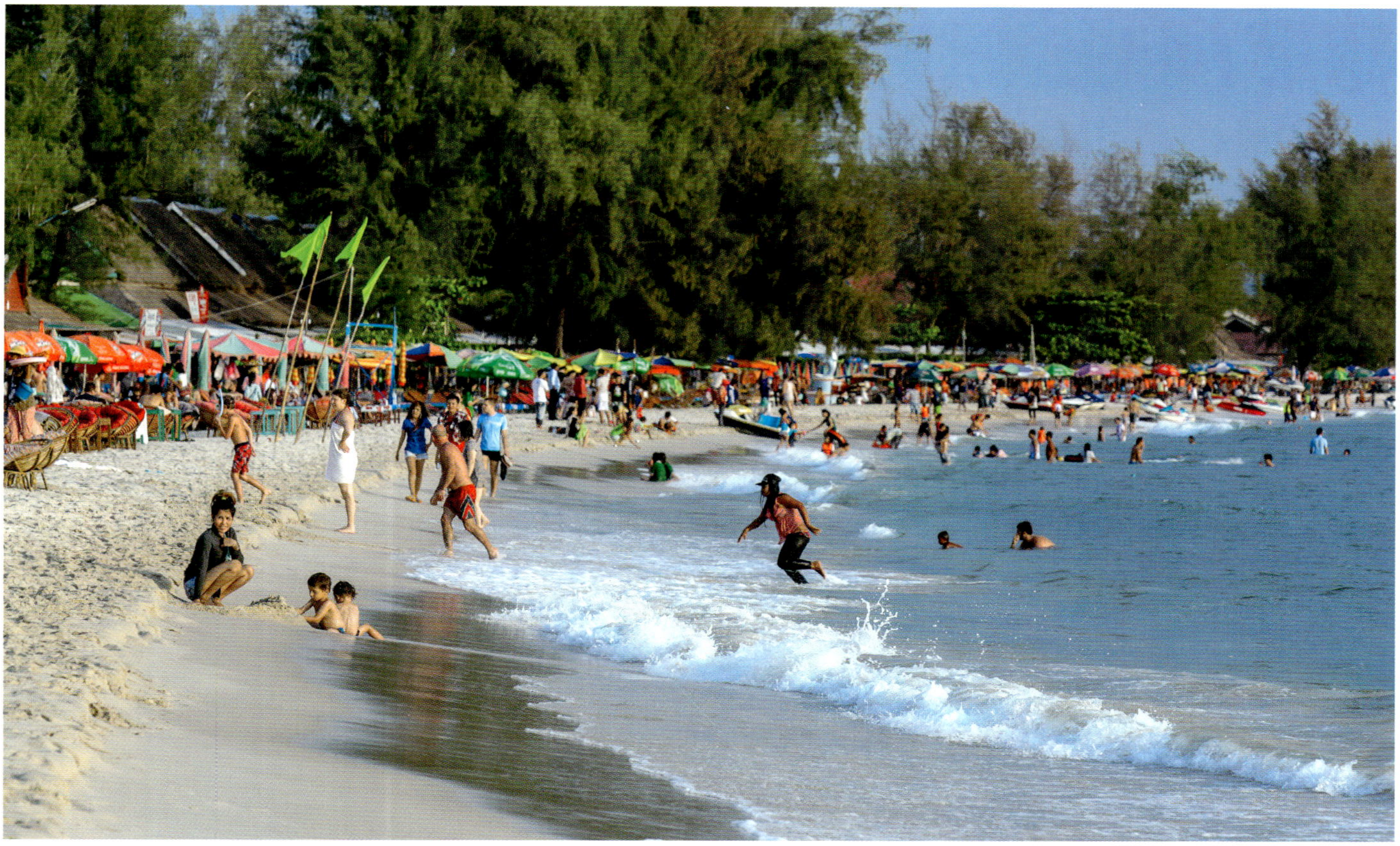

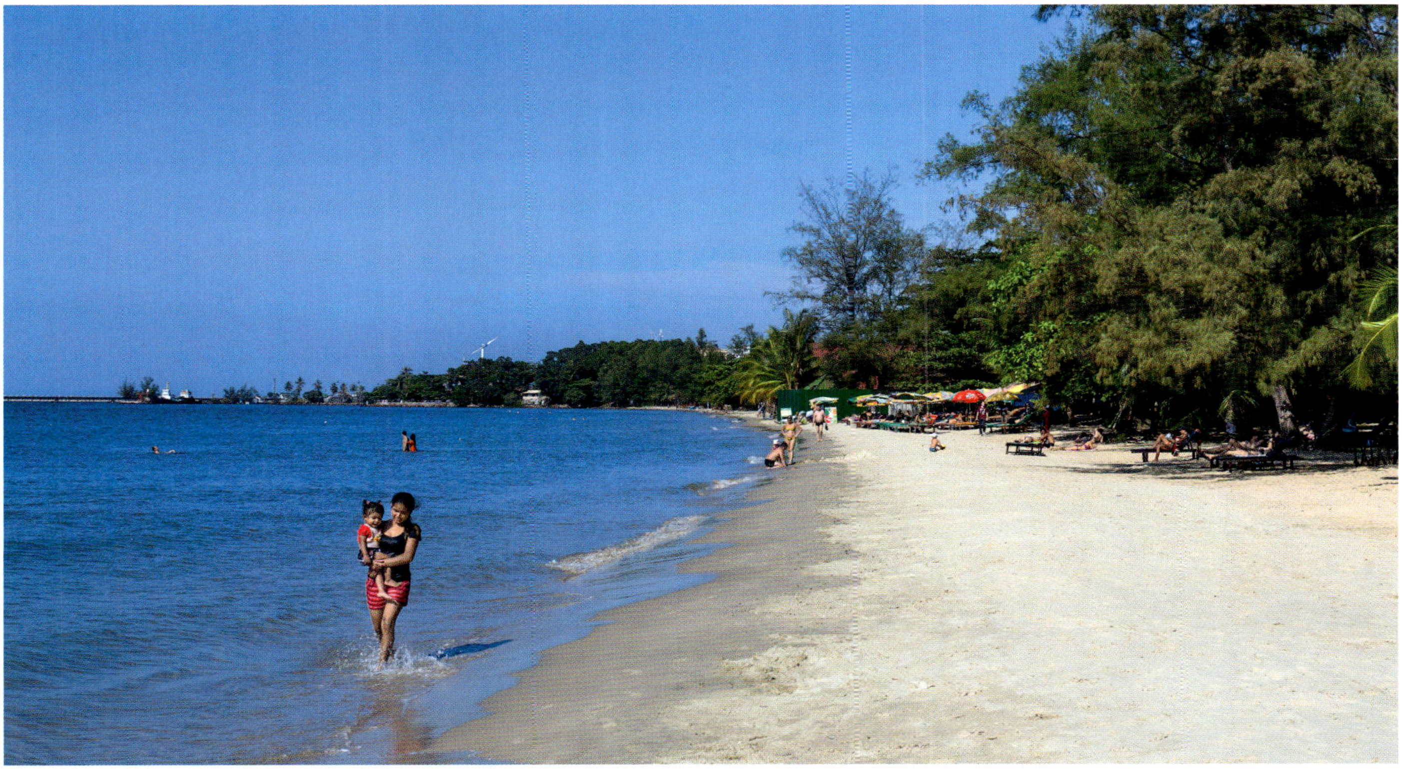

(2½-mile) stretch of sand lined with laidback bars fronted by groves of umbrellas and deckchairs. In the early evening the beach attracts holidaymakers who come to feast on seafood ordered from the restaurants or bought from freelance vendors walking the strip with baskets of delicious cooked crab, shrimps and rock lobster. An additional attraction is that Occheuteal, due to its orientation, is a sunset beach.

Quieter beaches include Otres which lies just south of Occheuteal but it, too, is starting to ride a wave of development and attracting increasingly more resorts and bars. One of the nicest beaches is the privately owned Sokha. All but the eastern end is managed by the Sokha Beach Resort but non-resort guests are welcome free-of-charge though they will be expected to order a drink or food.

There are several dive shops and tour operators on the main beaches and it is easy to arrange day or overnight diving and fishing tours. North-west of Sihanoukville in the Gulf of Thailand is Koh Kong, a beautiful island with several pristine beaches that is experiencing rapid development. The emerald waters are also scattered with another 60 islands including Koh Tang, now a deserted island loved by scuba divers who arrive on live-aboard boat excursions to explore the coral reefs and an abundance of marine life. There's also the more accessible Koh Ta Kiev, a one-hour boat ride from Sihanoukville and renowned for its peaceful, tree-lined beaches and its sprinkling of low-key resorts.

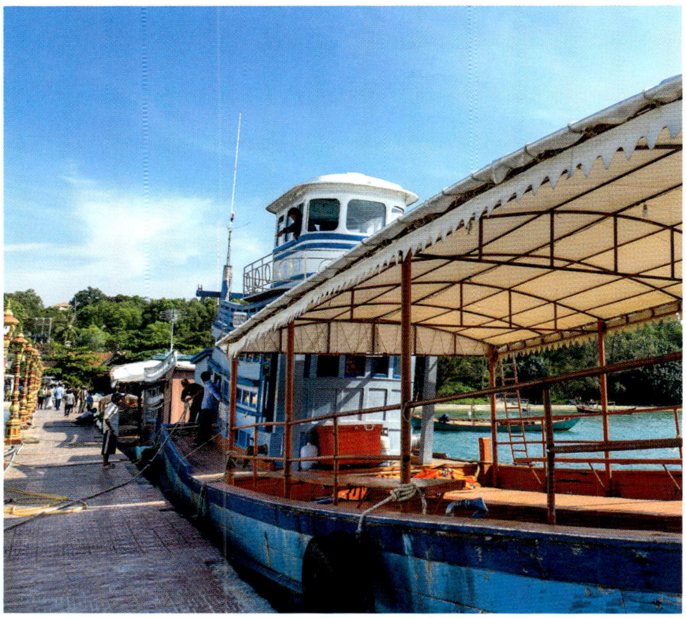

KAMPOT

The continued development of the south coast and the increasing numbers of tourists it attracts have made some Phnom Penhites and expats shy away from Sihanoukville and turn their attention to Kampot. Located 100 km (62 miles) east of Sihanoukville and just 159 km (99 miles) south of Phnom Penh, the sleepy riverfront town has an enchanting ambience conducive to several days' rewarding rest and relaxation. Its quiet streets are lined with cafés and bars in French colonial-era buildings and it is easily explored on foot or by bicycle. Beyond the immediate environs there is much to explore including Bokor National Park, Cham Muslim fishing villages and the famous pepper farms.

BOKOR HILL STATION

One of the main attractions of Preah Monivong National Park is Bokor Hill Station, a French-era hotel and casino that featured as a setting in the movie, *City of Ghosts*, starring Matt Dillon. However, those who have watched the movie and ascend the Damrei Mountain on which the hill station sits in the hope of exploring an atmospheric relic of the past will be disappointed. In 2008, the government-owned site was leased to the Sokimex Group, which also controls Angkor. They rendered and whitewashed the venerable building thereby, with the stroke of a brush, erasing a century of character from its walls.

Construction of the hill station began in 1921 and when completed featured the Bokor Palace Hotel and Casino, a church, a post office and a royal residence. However, the site was abandoned by the French in the 1940s.

With a new surfaced road, Bokor Hill Station is easily reached by car or motorcycle. The Sokimex Group's ambitious development plan for Bokor City has already seen the opening of a new hotel and casino but the multi-million dollar project also includes more hotels, apartments, restaurants and golf courses, all within the national park.

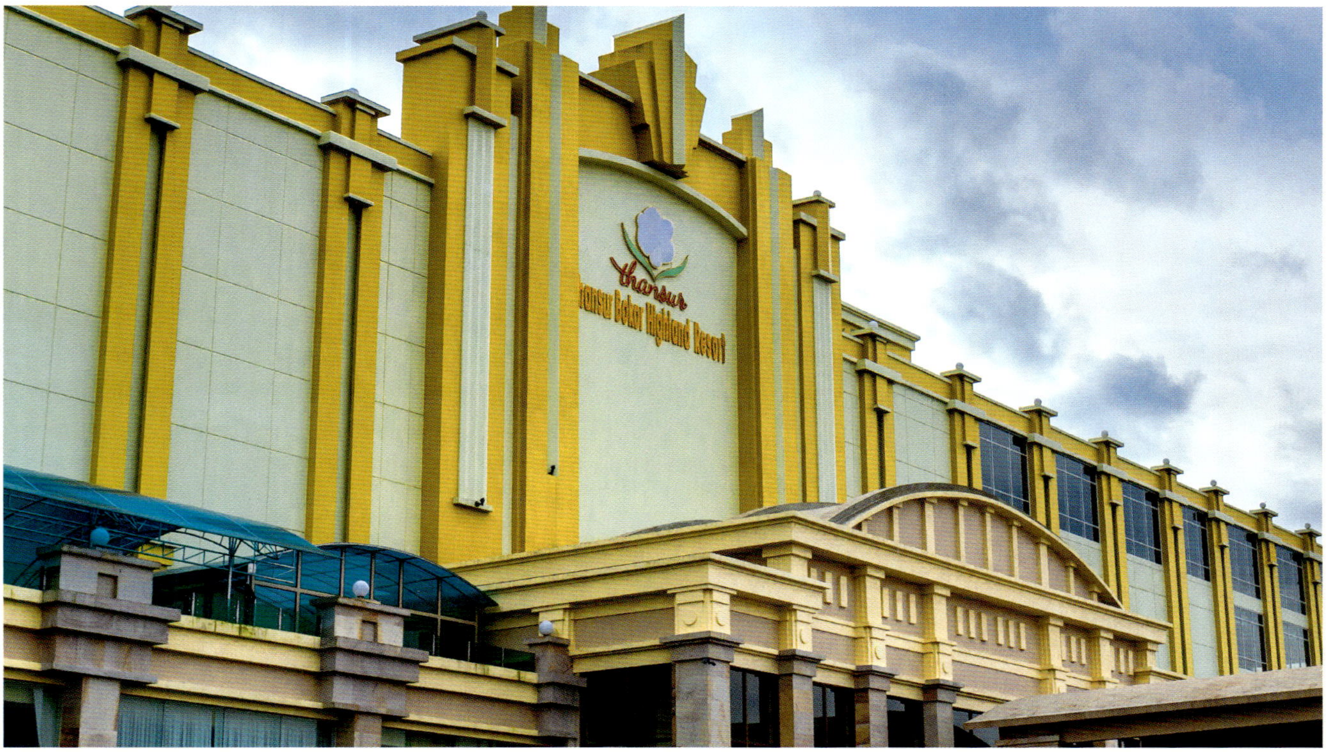

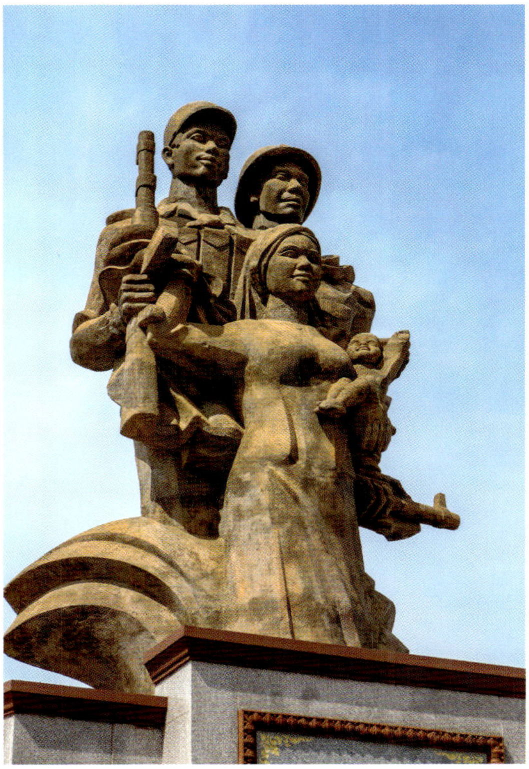

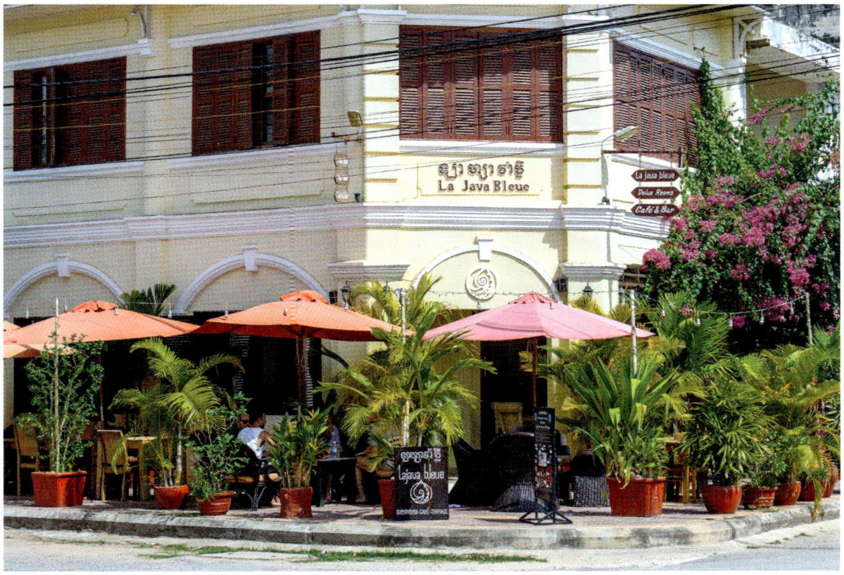

Above and below: Many of the French colonial-era villas and shophouses in Kampot have been restored as bars, restaurants and hotels.

Left: The Cambodia-Vietnam Friendship Monument in the centre of Kampot commemorates Vietnam's help in liberating Cambodia from the Khmer Rouge.

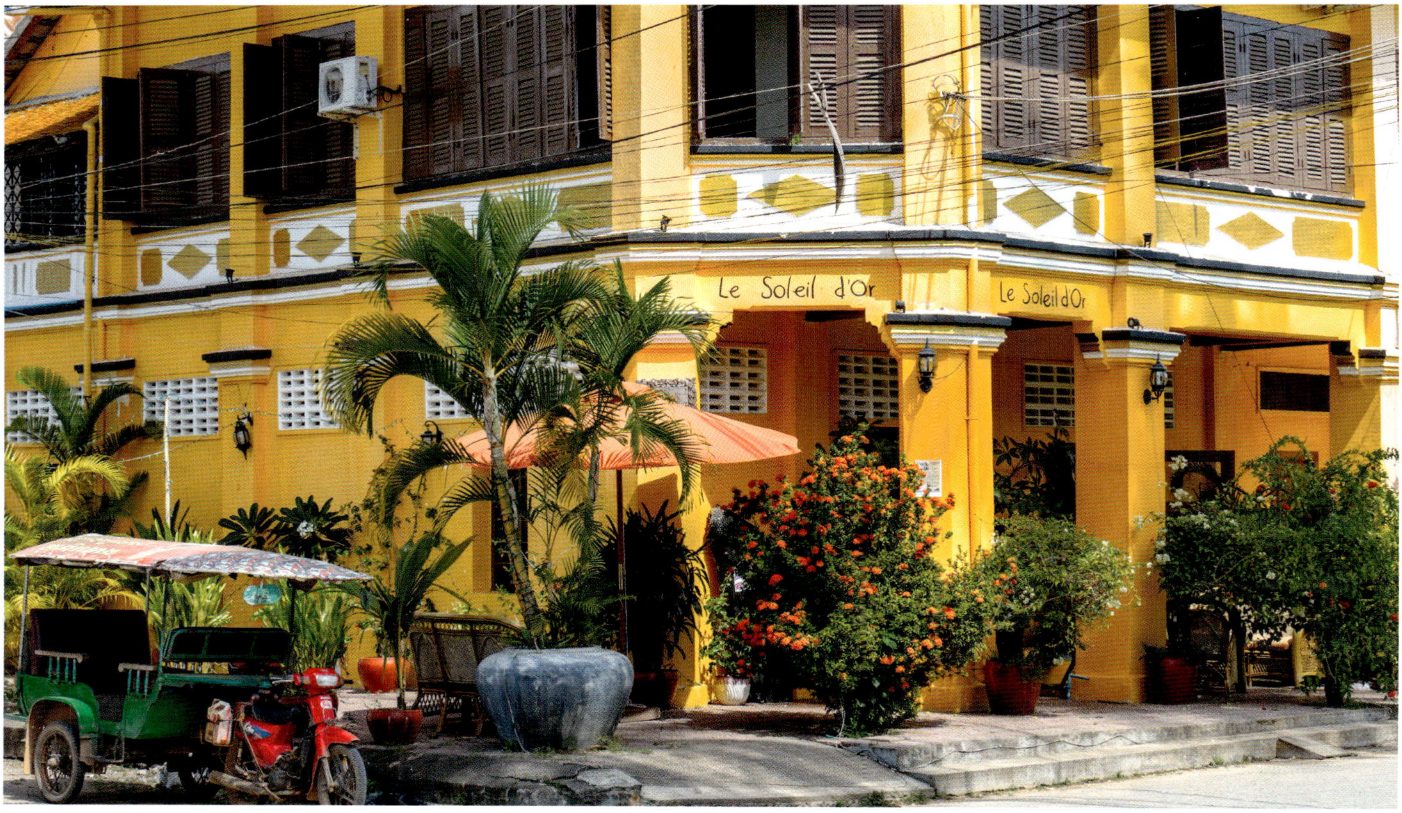

KAMPOT PEPPER

The revival of Kampot pepper is a combination of quality and shrewd marketing. There are many pepper farms in the gently rolling country between Kampot and Kep that are believed to have been started by Hainanese immigrants from China. However, there are also historical references in Zhou Daguan's 13th century accounts that refer to the cultivation of a spice which some believe could have been pepper.

At the tail end of the 19th century under French occupation when demand for pepper from Europe was high, production reached upwards of 7,260 tonnes (8,000 tons) a year. Today, after experiencing a steep decline in production due to years of strife in the country, Kampot pepper is enjoying a resurgence in popularity around the world. It is the first Cambodian product to be given Protected Geographical Indication (PGI) status from the Cambodian government and the European Union, an award that links quality and reputation to a specific area. The production of genuine Kampot pepper is restricted to a handful of districts around Kampot and Kep. Fuelled by the success of the PGI status, demand for pepper outstrips production but farms are expanding. In 2012 there were just 20 hectares (49 acres) under vine but this increased to 41 hectares (101 acres) in 2013. Crop yields have increased substantially from 21 tonnes (23 tons) in the whole of 2012 to 24.5 tonnes (27 tons) in just the first three months of 2013. Of this just over half met the PGI quality standard and the majority of that went for export.

There are 152 pepper-growing families in the Kampot area and they plant two varieties; *kamchay* and *lampong*, known locally as simply 'big leaf' and 'small leaf'. Strict PGI criteria forbid other varieties from being grown as Kampot pepper.

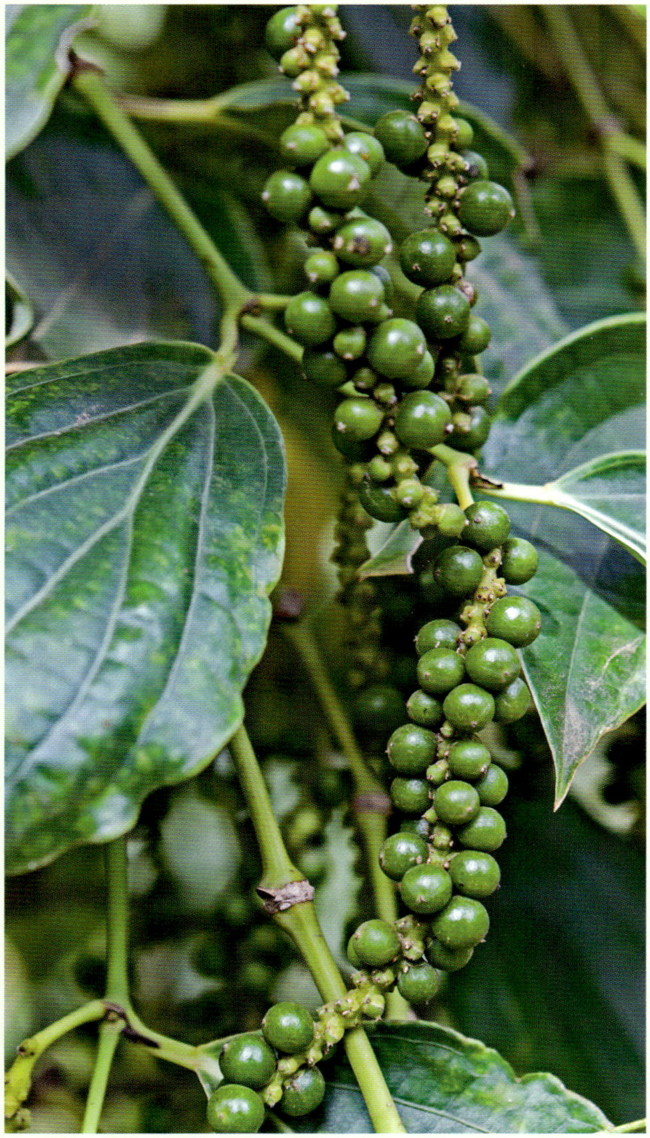

Pepper vines are shade lovers but also thirsty and during the dry season require up to 15 litres (32 pints) of water every three days. Picked from February to May, farms produce four kinds of pepper, each with distinctive characteristics. Green pepper is picked from the vine when still young and used within days of harvest. It displays powerful aromas, hints of citrus flavours and mild pepperiness. To make black pepper, the young green peppercorns are sun-dried for up to four days, a process that intensifies the flavour. White pepper is also produced from fully ripened berries but when they are picked the peppercorns are immersed in hot water to remove the skins. The core is then sun-dried for three to four days. The less common red pepper, a different species, is also sun-dried but using fully ripened peppercorns. The flavour is more rounded and less peppery than black.

The renewed interest in the high quality pepper and its recognition on the international market is one of Cambodia's many small, yet significant, success stories.

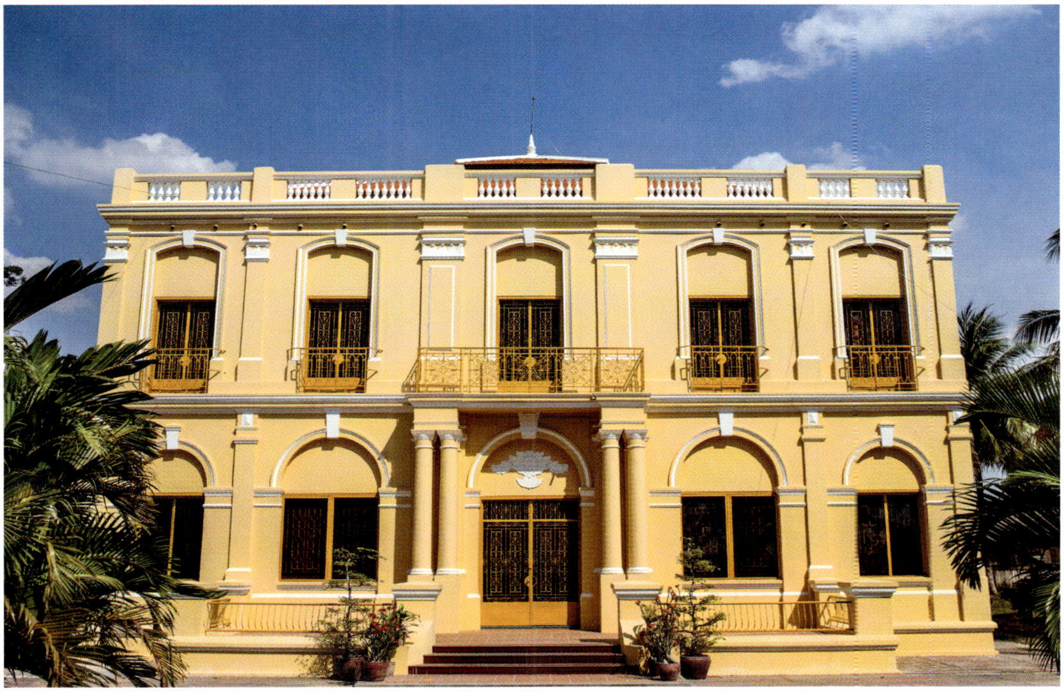

Left: The Governor's Mansion is one of many fine old buildings in Kampot.

Below: A small passenger boat offering sunset cruises moored near the old French bridge which spans Kompong Bay River in Kampot. A new bridge was opened further upstream in 2007.

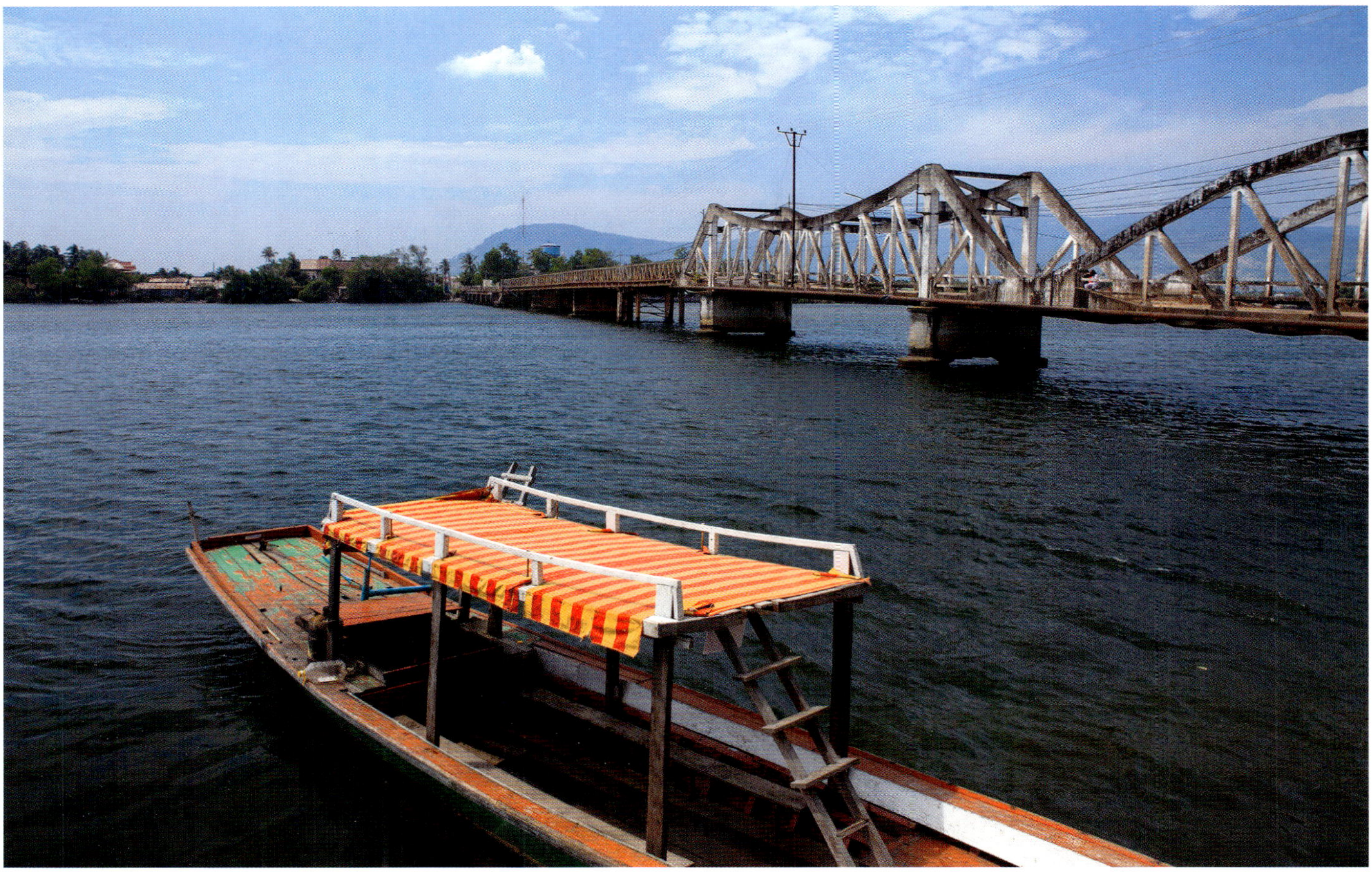

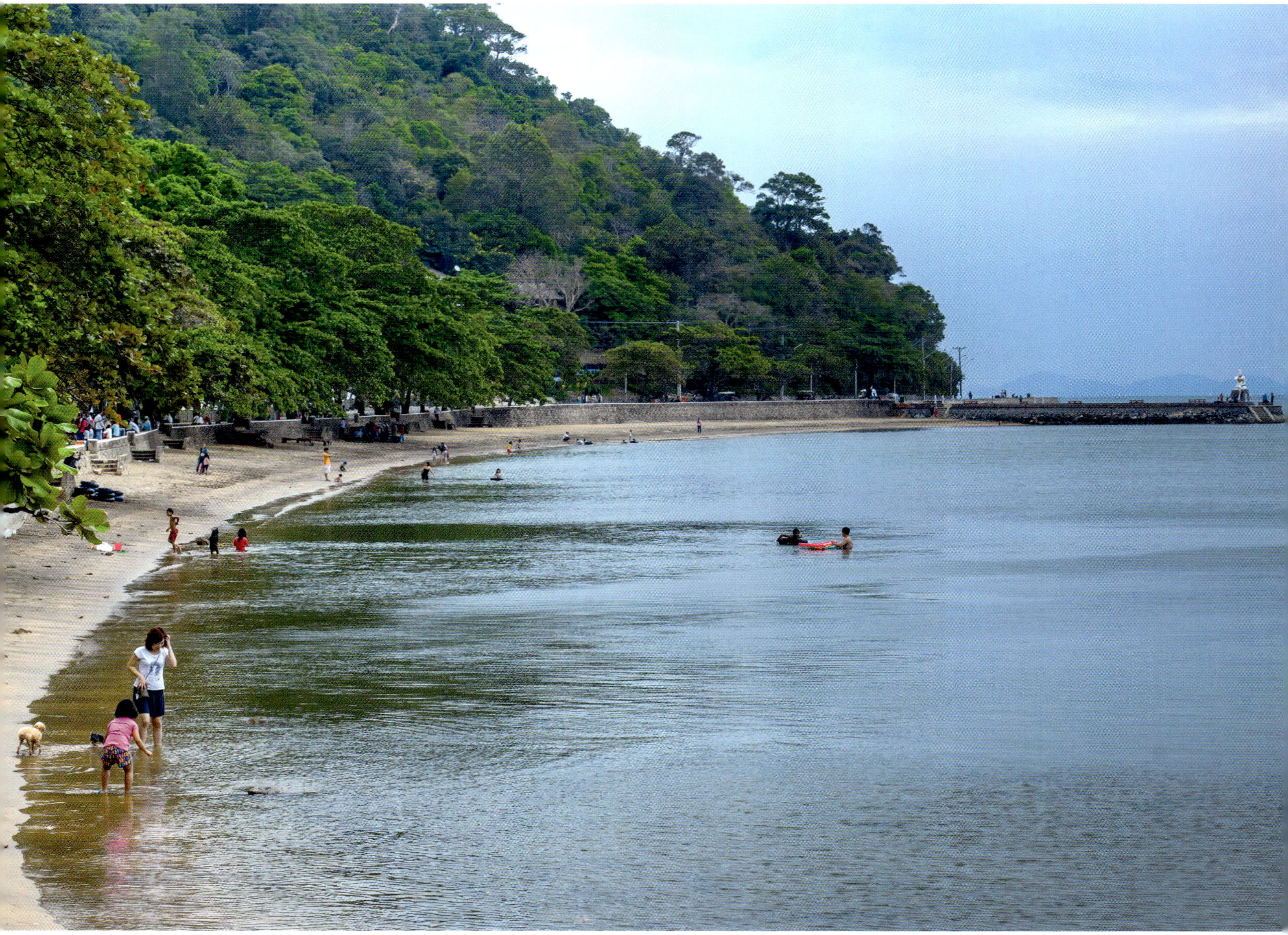

KEP

Kep is a laidback beach town on a small peninsula 25 km (15½ miles) from Kampot. It was once a popular weekend retreat for the French during the early 20th century and later for wealthy Cambodians in the 1960s but today the abandoned villas that line the beach road are the only sign of its glory days. It's a town ripe for development but it lies in waiting. There's actually not much to Kep and although it may suit those longing for a few quiet days, it is perhaps best enjoyed as a day-trip from nearby Kampot. The town's main claim to fame is the colourful crab market, that and the fact that is close to the popular Koh Tonsay or Rabbit Island. Lying just 4.5 km (2¾ miles) to the south-west, this popular destination is known for its beautiful beaches and shallow waters ideal for swimming. Kep's shallow coastal waters lap pebble-strewn beaches and are far from Cambodia's finest but there are some pleasant resorts and plenty of great seafood restaurants to explore.

Above: Kep's beaches are rather stony but the town is another that is becoming increasingly popular at weekends. A pleasant time can be spent strolling the promenade and feasting on local crab dishes.

KEP CRAB MARKET

One of the highlights of the beachfront resort town of Kep is the daily crab market. Every morning crowds of locals gather on the seafront promenade to bargain with Vietnamese girls hauling baskets full of live crab onto the quayside. It's a colourful scene with plenty of boisterous banter and customers prodding the crabs to check for quality and keeping a sharp eye on the scales as the blue swimmer crab are weighed out. A quick chat with buyers, however, reveals that the quantity of the daily catch and size of crabs have greatly diminished in recent years due to over fishing. Nearby, there's a row of restaurants on stilts overlooking the sea that serve up fresh seafood including squid, prawns, fish, and, of course, Kep crab. A firm favourite on the menu is a dish made with the local speciality crab accompanied by a piquant dipping sauce made with the renowned, locally grown Kampot pepper and lime juice.

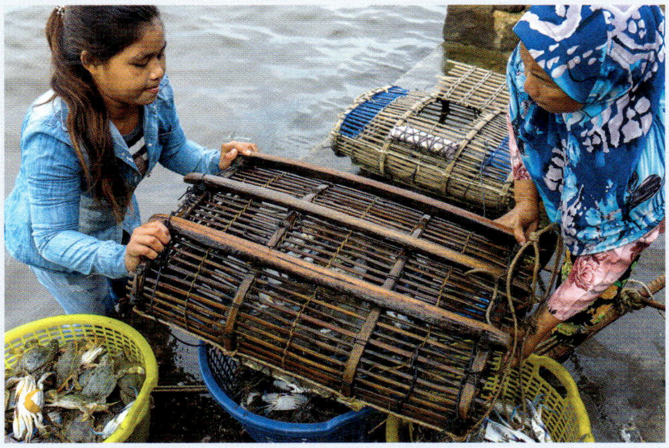

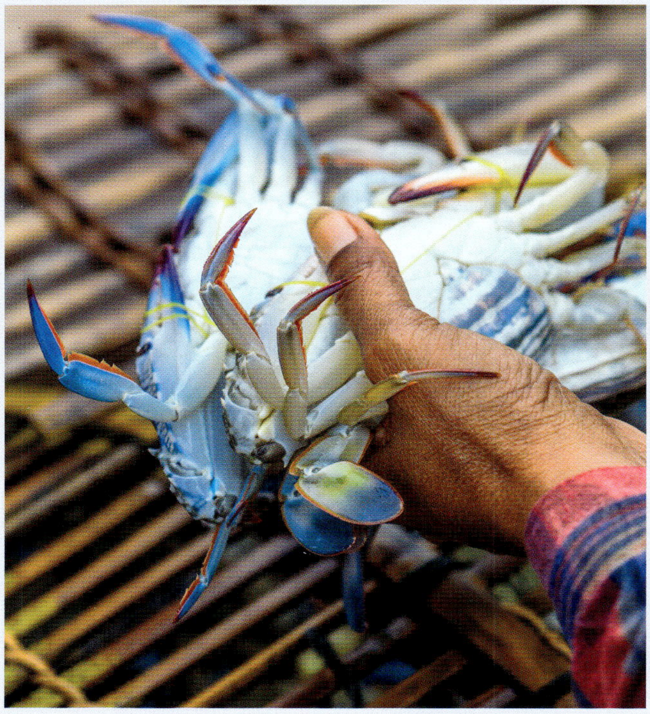

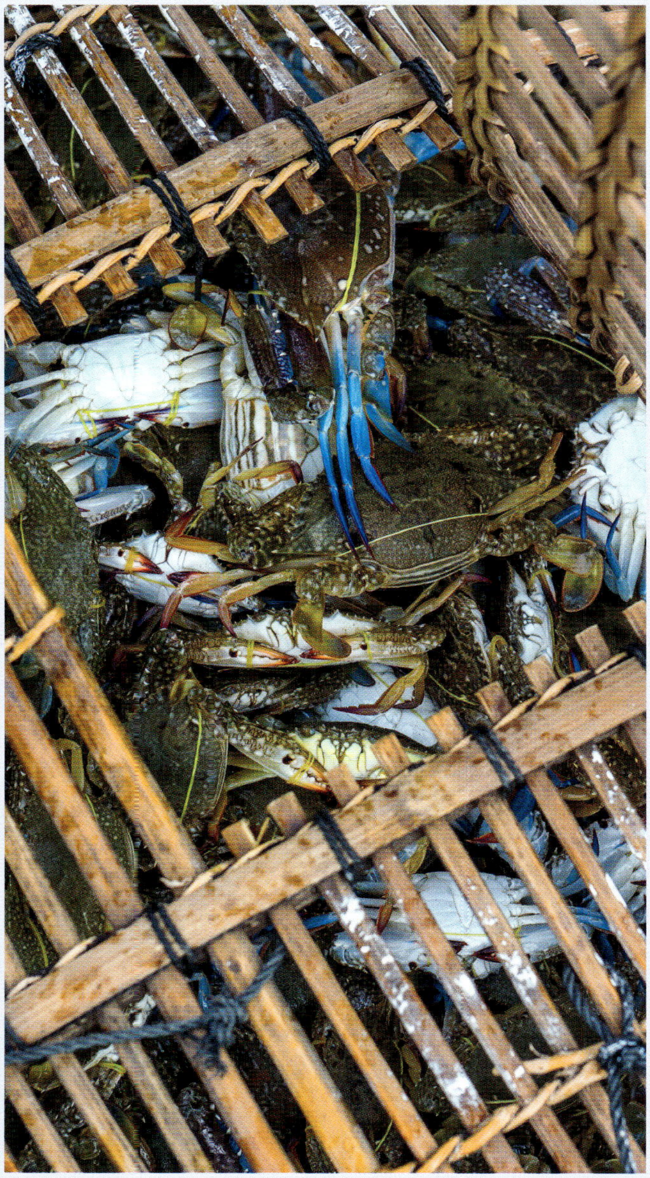

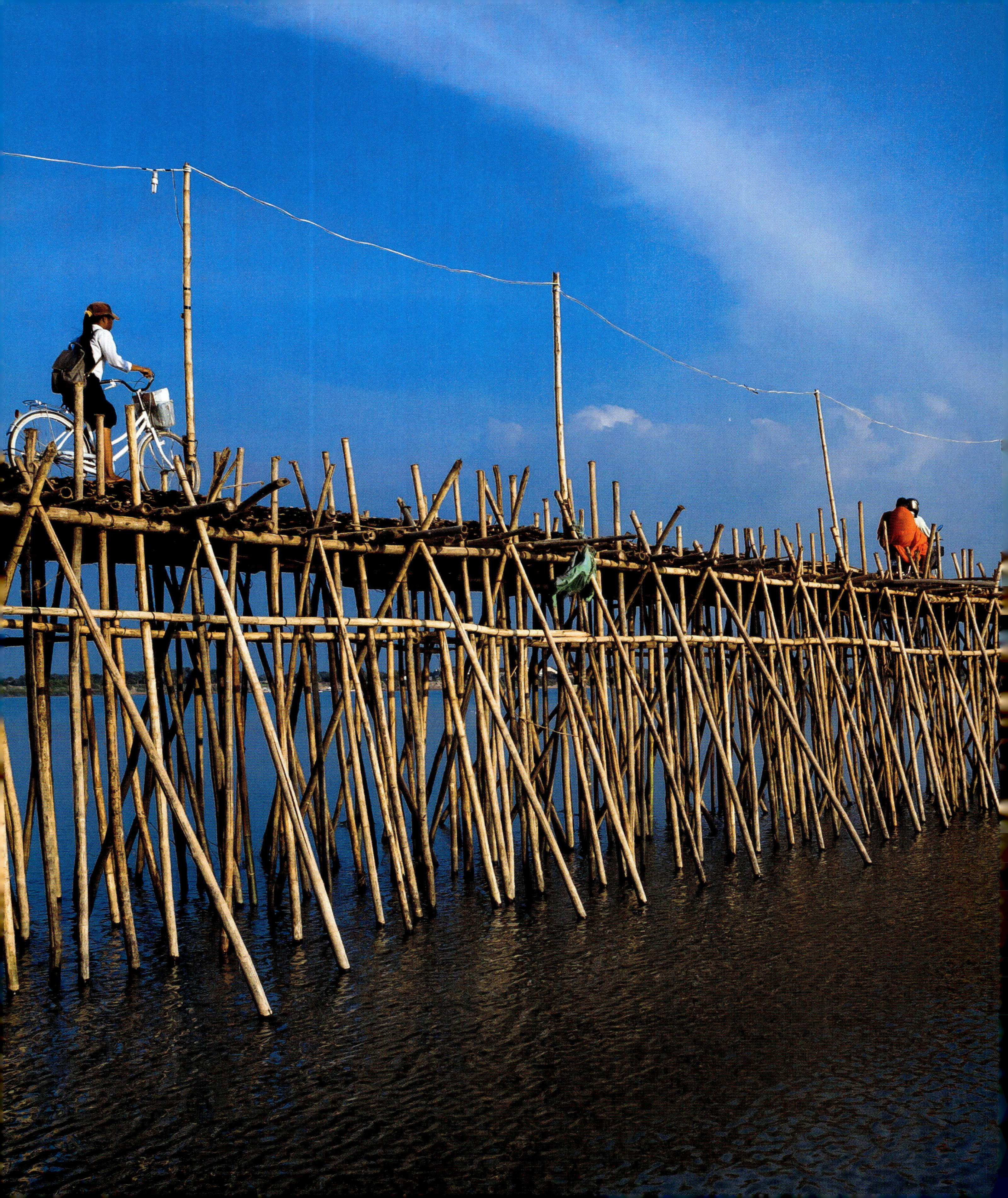

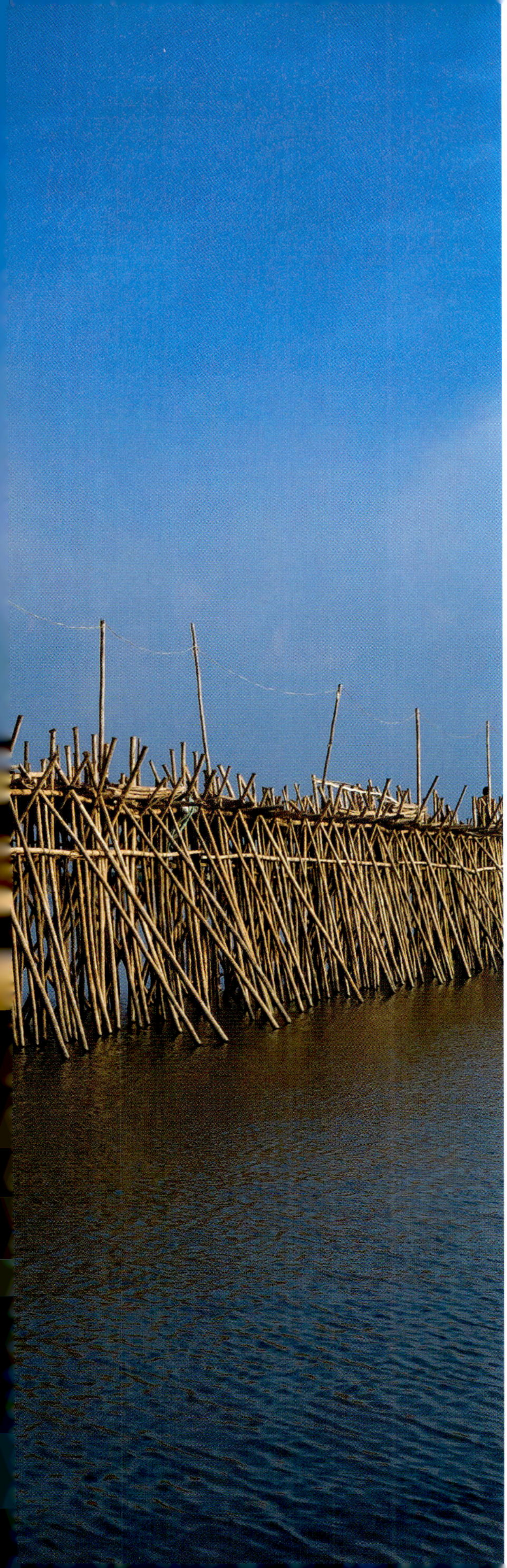

CHAPTER VI

The EAST

Beyond the Mekong

From Phnom Penh, national highway number seven runs north-east, carrying travellers on a journey to the riverfront town of Kompong Cham and on to Kratie, which also sits beside the Mekong River. Continue north through Stung Treng and the road leads east to Ratanakiri Province and the town of Ban Lung. This area is known for the trekking tours that pass through lush national parks to ethnic hill villages and volcanic lakes. East of Kratie is Mondulkiri. Here the dusty, wind-swept, hill-top town of Sen Monorom is used as a base for excursions to waterfalls and for discovering Cambodia's elephants at the eco-tourism Elephant Valley Project.

Left: One of the manmade wonders of Kompong Cham is the bamboo bridge that stretches across a section of the Mekong River, connecting the town to the island of Koh Paen. The bridge is washed away by the river's strong current at the height of the rainy season and rebuilt when the water recedes.

KOMPONG CHAM

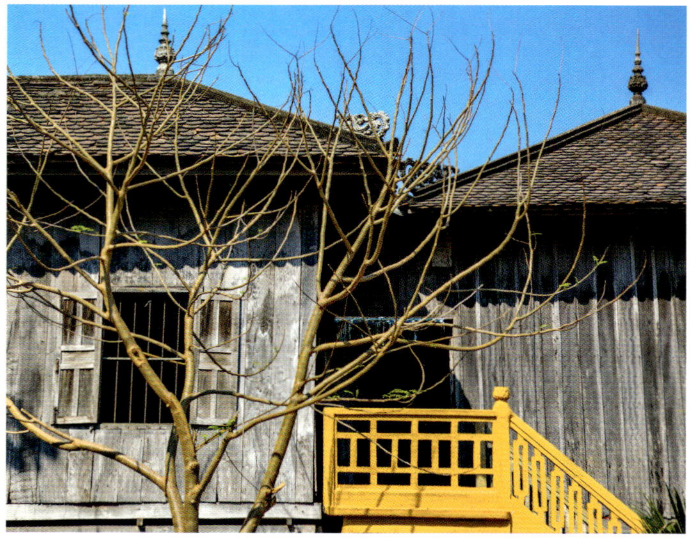

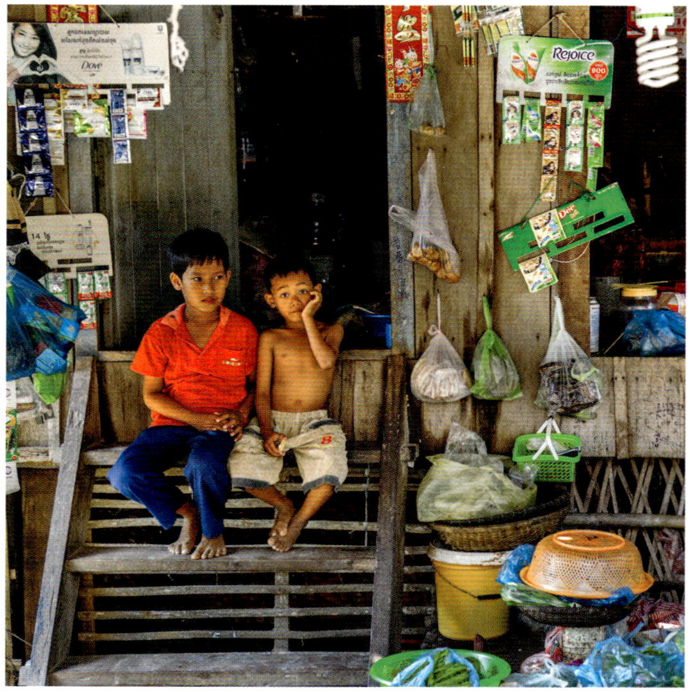

At first glance Kompong Cham appears to be in a comfortable slumber on the banks of the Mekong River but step back from the backpacker guesthouses and restaurants that line the riverfront and there are bustling markets to explore and architectural gems to admire. The town takes its name from the Cham Muslims who have a sizeable population in the area. The town is the perfect destination for a few lazy Mekong days. There are Cham fishing villages to discover on both sides of the river.

One of the highlights of time spent in Kompong Cham is to take a day to explore nearby Koh Paen. During the cool and dry seasons it can be reached by a bamboo bridge which stretches for almost one kilometre (two-thirds of a mile) and is wide enough and strong enough to take the weight of small trucks. The bridge has to be rebuilt every year as it is washed away by the Mekong's powerful current in the rainy season. In the late afternoon a pleasant hour or two can be spent at the bridge observing the to-and-fro of locals, and watching fishermen cast their nets into a river illuminated by the setting sun's fiery glow.

Once across the seasonal toll bridge, the network of roads passes through several welcoming villages. The island's lifestyle and economy are distinctly rural with many of the inhabitants making their living working the land. The main cash crops are sweetcorn and tobacco. The process of preparing the harvested tobacco leaves for drying in special, house-like kilns can be observed around the island.

In recent years there has been considerable investment in Cambodia's rubber industry. The majority of the country's smallholder plantations are in the Kompong Cham area. It's a regimented landscape of equally spaced trees, each bearing the scars of rubber tapping. The first rubber seedlings were planted in Cambodia by the French in 1910 and the first successful 150-hectare (370-acre) plantation established four years later. This was followed in the 1920s by a number of large-scale plantations in Kompong Cham Province. Today, rubber is a controversial issue as large areas of forest are cleared to develop plantations. In addition to smallholders, there are now huge plantations established through concessions offered by the government. The government has also announced that it plans to increase the area of land used for rubber plantations to 400,000 hectares (one million acres) by 2020. This acreage will be capable of producing 272,000 tonnes (300,000 tons) of rubber latex annually for export to Vietnam, Malaysia, China and Singapore. Each day, as early as 2 a.m. when the cooler climate encourages the latex to flow more easily, a rubber tapper will remove a slither of bark from the tree in a spiral around the trunk. The white milky liquid drips into a pot strapped to each tree where it coagulates and is collected later in the day to be taken for processing.

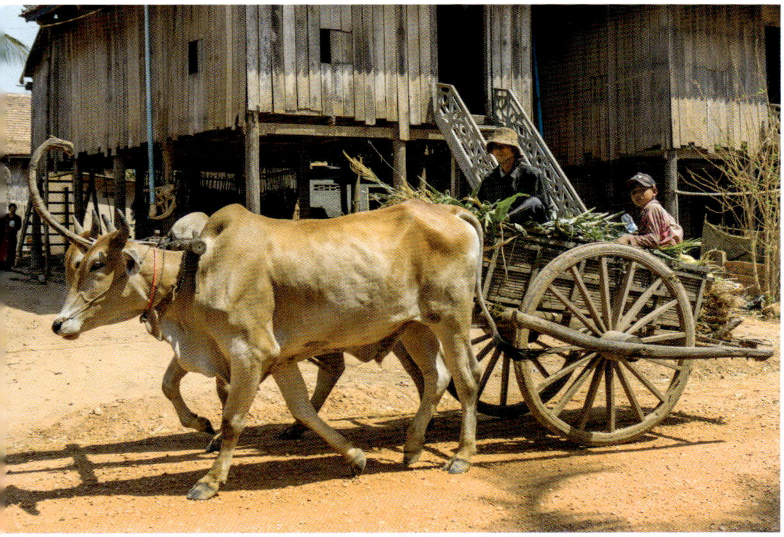

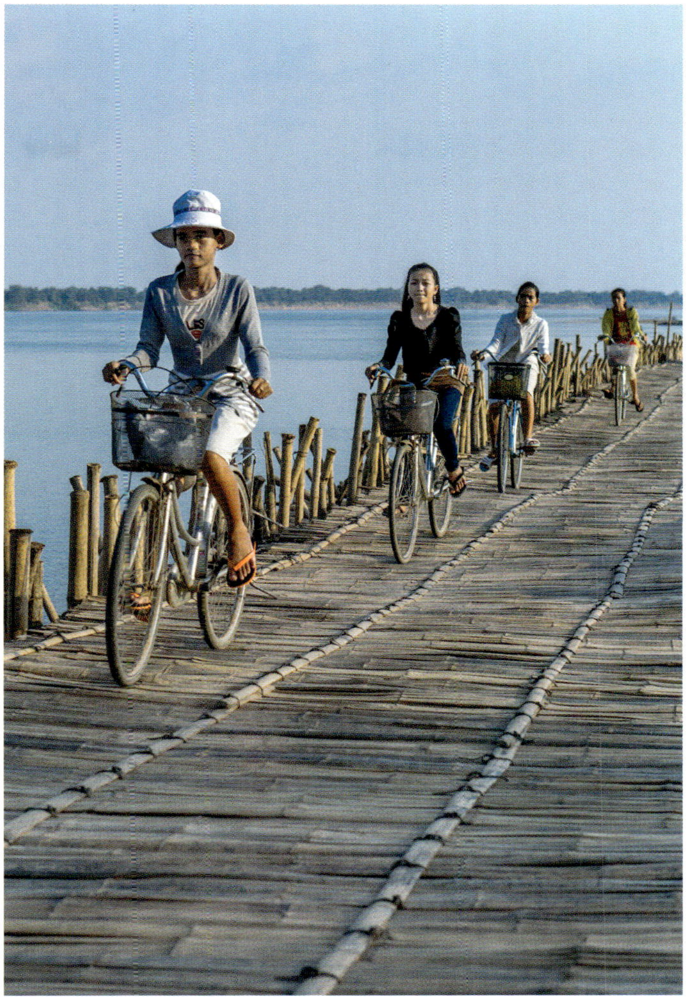

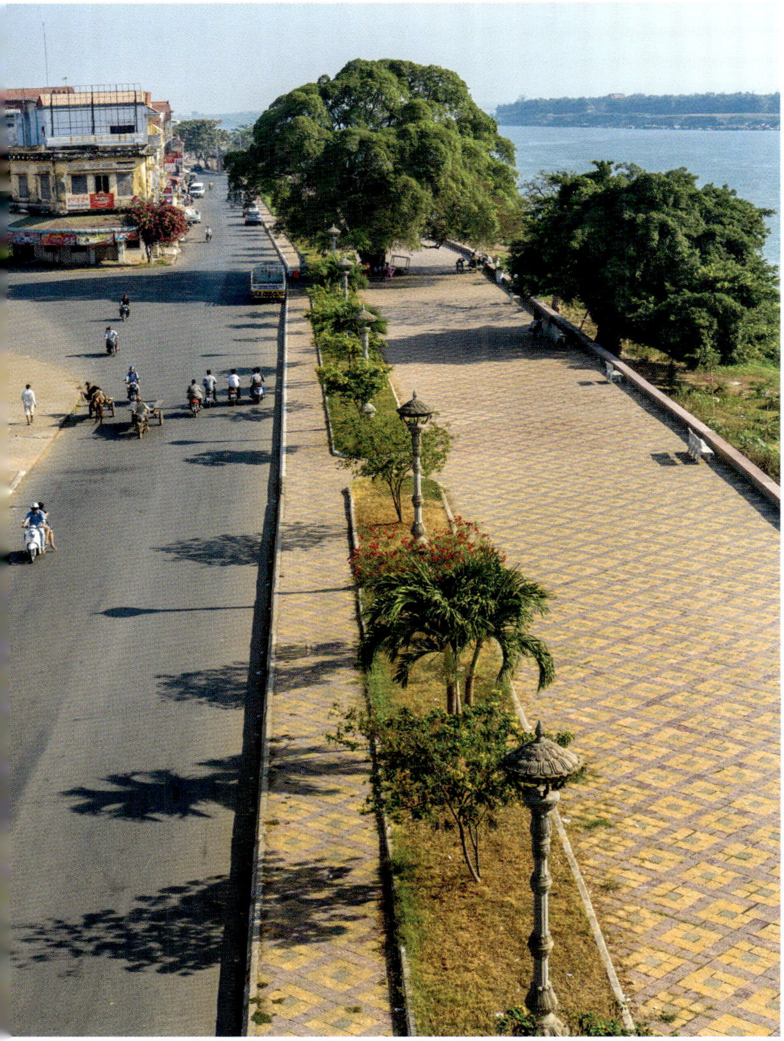

Above: In the dry and cool seasons, many locals cross the bridge to go tubing in the shallows and play on Koh Paen's beach.

Above left: The majority of villagers in the area are poor farmers who make a living from crops such as tobacco, peanuts and sweetcorn. Oxcarts are a common means of transport and essential for moving crops at harvest time.

Left: The view of Kompong Cham's riverfront road and broad promenade. Several guesthouses, restaurants and bars are located here.

Opposite top: Traditional wooden houses on Koh Paen.

Opposite below: Two young boys sitting on the steps of the village shop on Koh Paen. Life among the rural communities moves at a sedate pace.

KRATIE

For most travellers, Kratie is a popular stopping-off point en route to or from the border-crossing with neighbouring Laos. From Kompong Cham, Kratie can be reached by the national highway, or more interestingly, by an old French road that runs alongside the Mekong River. It's a dusty journey along unsealed roads and badly degraded tarmac but one enjoyed by serious cyclists and those travelling by motorcycle. The ochre-coloured thread winds its way through beautiful countryside knotted with dozens of small villages. Broken only by a Mekong ferry crossing, it is pulled passed crumbling riverfront building in charming Chhlong and on to Kratie.

Like Kompong Cham, Kratie's appeal lies in its Mekong riverfront location. It has the usual, intriguing, tumble-down colonial buildings with the incongruous addition of brash modern signage circling a boisterous market. The town is a good base for exploring several attractions in the area, the highlight being the chance to see the endangered Irrawaddy Dolphin.

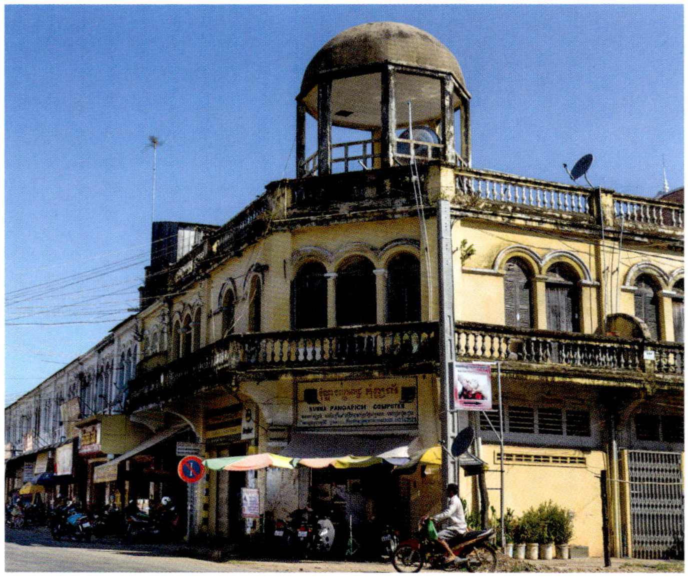

Below: The Mekong River island of Koh Trong lies directly opposite Kratie town and can be reached by a short ferry ride. Once on the island, it can be explored by bicycle.

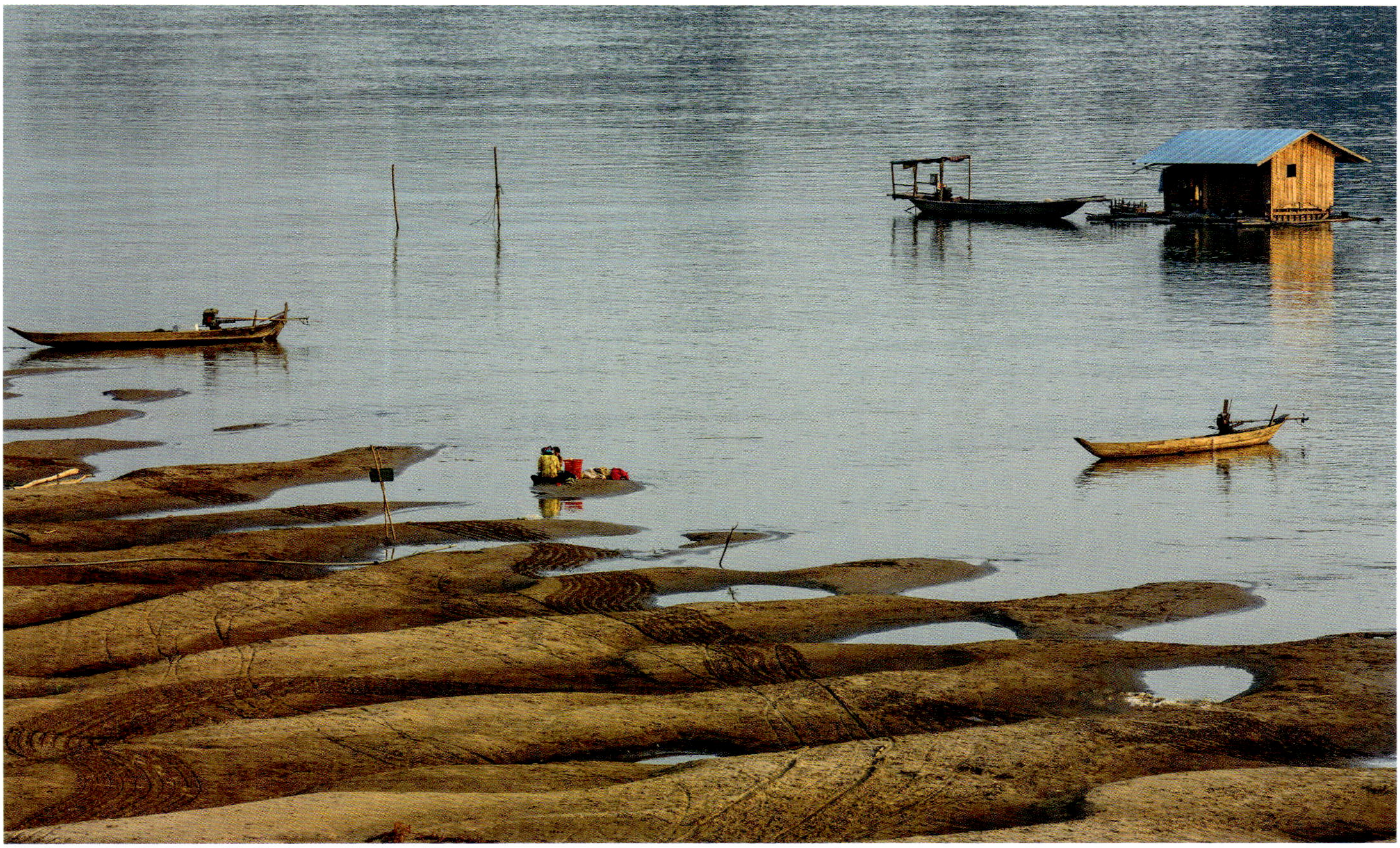

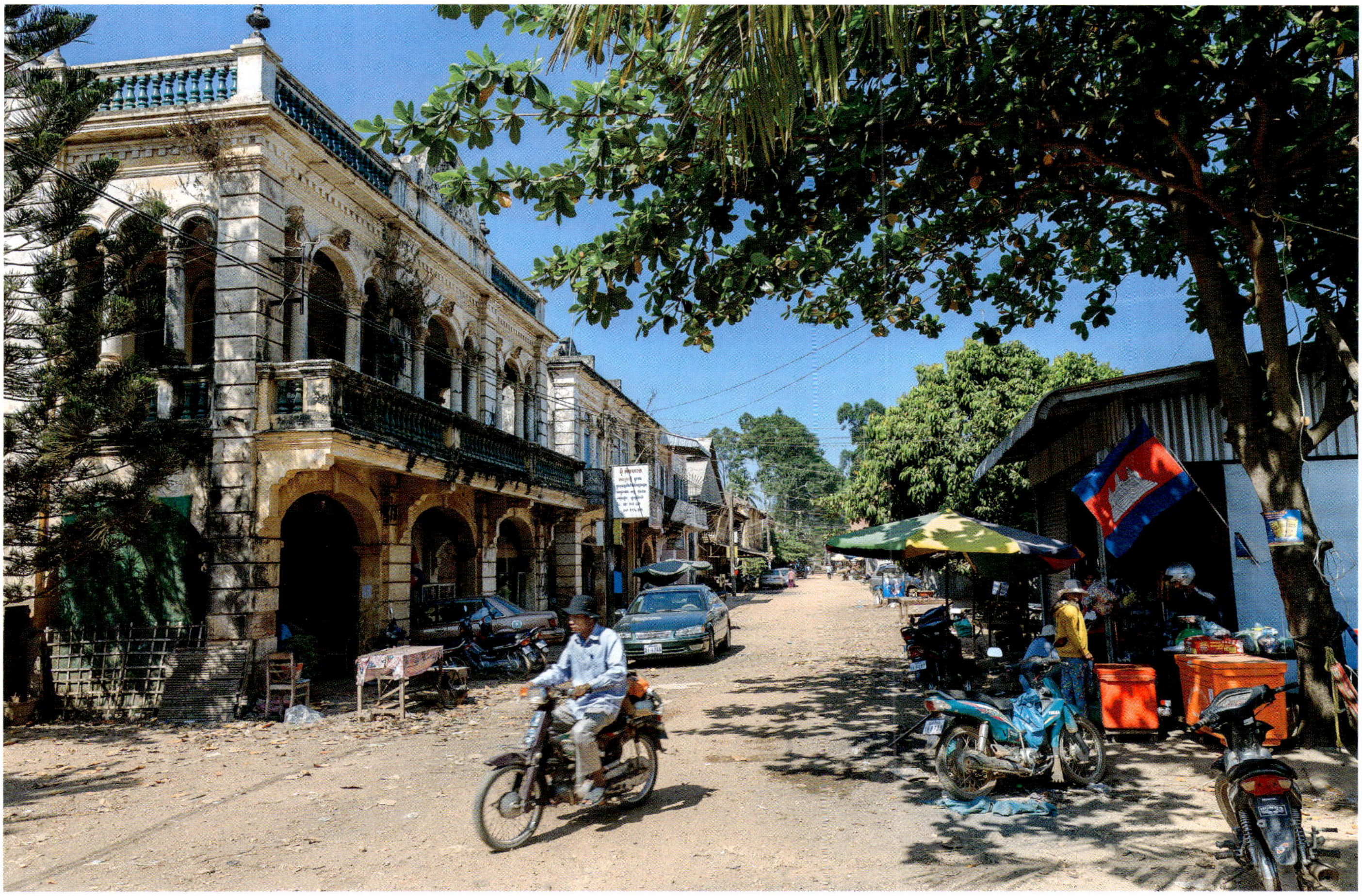

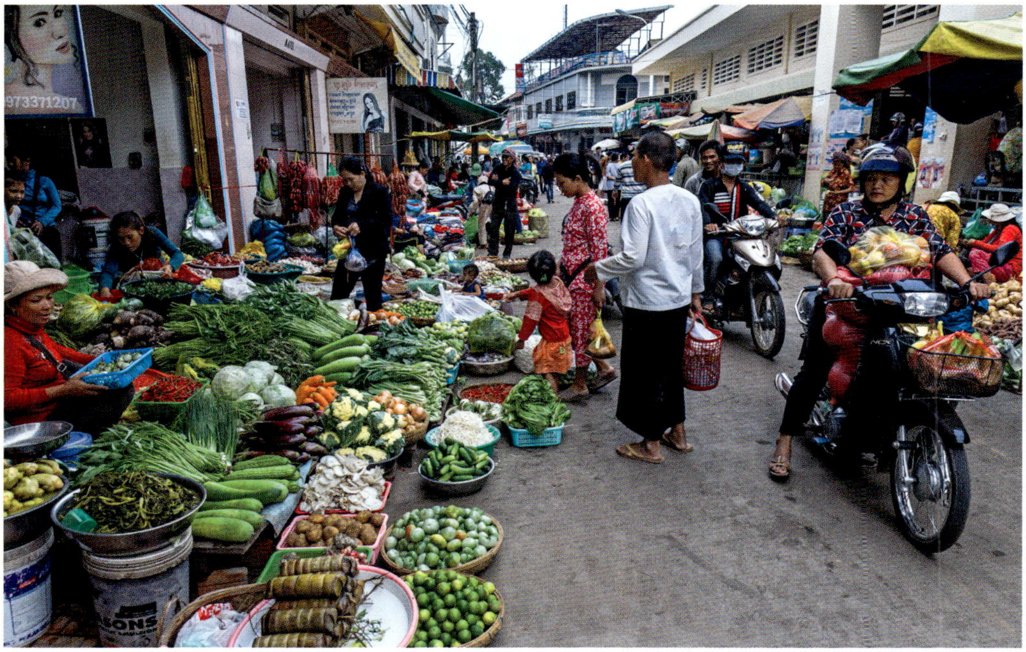

Above: The old road from Kompong Cham to Kratie passes through the town of Chhlong. It's a good place to break the journey but has little to offer beyond crumbling French buildings and a small fresh food market.
Opposite top: Kratie has the distinction of being one of the first towns to be freed from the grip of the Khmer Rouge by Vietnamese troops in 1978.
Left: Kratie's daily market in the centre of town sells a veritable cornucopia of fresh fruit, vegetables, fish and meat, and much more besides.

The Irrawaddy Dolphin acts as a barometer for the health of the Mekong River as it is extremely sensitive to any change in its environment. To thrive, the dolphins need clean and undisturbed water, an abundant supply of food and no disruptive human activity.

The shy Irrawaddy Dolphin is dark grey in colour with a blunt, rounded head and small dorsal fin. When mature, it can reach lengths of up to three metres (10 ft) and weigh in at 150 kg (330 lb). According to the World Wildlife Fund (WWF), the dolphins, which inhabit a 190-km (118-mile) stretch of the Mekong River between Kratie and the Khone Falls on the border with Laos, number fewer than between 78 and 91 individuals and are a Critically Endangered species.

The best place to observe the dolphins is at the town of Kampi, 15 km (9 miles) north of Kratie and easily reached by hired bicycle or motorcycle. Alternatively, most hotels and guesthouses offer daily tours that take in a dolphin-watching trip. Once at Kampi, there are dozens of river boats that can be hired for $US9 an hour. The dolphins are not as elusive as might be expected and are easily spotted as they surface, albeit fleetingly, for air. Once out in the middle of the river, the eagle-eyed boatmen kill the engines and drift so as to cause as little disturbance as possible. The dolphin-spotting project has proved to be a major eco-tourism success story and the income it generates for the boatmen has encouraged them to stop harmful fishing practices in the area.

In recent years, already dwindling populations have been adversely affected by the use of gillnets by local fishermen resulting in many deaths each year. As part of an urgent need

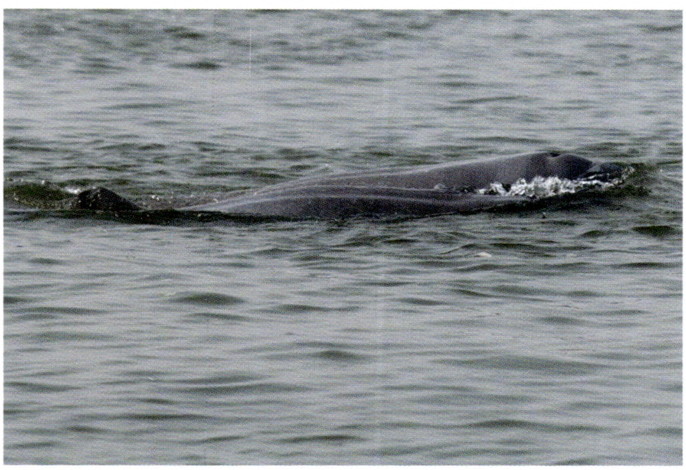

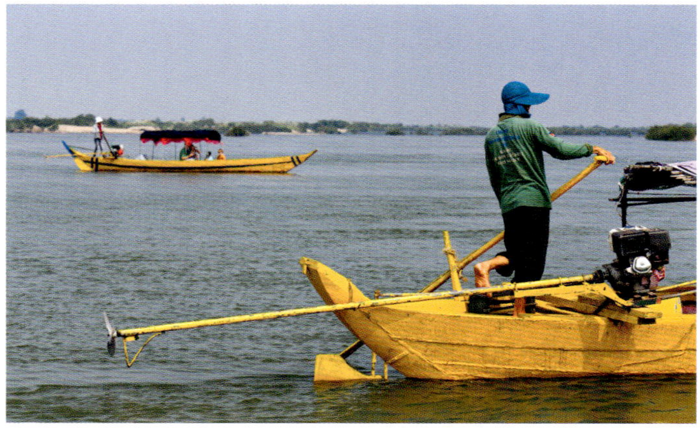

to prevent further decline in dolphin numbers, the Cambodian Mekong Dolphin Conservation Project (CMDCP) was created as a collaborative initiative between WWF, the Cambodian Rural Development Team (CRDT) and the Fisheries Administration. A major success was an agreement by local government agencies to work with WWF in trying to protect dolphins. The Cambodian government also banned the use of gillnets along a 175-km (110-mile) stretch of the Mekong River, giving the rare mammals a chance to increase their numbers. However, it remains to be seen what effect damming the Mekong River in Laos will have on the Irrawaddy Dolphin.

Opposite Kratie town, the huge island sandbar of Koh Trong basks in the Mekong sun. It is reached by a five-minute ferry journey from Kratie's quayside. Once on the island visitors can hire bicycles and navigate the nine-kilometre (5½-mile) trail that winds through sleepy villages, past temples and through an interior carpeted by rice fields. Best explored in the late afternoon, a floating village at the rear of the island can be reached just before sunset. Here, as the sun descends below the tree line, skeletal ribs of exposed sand are separated by pools of vermilion water. From homes anchored in the shallows, smoke rises from wood-burning stoves as women prepare supper, men cast nets hopefully into the river and there's the happy sound of children playing.

Above: Thanks to the Irrawaddy Dolphin conservation project, local fishermen are able to make a good living offering boat trips for dolphin watchers.

Left: An Irrawaddy Dolphin surfaces for air. Sightings are common but fleeting.

HAND-PAINTED SIGNS

One of Cambodia's many endearing idiosyncrasies is the hand-painted signage that can be seen all over the country. In the Kratie area, however, there seems to be a proliferation of these colourful boards. The quirky signs advertise anything from massage to motorcycle repairs, beauty salons to butchers. There are also warning signs, such as 'Beware of the Dog', and much more besides. Travelling through rural Cambodia, it is fun to keep an eye out for the signs, many of which date from the early seventies. The heyday of the hand-painted sign seems to be over but there are also plenty of colourful modern versions around that often use a collage of photographs and stencils to get customers' attention.

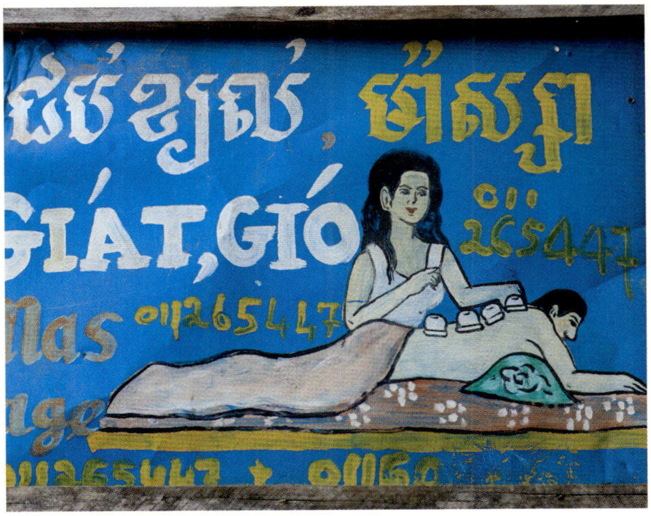

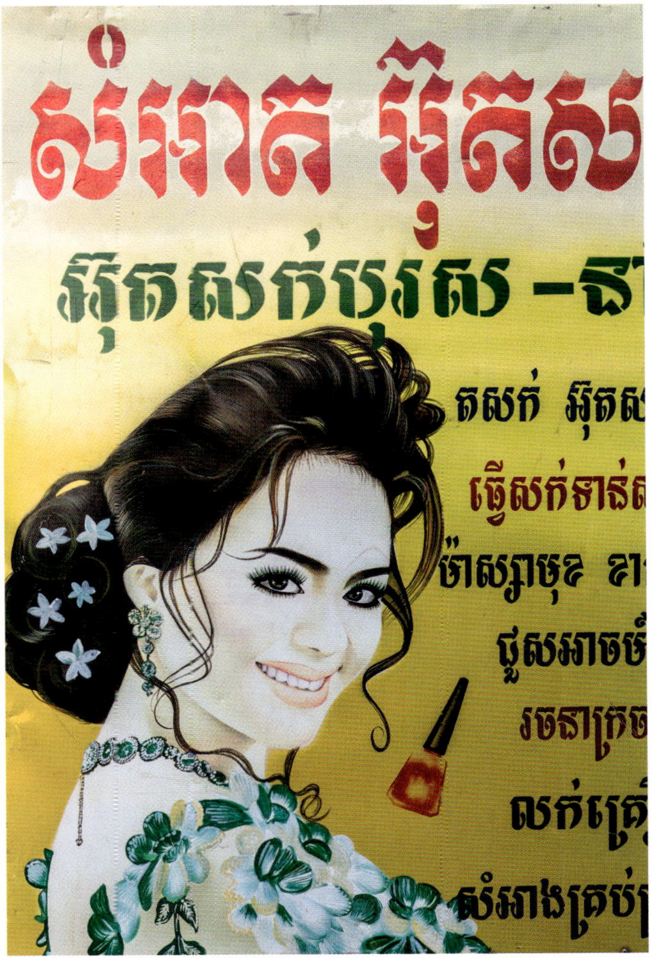

RATANAKIRI

The rural province of Ratanakiri is known as the north-east frontier. Home to the majority of Cambodia's ethnic minorities who populate its beautiful rolling hills, the area attracts nature lovers and adventure tourists alike. Getting there, however, is a bit of a trek as it is 640 km (400 miles) from Phnom Penh. Bordered by Laos to the north and Vietnam to the east, Ratanakiri is sparsely populated and rich in natural resources including gold and gemstones.

Most visitors stay at the provincial capital of Ban Lung, a busy market town in easy reach of the hill villages. Highlights include the Yek Lom crater, five kilometres (three miles) south-east of the town. The waters of the 50-m (165-ft) deep lake are crystal-clear and attract day-trippers who come to enjoy swimming, then eating at huts set up around the shoreline.

Resort and tour operators in Ban Lung can also organize treks in the forest-covered Virachey National Park which begins just 20 km (12½ miles) from the town and stretches to the borders. Typically treks will take in ethnic minority villages and scenic waterfalls. The peoples, who include groups such as the Chary, Kachok, Lan, Pnong and Prouk, can sometimes be seen in Ban Lung's morning market.

MONDULKIRI

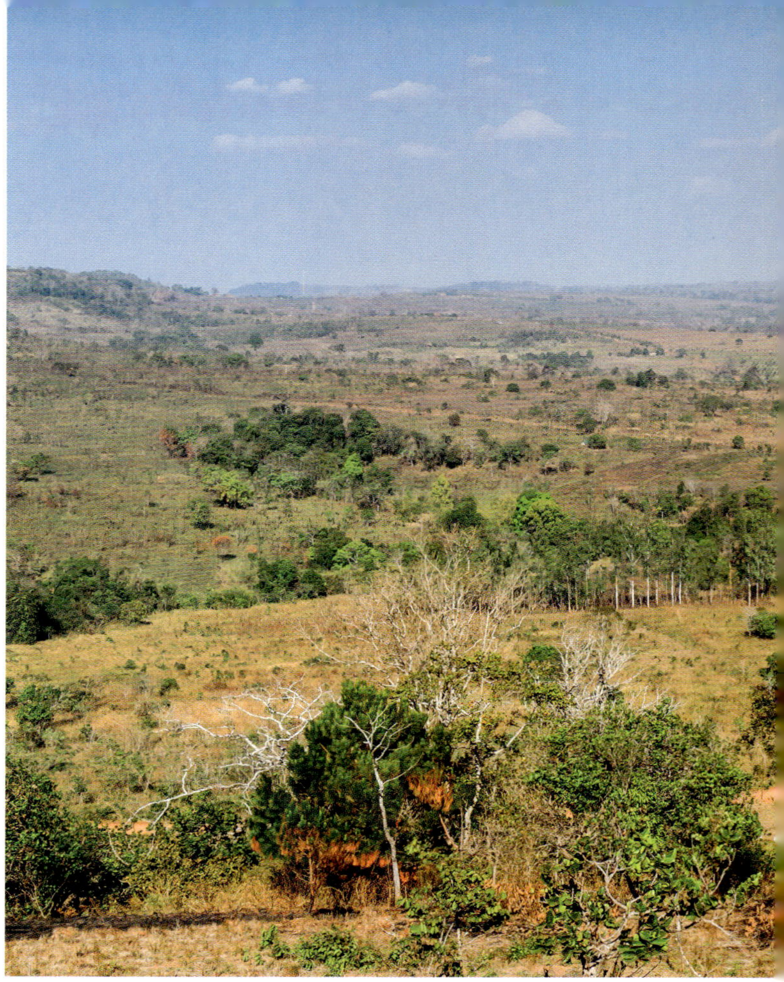

The rolling hills and mountains of Mondulkiri Province are windswept and in places badly deforested. The principal town is Sen Monorom, which sits on a hilltop at an elevation of 800 m (2,625 ft), meaning that it enjoys pleasantly cool mornings and evenings. Although the town has little to offer, it does make a good base for exploring the surrounding area which has some stunning countryside for trekking, numerous impressive waterfalls in the wet season and ethnic villages, particularly of the Buong minority. Like Ratanakiri, the province is sparsely populated and Sen Monorom only has a population of around 8,000. There are few hotels and restaurants but as the area slowly establishes a reputation as an eco and adventure tourism destination, it is gradually starting to develop. The most beautiful waterfall is Busra, about 43 km (27 miles) north-east of Sen Monorom. The two-tier falls have a 10-m (33-ft) drop on the top level and a dramatic 25-m (82-ft) cascade into a gorge on the lower level. Busra waterfall is a popular bathing and picnic spot for locals and tourists. For those who wish to stay in the area, there is a basic guesthouse run by Pnong hill peoples in Pichinda village.

The big attraction in Mondulkiri is the Elephant Valley Project. Unlike the majority of elephant camps in Asia that use domesticated elephants for financial gain, the inspirational Elephant Valley Project has the welfare of its charges at its heart. The camp is situated 11 km (seven miles) from Sen Monorom, close to the border with Vietnam. The project's land is made up of forest and grassland, an ideal setting for the conservation and rehabilitation of elephants. Visitors to the sanctuary are welcome for full- or half-day experiences that include watching elephants from a distance as they enjoy as natural a life as is possible for a domesticated animal. The stated goal of the project is to not only to help the elephants enjoy life in a safe environment but also to provide their mahouts, members of the Pnong peoples, with a decent income. The Elephant Valley Project also runs a volunteer programme for those wishing to make a lasting contribution to elephant conservation in Cambodia.

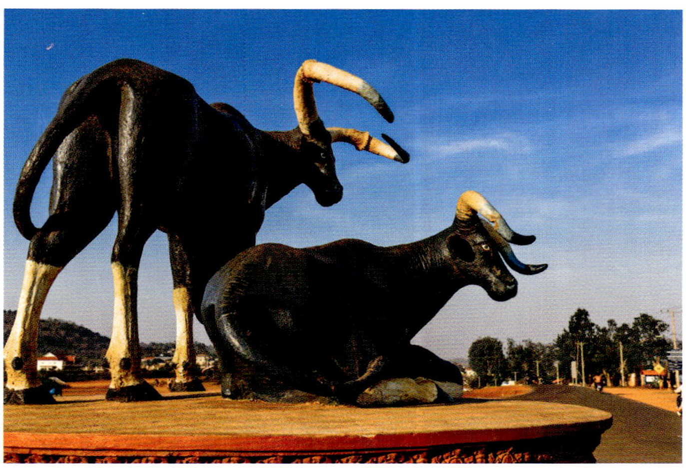

Above: The countryside around Sen Monorom is badly deforested but travel further afield and nature lovers can visit impressive waterfalls and trek to remote hill villages.

Left: A statue of Wild Water Buffalo in the centre of Sen Monorom. Mondulkiri province is one of the few places that the Critically Endangered species can still be found.

Opposite: In Cambodia, there are thought to be as few as 400 elephants left in the wild and just over 200 in captivity.

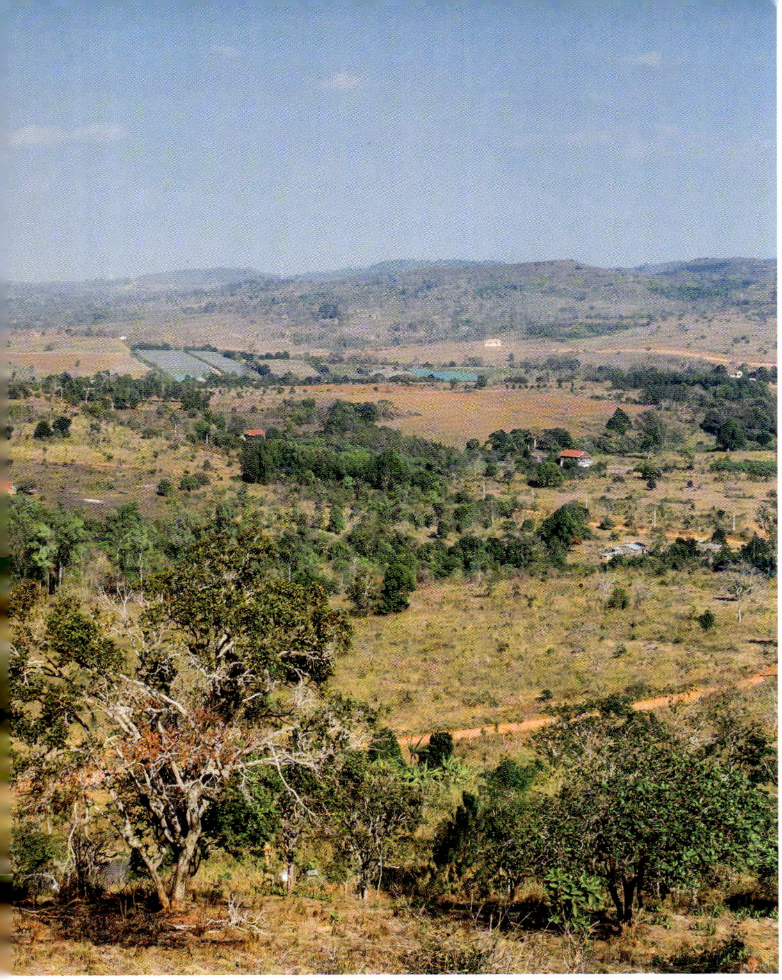

MOUNTAIN BREW

In the far north-eastern provinces of Ratanakiri and Mondulkiri rural farmers are finding that growing coffee can provide a much-needed boost to their income. Although in its infancy, Cambodian coffee has already found favour with coffee lovers in Japan and Korea and is increasingly discovering new markets abroad. As Phnom Penh booms and lifestyles change, the home-grown mountain brew is also gaining ground within the domestic marketplace. In fact, with only 30 hectares (75 acres) currently farmed in Mondulkiri, demand is outstripping production.

Coffee was first introduced to Cambodia, Vietnam and Laos by the French. Although much of the coffee grown in Cambodia is the high-yielding *robusta* coffee, the superior flavoured *arabica* bean is also now being farmed at higher elevations. The farmers in the highland areas of Ratanakiri and Mondulkiri are predominately indigenous hill peoples.

Cambodian coffee can be bought when in the two north-easterly provinces and also from supermarkets in Phnom Penh.

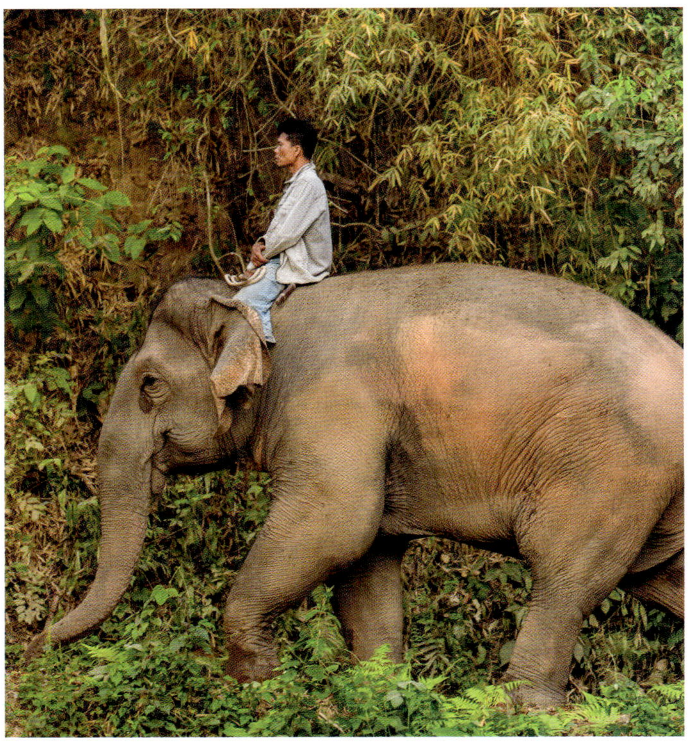

BIKE HIRE

With few asphalt roads and little development, Cambodia is perfect for adventure motorcyclists. For those who wish to travel independently, dirt bikes can be hired in Siem Reap and Phnom Penh. The typical machine is a Honda Baja 250cc or Honda XR 250cc, both light and nimble, and ideal for the rough terrain. Those unfamiliar with Cambodia will probably find the most rewarding way to explore the country by motorcycle is with an organized tour of fellow enthusiasts. There are plenty of companies to choose from but standards vary greatly. Check over the machines carefully and ensure that the company provides plenty of back-up in the form of a decent mechanic or a support vehicle. A licence is required to ride a motorcycle in Cambodia and an international driver's licence is not recognized. A reputable hire company should be able to arrange for a licence within a few days.

RESOURCES

Surviving the Killing Fields
Haing S. Ngor and Roger Warner
Chatto & Windus, 1988

Angkor: Cambodia's Wondrous Khmer Temples
Dawn Rooney
Odyssey, 2011

Traditional Ceramics of South East Asia
Mick Shippen
A&C Black, 2005

A Record of Cambodia: The Land and Its People.
Zhou Daguan, translated by Peter Harris
Silkworm Books, 2007

Lonely Planet Cambodia
Nick Ray
Lonely Planet Country Guides, 2012

From Spiders to Water Lilies; Creative Cambodian Cooking with Friends
Gustav Auer and Sok Chhong
Friends International.

Cambodian Cooking
Joannes Rivière
Periplus Editions, 2008

The Cuisine of Cambodia
Nusara Thaitawat
Nusara & Friends Co. Ltd., 2000

Dance in Cambodia
Toni Samantha Phim and Ashley Thompson.
Oxford University Press, SouthEast Asia, 1999

Dance of Life: The Mythology, History and Politics of Cambodian Culture
Julie B. Metha.
Singapore: Graham Brash Pte. Singapore, 2001

A Dragon Apparent: Travels in Cambodia, Laos and Vietnam
Norman Lewis
ElandPublishing Ltd., reprinted 2003

Sthapatyakam - The Architecture of Cambodia
An Danhsipo, Bo Sakalkitya, et al
Royal University of Phnom Penh, 2012

Theatre in South East Asia
James R Brandon
Harvard University Press, 1974

Hand-Painted Signs of Kratie
Sam Roberts
CreateSpace Independent Publishing Platform, 2012

Carving up Cambodia
The Cambodia Daily Weekend, Issue 730, 2012

International Rice Research Institute www.irri.org

www.battambang-heritage.org

United Nations Collaborative Programme on Reducing Emissions from Deforestation and Forest Degradation in Developing Countries www.un-redd.org

MOTORCYCLES

Red Raid
www.motorcycletourscambodia.com
and www.bicycletourscambodia.com
The best and most reliable company for motorcycle hire is Red Raid. Based in Phnom Penh, the adventure tourism enthusiasts set up business back in 2001 and have an excellent track record. They provide a support vehicle and mechanic for all tours. Back at base, a professional workshop and knowledgeable mechanics keep the fleet of bikes in tip-top condition to ensure the peace of mind required if travelling solo. Red Raid offers tour all over Cambodia. In addition to the 250cc bikes, they also have larger 650cc touring machines.

INDEX

Page numbers in italic type represent images.

ACKNOWLEDGEMENTS

My sincerest thanks to Daryl Hissey of the Angkor Sayana Hotel & Spa, Corner River Road & Samdech Tep Vong Street, Wat Bo Village, Sala Kamroeuk Commune, Siem Reap. Tel: +855 (0) 63 96 94 94. Fax: +855 (0) 63 96 94 93 Email: ask@angkorsayana.com. Website: www.angkorsayana.com

Sayana ANGKOR SAYANA HOTEL & SPA

my home away from home in Siem Reap. This book would not have been possible without his kindness. Hats off to you mate – this one's for you. Thanks also go to Shanthi Regupathy at Grebstad Hicks Communications in Singapore, the La Résidence d'Angkor Siem Reap, and Orient Express hotel, www.residencedangkor.com, Richard Bias, Executive Chef at La Résidence d'Angkor Siem Reap, Sofitel Angkor Phokeethra Golf and Spa Resort, Siem Reap, www.accorhotels.com and Madam Hao Dinh, the little girl with the big camera who shared the journey in Kompong Cham.

ABOUT THE AUTHOR

Mick Shippen is a freelance writer and award-winning photographer who has been based in Southeast Asia for 15 years. He travels extensively throughout Asia conducting research for articles and taking photographs for local and international newspapers and magazines.

He is the author of six titles in the 'Enchanting Asia' series: *Enchanting Cambodia, Enchanting Laos, Enchanting Thailand, Enchanting Myanmar, Enchanting Chiang Mai & Northern Thailand* and *Enchanting Bangkok*, and of *The Traditional Ceramics of South East Asia*.

He has provided content and images for several leading guidebooks, and his work has appeared in numerous magazines, the Bangkok Post, and the Australian Sunday Telegraph.

His images are represented by Gallery Stock, www.gallerystock.com, and StockFood, www.stockfood.com, and can also be viewed at www.mickshippen.com

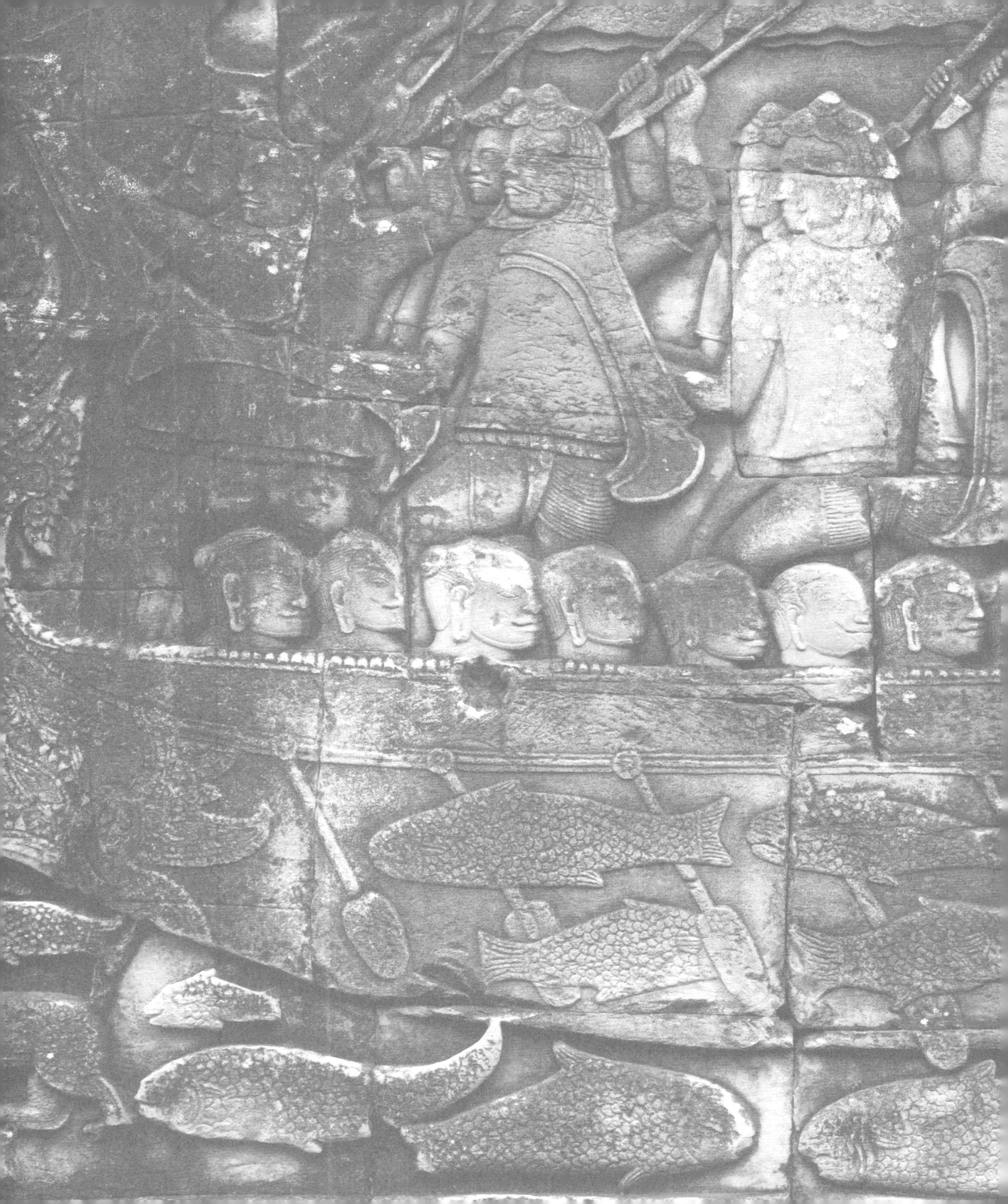